88

THE SPIRIT OF REVOLUTION
IN 1789

The Spirit of Revolution in 1789

A Study of Public Opinion as Revealed
in Political Songs and Other Popular Literature
at the Beginning of the French Revolution

BY CORNWELL B. ROGERS

PRINCETON NEW JERSEY
PRINCETON UNIVERSITY PRESS
1949

PRINTED IN THE UNITED STATES OF AMERICA
BY PRINCETON UNIVERSITY PRESS AT PRINCETON, NEW JERSEY

To
E.M.R.

✡ PREFACE ✡

AGAINST a rich background of research and writing, James Harvey Robinson came to the conclusion that the French Revolution is "perhaps the most difficult theme that a historian can select." There are doubtless many who will dispute this claim, and I, for one, would not know how to defend it.

But no one who has attempted to study the Revolution at first hand, and to deal with the many problems of interpretation that arise, can fail to be impressed by the immensity of the subject, or to be comforted by Robinson's verdict.

Fortunately, in undertaking a study which presents many obstacles and pitfalls, I have been generously aided—as the acknowledgments which follow will suggest.

The extraordinary interest of the French Revolution and its far-reaching and enduring effects were first forcibly brought to my attention as a graduate student by Professor Carlton J. H. Hayes of Columbia University; and I am happy to be among the many former students of Professor Hayes who have had an opportunity to express a word of grateful acknowledgment.

Similarly, I acknowledge a debt of long standing to the late Professor Charles Downer Hazen, whose seminar on the French Revolution afforded a valuable opportunity to profit by his careful study of the period.

The research on which this work depends was made possible in the first instance by an American Field Service Fellowship, administered by the Institute of International Education. I wish gratefully to acknowledge the help and encouragement received from both these organizations, and from Dr. Horatio Krans, who for many years represented the Institute in Paris.

The encouragement and generosity of my father, the late Noah C. Rogers, enabled me to make a more protracted study than would have otherwise been possible, and to assemble a documentary collection which makes a modest, though not inconsequential, addition to previously known sources of the French Revolution, and part of which has contributed to the preparation of this book.

In the matter of authorship, I owe my greatest debt to Professor Jacques Barzun of Columbia University. While Professor Barzun suggested many possibilities of inquiry and revealed innumerable ways of improving the text, he nevertheless did nothing to diminish my own sense of responsibility in such matters. Under the circumstances, I can acknowledge my profound indebtedness and lively appreciation without disclaiming any smallest degree of responsibility for whatever shortcomings the book may have.

Valuable criticisms of various parts of the manuscript were given by Professors Austin P. Evans, John Bartlet Brebner, Henri F. Muller, and Thomas P. Peardon, of Columbia University, and are gratefully acknowledged.

I wish, also, to mention with especial thanks several former colleagues on the teaching staff of Columbia College: John H. Berthel, now Librarian, Columbia College Library; Dr. Reinhard H. Luthin, now Bibliographer of American History, Columbia University; and Professor Paul H. Beik of Swarthmore College. Another former colleague, John A. Scott, made a particularly careful examination of most of the manuscript and offered many challenging and helpful suggestions.

For an appreciation of certain psychological trends in history, and especially of the complexity of eighteenth-century culture, I am indebted to conversations and correspondence with William Stanley Dell, translator of C. G. Jung. It is only fair to say, though, that no part of the finished work has had the benefit of his criticism. For various helpful suggestions I am indebted to Stuart Chapin of Wiscasset, Maine.

My friend and former editorial associate, James Fletcher Smith, read most of an early draft and all of the finished manuscript. Much from the standpoint of accuracy was gained as a result of his careful reading, and I have him to thank, besides, for many improvements in structure and style.

Elsewhere in the present work my great indebtedness to libraries in this country and abroad will be evident. Here I wish only to express admiration of the patience and courtesy of library people, and to say as a matter of record that the major part of my investigation was carried on at the Columbia University Library, the New York Public Library, the Bibliothèque Nationale, the Bibliothèque de la Ville de Paris, and the Bibliothèque du Sénat.

The careful and skillful attentions and many courtesies of the Princeton University Press are gratefully acknowledged.

Part of the Introduction of this book was published as an article in *The Public Opinion Quarterly*, vol. 12 (1947), pp. 436-44. Permission to reprint this material is acknowledged with thanks, as is permission to quote at length from works published by Henry Holt and G. P. Putnam, New York; Librairie Hachette, Paris; and Methuen, London. The design on the jacket is reproduced from P. Sagnac and J. Robiquet, *La Révolution de 1789*, by permission of Les Editions Nationales, Paris. The illustration preceding the Introduction came to my attention through the kindness of A. Hyatt Mayor, of the Metropolitan Museum of Art.

My wife has been a gallant partner in the preparation of this book. Her generous share in tasks of the most exacting sort and her encouragement of the project as a whole have been of immeasurable help. The dedication of this book to her is a fitting, though incomplete, expression of my thanks.

CORNWELL B. ROGERS

New York, N.Y.

☼ A NOTE ON DOCUMENTATION ☼

Many of the documents cited hereafter are rare, and some take on added significance when considered in connection with their full titles and the circumstances of their publication. To avoid duplication, however, complete data are provided only in the Bibliography, of which there are five parts:

Part I is a catalogue of the political songs of 1789; it discloses full titles, airs, and other data, including mention of editions.

Part II is a survey of the various publications in which such songs appear.

Part III is devoted to Revolutionary song materials for years other than 1789.

Part IV lists primary sources other than the above (including modern documentary collections), with full bibliographical data on items that are in any way esoteric.

Part V consists of secondary works.

Throughout the book, reference is made to special parts and subdivisions of the Bibliography by use in the footnotes of the following symbols:

Abbreviated song titles of 1789 are followed by arabic numerals in parentheses—e.g. (1), (2)—these corresponding to the numbered items in Part I (Catalogue).

Abbreviated titles of other original materials are followed by Roman numerals and capital letters—e.g. (II, A), (III, B).

(Titles of documentary collections and of secondary works are not similarly referred to Parts IV and V; but they are, as a rule, given in full when first mentioned.)

The French originals of songs and other Revolutionary writings, when reproduced in this book, appear—in so far as possible—unaltered. Variations and inconsistencies of orthography and apparent textual errors are retained as a matter of course and without comment, except where comment seems necessary to avoid misunderstanding. A similar principle has been applied in reproducing the titles of such materials. This procedure sacrifices stylistic regularity, but it serves to reflect the conventions of the Revolutionary epoch and to suggest here and there a shade of meaning or emphasis which might otherwise be lost.

☼ CONTENTS ☼

THE SPIRIT OF REVOLUTION
IN 1789

"Le Peuple parcourant les rues avec les flambeaux"
By A. Sergent-Marceau, 1789

An aristocrat looks down on the movement and menace of an aroused citizenry. Although the massive walls of her splendid establishment symbolize the strength of a great tradition, her silhouette at the window betrays an anxious concern. Below, "the people"—substantial burghers as well as ragged poor—make common cause against the Old Regime. Here, then, are pictured the two worlds of the French Revolution in its first phase.

✵ INTRODUCTION ✵

THE outbreak of the French Revolution in 1789 is taken by historians to symbolize the end of the *ancien régime* in France and the beginning in modern Europe of rule by the people. Popular government was not at first put into practice by the Revolutionists, but its basic ideals were launched with so much official endorsement and general approval in 1789 that one is justified in attributing to that year the birth of the Revolutionary spirit.

That spirit—epitomized by the First Republic in the slogan "Liberty, Equality, Fraternity"—is very much alive today. After the passage of over one hundred and fifty years, it serves as a torch —by no means the only beacon, but one of the best—which lights the way for the democratic peoples in their effort to preserve popular government and safeguard the freedom of the individual.

In 1789, Frenchmen projected a new order of society, in which economic, political, and religious enthusiasms blended in a common set of purposes. Their program of regeneration might today be called an "ideology." In the present study, however, I have avoided the word, since it was not used by the Revolutionists themselves and, especially, since it has current connotations which might be misleading. But it is a word that I abandon with reluctance, for it conveys the idea of an organic interrelationship of dogmas and sentiments. It is like the word "faith," as applied to a religion, which embodies many different tenets articulated in relation to a total outlook on life. In using the word "spirit" in the title of this book, I wish to imply an equally all-embracing mood— and by no means a single and isolated trend of spontaneous enthusiasm. For the spirit of an age, it seems to me, is never a simple melody, but rather a symphony, with certain dominant notes that ring out clearly in an atmosphere of contrast and dissonance, and with somewhat elusive overtones that are often as revealing as the main theme. It has been in the expectation of finding contradiction and frustration, as well as achievement, that I have examined the emotional and intellectual trends which together, in their dynamic interdependence, come to life as the spirit of 1789.

The end of the old regime was proclaimed in that year, but at first reform was relatively moderate. The men of 1789 still took for granted the continuance of monarchy; hoped to preserve peace abroad; foresaw no terror at home; abhorred such dictatorial methods as Robespierre later used; and extolled popular government only in abstract terms, believing that actual control belonged in the hands of the bourgeois class. But in blasting their way through the barriers of the old regime, they dared to use far more intellectual dynamite than was safe from the standpoint of their somewhat restricted interests. Though concerned primarily with their own rights, they invoked the rights of "man." Hoping by their attack on privilege to install themselves as the dominant class, they proclaimed the rule of "the people." They thought, quite rightly, that the illiterate masses would welcome liberation from the feudal dues and injustices of the old regime, and would want to aid the middle class in a common attack upon them; but they supposed with questionable wisdom that these same masses, once their conditions were improved, would know how to thank their benefactors, and to recognize their betters. They overlooked what the lowly might eventually hope to gain by "a second fit of Revolution."

Despite misjudgment, some hypocrisy, and much self-deceit, the reformers of 1789 were swept along by a remarkable zeal and a great wave of honest conviction. It will appear to their credit that they projected much of what has been durable in the French Revolution. This matter will be developed in later chapters. On the other hand, it will be suggested in the course of the present work that many of the characteristic aberrations of the climax of the Revolution were also present—at least by implication—in the faith of 1789.

The use that I have made of political songs in this investigation is somewhat of a departure in historical writing, and requires a word of explanation. In the first place, this is a work on popular opinion. The customary sources of historical information—legislative records, official papers, and the like—are indispensable guides in such a study, but for the most part they take one only to the outer limits of the field. To understand the reactions of the masses to events, or to appreciate the influence of public opinion on the course of the Revolution, one must go beyond state papers to popular forms of expression.

Critics frequently deplore the low literary and artistic standards of the period, but the fact remains that the people in France at the end of the eighteenth century were highly articulate and found innumerable outlets by which to express the enthusiasm of the moment. Political journals multiplied in number as the Revolution progressed, and exerted a wide influence. It was not long before patriotic themes were set forth in plays, and the theatre thus contributed its share to the output of Revolutionary literature. There were books of all descriptions, but even more popular were pamphlets, which came out in great profusion. Being less subject to official control than the journals, these pamphlets provided the radicals a ready outlet for information surreptitiously gained and for special pleading of the most extreme sort.

The extent and variety of this literature is bound to embarrass the student of popular opinion. He is obliged to extract the Revolutionary spirit from a mass of purely descriptive writings—eighteenth-century journalists were the forerunners of the indefatigable chroniclers of the modern press—and from a mass of literature unrelated to politics, as well as from tracts containing gossip, the expression of personal animosities, the elaboration of petty incidents, and so forth, to say nothing of the numerous and lengthy disquisitions of a pedantic nature.

After making a survey of popular writings, I felt that there was one literary source which contained the essence of the spirit of the French Revolution, largely without extraneous matter. This was the lyrical output of the period, which found its most vigorous expression in political songs. A study of this literature revealed that almost every event of any importance throughout the Revolution occasioned the writing of songs, and that nearly every phase of reform and every aspect of Revolutionary faith found expression either in them or in the more elaborate hymns which were composed as a part of the Revolutionary cults. Here in convenient compass was a distillation of what people felt in the course of great social and political changes. The use of this medium during the Revolution was anything but an incidental pastime: songs were, as we shall see, perhaps the most potent form of self-expression then existing, and were exploited by the Revolutionists of all parties as a major agency of propaganda.

Such a vogue was unprecedented. It is true that from earliest times there had been songs to celebrate acts of heroism, great victories or battles, and notable occasions of state. It is true, besides, that songs had been much used in France for political satire: they were an impressive part of the *Mazarinades* in the seventeenth century, and were used both before and after Mazarin to lampoon court favorites and even unpopular rulers.[1] They had thus served as a potent weapon for the opposition; but not until Revolutionary times was a vast song literature used, in a positive way, to embody the beliefs and aspirations of a people.

It is strange that this subject—despite its interest and importance —has not been extensively treated by historians, especially in view of the fact that many years ago pioneer bibliographical work was undertaken on an impressive scale. In 1898, the Municipality of Paris—to which scholars are indebted for the monumental bibliographies of Tourneux and Tuetey—provided for a similar work by Constant Pierre on the songs and hymns of the Revolution. Pierre thereupon brought to light the existence of some three thousand songs of a political nature which came out in the period between 1789 and 1800.[2] Despite this important beginning, no history of the part which this literature played in the Revolution has been written.[3] Accordingly, it seems advisable to introduce the

[1] Representative songs from the twelfth through the sixteenth century are collected in Leroux de Lincy's *Recueil de chants historiques français depuis le XIIᵉ jusqu'au XVIIIᵉ siècle*, Paris, 1841-42, 2 vols. Though the title indicates coverage of the seventeenth century, the work was carried only to 1600. I know of no comparable collection for the seventeenth century. Of the many contemporary items, attention may be called especially to the *Recueil général, de toutes les chansons mazarinistes. Et avec plusieurs qui n'ont point estées chantées*, Paris, 1649, 27 pp. This work (No. 3055 in C. Moreau, *Bibliographie des Mazarinades*) contains twenty-seven songs. It is preserved in the Talleyrand Collection of the New York Public Library. For the later period, previous to the Revolution, there is the *Chansonnier historique du XVIIIᵉ siècle* . . . , edited by E. Raunié, Paris, 1879-84, 10 vols.

[2] *Les hymnes et chansons de la Révolution, aperçu général et catalogue* . . . (Ville de Paris, Publications relatives à la Révolution française), Imprimerie nationale, Paris, 1904, 1040 pp.

[3] There are, however, writings which treat or touch on various phases of the subject. A considerable number of these are listed in Bibliography v of the present work. Mention may be made here of J. Tiersot's *Les fêtes et les chants de la Révolution française*, Paris, 1908, which serves as an introduction to the ceremonial of the Revolution. The best-documented discussion of the use of political songs during the Revolution appears in the *Aperçu général* of Pierre's *Les hymnes et chansons* . . . , pp. 1-151. His introduction, which is a topical analysis, not strictly speaking a history, offers a wealth of factual detail. Though I have referred to source material where possible, I owe a general acknowledgment to Pierre, in addition to particular acknowledgments subsequently made, for the abundance of references which he cites and the vistas which he opens.

present work, which considers the songs of a particular year, by at least a brief account of the subject as a whole.

The vogue of Revolutionary songs was occasioned by the revival, in the spring of 1789, of the Estates General, a parliamentary body that had been suspended for more than a century and a half. A list of songs inspired by that gathering, by the subsequent capture of the Bastille, and by other events of the year 1789, is given at the end of the present work,[4] and most of the pieces mentioned are discussed in chapters which follow.

To a remarkable extent, songs served during the Revolution as a means of enlightenment, and from 1793 they were exploited by Revolutionary governments as a primary agency of propaganda. But in the beginning the vogue was spontaneous.

The Revolutionists took to singing political songs for pleasure, as they had previously sung folk songs or other popular airs. The *Chronique de Paris* made mention from time to time of their increasing popularity. It noted on May 18, 1790, that "Songs within the reach of the people and made in the spirit of the Revolution are current in the streets." The editor reproduced verses to which the people had listened "with great satisfaction."[5] In a subsequent issue of the same journal, mention was made of a patriotic song which had been sung on the Pont-Neuf "to the great pleasure of all those present and of the singers, who made a considerable sale."[6] What the street singers sold were brochures—or else *feuilles volantes*, leaflets of two or four pages—which carried the words, but rarely the music, of the pieces of their repertoire, and included occasionally a note on the singers themselves. Ladré, an indefatigable composer and singer, used to go about, as one of his publications bears witness, "accompanied by his son."[7] Other street singers frequently went in pairs, as the citizens "Beauchant" and "le Divertissant," who announced that they were at the Tuileries every evening, "either on the terrace of the Feuillants, or in the garden, from five until nightfall to teach the airs of their songs" to "true Republicans."[8] Among other picturesque accounts of this form of out-of-door entertainment is the following record left by a con-

---

[4] See Bibliography I.   [5] *Chronique de Paris*, vol. ii, pp. 549-50.
[6] *Ibid.*, March 19, 1791, vol. iii, p. 310.
[7] Ladré, *Le chansonnier patriote* . . . , p. 1. (III, F)
[8] *Recueil de chansons patriotiques* . . . , *par les Citoyens Leveau, dit Beauchant, et Baptiste, dit le Divertissant*, p. 1. (III, F)

temporary: "Yesterday evening I passed by the Pont-au-Change. I saw a man on a platform surrounded by a great crowd of spectators of all ages and of both sexes, one Belle-Rose, who every evening entertains the public free, plays the violin and sings prettily enough familiar airs and patriotic stanzas."[9]

In the summer of 1790 the first of the great festivals of the Revolution took place. The occasion was the anniversary of the capture of the Bastille. Delegations of citizen-soldiers of the new National Guard converged on Paris from all the provinces. Travel was done on foot, and it took many of the delegations weeks to complete the pilgrimage. The climax of the whole gathering was the Festival of Federation at the Champs de Mars, July 14. For a long time in advance, the Parisians were ardently engaged in preparing the great field and the elaborate stands. People of all ages, women no less than men, repaired in their spare time to the Champs de Mars with shovel or spade. They interspersed their work with dancing and singing. The gay Revolutionary song, *Ça ira*, had just come out.[10] To say that the tune was catchy is to say too little; *Ça ira* was irresistible. People sang it over and over, and danced to it in groups indiscriminately formed on the spur of the moment. "Ça ira!" was the theme of the whole affair. By the time the volunteer workers at the Champs de Mars were through, they had prepared an area to accommodate three hundred thousand people, and had liked doing it.

In making these preparations, Frenchmen were under the illusion that the success of the Revolution had already been secured. Convinced that the democratic cause heralded a new day for mankind, they opened their hearts to one another without reserve, as if brotherhood and good fellowship had come to stay. The light-

[9] *Chronique de Paris*, February 17, 1792, pp. 190-91. This article, signed "P. D - - - - - - ," protests against the obscenity of certain songs in the repertoire of Belle-Rose, and recommends interference by the police.

[10] The lyrics of *Ah! ça ira* were written by the street singer Ladré, to a popular new dance tune, *Le carillon national* of Bécourt. The optimistic expression "ça ira" ("it will succeed," or in the idiom of today, "it will go over") was a favorite of Benjamin Franklin, to whose influence has been attributed the popularity of the slogan in Paris. The song *Ça ira* remained in vogue throughout the Revolution; it appeared in a great number of editions and parodies, the words being revised and adapted to changing circumstances. The text, at first cheerful in tone, became sinister indeed in certain of the later versions. For further consideration of this piece, and concerning the problem of dating its origin, see Appendix A, no. 315.

heartedness of the Parisians was shared by the provincials. Those who went to Paris, *fédérés*, as they were called, were feted all along the way; those who remained at home arranged their own local celebrations of the Bastille anniversary. To meet people and to be able to sing with them was one of the most cherished opportunities afforded by this mood of national rejoicing.[11]

There are numerous local accounts which give some idea of the singing strength of France at that time. Especially entertaining and instructive in this regard is a description by one Bagneris of the experiences of the deputation from Rouen.[12] In their progress toward Paris, they too were singing *Ça ira*. This was but one of the patriotic airs which kept the feet of the marchers light and their hearts gay. Not only did they sing on entering villages and on leaving them, but they took part in local celebrations, sharing in the singing, dancing, and patriotic ritual of fellow citizens in such towns as St. Germain[13] and Versailles.[14] The climax of the whole pilgrimage was, of course, Paris. Accounting amply for the various formal celebrations at the capital, Bagneris describes also impromptu occasions, such as this: "But what new songs of joy are heard . . . ! Brothers-in-arms are arriving in a throng. They ask us to join them, and to sing with them." Admitting that not all of the songs were of the highest literary merit, Bagneris contends that a whiff of patriotism is worth all the wit that one can put into the most studied couplet.[15]

When in the preceding year the patriots celebrated the capture of the Bastille three days after the event, they gave thanks at Notre Dame by singing the *Te Deum*. Shortly thereafter there were protests against this dependence on church ritual and the use of Latin. It was proposed that the patriots express their thanks to God in a language that could be understood by all. To this end, Marie-Joseph Chénier, brother of André, wrote a hymn in the French vernacular to celebrate the anniversary of the capture of the Bas-

11 Pierre refers in his Introduction (*op.cit.*, p. 36) to "more than sixty" songs written to celebrate the Festival of Federation. In the *Catalogue* itself he lists over eighty items occasioned in one way or another by that event (for a further word on this subject see below, p. 223, including footnote 58). In addition, I have come across several songs on the Federation which Pierre does not mention.

12 F. A. Bagneris, *Récit de tous les incidents qui ont dû intéresser les Députés de la Garde-Nationale de Rouen . . . , 1790.* (III, D)

13 *Ibid.*, p. 17.   14 *Ibid.*, p. 31.   15 *Ibid.*, pp. 68-70.

tille.[16] As it turned out, Chénier's lyrics were not ready in time; but a "sacred drama" in French, entitled *La prise de la Bastille*, was performed by opera singers in Notre Dame Cathedral on the eve of the Federation.[17] The narrative, carried by a single voice and several choruses, traced the first success of the Revolution in · phrases borrowed from Scripture. This "sacred drama" is an early and remarkable instance of the adoption by the patriots of religious forms, which came to play an increasingly important part in the civic ceremonies of later years. As for the vast gathering at the Champs de Mars on the following day, innumerable observers have paid tribute to the grandeur and sublimity of the celebration, the people assembled apparently having been inspired by a patriotic enthusiasm akin to religious fervor.

Although original music was composed for ceremonial pieces of the type referred to above, and for many casual songs as well, the general practice was to adapt new words to airs which were already popular (i.e., folk songs and other pieces which had survived in France for varying lengths of time, some of them very old)[18] and to publish simply the words with the familiar airs indicated. The reason why more songs did not have original musical settings is explained by Pierre in the following interesting passage: "Granted the inaptitude of the public to learn new melodies easily and its very marked preference for airs which had become familiar as a result of being frequently heard throughout many years, there could be no direct collaboration—save for rare exceptions, which we have cited—between the lyrist and the musician. For centuries, music had been assigned an accessory role, with the result that nonsense and anomalies frequently resulted from adaptations which were made at random and without discernment. A number of song writers were aware of this, but they preferred to yield to

---

[16] *Le Chant de 14 juillet, par M.-J. Chénier, musique de Gossec.* See Pierre, *op.cit.*, pp. 197-205. This was the first of about thirty such hymns that Chénier wrote to further the progress of the Revolution.

[17] *La prise de la Bastille, hiérodrame tiré des Livres saints, suivi du cantique en action des grâces, Te Deum laudamus, par Désaugiers.* See Pierre, *op.cit.*, pp. 185-94, and J. Tiersot, *Les fêtes et les chants de la Révolution française*, pp. 27-30.

[18] The predilection for popular songs appears to have been particularly strong in France; at least, Frenchmen felt this to be the case. Rousseau, for example, having once come across a collection of *chansons populaires* which had been circulated in a town, exclaimed: "These are memoirs for the history of France which one would scarcely conceive of in any other country."

the popular requirements rather than to compromise the success of their works. . . . Those who tried to free themselves from this tyrannic custom by composing new airs for their songs, protected themselves against the ignorance or prejudice of the public by indicating at the end of their compositions familiar airs which might also be used."[19]

Club meetings, banquets, and reunions of various sorts afforded the patriots ample opportunity for singing in unison, a form of expression which they particularly enjoyed. In this connection, an interesting custom developed at the theatres. Early in the Revolution actors adopted the practice of singing one or more patriotic songs in the course of a performance.[20] It was usually intended that only the performers should sing, but the audience could not resist taking part. "The desire to sing in concert with the actors is so compelling in France," an English observer was reported to have said, "that in the case of a *well-known song*, he had sometimes seen the music leader of a theatre play almost the same role as the precentor in the churches, who serves only to intone the psalm and whose voice is then absorbed by that of the entire audience."[21] Thus, political songs came to be sung in almost all the theatres and at the opera as well. This vogue, at the height of the Revolution, transformed these places of entertainment into centers of great political excitement.[22]

There were many amateur enthusiasts who did not stop at singing; regardless of literary qualifications, they went in for the art of

[19] Pierre, *op.cit.,* p. iii. Of the approximately 3,000 songs of the French Revolution which are known, but 150 were written to new music. The rest were put to familiar airs, some old, such as *Aussitôt que la lumière*, which served for nearly seventy of the songs. Certain new airs, too, were used repeatedly, the tune of the *Chant du départ* serving for forty Revolutionary songs, and that of the *Marseillaise* being the most frequently re-used of them all. Pierre has found that over 650 different airs, including both old and new, provided the musical settings for the songs of the Revolution. See *op.cit.*, p. 50. In Bibliography I of the present work, mention is made of the airs which were used in 1789.

[20] This custom had already commenced in 1789; see Bibliography I, 43 and 44.

[21] Reported in the *Chronique de Paris*, October 19, 1792, p. 1170.

[22] The reference above is particularly to the custom of singing patriotic songs in the intermissions. By 1790, propaganda plays with Revolutionary themes were produced, and in the course of many of these, patriotic songs relating to the development of the story were interpolated. For a catalogue of music in plays of this character, see Pierre, *op.cit.*, pp. 822-38. In an interesting article on the Paris theatre during the Reign of Terror—*Journal of Modern History*, vol. xvii, no. 4 (1945), pp. 332-55—Beatrice Hyslop gives considerable attention to songs.

composition. This they sometimes did with official encouragement, as the following account of a ceremony at Arras suggests: "The citizens had been invited also to compose songs for the occasion. Several bright spirits had given free play to their poetic gifts, with the result that the singers were confronted by an embarrassment of choices. Each began to sing the hymn that suited him best, something which was bound to produce a fair degree of cacophony. But the harmony of good feeling took the place of perfect musical accord."[23] Details of a ceremony held the same evening indicate that these compositions, apparently so spontaneous, were made to some purpose, contributors having been instructed to instill into their songs "all the energy of patriotism, in order to express the horror which tyranny inspires in free men."[24]

The Arras celebration was in 1792. It was a fateful year—not only for France, but for Europe as well; for on April 20 the new constitutional monarchy of the Revolution declared war on reactionary Austria. Prussia was allied to the Hapsburg power, and before long the armies of both countries were invading France. In the face of this advance, the Legislative Assembly, July 11, made its stirring declaration that *la Patrie* was in danger. Of the patriots who responded, perhaps the most notable were those from Marseilles who arrived in Paris on July 30, singing the great song that was to become the national anthem of France. These new arrivals played a prominent part in the insurrection of August 10, by which Louis XVI, already discredited, was virtually overthrown. By the end of September, 1792, France had become a Republic.

War heightened the popularity of patriotic songs, and altered their tone. More than ever they became nationalistic and militant. Not that this hard quality was entirely new, for a struggle between Revolutionary France and her predatory neighbors had in a measure been foreseen. The battle hymn *Veillons au salut de l'Empire*, for example, was written weeks before war was declared. It appeared shortly thereafter in a Paris journal,[25] with this injunction: "May the songs of liberty echo in all places, and fill the tyrants of the earth with profound terror."

[23] E. Lecesne, *Plantation de l'arbre de la liberté à Arras, en 1792*, pp. 300-1.
[24] *Ibid.*, p. 301.
[25] Under the title "Romance patriotique," in *Annales patriotique et littéraires* . . . , May 3, 1792, p. 550.

The "tyrants of the earth" were not so easily intimidated, and they persisted in their attitude of proud contempt toward the beginnings of popular government in France. Nevertheless, there were French enthusiasts who seemed to suspect that the song was mightier than both the pen and the sword. Poets had expressed, in one piece or another, certain of the stirring sentiments that are known to us today through the *Marseillaise*, but none of them had quite encompassed in one work the elements of the war crisis which confronted France. It was Rouget de Lisle's good fortune— and one great achievement—to combine the reforming spirit of the Revolution and the militant spirit of nationalism in a balanced and vigorous text, and to find for it, a suitable—one might almost say, the inevitable—air.[26] It was as though a human organism had in one brief interval caught the meaningful vibrations of an age and conveyed them—more as agent than creator—in a musical pattern so expressive and authentic that it met instant recognition.[27]

The success of the *Marseillaise* was such that astute observers began to foresee that some deliberate use might be made of it and of other patriotic songs to spread the spirit of the Revolution. "I propose," wrote a contemporary, "to add our songs to our cannon; the former will be for the peasants' cottages, the latter for the châteaux. . . . Songs will have a more prompt effect than writings, will be their precursors, and will scatter sparks of light in advance. The *Marseillaise* at once enlightens, inspires and cheers; it alone sufficed to subjugate the entire youth of Brabant. I conclude to the effect that four singers be attached to each of our armies."[28] The Convention did not follow exactly the terms of this proposal; but it presently acted on the conviction that the song could be ex-

[26] The *Marseillaise* is a paean of balanced emotions: of love of Revolutionary France, on the one hand, and of hate of her enemies, on the other. So violent is the language of this Revolutionary hymn that it has served to prompt Frenchmen to ruthless acts of hatred and vengeance in the course of civil strife, as well as to incite them in their national struggles to sublime acts of patriotic devotion.

[27] Rouget de Lisle did nothing else of comparable importance. For a time he served with distinction in the army, but, except for this brief success, he seemed fated, by his arrogance and irascibility, to block the many avenues of advancement that were open to him. For more than thirty years after the Revolution he lived in obscurity, much of the time in poverty. At last, when he was past seventy, substantial pensions were granted him under the July Monarchy in recognition of his service to France as the author of the *Marseillaise*. He died in 1836.

[28] Roussel, in a communication to the *Chronique de Paris*, October 29, 1792, pp. 1210-11.

ploited to quicken the spirit of the fighting forces of France and to stimulate among foreign peoples a universal uprising.

At this point, it may be of interest to consider the numerical increase in political songs. The figures which follow are based on the *Aperçu général et catalogue* of Constant Pierre.[29] They take into account the numerous items which Pierre found in libraries and collections, but afford no indication of the vast amount of material which may have been lost in the course of years. Furthermore, it must not be assumed, even in regard to such items as are extant, that the totals given below are all-inclusive. There are certainly many songs in the libraries of the French provinces and elsewhere which did not come to Pierre's attention.[30] Nevertheless, the figures at hand are based on extensive investigations, especially at Paris, and—subject to certain qualifications[31]—they may be regarded as representative of general trends. It appears that the vogue of political songs reached its height under the Convention. Whereas Pierre's summaries for the first four year of the Revolution indicate an average annual output of slightly over 250 new political songs, his total for 1793 is 590, and for the following year 701, after which there was a decided falling off.[32] One important factor Pierre fails to take consistently into account. In the early years (1789-1792) many of the songs—perhaps a third—were the work of the aristocrats. When this group of anti-Revolutionary pieces is discounted, the relative numerical preponderance of the two later years becomes even greater.[33] It should also be mentioned that Pierre misdates many items, especially among those which he attributes to the pre-Republican period, his tendency being to fix the date too early.[34] A revision of his work would therefore involve assigning a considerable number of entries to years later than

[29] In that author's *Hymnes et chansons de la Révolution*, referred to above.

[30] In my research I have come across a considerable number of items that Pierre does not mention; those ascribable to 1789 are included in Bibliography I, where they are signalized as "Addenda."

[31] Such as are stated in the course of the paragraph above, and on page 31.

[32] Pierre gives figures for each year from 1789 through 1800. See *op.cit.*, p. 34. Concerning his analysis of the songs of 1789, see "Critique of the *Catalogue* of Constant Pierre," Appendix A.

[33] It is true that some songs of 1794—those of the Thermidorian reaction—should likewise be discounted as anti-Revolutionary, but their number is relatively small.

[34] These errors, in so far as they apply to 1789, receive detailed consideration in Appendix A.

those under which they now stand in the *Catalogue,* and this change would further emphasize the increased vogue of the songs as the Revolution reached its height.

The significance of this vogue is expressed in the numerous almanacs and handbooks which were devoted in whole or in part to political songs. The most typical of these were called *almanachs chantants,* or *chansonniers.* These anthologies were offered by their editors as containing the essence of the Revolutionary spirit. Many of them carried prefaces which throw light, not only on the singing habits of the Revolutionists, but also on their ideals and aspirations.

Le chansonnier patriote . . . , published in the first year of the Republic, carried the following introductory notice: "There is need for an anthology in which the best patriotic songs that have appeared since the Revolution are brought together; we have been confident of rendering a service to liberty and its friends by presenting such a work. . . . Here one sings only hatred and contempt of kings; ridicule is directed only against their partisans, against traitors and against false patriots."[35]

About the same time an anthology was published at Commercy. The editor explained his work, in part, as follows: "The song stimulates courage and celebrates virtue. All famous peoples have had their Poets and Musicians. The French, more than any other, know how to intersperse the garlands of glory with the flowers of enjoyment. Every phase of their beneficent revolution is marked by Hymns. This sort of chronology electrifies Republican souls, and depicts the happy public spirit."[36]

The editor of the *Almanach républicain chantant, pour l'an 2,* expressed the hope that "the aristocrat, the federalist, the counter-Revolutionary" would read, and even sing, the patriotic couplets which he had compiled.[37] He pictured these reactionaries as "the most unhappy of men on account of their opinions," and apparently had little doubt that through the influence of patriotic education they would be converted to the Revolutionary cause.

---

[35] *Le chansonnier patriote, ou Recueil de chansons . . . par différents auteurs, Paris, an I*er *de la République.* (III, F)

[36] *Recueil de chansons civiques et martiales, Commercy,* n.d., p. 2. (III, F)

[37] *Almanach républicain chantant, pour l'an 2 . . . , par le citoyen B - - - , Paris,* p. 2. (III, F)

This would dispel the "grief and despair" and "chagrin" from which he presumed they were suffering. Accordingly, the Revolutionist could afford to pity, perhaps even to love, his enemies. This hope of reforming the aristocrats, which was frequently expressed by the patriots, is an instance of what the psychologists call a projection, i.e., a superimposing of some phase or adaptation of one's own views on another. It was assumed that the Revolution was an expression of absolute truth and justice, long awaited, and that men generally, including the aristocrats, would in time see the light. Strange as such optimism may seem from the political standpoint, it is entirely understandable in terms of the history of religious experience. The devout generally suppose that their particular faith will eventually win the allegiance of men everywhere, will become universal. This is the highest aim of "conversion," and was what many of the Revolutionists were hoping to achieve.[38]

Also of interest is the preface of the *Nouveau chansonnier patriote . . . , l'an 2ᵉ*, which contains the following significant passages:

"Popular songs are with the French what morality is with other peoples: there are no events or remarkable deeds which have not been put into couplets. It is therefore to give to posterity a new proof of that delightful frenzy which fills the heads of all Frenchmen, that we have gathered together in an anthology the best productions of this kind.

"A eulogy of the martyrs of our revolution appears at the beginning of this collection: this eulogy . . . was read in all the sections of Paris and was everywhere greeted with transports of patriotism. . . .[39]

[38] In practice they had to be satisfied with much less. As the Revolution progressed, new converts were not won from the aristocracy, and the enemies of the Revolution proved obdurate indeed. This situation filled the patriots with righteous indignation comparable to that felt by the Crusaders toward infidels, or by Medieval inquisitors toward heretics. As Robespierre put it, in the climax of his famous report of May 7, 1794, on the Worship of the Supreme Being: "Commandez à la victoire, mais replongez surtout le vice dans le néant. Les ennemis de la république, ce sont les hommes corrompus" (*Moniteur*, vol. x, p. 932). The *guillotine*, accordingly, was busiest at the height of the Reign of Virtue.

[39] By no means an unusual occurrence, for by this time the Revolutionists had their own martyrology. The allusion in the text above is to Marat and Le Pelletier. Interesting in this connection is an engraving of "the Seven Martyrs of Liberty," which serves as the frontispiece of the *Chansonnier de la Montagne . . . , l'an III.* (III. F)

"People of all nations . . . unite with the French. Blush to wear your chains any longer, and, in imitating us, hasten to become worthy of liberty."[40]

This was world revolution.

The amazing successes of the armies of the French Republic, which by 1793 were battling the forces of Sardinia, England, Holland, and Spain, as well as those of Austria and Prussia, and which a year later were driving them all back, naturally added fuel to the flames of patriotic self-confidence. The early humanitarian impulses of the Revolution persisted, but, as the war progressed, they became inseparably fused with national pride and intolerance. All the new, as well as the old, impulses found a natural expression in song. Frenchmen took pride in their habit of singing and regarded it as one source of their success. We read in the preface of the *Chansonnier de la République* (for the year III) this relevant and rather striking paragraph: "A nation which has known how to combat all prejudices at once, which has made Europe ring with the sound of its exploits, and of its songs of victory, and which has proven to the universe that heroism can be linked with gaiety, is, for philosophy, a touching spectacle. What will the ferocious reactionaries, who accuse the French of levity, say when they see them equal the heroes of antiquity, in singing the *carmagnole?*[41] What will they say when they hear on the battlefields of the republicans these patriotic refrains, which precede and follow the most bloody combats?"[42]

By 1793 the National Convention was fully aware of the important effect of songs on morale, and began to use them, somewhat as radio is used today, to reach and arouse the masses. Although in Revolutionary times the democratic press had made a notable beginning, its field was limited, because of the fact that the French people were still largely illiterate. Much of the propaganda of that day had, therefore, to be oral; and apparently lyrics

[40] *Nouveau chansonnier patriote ou recueil . . . ; Lille, Paris, l'an 2e.* (III, F)

[41] The *Carmagnole*, which took its name from a popular dance, appeared in August or September, 1792. It expressed contempt and mockery of Louis and Marie Antoinette. Following are the opening lines of an oft-quoted version:

> Madame Veto avait promis
> De faire égorger tout Paris.

[42] *Chansonnier de la République pour l'an III . . . , Bordeaux et Paris,* p. 1. (III, F)

remembered for enjoyment's sake proved to be at least as stimulating as the reasoned arguments of political discourse.

The members of the Convention had ample opportunity to gain firsthand knowledge of the "delightful frenzy" of popular singing. They entertained at their sessions numerous delegations representing both sexes, all ages, and most classes of French society, and they frequently permitted these visitors to sing in their presence. Just as the theatres were transformed into centers of political excitement, so on occasions did the Revolutionary parliament become an arena of theatrical effects. The sessions of July 4 and 5, 1793, may serve as an example. On the former day, groups of "jeunes citoyennes" twice regaled the Convention with song: five girls rendered "an invocation to the love of *la patrie* and the hymn of the men of Marseilles"; presently, another group of girls sang "patriotic hymns" to the legislators.[43] They had come with deputations from the forty-eight sections of Paris to pay honor to the Constitution. On the following day several delegations together sang a "Hymn to Liberty" and other patriotic lyrics, "accompanied by drums and musical instruments."[44] One of the deputations included some of the best operatic talent of the capital. No doubt, a striking effect was attained when the opera star Chenard, after singing the *Marseillaise*, turned to the benches of the dominant Jacobin party and added a new stanza to the "true defenders of the people."[45]

The legislators occasionally enjoyed an advance audition. For example, on November 8, 1793, the band of the National Guard played for the Convention a new "Hymn to Liberty" two days before it was heard at the remarkable Festival of Reason in Notre Dame Cathedral.[46] The words of the hymn were by Marie-Joseph Chénier; the music, by Gossec. Both Chénier and Gossec, together with an important delegation of musicians and officials, attended the session. The account in the *Moniteur*[47] tells of repeated applause by deputies and spectators. Also present on this occasion was a group of pupils of the band, who were introduced as being

---

[43] *Moniteur . . .* , July 6, 1793, p. 806.

[44] Quoted by Pierre, *op.cit.*, p. 7, who refers to the *Procès-verbal* (mss.) at the Archives Nationales.

[45] *Moniteur*, July 7, 1793, p. 809.

[46] To celebrate the new Revolutionary religion, called at first the Worship of Reason.

[47] *20 brumaire, an II* (November 10, 1793). p. 202.

among "the poorest citizens of each section." They, too, were given a chance to play in the presence of the legislators. One purpose of the visit of the musicians was to request that a national institute of music be created. Acting as spokesman, Chénier called the attention of the Convention to the influence which music had exerted "on the patriots at Paris, in the departments, on the frontiers." Chénier's proposal was approved in principle, and the National Institute of Music, renamed in 1795 the Conservatory, was brought into being.

When on January 15, 1794, a deputation of boys, "pupils of *la patrie*," went before the Convention on behalf of the Section des Piques, and one of them sang a patriotic song, Laloi, a member of some prominence, demanded that the lyrics be inserted in the *Bulletin*. Danton protested that this publication was not intended "to circulate verse in the Republic, but good laws written in good prose." His objection prompted another member, Dubouchet, to give the following interesting testimony: "Nothing is more appropriate than patriotic hymns and songs to electrify the souls of Republicans. When on mission in the departments [i.e., administrative divisions of France] I was witness to the prodigious effect which they produce. We used always to end the meetings of official bodies and of the popular societies in singing hymns, and the enthusiasm of the members and spectators followed as an inevitable consequence."[48] Danton, without denying the efficacy of the songs, nevertheless insisted that the Convention could not pass judgment on the sense and words of a song that had not been well heard. He urged that the matter be referred to the Committee of Public Instruction.[49]

This proposal was accepted, but the custom of interrupting the sessions of the Convention with song continued. On March 16, twenty days before his death, Danton rose to protest again. A delegation from the Section of Mont-Blanc had congratulated the Convention on the firmness with which it had struck down the Hébertist "traitors." The spokesman of the delegation then undertook to sing a song of his own composition. Danton stopped him. He denounced the practice of permitting the work of government to be thus delayed, and concluded as follows: "I do justice to the civic

[48] *Moniteur, 27 nivôse, an II* (January 16, 1794), p. 471.   [49] *Loc.cit.*

devotion of the petitioners, but I demand that from now on one hear at the tribunal only reason in prose."[50] A motion to this effect was passed. From then on there were auditions, but only of a more dignified sort, as when the Convention had certain festivals celebrated in the midst of its deliberations. On such occasions hymns were played or sung by members of the National Institute or of its successor, the Conservatory.

In May, 1794, a new Revolutionary cult, the Worship of the Supreme Being, was established by the Convention at the behest of Robespierre. This was a modification of the Worship of Reason, inaugurated the year before. In both these cults patriotic festivals of the type already referred to played an important part. It was hoped that the Revolutionary religion would take the place of Christianity. Much of the reforming zeal of the late eighteenth century was pagan in spirit; and during the Revolution—when a bitter struggle between the patriots and the Church developed— paganism, accompanied by the highest moral pretensions, gained in strength.[51] The Revolution produced four cults, a fact which has been confusing to later generations, for it is often assumed that these cults represented a somewhat haphazard growth of scattered sects. Actually, they appeared successively; it is true that the last two overlapped, but in general the cults replaced one another as a continuing expression of the Revolutionary religion. There were changes in name and ritual, but, as Mathiez has amply demonstrated,[52] there was but one system of faith which was embodied in these successive forms of worship. The essence of the faith was the equality and liberty of man, revealed by Nature, fostered by the State (la patrie), kept alive through brotherly love (fraternité), and consecrated by patriotic devotion and sacrifice—if need be, by death. The new paganism—introduced as the Worship of Reason

[50] Moniteur, 27 ventôse, an II (March 17, 1794), p. 716.

[51] Although this paganism was a protest against Christianity—many elements of which had supported the old regime and obstructed the Revolutionary cause—it paralleled Christianity in numerous respects, as Carl Becker has charmingly and entertainingly shown in The Heavenly City of the Eighteenth Century Philosophers (New Haven, 1932). The use of the word "pagan" is mine. Professor Becker refers to the Revolutionary worship as "a civic and, as one may say, secular religion of humanity" (p. 156), or simply as "the new religion of humanity" (p. 158).

[52] See especially Contributions à l'histoire religieuse de la Révolution française, Paris, 1907; Les origines des cultes révolutionnaires (1789-1792), Paris, 1904; and Le Théophilanthropie et le Culte décadaire . . . , Paris, 1904.

and revised in May, 1794, as the Worship of the Supreme Being —survived under the Directory as the Decadal Cult and Theophilanthropy.[53] Furthermore, as Mathiez has shown,[54] this Revolutionary faith was already a potent religion before Robespierre settled on certain of its forms and won for it official recognition. Many of its first impulses date, as I shall later have occasion to show, from 1789.

The members of the Convention, affected by the growing religious fervor of the Revolution, and confronted by a vast task of indoctrination, were quick to make use of music as part of their extensive propaganda. They not only subsidized patriotic songs for a great variety of occasions, but also undertook to promote their influence by mandatory legislation. On November 24, 1793, for example, the Committee of Public Safety decreed that the *Marseillaise* should be played at all theatrical performances in the Republic, "regularly on all the *décadi* [the tenth day, or day of rest, under the new Revolutionary calendar] and at any time the public may demand it."[55]

Government subsidies undoubtedly contributed greatly to the spread of patriotic songs and hymns. The Convention had commenced to spend money for this purpose even before the inauguration of the Worship of Reason.[56] It bought, for example, at a cost of over two thousand livres, 2,500 copies of Imbault's elaborately prepared edition of hymns sung at the Festival of August 10, 1793.[57] An indefatigable song writer, T. Rousseau, requested the Committee of Public Safety to commission him to bring out a new edition of 40,000 or 50,000 copies of one of his works, for

[53] The Decadal Cult was embodied in decrees passed after the fall of Robespierre, by the Convention, and later by the Directory. It salvaged elements of the Worship of the Supreme Being. Theophilanthropy was a cult of private origin, which the government adopted in 1797; but the following year the Directory again made the Decadal Cult the official religion.

[54] See especially *Les origines des cultes révolutionnaires.*

[55] *Recueil des actes du Comité de salut publique* . . . , vol. viii, p. 670.

[56] The possible use of songs as propaganda had caught the attention of officials in France as early as 1791. In that year the intendant Laporte projected an agency, involving an expense of 2,400,000 livres a year from the civil list, to influence leaders and molders of opinion. The plan, which according to Sagnac reflected the thought of Rivarol and Mirabeau, was submitted, February 23, to the King. Among the several classes of persons who were to receive payments under this scheme were "des auteurs et des chanteurs de chansons." P. Sagnac, *La Révolution (1789-1792)*, Paris, 1920, p. 273.

[57] According to Pierre, *op.cit.*, p. 119.

distribution "in all the communes attacked by the leprosy of fanaticism, royalism, or federalism."[58] Though the Committee appears not to have acted on this proposal, it is interesting to note, in connection with Rousseau's request, his claim that the work in question had been distributed to all the armies and had run to nearly 100,000 copies.[59]

An important request came from a music publishing association which had been organized late in 1793 by members of the newly created National Institute. This Association—the "Magasin," as it was called—hoped to bring out, in the form of a monthly serial, scores for the decadal and national festivals, and proposed that the government subsidize the undertaking. The musicians complained that under existing circumstances merchants were paying composers a mere two or three hundred livres for the manuscripts of works on which they (the merchants) later realized as much as forty or fifty thousand. The memoir of the Association suggested various patriotic reasons why the Convention should occupy itself with the matter. The Committee of Public Safety examined the proposal, and pronounced it "important in revolutionary connections"; it would, according to their analysis, improve public spirit, arouse courage, and offer a means of strengthening the moral effect of civic festivals. The Committee accordingly decreed that the Association should provide the government, each month, 550 copies of the proposed serial, which was to be published in quarto. In return, the Association was to receive from the government a sum of 33,000 livres.[60] The enterprise developed tardily, but essentially as planned. The new publication, *Musique à l'usage des fêtes nationales*, consisted of twelve issues, and contained scores by Catel, Cherubini, Gossec, Lesueur, Méhul, and others, some of the scores being known today only through this series.[61] The first num-

---

[58] "Fanaticism"—a word often used by the Revolutionists to denote Catholicism. "Federalism" refers to the program of the Gironde party, which was bitterly opposed by the Jacobins, who favored a strongly centralized government.

[59] Pierre, from whom I have borrowed the account of Rousseau's proposal (*op. cit.*, p. 32), cites as the source of his information a document in the handwriting of Barère at the Archives Nationales.

[60] Session of 27 *pluviôse, an II* (February 15, 1794), *Recueil des actes . . .* , vol. xi, p. 157. The preceding month, the Committee of Public Instruction had reviewed the proposal of the Association and had approved it in principle. See *Procès-verbaux du Comité d'Instruction publique*, vol. iii, pp. 299-301 and 303-4.

[61] The *Musique à l'usage des fêtes nationales* is itself rare. Pierre reported the existence of only one complete set of the twelve issues, that at the Conservatoire, Paris.

ber having appeared on April 9, 1794, a deputation of artists, headed by Gossec, went before a meeting of the Jacobins the following day, to announce the arrival of the new publication and to present the Society with one of the first copies.[62]

This activity of professional musicians was evidently not sufficient. On May 7, the Convention asked that all with talents "worthy of serving the cause of humanity" contribute civic hymns and songs to the successful establishment of decadal and national festivals.[63] Ten days later, the Committee of Public Safety repeated the invitation, calling on all composers and others interested in music to provide for these festivals "plays, martial music, and whatever else their art might offer as being best suited to recall to republicans the most cherished sentiments and memories of the Revolution."[64] These promptings no doubt account in part for the record number of songs—Pierre found 120—which were written to celebrate the Festival of the Supreme Being, June 8, 1794.

The *Magasin*, encouraged by its success in obtaining a subsidy for its serial publication of music for festivals, before long projected a second enterprise. The new plan called for the issuance of "a collection of songs and *romances civiques* in the form of a journal," to be underwritten by the government. The Committee of Public Safety viewed the proposal favorably, and on July 9 decreed that "the Association of Artists, Musicians, and Composers shall distribute to the various armies of the Republic, on land and sea, 12,000 copies of patriotic songs and hymns such as are suitable for propagating the republican spirit and the love of public virtues." The decree bears the signatures of an important company of Jacobins: Carnot, Barère, Billaud-Varenne, Collot d'Herbois, C. A. Prieur, and Saint-Just.[65] For the support of this journal for one year the government paid in installments a total of over 60,000 livres.[66]

In addition to the serial issues which it supported, the Conven-

[62] *La Société des Jacobins, Recueil de documents* . . . , vol. vi, p. 63.

[63] This call was part of the decree of *18 floréal, an II* (May 7, 1794) relative to the institution of decadal and national festivals. *Moniteur, 19 floréal, an II*, p. 932.

[64] *Recueil des actes* . . . , vol. xiii, p. 572.   [65] *Ibid.*, vol. xv, pp. 25-26.

[66] Pierre, *op.cit.*, pp. 122 and 129. Subsequently, May 27, 1795, the Committee indemnified the Association for losses on its periodical publications (caused, it was held, by the repeal of the Law of the Maximum) to the amount of 47,525 livres. *Ibid.*, p. 136, and *Recueil des actes* . . . , vol. xxiii, p. 581.

tion provided for the publication and dissemination of hymns and songs in connection with particular occasions. For the festival of July 14, 1794, for example, it subsidized the distribution of 8,000 copies of *La Bataille de Fleurus* and of the *Chant du départ*.[67] The battle of Fleurus had been won by the army of Jourdan on June 26. This decisive victory saved France from invasion and opened Belgium to conquest by the Republican armies. One of the soldiers who took part wrote exultantly, "We fought one against ten, but the Marseillaise was fighting beside us!"[68]

The few instances already cited may serve to suggest that by 1794 the Convention was using hymns and political songs as a primary agency of its propaganda. The first half of that year was the period of Robespierre's greatest influence. He not only determined party policies, but was the outstanding leader in matters of Revolutionary culture and morale. On July 24, a few days before his sudden fall, the Committee of Public Safety was expressing concern over the need for speed in the circulation of patriotic songs, shipments of which had been ordered by the Committee to be sent "to the departments and to the armies of the Republic."[69] It may be added, as a matter of incidental interest, that Robespierre himself contributed to the production of songs by his death, which was followed by an outburst of lyrics blatantly celebrating the fall of the forsaken leader, whom, a short time before, few would have dared to criticize.

The Convention continued in existence for a year and three months after the overthrow of Robespierre. During this period, July 27, 1794, to October 26, 1795, decisions in regard to music were relegated, for the most part, to the Committee of Public Instruction. This Committee paid one Perrin twelve hundred livres

[67] Pierre, *op.cit.*, p. 133. In his commentary on the hymn on the battle of Fleurus (pp. 322-26), Pierre refers to several editions, all of them with musical scores. There is, besides, an edition giving words only, entitled *Chant Républicain, sur la bataille de Fleurus*, published by l'Imprimerie de la Commission de l'Instruction Publique. This *feuille volante* carries an imprint repeating an order of the *Commission* [sic], *16 messidor, an II*, requiring that the song be distributed to "the Armies, Departments, Districts, Municipalities and Popular Societies of the Republic." In making a collection of Revolutionary songs, I had the good fortune to come across this item; so far as I know, it is the only copy extant. (III, B)

[68] L. Madelin, *The French Revolution*, New York, 1927, p. 402 (translation by F. S. Barr, of *La Révolution*, Paris, 1911). By and large, the French forces at Fleurus were not greatly outnumbered by those of the Coalition.

[69] *Recueil des actes . . .* , vol. xv, p. 398.

to enable him to furnish to the forty-eight sections of Paris 12,000 copies of his hymn in honor of Jean Jacques Rousseau.[70] On another occasion, the Committee—at the instance of the National Institute—provided for 1,000 copies of engraved music to be sent to each of the fourteen armies of the Republic.[71] There is no need to multiply examples. They all point to the same fact: that the Convention regarded music as highly effective propaganda, and was willing to pay well for it.[72]

The Convention hoped to propagate Revolutionary ideas even in foreign countries through the influence of songs. Perhaps it was encouraged in this expectation by the report of contemporaries that in some areas the *Marseillaise* had caught the imagination of foreign populations and had helped to convert them to the cause of the Revolution. In any case, on June 26 the Committee of Public Safety exempted engraved music from the ordinary customs regulations, in order to facilitate its distribution abroad.[73] It is known that boxes of patriotic music were shipped to Zurich,[74] and it may be that similar shipments were made elsewhere across the borders. The fact that evidence on the subject is scanty suggests that the business of exporting music did not become very considerable.[75] It stands, however, as one of many interesting instances

[70] According to Pierre, *op.cit.*, p. 77.

[71] An additional 4,000 copies were ordered "for the Convention and the citizens." *Procès-verbaux du Comité d'Instruction publique; Séance du Ier jour des sans-culottides, an II* (September 17, 1794), vol. v, p. 54.

[72] It should be added that songs were distributed not only by the national government, but also by localities and clubs. Of interest in this connection is a brochure containing a *Chanson nouvelle* . . . , which is accompanied by the following extract from the minutes of the Section of the French Pantheon (October 31, 1793): "Having heard this patriotic hymn, the general assembly, being equally desirous of rendering homage to the lyrical talents of its author, and convinced that the spirit of patriotism and the thirst for glory which characterize republican souls are propagated especially by patriotic and warlike songs, orders its printing up to a cost of 50 livres, and its distribution to the 47 Sections and to the Popular Societies." This piece—the subtitle explains—had originally been sung "by a soldier of the revolutionary army, at the republican society of Provins." This citation may serve to suggest the range of activity which made the diffusion of songs so widespread. *Chanson nouvelle, chantée par un soldat de l'armée révolutionnaire. . . .* (III, B)

[73] *Recueil des actes* . . . , vol. xiv, p. 538.   [74] Pierre, *op.cit.*, p. 135.

[75] The French habit of using songs to express Revolutionary enthusiasm had already exerted influence abroad. At the British Museum there is a sizable collection of Revolutionary songs published at Brussels. As far as I am aware, no study has been made of this literature, but one would be safe in assuming that it owed much to French influence. We know, for example, that on government orders singers from

of the conviction of the Revolutionists that their program would be favorably viewed by all other nations, or, as people said in those days, by the "entire universe."[76]

An extraordinary development in the use of Revolutionary songs occurred in 1795-1796. In those years of reaction and uncertainty, France was rent by a bitter struggle between the Republicans and the Royalists. Each of the opposing parties chose for its battle cry a song, the former cleaving to the *Marseillaise*, the latter adopting the *Réveil du peuple*. In an interesting study of the subject,[77] Aulard explains the effectiveness of these songs as follows: "In this war of the old spirit against the new, the two opposing parties fought one another not merely by newspaper articles and discourses from the rostrum. They would thus have influenced only the literate élite when it was a question of winning the mass of the population, who generally did not know how to read. . . . It was by the political song, sung in the theatre, in the cafés and in the street, that the Royalists and Republicans succeeded, principally at Paris, in influencing the people."[78] Rival leaders exerted this influence so effectively that the singing in public of either the *Marseillaise* or the *Réveil* was sure to lead to confusion, and not infrequently it resulted in riots that had to be put down by armed force. Both the songs had sanguinary associations: the former had been sung by Jacobin enthusiasts around the scaffold; the latter, during the White Terror following the fall of Robespierre, had been used in the south of France by the Royalists as "the signal for proscriptions and the song of assassination."[79] As the words of the

---

the Paris opera toured the chief cities of Belgium in December, 1792, to sing the *Marseillaise* and other Revolutionary airs (Pierre, *op.cit.*, p. 236).

No doubt this mission of song was without benefit of envoys to the New World, but the fact remains that a few weeks later (January 24, 1793) the citizens of Plymouth, Massachusetts, were singing an *Ode to Liberty* at a "Civic Feast to Celebrate the Victories of the French Republic." See Chandler Robbins, *Address at Plymouth . . .*, p. 19. (IV, C)

[76] Mathiez' *La Révolution et les étrangers* (Paris, 1918) provides an excellent brief introduction to this subject.

[77] *La Querelle de la "Marseillaise" et du "Réveil du peuple"* by A. Aulard, first published in *La Grande Revue*, October 1, 1899, and reprinted in the author's *Etudes et leçons sur la Révolution française*, vol. iii, Paris, 1902. In a more meticulous but less engaging account, Pierre (*op.cit.*, pp. 10-24) covers much the same ground.

[78] Aulard, *Etudes et leçons . . .*, vol. iii, pp. 241-42.

[79] From a report by Delaunay before the National Convention, July 19, 1795. *Moniteur, 6 thermidor, an III*, p. 1232.

original texts wore bare through repetition, parodies began to
appear, by which it was possible to express the existing antipathies
even more pointedly than before. The Republicans might be
heard to sing (to the tune of the *Réveil du peuple*, by the way):

> En écrasant les terroristes,
> Les fripons, les assassins,
> Nous frapperons les royalistes,
> Avides du sang des humains. . . .[80]

The Royalists—in their turn resorting to parody—pretended to
convey the Republican outlook, to the strains of the *Marseillaise*:

> Des poignards, mes amis! Dressons des échafauds!
> Couvrons [*bis*] le sol français de morts et de bourreaux![81]

Aulard states that by the late spring of '95, the *Réveil* had triumphed in Paris. The Convention, alarmed at the success of the
reaction, thereupon made the singing of the *Marseillaise* compulsory under certain conditions.[82] This did not produce the desired
results, and the Committees of Public Safety and General Security
then undertook to suppress the *Réveil* by law.[83] But Parisians continued to sing it at the opera and in all the theatres, and the Convention, powerless in the matter, adopted a policy of *laissez faire*.
It even tried to reconcile the opposing parties. This failing, it gave
the *Marseillaise* the benefit of mild legislative support, and in the
last days of the Convention that song momentarily enjoyed what
Aulard calls an "official triumph."[84]

As soon as the Directory took office, Royalist opposition reap-
peared, and the singing of the *Marseillaise* again became the occasion of hostile demonstrations and public disorder.[85] The theatres
were the chief storm centers. The Directory thereupon decreed
that "All the directors, promoters and proprietors of theatrical
performances at Paris are required, on their own responsibility, to
have the orchestra play every day before the rising of the curtain,
airs cherished by Republicans, such as the *Marseillaise*, *Ça ira*,
Veillons au salut de l'Empire, and the *Chant du départ*. In the

---

80 Aulard, *op.cit.*, p. 257.   81 *Ibid.*, p. 260.   82 *Ibid.*, pp. 250-51.
83 *Ibid.*, p. 253.
84 That is, after October 5, 1795, when the Royalist insurrection of Vendémiaire
was suppressed. *Ibid.*, p. 261.
85 *Ibid.*, p. 263.

interval between two plays, the hymn of the *Marseillaise*, or some other patriotic song, shall always be sung. . . . It is expressly forbidden," the decree continued, "to sing, to have sung, or to allow to be sung, the homicidal air, *Le Réveil du peuple*."[86]

Such legislation was of no avail. The Paris crowds were out of hand, and, despite this decree and others which followed, continued for some months to battle over their rival songs. This fanatical preoccupation with song came to an end in the summer of 1796, not as the result of government action but only because the old enthusiasms were spent. Under the Directory a general laxity of morale became increasingly evident both in private and public life. As Mathiez writes, "The people . . . no longer believed in the virtue of its representatives."[87] The atmosphere of a few years before, when the representatives had been "the priests of social happiness," was gone. People, having either embraced, or endured, civic virtue under the Terror, were ready to relax. The "gilded youth" of the Directory replaced the Spartan youth which had responded to the call of Danton and Robespierre. But even this mood of leisure and laxity was not peace. The struggle between the new men of the Revolution and the conservatives continued, and became increasingly complicated. Some of the former, led by the extreme radical Babeuf, alarmed their fellow Republicans by advocating a "society of equals" based on a leveling of fortunes. The Royalists were perhaps more uniform in their views, but still there were those who would have preferred almost any regime to the misgovernment of the Directory, and who might be attracted by any strong leader, should one appear.

It is true that the Directors tried to preserve the cult and, to some extent, the spirit of the French Revolution. They continued the patriotic religion by keeping alive the decadal festivals. There were hymns and songs, as before, though in diminishing numbers.[88] Finally, by superimposing the cult of Theophilanthropy on

---

[86] Session of *18 nivôse, an IV* (January 8, 1796), in *Recueil des actes du Directoire exécutif* . . . , vol. i, p. 391.

[87] *La Théophilanthropie et le Culte décadaire* . . . , p. 37.

[88] The following figures given by Pierre (*op.cit.*, p. 34) are indicative of the trend, though they are subject to allowance for error and to the general qualification concerning statistical summaries which is made subsequently in the text above. For 1793, Pierre lists 590 songs; for 1794, 701; for 1795, 137; and for later years, through 1800, 126, 147, 77, 90, 25.

the established decadal worship, the Directors formalized and attempted to perpetuate the moral preachments of the eighteenth century, but to no avail. The spontaneous enthusiasm of the patriots was gone, and it did no good to try to replace it by dull reminders of duty. The songs which we have considered had been the manifestations of a faith, and on it their life depended. Once disillusionment set in, as it did under the Directory, their vogue was over.

The fraternal spirit of the first stage of the Revolution, with its promise of unity, thus vanished in a maelstrom of bitter hatreds. The five-year period from the fall of Robespierre (1794) to the assumption of power by Napoleon (1799) opened with civil war and threatened to end in anarchy. It has been said that the genius of Napoleon was to externalize an internal conflict: by sending Frenchmen abroad in foreign wars of conquest, he prevented them from killing each other at home. In this sense, one may think of him—with reservations, to be sure—as a Mephistopheles with whom the French people had made a Faustian compact. In accepting his rule, Frenchmen signed away their precious liberty. In return, they gained power—power through guaranteed order and civil equality, and to compensate further for their lost liberty, power over others, in short, glory.

When new enthusiasms crystallized around Bonaparte—as they did progressively with the arrival in France of the news of Lodi, Arcola, Rivoli, of Malta and Alexandria, and of Marengo—they expressed, not the passions of popular government, but the devotion of men in a mood to be led. There was scope under the Empire for patriotism and for pagan worship as well, though in the latter regard the catechism of 1806 struck a new note: "To honor our Emperor and serve him is therefore to serve God himself." Yet whatever was salvaged, one thing at least, popular responsibility for government, was lost. People might again sing, as in an earlier day, of love, glory, and wine, but no longer would they look to the delightful frenzy of song as one means of remaking France and redeeming humanity.

In considering the year 1789, one cannot claim that political

songs enjoyed a popularity comparable to that which they had in
later years, and it is furthermore true that songs were not at first
used as official propaganda. Nevertheless, the lyrics which appeared
in 1789 were an integral part of the vogue which later developed.[89]
One can find among them the prototypes of the patriotic couplets,
of the canticles of worship, and even of the battle hymns, that
followed for the next five years in increasing numbers and with
increasing effect. They serve admirably to convey the initial atmosphere of Revolutionary enthusiasm, which before long achieved
a break with the aristocratic regime and launched Europe on its
new course of democratic nationalism.

A word may be added about the difficulties that arise in connection with the use of political songs as an index of public opinion.
Many of the Revolutionary songs appeared in brochures or *feuilles
volantes*—items which at first disclosed little, if any, bibliographical
information. Only in the later years of the Revolution does one
commonly find a publisher's imprint on songs released in this way.
For the identification and dating of such material, internal evidence must usually serve as the decisive factor. Difficulties are
bound to result. But fortunately this is not the whole story; many
other songs, even from the beginning of the Revolution, appeared
with information concerning the circumstances of their composition, publication, and dissemination. Besides, journalists frequently
made mention of songs, and their comments often establish dates
or other information that it would otherwise be impossible to
obtain. From the materials about which there is positive knowledge, the development of the song literature can be reconstructed.

[89] Of the songs known to me at first hand, there are seventy-nine which can be
ascribed to 1789 with reasonable certainty, and another five with high probability.
Several more, known to me only by their titles, appear to have belonged to that year.
These materials are listed in Bibliography I.

This body of literature no doubt comprises but a small part of the contemporary
output. The proportion of songs lost as the result of neglect appears to have been
greater for 1789 than for later years, when the patriots became increasingly concerned with preserving Revolutionary records for posterity. The result is exemplified
in the bibliographical findings of Grant-Carteret. His work shows that whereas most
of the *almanachs chantants* known to have been published under the Convention
have been preserved, most of those for 1789 apparently are not extant, their titles
being followed by the explanation that the entries were made "d'après un catalogue
de l'époque." (See Grand-Carteret, *Les Almanachs français*, items 895, 900, 920, 942,
943, 954.)

Once this development is clear, many doubtful pieces take their place.[90]

The statistical summaries which Pierre presents, though requiring revision, are not without interest, and I have cited them as indicative of general trends,[91] but one should be wary of placing too great dependence on numerical totals. A single song of great popularity may outweigh a large number of others of no particular appeal. The song material has, therefore, to be broken down on the basis of its merits, and, once this is done, so many factors of individual judgment may have been involved that absolute comparisons of a statistical nature become invalid. The difficulties inherent in the situation are only increased when by 1791 and 1792 certain writers, no longer content with composing single songs for particular occasions, began producing sizable collections—thereby at times enlarging, without proportionately enriching, the song literature. For example, the writer who signed herself "the citizen widow Ferrand," brought out a book of her own lyrics entitled *Le Triomphe de la Liberté et de l'Egalité*.[92] In this work there are thirty songs. None of them was ever reprinted, so far as is known, and there is no indication that any of them was ever sung. Yet each of them counts in Pierre's catalogue as a separate item. Statistically, they are thirty. Actually, their influence may have been negligible. This is admittedly an extreme example of the unreliability of mere numbers when it comes to an analysis of the singing habits of the Revolutionists. Furthermore, extant material alone can be taken into account; one can only guess how much may have been lost in the course of time.

For these and other reasons—including the fact that the songs of 1789 are relatively not numerous—it has seemed that a statistical approach would be unsuitable to the present work. Nevertheless, a full description of material used is very much in order. Such data as are available concerning separate songs are therefore pro-

---

[90] In these matters I had expected to depend on the bibliography of Constant Pierre, to which reference has already been made. But Pierre's work, though providing an immense amount of valuable information, proved in many respects undependable. Its importance and limitations are discussed in my "Critique of the *Catalogue* of Constant Pierre." See Appendix A.

[91] See pages 14-15.

[92] With subtitle, *Almanach Républicain, chansons analogues aux années 1789, '90, '91, '92, par la citoyenne veuve Ferrand.* (III, F)

vided—occasionally in the narrative or in the footnotes, and systematically and fully in Parts ɪ and ɪɪ of the Bibliography. At this
point it is perhaps well to state explicitly what has already been
implied, that it is not the aim of this book to discuss songs as such,
far less to describe the historical development of song literature.[93]
Though these matters are important and relevant, they are subordinated here to the primary purpose of considering lyric expression in relation to popular opinion.

This is a task which calls for a special approach and considerable caution. Therefore, by way of checking results, I have undertaken in the following pages to correlate findings concerning popular opinion that are obtained from the songs with the knowledge
of popular opinion that is obtainable from other sources. This
correlation, far from raising new problems, has been a simple and
satisfactory undertaking, since the attitudes expressed in the lyrics
are those which are on record, in their main outlines, in an abundance of other material. The service of the songs is to convey in a
freer way, and frequently in phrases that are particularly revealing,
the beliefs, the fears, the hopes, and the illusions of the people.
The spontaneity of this form of expression brings to life Revolutionary moods and impulses which, when described in detachment
by writers living years after the event, lose their freshness and seem
sometimes to lose even their reality.

The reader must by now be aware that this book on the spirit
of 1789 is not primarily an investigation of the so-called "facts" of
the Revolution. It is rather a study of contemporary thought and,
to an even greater extent, of human emotions. Whereas the methods of research and of presentation are historical, many of the implications of the subject fall into the field of psychology. This has
not induced me to use psychological jargon or to try to use the
techniques of psychological exposition. The fact is that no "psychological history" has been developed in the sense that there has
been a fruitful "intellectual history," an "economic history," and

---

[93] The basic problems involved, however, have received careful consideration, some
of the results of which are embodied not only in the parts of the Bibliography referred to above—and in Part ɪɪɪ as well—but also in the critique of Pierre's *Catalogue*
for 1789 (see Appendix A) and in the two following appendices. As a matter of fact,
my inquiries have taken me considerably further than these references indicate; but,
in accordance with the scope of the present work, only such findings as relate to 1789
are included.

so forth. Yet any historical study of thought and feeling should in this day and generation owe something to the pioneer work of anthropology and psychology. While I am aware of the dangers of treating history from the standpoint of any particular school of thought, and have tried to avoid doing so, I cannot refrain from acknowledging a debt to certain investigators and experimenters in the field of human emotion, notably to Frazer for *The Golden Bough*, to Boas for his *Mind of Primitive Man*, to William James for *The Varieties of Religious Experience*, and to Freud, Otto Rank, C. G. Jung, and many others who have made available new insights into human nature. As a matter of fact, at no time in modern history have the extremes of emotional behavior which such writers explore been more operative—or, at least, more apparent—than in the period of the French Revolution.

Finally, it may be admitted that one who attempts to portray the "spirit" of an age courts difficulties from the standpoint of scholarly presentation. In his case, customary monographic procedures are of little avail. For it must be obvious that to isolate evidences of "spirit" gathered in the course of research and to present them in compact monographic form would result in an unintelligible product. A quite contrary procedure is called for. Indeed, an investigator who would revive the atmosphere of a past epoch cannot be content merely with allusions, however pointed, to the history of the period—far less can he take it for granted. His task is to recreate history, and along the broadest lines. Otherwise, there is no room and setting for spirit, nothing from which it derives.

Accordingly, in treating of the spirit of 1789, I have had occasion to trace in narrative form many of the developments of that year—in a measure, to retell a story that has often been recorded. The method observed in the present work is to open chapters that concern political developments, such as the gathering of the Estates General, the fall of the Bastille, and the capture of the King, with a description of events and of the main and obvious trends of public opinion, and then to introduce little known materials—particularly the political songs of that era and prose writings as well—in an attempt to throw new light on the intricate pattern of Revolutionary thought and feeling.

This pattern continues to play an important part in the tradition of popular government, as was suggested at the outset of the present chapter, which opened on the large subject of political democracy. But the situation becomes complicated when we consider that modern dictatorship—as well as free government—stems in a measure from the French Revolution.

In considering this other aspect of the Revolution, one is apt to recall the Jacobin regime or the despotism of Napoleon; but it will appear in the course of the present work that inherent in the earliest of the Revolutionary impulses were elements inimical to freedom.

The consequences are alarming; for in so far as the volatile ideals of the French Revolution have served to justify, on the one hand, popular government, and on the other, dictatorship, they have tended to divide the new world which they helped to bring into being.

Thus, not only interest in the past, but also concern for many of the major issues of the present, encourage one to probe the record of democratic beginnings in the France of 1789, in the hope of better understanding the spiritual and emotional forces that were released at that time.

POPULAR opinion as expressed in the early months of 1789 was in some respects less radical than one might expect. It was certainly less clear-cut and rational than is generally supposed. Indeed, many of its simplest trends turn out to be devious, and even its general meaning is unintelligible except against the background of certain underlying historical forces. Accordingly, it is necessary—before turning to political songs and other expressions of Revolutionary enthusiasm—to consider the condition of France and the outlook of Frenchmen in the years immediately preceding 1789.

The explanation of the French Revolution as the violent and almost inevitable answer of oppressed humanity to conditions that had grown unbearable has long been rejected by scholars. To be sure, Carlyle, Michelet, and other early interpreters of the period wrote as if this had been the case. But in recent decades economic historians have exposed the fallacy of this view. Having examined the eighteenth-century world as a whole, they have demonstrated that many countries of Europe suffered from conditions far worse than those which prevailed in France, and yet experienced no revolutions at all. Besides, numerous investigations have combined to show that while the government of France in the eighteenth century was falling into political decadence and financial ruin, the economic resources of the country, as expressed in trade and industry, were increasing. As Mathiez writes in summarizing this growth, "The Revolution was not to break out in an exhausted country, but, on the contrary, in a flourishing land on a rising tide of progress."[1]

This rising tide of progress, which one might think would have allayed discontent, served actually to hasten a crisis, because it precipitated a breach between the growing business interests and the failing government. The royal administration had been weakened by ill-conceived political ventures, as well as by routine mismanagement and lavish waste. The treasury, far from having strengthened its position in response to the new national wealth,

[1] A. Mathiez, *The French Revolution*, London, 1929, p. 12 (translation by C. A. Phillips of *La Révolution française*, Paris, 1922-27, 3 vols.).

was drifting toward insolvency. In this respect matters were especially bad toward the end of the century. Though taxes had been drastically increased in the first fifteen years of Louis XVI's reign, in the same period the national debt had tripled. By 1790 the service of the debt alone required a sum considerably more than half the total annual budget.

This deficit financing, which to some historians has seemed so fatal to France at the end of the eighteenth century, did not of itself—if we may judge from recent fiscal experience—render the condition of the country desperate.[2] What aggravated the situation, and perhaps made it hopeless, was the fact that the Bourbon government could not, or in any case did not, command the respect of the business interests, which had grown to a position of great strength. Capitalism had been developing for generations in France; it is probably true that the chances for the French subject to make money were better, as the eighteenth century progressed, than they had ever been before. And yet the government kept the business interests in a turmoil for want of any policy, present or prospective, which might make investments safe; and, accordingly, enterprisers were touchy and restive. The middle class, which had steadily risen at the expense of the aristocracy, was out of patience with old regime inefficiency and had to be reckoned with.

Blocking the progress of the middle class were the nobility and the clergy, whose favored position was entrenched by privileges inherited from the past. That both these groups should have been largely exempt from the heaviest tax of the kingdom (the *taille*) is simply one indication of the enormous favoritism which they still enjoyed on the eve of the French Revolution. Changed conditions of life had rendered the original justification of specific privileges largely obsolete. Even among the nobles there was some stir of reform, though in general it may be said that the pride and self-interest that attach to class remained dominant. But whereas privilege had once been a stimulus to national well-being and had been taken for granted, it was now condemned by the rising middle class as an obstruction to general prosperity, and as being contrary to new standards of justice and equality.

[2] Jacques Bainville takes this position, namely that the ruinous effect of the deficit in bringing about the collapse of the old regime has been overestimated. See his *Histoire de France*, Paris, 1926, vol. ii, pp. 27-28.

Even traditional religion, in which it is often maintained on high authority that French society was grounded, was losing its hold. Subjects, whether religiously minded or not, were disturbed by countless rumors and abundant evidence that throughout the higher clergy there was much corruption. This was a serious matter from the material as well as from the spiritual standpoint, for the Catholic Church possessed much land and great sources of income.

Beneath the middle class were the artisans and proletarians, a population that was considerable not on account of its size (because it was relatively far less numerous than today) but on account of its concentration in cities and towns. Many of its members lived near the line of subsistence and were doubtless more interested in bread than in ideas.

Finally, there were the peasants. Though in France their lot had steadily improved, it was often dreary and sometimes desperate, thanks to a degenerate feudalism. To be sure, the peasants of neighboring countries—of Spain, Italy, and the German states—were worse off, but being even more ignorant than the French, they were helpless. The French peasants were advanced in this sense at least, that they were capable of grasping the idea of organized revolt, and the idea was everywhere about them. In the course of widespread exploitation, there was some protection for the bourgeois and for the artisans, who, subject to restrictions, could perhaps increase their product or vary the price of their wares. The overwhelming burden of an inefficient system fell finally upon the peasants, who numbered twenty-one million, or nearly nine-tenths of the population.

The peasants were subject to every sort of petty and grievous tax; and since in many cases the upper classes were tax-exempt, we have in the France of that day the spectacle of a tax program which operated against those least able to pay—a system of taxation that, in the language of economists, was "regressive." Today, even in conservative countries, we are accustomed to a graduation against high incomes, to a "progressive" tax which, instead of protecting the great fortunes, operates against them. Nothing of the sort, but merely proportional taxation, was all the reformers asked or at first dreamed of desiring; and yet they were often harshly criticized for opposing a regressive tax regime which today seems utterly inimical to good sense and justice, and from which modern democracies are now twice removed.

Thus, matters of bare survival, subsistence, and self-interest were prompting the Frenchmen of the eighteenth century to call the privileged classes to an accounting and to demand an alleviation of abuses.

There were other motives for reform that were affecting men and women throughout France, and since these were derived from a new and more hopeful outlook on human life, we may call them spiritual. These spiritual motives, which had been stimulated by the philosophers of the eighteenth century, we shall consider in subsequent chapters.

Louis XVI was thirty-four years of age when the Revolution broke out in 1789. There still attached to the Crown—eighteenth-century skepticism notwithstanding—much of that reverence which Frenchmen traditionally held for their rulers. It is conceivable that there would have been no French Revolution had Louis XVI resolutely carried through certain reforms which he either instituted or favorably considered in the early years of his reign. The interests of the King and of the rising middle class were much more in accord than is generally supposed.

For a statement of the King's policy, it is safe to turn to Aulard, since, in view of his devotion to the Republican tradition, there is no likelihood that he was subject to prejudice in favor of monarchy. He credits the royal policy with having been directed toward certain ends, all of which were highly popular.[3]

In the first place, the King was reconciled to the revival of the Estates General—a representative parliament dating from the Middle Ages. Its memory was still cherished by Frenchmen, though it had not met since 1614. Louis, however, was not sufficiently mindful of the fact that no institution is today what it was yesterday. He did not seem to realize that the Estates General, meeting after seventeen decades of neglect and in a country which had undergone the influence of "enlightenment," might bear scant resemblance to that institution as it was when Europe had taken little more than

[3] A. Aulard, "Le programme royal aux élections de 1789," in *Etudes et leçons* [*première série*], Paris, 1893, pp. 41-54.

first strides away from feudal living and feudal thought. Nor did the King regard the gathering of the Estates simply as an emergency measure; he was prepared to approve regular meetings at settled periods. In this he shared the advanced thought of the times, which held that there was something highly constitutional about regular meetings of the people's representatives. This view was finally supported by the judiciary—that is to say the *Parlements* —and by the so-called Notables of the Realm; for, having lost influence through their reactionary blunders, they hoped to regain popularity, as well as to avoid responsibility, by advocating that the voice of the nation[4] be heard at a time when all other voices, including their own, were beginning to sound dangerously off key.

Louis XVI seemed also to side with the people in his view of the economic situation; at least in his desire for a budget and the proper financing of the state, he had necessarily to advocate measures which were in accord with the popular clamor for reform. Privileges and exemptions based on outworn formulas, aside from putting the burden of taxation on those least able to bear it, and thereby causing popular discontent, cut the state off from important means of revenue and were a constant source of embarrassment to the King and his ministers. Equal taxation for all was the rational solution, and it was accepted in theory as part of the royal program, even though it meant the denial of what had gone before, of generations—indeed centuries—of economic discrimination. Furthermore, the King favored putting an end to the arbitrary powers of ministers in respect to expenditures, and was reconciled to restoring to the nation the power of consent to taxation. In short, the royal policy (when uncorrupted by Court pressure) did not run counter to the popular longing for a more equitable society. For this, if for no other reason, it offended many nobles and high churchmen, who, in their unwillingness to sacrifice anything, were destined to lose all.

In favoring the suppression of *lettres de cachet*, the King was again on the side of the people. He even advocated—though none

---

4 The word "nation" was being used at this time to denote a France that was regenerated, or about to become so—and especially the French people as a whole, regardless of class distinction. It thus had a Revolutionary connotation, and tended among the advocates of reform to replace the word "kingdom," with its old associations of privilege.

too heartily—freedom of the press. There was one other respect in which a strong popular tendency won the acquiescence of the King: his approval of the creation of permanent provincial Estates. This approval of an increasing number of local legislatures seems especially reckless, unless we remark that it was almost a necessary concession. In 1788 the province of Béarn had taken an independent stand, regarding itself as linked to France only through the Crown,[5] and that of Dauphiné had revived its own provincial legislature despite the prohibitions of the King's officers, who themselves finally yielded as a matter of expediency. Of course, the problem of the specific powers of the King over the various parts of his realm, and the whole question of centralization or decentralization, were among the issues at stake. But contributing to the same ferment was the desire of individuals at the end of the eighteenth century to express themselves politically, to become active in the arrangement of human affairs instead of being merely acted upon. Thus, by approving the provincial Estates, the King was encouraging not only regression toward feudal sectionalism, but also political self-consciousness among the people.

Whether Louis was foolhardy or was simply accepting the inevitable, he was, in either case, taking the popular stand and moving along in a trend which might be called a revolution against the old regime. As regards the ends to be achieved by reform, he presented himself in the first instance as a friend of the people. He was an acquiescent, if not an energetic, innovator.

From the standpoint of objectives, then, we may say that the greatest revolution of all modern history previous to the twentieth century grew to a considerable extent out of an identity rather than out of a conflict of interests. It was this ready agreement as to ends, albeit ill-defined ones, that made the year 1789 a time of such happy political exaltation in France and allowed the mood of experimentation to develop with such remarkable rapidity.

What produced the rift which divided France, and led eventually to a death struggle, was the matter of the means by which the reforms were to be effected. Who was to be the reformer? The King? The nobles? The people? It is not surprising that in the dis-

[5] Interesting details concerning the important movement in Béarn appear in P. Moulonguet's *La souveraineté de Béarn à la fin de l'Ancien Régime*, Toulouse, 1909, pp. 188-201.

organized regime out of which the Revolution grew, this question led to confusing and conflicting answers.

Great changes for France were imminent, yet to Louis' mind these changes should come not from the people but from him, as emanations of the sovereign power of the Crown. This was unfortunate, because the King was under the pressure of self-interested factions—pressure which would have tried the strength of even a naturally great ruler. Louis was far from that. Owing to a combination of outside influences and of his own personality, he could not exert sufficient force to achieve national ends. In retrospect, it appears that most of his cherished reforms were either half-tried and revoked, or not tried at all. Just as in later years Louis could not suppress a revolution from below, so from the outset he was incapable of initiating one from above. Yet instinctively he clung to an authority that he could not effectively use. An effort will be made in the course of the present work to explain these traits. For the present, however, it may suffice to repeat the striking, although perhaps too epigrammatic, comment with which Madelin draws to a close his characterization of Louis XVI, "He was not born a king."[6]

Such reforms as were enacted during the early years of Louis' reign were, consequently, mere palliatives which did not reach the heart of the national distress. Thoroughgoing reform, as already suggested, was obstructed by groups representing the special interests of the nobility and the clergy. Even the reformers themselves— for the most part members of the middle class—seem on certain occasions to have lost their sense of direction and to have stood in the way of measures which promised general benefits. Thus there developed, in the years immediately preceding the Revolution, a complicated political rivalry, which resulted in frequent changes of ministry.

The last of the pre-Revolutionary ministers to fall was Loménie de Brienne. Unreasonably discredited in several attempts to achieve reform, Brienne tried as a last resort to win over the opposition by declaring, in July and August, 1788, that the Estates

[6] L. Madelin, *The French Revolution*, New York, 1916 (translation by F. S. Barr of *La Révolution*, Paris, 1911), p. 34.

General would shortly be summoned. May 1, 1789, was the date finally fixed for the gathering. Presumably such an announcement would have assured the popularity of a minister. But the indignation against Brienne was by this time too great to be dispelled by even so momentous a concession. The financial situation had become increasingly bad, and on August 16, 1788, the treasury was obliged to suspend payment on notes which were legal tender. Even members of the wealthy class who had hitherto taken no part in the opposition to Brienne now saw their property threatened and joined in the attack on his ministry. The government, on the verge of financial ruin, had lost every source of support.

The resignation of Brienne, on August 25, freed the King from the encumbrance of an unpopular policy. His Majesty appointed as the new minister, Jacques Necker, a wealthy Swiss banker, who, in contrast to Brienne, was reputed to be both a genius in matters of financial reform and a staunch friend of the popular cause. This changed situation permitted the people to revive an orthodox political view—namely, that whatever might be thought of a given minister, the King himself could do no evil. In this atmosphere of indulgent respect the people credited Louis, where they had not credited Brienne, with spontaneous leadership in the matter of summoning the Estates General.

But for the moment widespread reform seemed much less urgent than the restoration of government credit. That was the crisis of the hour; and it was confidently believed that Necker was the man to meet it. Though a foreigner, Necker had once before been minister of France, and he was trusted above all others by the prosperous members of the middle class. Since their approval of him was contagious, his recall did, for a few days, revive public confidence. The particularities of this situation, especially the incongruity of Louis' choice, were described at the time by a keen observer, Mallet du Pan:

In a kingdom of twenty-four million inhabitants, it has been necessary to have recourse to a foreigner, who is a Protestant, a republican, who was dismissed seven years since, who was banished last year, who is personally odious to the sovereign, and whose principles and character are entirely opposed to those of the Court. M. Necker once nominated, Paris, especially the Palais Royal, the fund holders, etc., gave vent to their delight. On the morrow, the effigy of M. [de] Sens [i.e.,

Brienne] was burned in the Place Dauphine, and similar illuminations took place in the Palais Royal and various other spots.[7]

The immense satisfaction over the change of ministry was almost as short-lived as the bonfires which celebrated it. A week later the following entry appears in Mallet du Pan's memoirs:

September 2nd—Since M. Necker's return, nothing has been done, and murmurs have been renewed. The satirists in their jeremiads, the quidnuncs, and simpletons of every kind are astounded that M. Necker should not have restored the national finances within three days after coming into office. . . . The funds, which rose on the return of M. Necker, have again fallen.[8]

By October first, Mallet du Pan took note of the "perfect inundation of pamphlets,[9] abusive, meaningless attacks against the new minister."[10] This was Necker, whom at the time of his triumphant return to power, Mirabeau had characterized as "king of France."[11] Even so, misgivings about Necker quickly disappeared, and his popularity was to become greater than ever by the spring of 1789.

Once the hope of restoring credit through some financial magic of the Minister was gone, interest shifted to fundamental reform. Despite the recent setback to popular enthusiasms, it was now supposed that the Estates General, summoned August 8, 1788, to meet in the spring of the following year, would put an end to the financial distress in the course of a far-reaching reformation.

Hopes were thus centered on an institution that had been in disuse for over a century and a half. The institution had been rather complex and variable in its day, and no one knew exactly what the composition and procedure of the revived Estates should

[7] Mallet du Pan, *Memoirs and Correspondence*, A. Sayous, ed., London, 1852, vol. i, p. 157.

[8] *Ibid.*, p. 160.

[9] Considerable freedom of the press had been permitted by the royal order in council of July 5, 1788.

[10] Mallet du Pan, *op.cit.*, pp. 167-68. In this brief survey it has not seemed feasible to discuss the important role played at this time by the *Parlements* (or courts of France); but what Mallet du Pan has to say concerning the judiciary of Paris, in lines which immediately follow the above quotation, is interesting as revealing further the prevailing instability of public opinion. "The *Parlement* was the idol six months back; now every one detests and insults it: Epremesnil, the avenger of the nation, the Brutus of France, on whom they have lavished their enthusiasm, is vilified everywhere. This is what in France is called the noble empire of opinion."

[11] In a letter to Mauvillon, August 27, 1788, according to A. Chérest, *La chute de l'Ancien Régime (1787-1789)*, Paris, 1884-86, vol. ii, p. 163.

be. As there were rival groups which hoped to dominate the forthcoming convocation, the matter of procedure was of supreme importance.[12] There seemed to be nothing to do but to re-examine
the old records, and there was an eager and interested search for
precedents, for the discovery of which it was necessary to go back
at least to the seventeenth century.

Since the privileged classes, the clergy and nobility, were believed to have more or less identical interests, the reformers held
that the unprivileged, the Third Estate,[13] should have double representation, so that it might cope on an equal basis with the other
two orders. On December 27, 1788, the King's government, ending
a period of considerable uncertainty, came out in favor of this view.
By this decision Louis and his minister Necker seemed to have
espoused the cause of the Third Estate.

There was, as a matter of fact, some precedent for double representation. In most of the fourteenth-, fifteenth- and sixteenth-cen-
tury sessions of which the facts are known, the representatives of
the Third Estate outnumbered those of either of the other two orders, and in at least two sessions, occurring in 1356 and 1560, its
delegations were larger than those of the other two orders combined.[14]

But after all, since common action was traditionally decided by
the votes of each of the orders acting as separate entities, neither
double nor quadruple nor any other increase of representation
could have lifted the Third Estate out of the minority position;
for if decisions followed the lines of class interest, as was anticipated, the Third Estate would always be outvoted two to one. It
had become established before 1614 that a unanimous vote of the

[12] A special study of this subject has been made by M. B. Garrett, in his *The
Estates General of 1789; The Problems of Composition and Organization*, New York,
1935. This work, which is an analysis of public opinion, contains a notable bibliography of several hundred pamphlets which appeared between July 5, 1788, and
January 24, 1789.

[13] Of the three classes which composed French society, the Third Estate is the
least clearly defined and the most difficult to envisage. It was often referred to by
the blanket phrase "the people." It included several disparate groups: the "middle
class," with its money power; wage earners and laborers of all kinds in the cities; and
the peasants, who comprised over ninety percent of the population.

[14] See R. Jalliffier, *Histoire des Etats généraux (1302-1614)*, Paris, 1885, pp. 151-52;
and G. G. Andrews, "Double Representation and Vote by Head Before the French
Revolution," in *The South Atlantic Quarterly*, October, 1927, vol. xxvi, pp. 373-91.

three orders was necessary for most measures; and, though the traditional system would thus permit the Third Estate to block such measures as it disapproved, it would not enable that body to carry through the reforms which it might deem essential. Therefore it was strategically important to the popular cause that the three orders should merge, i.e., sit together and vote as a single body. In this case the Third Estate would on its own be equal to the other two, and it could, in addition, count on the support of many of the lower clergy, who were to be represented in the ecclesiastical body and who, as it turned out, gained two-thirds of the seats in that class. There were, besides, a considerable number of nobles who had put on record their liberal views and who conceivably might be relied upon to support the commoners.

But this business of sitting together had absolutely no precedent. There never had been a gathering of the Estates General where all met and voted as a single body.[15] Nevertheless, popular opinion was expecting of the forthcoming Estates General such an arrangement.

The issue was sufficiently dramatic; everything depended upon it. But neither the King nor his Minister would commit himself.[16] Even when it came time to vote, the people were not informed how the body to which they were electing representatives would be constituted. Those who called themselves "patriots"[17] took it for granted that their view would prevail; and they even had the audacity to make it appear that what they were urging represented a return to original liberties, and had real constitutional sanction. Nobody on the patriotic side, apparently, was ready to admit that the merging of the three orders had no relation whatsoever to the so-called constitution of the kingdom, except a revolutionary one.

[15] A few months earlier (July, 1788) there had been a gathering of the provincial estates in Dauphiné, in which the three orders had merged. This, of course, was not a legal precedent for the Estates General, but it strengthened the popular clamor for such a procedure.

[16] The clergy and nobles, however, were invited in advance by the King voluntarily to merge with the Third Estate. Louis hoped that this gesture of self-abnegation would take place "from their common love for the welfare of the State"; but nothing came of his effort to rule by request, rather than by command. Madelin, *op.cit.*, p. 38.

[17] Persons who were affected by the new ideas and who favored reform began from about this time to be known as "patriots"—as distinguished from aristocrats and others who favored the old regime.

On January 24, 1789, the first electoral regulations were announced. In effect, something resembling universal male suffrage was accorded the Third Estate.[18] Practically speaking, every shopkeeper and trader, every craftsman and every peasant of France, who was over twenty-five years of age and who paid taxes, was invited by Louis XVI to go to the polls and, through a system of indirect elections, vote for representatives to the Estates General. The King's memorandum to his agents was preceded by a preamble, which concluded as follows: "His Majesty . . . has determined to assemble the Estates General of his Kingdom at his own dwelling, not in any way to restrict the freedom of their deliberations, but in order to preserve in respect to them the character which lies nearest to his heart—that of counsellor and friend."[19]

What did this gracious statement mean? Did it mean that Louis was partially abdicating his sovereignty and turning to the nation as a partner in power? In so far as it meant this to the patriots, it served simply to arouse false hopes. Louis, as we have seen, was jealous of the prerogatives he had inherited, and they were very great. As Sagnac remarks in the sentence which opens his important volume on the early history of the Revolution, "At the moment when the Estates General were going to assemble after an interruption of one hundred and seventy-five years, the King of France was still, by right, the absolute monarch, in whom sovereignty resided uncontrolled and unshared."[20] Of his theoretically transcendent power Louis XVI was not unmindful.

On the theoretical plane, the King's sovereignty might still be unimpaired. On the practical plane, it was in danger of becoming a fiction. Constitutional historians are accustomed to insist that what an unlimited monarch ordains, he can disavow, and that a gathering summoned at his will can likewise be dissolved at his pleasure. But such reasoning has no reality when applied to the period now under consideration. New interests and new modes of

---

[18] Some five out of a possible six million men were entitled to vote. Special restrictions applied to the franchise in Paris. The somewhat complicated matter of electoral procedure has been well summarized by J. M. Thompson, in *The French Revolution*, New York, 1945, pp. 7-12.

[19] "Règlement fait par le Roi pour l'exécution des Lettres de Convocation du 24 janvier 1789," in A. Brette, ed., *Recueil de documents relatifs à la convocation des Etats généraux de 1789*, Paris, 1894, vol. i, pp. 66-101.

[20] P. Sagnac, *La Révolution (1789-1792)*, Paris, 1920, p. 1.

thought and life had developed since the sixteenth and early seventeenth centuries. In those earlier times, a king could make with impunity a summons that might be dangerous in 1789. As Lord Acton declared, "The States-General, which had not been seen for one hundred and seventy-five years, were the features of a bygone stage of political life, and could neither be revived as they once had been, nor adapted to modern society."[21]

Modern society had been affected, for one thing, by a new outlook in regard to the relation of the individual to the state. For centuries, Frenchmen had abided by the hierarchic ordering of society and found it good; it had seemed natural that in society's pyramidal arrangement, authority should be derived from the top and should extend down and out to the various lower ranges. Yet now French subjects had lost, or were losing, what we may call their hierarchic sense of form; they began to be affected by the feeling that they should find toward their fellow subjects some shoulder-to-shoulder relationship. This mood was shared even by certain of the "repentant" nobles and higher clergy, and was general among the progressive bourgeois, whose sense of congruity could not now be reconciled to the fact that there were others pyramided above them in an elaborate structure of social distinction and special privilege. There were few, if any, democrats à outrance—a man of affairs was not apt to apply his principles to the city poor or to the dull peasants. But a definite democratic trend was in the air.

It would be wrong to consider such a change of outlook as exclusively a revolution in thought. Thought is only one aspect of public opinion, and in eighteenth-century France there had been also a revolution in feeling. In the atmosphere of authority and formality which had characterized French life, and which is epitomized in the Age of Louis XIV, the expression of emotion had been suppressed. This seems to have been true in the simplest home—witness the stringently patriarchal father of the old provincial France[22]—just as it was true at Versailles. But by the second half of the eighteenth century, a much greater flexibility of moods was becoming general. There was a resurgence of emotional values.

---

[21] J. Acton, *Lectures on the French Revolution*, London, 1910, p. 46.

[22] Interesting examples of patriarchal authority and severity are given by Frantz Funck-Brentano in his *L'Ancien Régime*, Paris, 1926, Chapter II, "La Famille," pp. 25-113.

The earliest springs of a movement later to be known as Romanticism were beginning to bubble, not only in literature and the arts, but also in common life. Furthermore, in connection with the same trend, an attitude toward the state was arising which, without exaggeration, may be called political romanticism. Rousseau's views were a part of the general change. There were other and deeper influences, of which something will presently be said, but certainly one strain in Rousseau's doctrine may well be singled out at this point. In his *Social Contract* (1762), he had extolled the direct responsibility of everybody in government, in order that the people, whom he called "sovereign," might preserve the exercise of their rights. He commended, as the guarantee of their liberty, the personal participation of all—not, to be sure, in the routine functions of government, but in "periodical assemblies" (of a constituent nature).[23] "In a well-ordered city," he explained, "every man flies to the assemblies." This, he warned, might not be possible "unless the city is very small."[24] It was only, he made clear, under less favorable circumstances—including the "lukewarmness of patriotism" and the "vastness of States"—that there arose "the method of having deputies or representatives of the people in national assemblies."[25] Thus Rousseau, as he penned the *Social Contract*, was not unduly sanguine about the easy and widespread application of his ideal of popular sovereignty.[26] But his reservations were readily ignored by his enthusiastic disciples, who perhaps misconceived, and in any case oversimplified, the doctrine. By the end of the eighteenth century in France there were numerous people who wished to apply the notion of the "well-ordered city"

[23] The distinction is important. Rousseau did not propose that all the people take an equally active part in the everyday functions of government; it is in this strictly literal sense that he wrote of democracy, "So perfect a government is not for men." But he did call for "periodical assemblies" where people reassert, or if necessary restore, their sovereignty. These assemblies are rather shadowy in the *Social Contract*, but the idea of individual responsibility which they embody is an important part of the doctrine. (See *The Social Contract*, G. D. H. Cole's translation in Everyman's Library, especially pp. 58-59, and 80 and 89.)

[24] *Ibid.*, pp. 82 and 85.   [25] *Ibid.*, p. 83.

[26] Although in *Du contrat social* Rousseau discussed various forms of government with sympathy and insight, he maintained that liberty was possible in the larger and richer states only in a diminished degree. He was nevertheless glad to consider from the practical standpoint the best possible government for the larger nation, as is well shown in his *Considérations sur le gouvernement de Pologne*, in which, incidentally, he warned against the danger of sudden social change.

to the entire nation—not literally, of course, for this would have implied assemblies of several million persons, but in spirit, the idea gaining acceptance in some circles that every citizen might be as politically effective as every other citizen, and that all should take an equally active part, since in their totality the citizens constituted the ultimate power in the state. This notion, being a new thing under the sun when applied on a vast scale, was highly exciting to entertain.[27]

But at first this conception of popular government was by no means provocative of open rebellion; for, far from challenging the King, even the most zealous reformers tended to regard him as an ally. But in claiming sovereign power for the people, they were undermining the traditional authority of the Crown.

At the outset of the Revolution, inroads on the King's sovereignty were made step by step; from the standpoint of intellectual honesty one might almost say, clandestinely. Later, that sovereignty was to be openly questioned, then ruthlessly limited, and, finally, destroyed by cataclysmic changes in the whole social structure of France.

The first step in this transfer of sovereignty was the King's invitation to the people to vote for delegates who should elect—directly or indirectly—representatives to the Estates General[28] and draw up lists of grievances in the form of *cahiers*.[29] No sovereignty was transferred by intent, but the manner and mode in which the people accepted the King's invitation gave them the feeling that they were now related to the body politic in a new way. By participating in government, the voter in the winter of 1789 seemed in no small degree to have acquired the status of citizen, and, in so far as this was true, so much the less considered himself a subject. The Es-

[27] The reference is to the dawning consciousness of modern democratic nationalism. Citizenship in ancient times had been limited to small areas, as in the city states of Greece and in the Republic of Rome, or to particular classes, as in the later Roman Empire. In eighteenth-century America, which at first thought might suggest a parallel, suffrage in the newly formed states was for the most part highly restricted.

[28] The electoral arrangements for the Third Estate were highly complicated; there were sometimes only two, sometimes three, and sometimes even four, stages in the indirect election.

[29] There is no richer mine of information concerning conditions in France in 1789 than the *cahiers*, but these well-known materials do not figure prominently in the present work, because they take one only to the threshold of the Revolution, whereas we are concerned here with the progress of the movement in the first phase.

tates General had been called many times prior to 1614, but at no previous time had Frenchmen responded to the call in the same manner. What happened—the unforeseen thing—was this, that the people, as a nation, derived from the activity of voting some awareness of exercising sovereign power.

In short, thanks not only to the views of the day—to its undaunted criticism and unabashed hopes—but also to the re-creation of the Estates General, worlds were opened to the imagination of the people which a generation before had been dreamt of only by philosophers. Frenchmen, to be sure, were inexperienced in matters of citizenship, and, except for their familiarity with the abuses of the old regime, lacked firsthand knowledge of government. Yet they were about to rush into the realm of action, from which, by and large, the philosophers had been excluded.

Under the circumstances it was not likely that popular views would reflect disciplined thought. Everyone welcomed "ideas," but the ideas in vogue were charged with emotion. They were the product usually of sentimentalized attachments and impassioned hopes, sometimes of animosities and fears, but seldom of critical inquiry.

In the chapters which follow, we shall see how this excited state of opinion led to the popular acceptance of suppositions widely removed from the facts.

It will appear, for example, that Louis XVI was regarded by the people as a hero of the Revolution, though he never wholly accepted the patriotic cause and often publicly opposed it.

We shall find Necker, whose incapacities were before long discovered even by the patriots, placed temporarily on a pedestal and made a prime object of public adoration.

We shall observe that substantial members of the bourgeois class, who believed in man's peaceful regeneration through enlightenment, nevertheless applauded the first Revolutionary bloodshed; and that they viewed successive outbreaks of Revolutionary violence, not as auguries of further bloodshed, but as providential occurrences incidental to reform and to the attainment of a better order.

Finally, it will be shown that by the close of the year 1789, the Revolution, which had little more than been set in motion, was generally assumed to be over.

These are but a few of the many illusions that the people created, and by which, in turn, they were sustained.

Such views, though based in a measure on realities, were shaped to a notable degree by man's imaginative faculty. This compounding of the real and the ideal is, of course, the stuff of public opinion in any age. Thus the student of popular enthusiasms must interest himself in the imaginative, myth-making proclivities of man, as well as in events and man's formal estimate of them. From this standpoint, an accidental exclamation—when one can recapture it —is often more revealing than a parliamentary brief; and doggerel that has caught the popular fancy may likewise be more expressive than polished prose or verse. The political songs of the French Revolution are documents of this spontaneous character. They express the aspirations of a people who were becoming excited in a new cause. They do not always reflect the issues of the hour with literal truthfulness, and it is not for this purpose that we shall use them. But they serve a no less valid historical purpose if they lead us to understand a state of mind.

We are now in a position to consider the progress of events in 1789 and the spirit in which the Revolutionists both helped to create and undertook to interpret their changing world.

By the end of April, 1789, most of the deputies had arrived at Versailles, their convergence from all parts of France causing great excitement and expectancy. A question in everyone's mind was finally settled when on May 1 heralds announced His Majesty's proclamation that the initial gathering of the Estates General was to take place on May 4. The word was spread according to traditional procedure. After the sounding of three trumpet calls, a herald would shout to the attentive populace, "In the King's name!" This cry preceded the reading of the proclamation, and would be repeated, after another blast of trumpets, at the next open square.

Thus, as in olden times, was every decision of consequence to the state still given out as an expression of the royal wish. Although forces of discontent had been gathering during nearly a century, it was still assumed that the regeneration of man was to be achieved within the framework of benevolent monarchy.

There occurred from the start, however, slight provocations and antagonisms, of themselves of no importance but capable of revealing the gap of misunderstanding that separated the King from his people. At the gathering proclaimed for May 4, Louis, whose appearance was breathlessly awaited, kept the assembled deputies waiting, not a matter of minutes, but three hours. The ceremonies were being held some days later than originally planned, and the deputies were already discontented. One of them who belonged to the lowest of the three orders was heard to protest that "No single individual should keep a whole nation waiting!"[1]

"A whole nation." Here is an example of the use of words on the grand scale that prevailed from the very beginning of the Revolution. For those who waited were deputies of three distinct classes, a good third of whom never could have agreed with the majority as to the real meaning of this mystic entity, "the nation." Strong though the patriotic movement might be, there was no "whole nation" in the political sense that was intended. Note, also, the dethroning of a king by a phrase, "single individual." So Louis was to count only as one unit in a population of twenty-five mil-

[1] Cited in Madelin, *The French Revolution*, p. 52.

lion! These were modern ideas indeed! They were beyond Louis. He was destined never to understand them.

Though the commoners—that is to say, the representatives of the Third Estate—had been prodigiously feted at home, they were by no means flattered at Versailles. In contrast to the brilliant adornment of the higher orders, there was assigned to them a dress—plain black suits, muslin cravats, and cloaks of cloth—which signified that they were not to cut too brilliant a figure.[2] But feeling themselves to be entrusted with a mission, they remained proud. Flattery might have quickened good feeling, but the absence of it by no means diminished their sense of the importance of the roles they were filling. All of them, even the most humble, seem to have experienced in some mystical way the sensation of *being* France. It was almost a case of "L'Etat, c'est nous." And as we shall presently see, public opinion, which was steadily gaining force in the eighteenth century, supported them.

The purpose of the procession on May 4 had been to attend mass and to listen to a sermon. Whether or not the spirit of Roman Catholicism was already undermined by skepticism, its forms still wrapped themselves around all phases of ceremonial life.

The representatives of the three orders met the following day in their first political gathering. None of those who spoke—the great figures of the realm, the King, the Keeper of the Seals, and the Minister—had anything very pertinent to say, except Necker, who spoke exclusively of the finances. In an exciting atmosphere of reform, the deputies were left wondering how they were to go about their work. Those of the Third Estate expected a royal commitment in favor of a merging of the three orders. None was forthcoming; for by now the King was inclined to hold back. But an occasional sop was given to the commoners; presumably no harm could come from indulgence in the language of reform, if

[2] In the first of the *Lettres . . . à ses commettans* (May 10, 1789, pp. 21-24), Mirabeau published with his endorsement a communication from Salaville, which decried the costume assigned to the Third Estate as a "humiliation." Indeed, the writer held that there should be no distinction in costumes, and maintained, besides, that the decision should rest not on royal authority but with the Estates General. Contemporary illustrations of the various costumes and caricatures expressive of the rivalry between the classes appear in E. F. Henderson, *Symbol and Satire in the French Revolution*, New York and London, 1912, pp. 25-27 *et seq.*; and in A. Challamel, *Histoire-musée de la République française . . .* , 3rd ed., Paris (1857-58), vol. i, pp. 27-35.

it were sufficiently vague. It was perhaps in this spirit that the Keeper of the Seals included in his speech the following remark: "All titles are going to merge in the title of citizen."[3] Poor old Barentin—for that was his name—was inadvertently heralding, in one sentence, both a political and a social revolution.

While the administration gave lip service to the apparently innocent, but really devastating, jargon that was current, the commoners assumed that the King was on their side—that, despite his avoidance of the subject, he privately wished the three orders to merge. This supposition led to complications. But before coming to them and to the story of subsequent events, we must pause to consider further an attitude of mind which enabled the patriots to launch a revolution with no thought of failure, and with little anticipation of difficulties, though many were at hand.

France as it was in the spring of 1789 has been elaborately investigated and pictured by historians. Most of the accounts which we have lay stress primarily on material conditions and political occurrences—on what are sometimes called the "objective" facts.[4] Such a method is necessary if we are to know exactly *what* happened at any given time. The danger of this method is that the atmosphere of contemporary thought and feeling may be neglected. If this occurs, the *why* of events is lost. It is largely for this reason that people are forever finding the behavior of earlier generations

3 *Archives parlementaires* . . . , *première série (1787 à 1799)*, vol. viii, p. 5.

4 The allusion is less to works of recent years than to those of an earlier generation, when writers first felt the influence on history of the scientific method.

Still earlier writers—let Michelet stand as the classic example—did not have the preoccupation noted above; they were concerned with interpreting the Revolution, with conveying its spirit. To a considerable extent they succeeded. They fell down in not critically drawing a line between the inspirational aspects of their own age and of their own personalities, and those which pertained to the Revolution. Precisely as the phrase is used in the arts, one may say of Michelet that in expounding the French Revolution, he *expressed himself*.

This romantic approach to the subject, which was prevalent during much of the nineteenth century, frightened sober students into a false position, causing them to overlook the fact that the Revolutionists were themselves impassioned and partisan. In the course of this reaction, the French Revolutionists fared rather badly—being frequently pictured, alas, as without revolutionary zeal. Gottschalk (in his *Era* . . . , p. 465), for example, cites a criticism of the Cambridge Modern History (vol. viii, 1904), that the "authors knew a great deal about the Revolution without being aware that there was a Revolution."

No doubt, this magic of eliminating the essence of a historical period in the process of establishing its form is the romanticism of the age of science.

"strange." Such behavior appears natural only when the climate of opinion of a past epoch is revived. This is particularly true of the period we are considering. Admittedly, the Revolutionists frequently lacked full information concerning the development of events, but, in addition, they were disinclined properly to appraise, or even to face, many of the facts and conditions which actually confronted them. Accordingly, in order to understand the patriotic citizen when the Estates General was gathering, we have to appreciate not only his objective environment, but also the environment created by his imagination. The patriot lived in the latter to a considerable extent, with an inevitable effect on his conduct, and, indeed, on the progress of the Revolution itself.

The popular songs of the spring of 1789 well convey the atmosphere of opinion which prevailed in France at the dawn of the Revolution. Of the songs still extant, there are twenty or more[5] which appeared in the heyday of optimism, before any serious prospect of violence darkened the sky, before the Bastille had been attacked, and when it was still supposed that change was to be effected by peaceful evolution. Taken together, these pieces enable us to enter into a spirit which not only was general among lyrists, but also reflected the mood of the times as expressed in a great variety of popular writings. We cannot enter into that spirit primarily through the intellect. To share at all in the mood of the spring of 1789, one must have an emotional response. As we are reminded in one of the earliest of the songs, "already hearts begin to open";[6] and hearts continued to open in an efflorescence of human kindliness until they exposed themselves to rude and unexpected wounds. Furthermore, one must be capable of sensing in the Revolutionary enthusiasm a strong admixture of religious feeling; for there was a blending of the secular and the religious, partly in conjunction with the traditional forms of Catholic worship, but also in other ways, as will presently appear.

This resurgence of emotion was already evident in France—as suggested in the preceding chapter—by the middle of the eighteenth century, when expressions of sentiment and of mysticism became increasingly general. Such was the case even though many

---

[5] Items 1 through 25 in "A New Catalogue of the Political Songs of 1789," Bibliography I.

[6] *Hymne en l'honneur de la Résurrection* . . . (3), stanza 41.

of the century's leading spokesmen, the famous *philosophes*, proclaimed that theirs was an age of reason and science, with the result that the intellectual aspects of the eighteenth century have frequently been overemphasized in historical accounts. The fact is that the much-heralded "reason" of that day exerted its appeal on the emotional as well as on the intellectual plane, and that the *philosophes* were perhaps less united through a common science than through a common faith.[7]

The growing wave of mysticism which characterized the greater part of the eighteenth century was in part a reaction against the classic tradition of the *grand siècle* and certain aspects of the "rationalism"[8] which followed. But the movement was by no means merely negative. It had its own spontaneous growth, expressed in Freemasonry,[9] occultism, and the literary and artistic impulses that led to the schools of sensibility and to Romanticism. Accordingly, Voltaire, though the most brilliant of the critics of the outworn institutions of the *ancien régime*, cannot rightly be regarded as the embodiment of his century, even when full allowance is made for his mixed qualities. When he is taken, incorrectly, as the symbol of the triumph of the intellect over feeling, it is even more misleading to call him *the* man of the age. It must be remembered that the eighteenth century was preparing a revolution such as Voltaire never would have wanted and a romantic movement which, in some of its aspects, he would have detested. To be sure, the eighteenth century was, from one point of view, the age of Voltaire; but it was also, from an equally urgent though more subtle standpoint, the age of anti-Voltaire. Unless historians recognize this double trend, and, along with it, the equivocal character

[7] See A. Cochin, *Les sociétés de pensée et la démocratie*, Paris, 1921.

[8] "Rationalism" as applied to the eighteenth century should not be identified with the ideal of "scientific objectivity" which has permeated the social sciences since the end of the nineteenth century. Only one trend of eighteenth-century rationalism was "scientific"; the rest was dogmatic philosophy, shaped as much by individual predilections as by detached observation.

[9] Masonic lodges were first established in France about 1725. By 1789, there were seven hundred of them in Paris alone. Many of the leading lights of the eighteenth century joined the organization. In 1772, the Duke of Orleans was elected Grand Master. The society preserved a ritual and secret symbols which were centuries old, but was at the same time a potent agency in propagating the new ideas. It was from Freemasonry that Republican France borrowed its slogan, "Liberty, Equality, Fraternity."

of "reason" itself, they cut the Revolution off from one half of its roots.

Nor am I trying simply to insist on the place and mission of Rousseau. Though he was the greatest single personality in the trend toward emotionalism, he had at times a critical capacity and an analytical sense which disqualify him as its complete embodiment. The popularity in pre-Revolutionary Paris of the great necromancer Cagliostro and, during the Revolution, of the Abbé Fauchet,[10] may serve to indicate the erratic trend to which I refer. In other words, it is perhaps not too much to say that the stability of French culture was being threatened by widespread emotional disturbance, and that it would have been so threatened had Rousseau never lived. But this chapter in history involves a complicated story of human emotions which, to the best of my knowledge, has not yet been written.[11]

What brought the resurgence of feeling and sense of mysticism so conspicuously to the fore in the spring of 1789 was the gathering of the Estates General, which seemed to promise fulfillment of the hopes for reform cherished by most Frenchmen. The songs convey this enthusiasm occasionally in well-formed verses, but more often in homely poetry written in the language of the common man, or in the awkward phrases of the literary tyro who acted as his spokesman.

Typical of the spirit of rejoicing at this time is a song entitled *Hymn in Honor of the Resurrection of the Estates General.* As the

10 Claude Fauchet, who belonged to the society of the Illuminati, became a leading spokesman at patriotic and religious gatherings in Paris. It was his penchant to synthesize Christ's teachings and those of the Revolution. He declared in a sermon that "Jésus-Christ n'est que la divinité concitoyenne du genre humain." In *De l'Esprit des Religions*, 1791, he wrote "Tout est dans tout. . . . Il n'y a pour moi que . . . un même Dieu en trois personnes: moi, toi et lui." This suggests, but does not begin to encompass, the mystical undercurrent of the Revolution. One of its strangest manifestations was the sect of *la Mère de Dieu*, which during the Terror centered around the visionary Catherine Théot. See G. Lenotre, *Le mysticisme révolutionnaire; Robespierre et la "Mère de Dieu,"* Paris, 1926.

11 A succession of remarkable accounts, from Tocqueville's *L'Ancien Régime* (1856) to such less general and far more detailed works as Mornet's *Les origines intellectuelles de la Révolution française* (1933), could be mentioned as in one way or another describing developments involving emotional change; but none of them, so far as I know, attempts to provide a comprehensive analysis of new feeling values which in eighteenth-century France affected all classes in every social relationship, and which may be presumed to have acted according to certain dynamic principles and a discernible pattern.

words "hymn" and "resurrection" imply, something of the miraculous was sensed in the changes that were taking place. And the changes were considered far-reaching, as a stanza from the original may suggest:

> Vive ce moment fortuné,
> Ou tout ainsi qu'un nouveau-né,
> Le Royaume est régénéré!
> Alleluia.[12]

Thus it was assumed (no doubt somewhat prematurely) that, thanks to the revival of the Estates General, the kingdom had been transformed. But it is important further to note that the sense of new life occasioned by this single event was unconsciously extended throughout the whole cultural medium in which the French people were living: as proclaimed in the stanza which follows, man lives on "a new earth" and under "new skies."[13] According to the recurrent phrase of those days, the *siècle d'or*, the golden age, had at last arrived.

Not only man, but even nature, was thought to be participating in the general beneficence. Of this faith there is touching evidence in a song by one who signed himself "A. L. G.," which bears as its quasi-religious title, *New "O Filii" of the Estates General*.[14] In this long and curious hymn, one discovers such promises of abundance as the following:

> Les vignes qu'on croyoit être gelées,
> Présentent des grappes en quantité;
> Ah! quel miracle que celui-là!
> Alleluia.

There follows an even more homely stanza which one would hesitate to omit:

[12] *Hymne en l'honneur de la Résurrection* . . . (3), stanza 25.

[13] *Ibid.*, stanza 26. The none-too-gifted author of the *Alleluia du Tiers-Etat* (1) described the popular excitement on the eve of the gathering of the Estates General, as follows:

> Soudain l'Empire électrisé,
> Tout François fut magnétisé;
> Le pauvre Tiers ressuscita.
> Alleluia.

[14] *Nouvel "O Filii"* . . . (14). The date "le 23 Mai 1789" appears after the title.

On voit déjà dans les marchés,
Beaucoup de petits pois écossés,
Et tout le monde en mangera,
Alleluia.[15]

It is the supposedly manifest bounty of nature in the agriculturally impoverished year of 1789 that led the author of this song to conclude that "so rich a year" might usher in "the golden age."[16] Here indeed was hope which knew no bounds. But one thing at least, the plight of the royal treasury, should have occasioned an exception to the optimism in the France of 1789. A writer, certainly a song writer, might have passed over matters of national finance, to seek cheer in other directions. But "A. L. G." had a lyrical solution even for bankruptcy. He called attention to the threat of it in one stanza, only to promise that it would never more be mentioned, since Necker had found the remedy:

On n'entendra jamais parler
De la banqueroute si redoutée;
Necker a sçu remédier à cela,
Alleluia.

The next stanza prophesies the disappearance of even the deficit:

Le déficit disparoitra,
Et le Trésor se remplira,
Pour lors l'argent circulera,
Alleluia.[17]

---

[15] *Ibid.*, stanzas 39 and 41.

[16] *Ibid.*, stanza 43. This optimism is pathetic as we glance at it in retrospect. However abundant the *petits pois* may have seemed, there was a shortage of wheat; and by the end of June the deputies were discussing the "famine." Matters did not at once improve, as even the lyrists had to admit. A patriotic song written a few weeks later, July 17, sounded the following note of distress:

Heros! Voyez nos larmes:
La disette déjà
Nous fait tomber les armes:
Quel nombre périra!

These lines are from the *Chanson sur la prise des Invalides* . . . (29), stanza 7.

[17] *Nouvel "O Filii"* . . . (14), stanzas 6 and 7. The absence of an accent on "disparoitre" (line 1 of stanza 7) corresponds to the original. This is a discrepancy of the sort referred to in the "Note on Documentation" following the Preface of this book. It is well to recall at this point that, in the reproduction of the originals, orthographical errors and idiosyncrasies are retained without, as a rule, being signalized either in the text or in the footnotes.

There are in the songs many verses such as the above, which adapted the entire economic situation to the popular mood.

The author of the *Alleluia of the Third Estate*, written in anticipation of the gathering of the Estates General, assumed that the deputies would forthwith abolish tax abuses. This step, he felt, would introduce a new era of brotherhood:

> Alors l'égalité naîtra,
> Tout préjugé disparoîtra;
> Et chaque François chantera;
> Alleluia.[18]

Similarly high hopes were expressed in other songs of this time. *Le moment désiré*, by Déduit, which opens with the exultant "Happiness at last is going to be reborn," is a good example, as will subsequently appear.[19] A poet who signed himself "Mr. B." presented a *New Song on the Gathering of the Estates General* to the religious air *O Filii*.[20] His stanzas—brought to a close with repeated "alleluias"—were in the prevailing mood of optimism. One Jeanne Rocher, who described herself as "une demoiselle religieuse de 78 ans," has left behind in a manuscript preserved at the Bibliothèque Nationale, two songs to celebrate the Estates General.[21] Her verses, though lacking in literary merit, are notable for their ardent spirit. A composition entitled *The Third Estate*— sung, May 18, by a deputation of fishwives at the palace of the Archbishop of Paris—said of Louis XVI, "He wishes, he makes, he reveals to us, our happiness."[22] One might cite other pieces written in a similar vein.[23]

[18] *L'Alleluia du Tiers-Etat* (1), stanza 15. In this song (stanza 8) occurs the phrase "le feu sacré . . . du Patriotisme," which—appearing at this early stage of the Revolution—has a striking and prophetic quality.

[19] *Le moment désiré* (7). For fuller consideration of this song, see pages 84-98 passim. It is noteworthy that a "Vive Antoinette!" occurs in this piece (stanza 4). The patriotic songs did not as a rule include tributes to the Queen. Having once been an Austrian princess, she was supposed still to be under Hapsburg influence— which, in fact, was the case, as later disclosures were to prove.

[20] *Chanson nouvelle sur l'assemblée* . . . (8).

[21] *Chanson nouvelle sur les Etats-généraux* (9) and *Chansonnette sur les Etats-généraux* (10).

[22] *Le Tiers Etat* . . . (11), last stanza. The prevalent assumption that Louis was wholeheartedly in favor of the Revolution is discussed elsewhere; see especially pages 84-85.

[23] For example, *Arrêté des Habitans de la Grenouillère* . . . (5); *R'quête en magnier' d'écrit* . . . (6); and *Motion des Harangères* [sic] . . . (15). As their titles may

Occasionally a note of distress—or at least of concern—is sounded. The author of *Chanson très-nouvelle* pictures "a King whom justice inspires" as having rescued the Third Estate from "the abyss." But he thereupon decries the privileged position of the nobility, and demands whether the "cher Tiers Etat," as he affectionately terms it, will still permit itself to be abused by the upper orders. In closing, he exhorts the Third Estate forever to offset their "suffrage and power."[24]

At this point a cautious reader may object that the songs are perhaps a misleading guide—joy being the essence of a certain type of lyricism. What of the soberer arguments that might appear in other literature? What of the perhaps troubled views of the deputies who were attempting to carry the burdens of state? Were such responsible persons as sanguine as the poets? We shall see something of these men and take note of their optimism in later pages. As for the literature other than songs, one has only to turn to journals and pamphlets, which by this time were very numerous. Indeed, much of the prose is itself almost lyrical, and glows with an ardor similar to that of the songs. But, in general, the journalists and pamphleteers tended naturally to treat political developments in a more workaday manner. They exposed many crosscurrents of conflict, especially as the controversy over the composition of the Estates General became more protracted and bitter (from May 28 to June 27). This is admittedly true of the battle of words over immediate issues; but when the prose writers turned to a contemplation of the political scene as a whole and to philosophic generalization, they usually proclaimed the same optimistic hopes and beliefs as were expressed by the lyrists.[25]

---

suggest, these pieces were written in a special patois. Mention of them is made toward the end of the present chapter.

[24] *Chanson très-nouvelle* (12). Allusion is made above to stanzas 1, 5, and 7.

[25] Proof of this contention, admittedly, would require a much more extended documentation than it is feasible to give—especially in respect to pamphlet materials, which are voluminous. Representative items are cited from time to time in the pages which follow; but, in general, the reader must be referred—concerning not only the period under consideration, but also the remainder of the year 1789—to such materials as are listed in the *Bibliographie* of Tourneux (vol. i, nos. 679-1661; and items for 1789 appearing under various topics in vols. ii, iii, and iv); or to such materials as are readily at hand in special collections (for example, in the Talleyrand Collection, New York Public Library—for the year 1789, especially vols. lv-lxxiv and lxxvii).

Something, too, must be said of the anti-Revolutionary writings
of reactionaries—of those members of the upper classes who wished
to preserve privilege. Of such writings there was a comparative
dearth. In his chapter "La convocation des Etats généraux et la
crise des brochures," Chérest refers to the "small number" of brochures which he could call reactionary, and points out that the
burden of their argument was so out of tune with the times as to
be ineffectual.[26] Furthermore, of the privileged who did take up
the pen, a surprising number supported the patriotic cause. In his
Qu'est-ce que le tiers-état?, which appeared in January, 1789, Abbé
Sieyès observed, "It is a remarkable thing that the cause of the
Third has been defended with more eagerness and energy by
ecclesiastical and noble writers than by the non-privileged themselves."[27] There was, indeed, soon to be a vast anti-Revolutionary
literature; but at the outset the reactionaries were remarkably
careless of public opinion. Even after tempers had become exacer-
bated by the protracted deadlock between the orders, and when the
fate of upper-class privilege was clearly in the balance, anti-Revolutionary propaganda remained slight. This fact impressed Arthur
Young. Writing on June 9 of the profusion of pamphlets then
appearing, he observed that "Nineteen-twentieths of these productions are in favor of liberty, and commonly violent against the
clergy and nobility." He added, "Is it not wonderful, that while
the press teems with the most levelling and even seditious principles . . . nothing in reply appears."[28] In the light of this general
trend, one need not be surprised that among the songs published in
the first months of the Revolution, there is, it would seem, but one
text extant which bears an anti-Revolutionary character.[29]

26 A. Chérest, *La chute de l'Ancien Régime (1787-1789)*, 1884-86, vol. ii, especially
pp. 255-59.

27 *Qu'est-ce que le tiers-état? Seconde édition, corrigée*, 1789, p. 53. (IV, C)

28 A. Young, *Travels in France During the Years 1787, 1788, 1789*, Betham-Edwards,
ed., London, 1900, p. 153.

29 Ironically entitled *Le chansonnier du Tiers* (13). On May 19, the Third Estate
selected sixteen commissioners to negotiate with the upper orders. Among those
chosen were Barnave, DuPont de Nemours, Mounier, Rabaut Saint-Etienne, and Tar-
get. *Le chansonnier du Tiers* consists of a lampoon of all sixteen. As indicated above,
this is the only text of an anti-Revolutionary song previous to the events of October,
1789, of which I have firsthand knowledge. However, concerning a contemporary
reference in July to the anti-Revolutionary songs of foreign troops, see page 116, footnote 25.

The optimism of the patriot, being based, not on a true appraisal of facts, but on a partial view, was not altogether one of healthy confidence. It was elation of the sort that occurs when people assume more or less perversely that objectives which are complicated and difficult of attainment can be easily won. When obstacles and disappointments did arise—as was the case almost from the beginning—they did not greatly disturb the prevailing climate of opinion. On the contrary, unhappy disclosures merely incited the faithful to devise increasingly intricate patterns of thought and feeling by which to sustain their self-assurance. At this point it is well to take into account the actual position of the patriots, and to examine more closely the fabric of their views.

The fact is that the patriots, having enjoyed great political activity in the election of their deputies and in the framing of the *cahiers*—a novel and exciting experience in the Europe of the eighteenth century and one which represented in itself something of a revolution—thereupon found themselves to be in a relatively dependent position. With no further part to play for the time being, they had to await developments. They seem to have felt a little strange—as many evidences suggest—in the new world which they believed they were creating. Having given over their minds to radical criticism and to large hopes, they craved at the same time the old sense of an intimate and traditional security. This craving expressed itself in gentle emotions, which the people, with or without reason, presumed the leaders were capable of sharing. And in their quest for comfort and security, they placed especial emphasis on virtue.

One finds a writer addressing the enemies of the popular cause in the following benevolent manner: "O detestable envious ones! In spite of your injurious cries, Necker will know how to make you happy."[30] The expectation that selfish emotions would disappear and the almost religious confidence that all Frenchmen might be converted to the new cause, were prevalent assumptions. They are well expressed in the last three stanzas of the *New "O Filii"* . . . :

> L'envie, aussi la jalousie,
> Les plus grands maux de la Patrie,

---

[30] *Hymne en l'honneur de la Résurrection* . . . (3), stanza 14.

Dieu les reduira au trepas,
    Alleluia

L'orgueil et la sotte vanité
Sont des defauts bien empiétés,
L'Assemblée les déracinera,
    Alleluia.

Pour finir, prions le Seigneur
Qu'ils [sic] convertisse les mauvais coeurs,
Et la calomnie cessera,
    Alleluia.[31]

Clearly, a particular concern of the patriots was that the political and social regeneration of France be supremely moral. Perhaps this emphasis resulted in part from the fact that the reform movement was felt to be a departure from the artificialities of the old regime in the direction of the natural life, which was regarded by men of the eighteenth century as virtuous. In any case, an atmosphere of self-righteousness characterized the Revolution from the very beginning. In the *Hymn in Honor of the Resurrection of the Estates General* the author gives the essence of a suggestion that one finds recurrently, to the effect that it was through the absence of any moral turpitude that Frenchmen were destined to effect their great ends. A characteristic stanza follows:

Dans les trois Ordres confondus,
Ayant pour guide les vertus,
François réformons les abus.
    Alleluia.[32]

In the same song the deputies were expected, not only to make such reforms as were needed, but also to change human nature, making of it a better thing than it had hitherto been. So ambitious were the author's hopes that he directed them even toward his own craft. "May they [the deputies] accord humility to the authors whose vanity revolts society."[33] This jibe at rivals may represent on the part of the song writer a final twinge of that envy which was destined no more to rankle in the human heart. The same writer,

---

[31] *Nouvel "O Filii"* . . . (14), stanzas 44-46.
[32] *Hymne en l'honneur de la Résurrection* . . . (3), stanza 44.
[33] *Ibid.*, stanza 38.

whose hopes for a new day covered a very wide field, put in his song the wish that the deputies might "give an air of virtue to certain of our well-known women," whose honor is corrupted.[34] The song in question has an atmosphere of such obvious sincerity and naïveté that it is doubtful whether the author is humorous by intent when, in addressing the *sexe charmant*, he gives the assurance that if changes are prescribed for their *bonnets* and for their "flirtatious manners," such changes will be directed only to the worthy end of increasing their attractiveness.[35] The author of this "hymn," gentle though his spirit was, may be taken as a precursor of those who, in the full tide of revolution, revealed a fanatical regard for regulation as a means of attaining virtue.

The concept of virtue was closely associated with the passion for reform, and often had a highly practical import. One may consider in this connection a song entitled the *Cahier of the Marquis of Fulvy*, which embodies the views of a liberal nobleman.[36] While the Marquis felt that the distinction between the classes should be observed ("otherwise licence would make a chaos of France") he proposed the abolition of many abuses of the old regime—the remnants of serfdom, the hunting privileges of the nobles, the *lettres de cachet*, etc. In addition, he suggested some reforms which did not win general favor until the Revolution had gone to a more advanced, or radical, stage—for example, divorce, and "a gentler lot" for the Negroes.[37] In one stanza he proposed that every elderly man who was unmarried adopt a son. He wished that ladies of fashion might become more modest, the younger generation less heedless. This review of the *Cahier of the Marquis of Fulvy* does not begin to cover all the ideas which the author had for a better society.

Indignation against the churchmen—which, too, had a practical character—was expressed in many of the songs. According to one of them,[38] Paris was to be purged of its priestlets, the "base valets

---

[34] *Ibid.*, stanza 39.   [35] *Ibid.*, stanzas 45 and 46.

[36] *Cahier du Marquis de Fulvy* (4). The author is Philibert-Louis Orry, Marquis de Fulvy.

[37] Already considerable interest was taken in the Negroes, thanks largely to the propaganda of the Société des Amis des Noirs, founded in 1787. Beatrice Hyslop finds that protests against slavery or the slave trade appear in forty-nine of the general *cahiers. French Nationalism in 1789* . . . , New York, 1934, p. 142.

[38] *Hymne en l'honneur de la Résurrection* . . . (3). For the quotations which follow, see stanzas 19, 17, and 18, respectively.

of the prostitutes." In the growing enthusiasm for virtue, the members of the higher clergy fared especially badly. The popular attitude in regard to them is well expressed in an address to the "fine prelates." "Too long, alas! have we celebrated virtues which you do not possess." In an age of highmindedness, one was no longer to see such offenders, "ces grands vicaires superflus."[39]

Thus, in the light of popular sentiment, the patriotic cause was destined to succeed through righteousness. Virtue immediately attached itself to anyone who was regarded as furthering the changes that were occurring in France, and was supposed to inhere in the reforms themselves. This passion for virtue can be almost as compelling as the physical passion of hunger; and the economic historians of the French Revolution, though they see much—and things of invaluable importance—fail to see all if they do not give due regard to this moral yearning, which can be discerned from the very beginning, and which became a matter of life-and-death importance to the patriots as the Revolution progressed.

The few songs of the spring of 1789 which lack an atmosphere of gentleness and forbearance belong, for the most part, to a special and picturesque school of writing, the *genre poissard*. This literary genre, which dates from early in the seventeenth century,[40] ran parallel with the tradition of neo-Classicism, and was, as nearly as writing could be, its exact opposite. The language was that spoken in the markets and elsewhere in the humbler quarters of Paris. From the days of Mazarin until far into the nineteenth century, a line of gifted though mostly second-rate authors produced plays, prose, and verse in this lowly medium.[41] Their work, usually despised by the critics,[42] had enough vitality and popular appeal to withstand any amount of academic obloquy.

Although the *genre poissard* of Paris may in a general way suggest other forms of corrupted French, it had its own indigenous

[39] A fuller discussion of the attitude of the patriots toward the Church is reserved for Chapter IX.

[40] From about 1640. A considerable number of *mazarinades* were of this genre.

[41] The greatest single contributor to this tradition was Jean-Joseph Vadé (1720-57). He is sometimes incorrectly referred to as its creator.

[42] Of the outstanding critics of the eighteenth century, Fréron was perhaps the only one who found that the *genre poissard* was "not at all contemptible . . . but very agreeable." See A. P. Moore, *The Genre Poissard and the French Stage at the End of the Eighteenth Century*, New York, 1935, p. 6.

origin and character. It differs, for example, from the medium of François Villon, who in the fifteenth century made literary use of the language of thieves. The *genre poissard* is the language of honest folk—or folk as honest as need be—who, by and large, kept out of trouble and did all the heavy and humble work upon which the life of so great a city as Paris depended. These were market men and women, street venders, little shopkeepers, fishermen, boatmen, porters, and so forth. Their assault on French was largely an assault on grammar. It is said that in the *genre poissard* there were not more than a dozen words of *argot*.[43] But outlandish distortion of grammar, strange contractions and elisions, and the mangling of words, were in themselves enough to produce a speech with a definite claim to originality.

The writers who kept alive the *genre poissard* were for the most part obscure, but the plays and pamphlets which they wrote had at times an audience that extended up the social ladder, even to the Court. This was especially true toward the end of the eighteenth century. Market women were invited in 1777 to Marie Antoinette's Théatre du Trianon to coach noble actors in the correct pronunciation of *poissard*.[44] The Duke of Orleans had plays of this type produced at his private theatre, and he himself acted in one of them.[45] At the same time, this literature never drifted entirely away from the markets and back streets and alleys whence it sprang. The common people attended plays and sketches composed in their own rough speech, sang songs in *poissard*, and were in other ways familiar with the *poissard* literature. Furthermore, A. P. Moore, a recent investigator of this subject, cites certain writings in this genre which appear to have been the firsthand expression of the common people.[46] During the Revolution, *poissard* writings were particularly numerous, and there seems to me

[43] See Moore, *op.cit.*, p. 23. The derivation of the word *poissard* is apparently not from *poisson*, as is frequently supposed, but from *poix*, "pitch." In its adjectival form, it came to imply "besmired with slimy dirt." It was unflatteringly used to designate workers at Paris, and especially fishwives, who played a conspicuous part in the life of the *Halles*. For Moore's discussion of the word *poissard* and for other references on the same subject, see pp. 13-15.

[44] *Ibid.*, p. 291.   [45] *Loc.cit.*

[46] *Op.cit.*, pp. 287-88. The work of Moore is not so strictly confined to the theatre as its title would suggest; it furnishes a good general introduction to the subject of *poissard* writings. See also in this connection, C. Nisard, *Etude sur la langue populaire ou Patois de Paris et da sa banlieue*, Paris, 1872.

to be no doubt that many of them hailed from the markets—which had their own spokesmen—and were the forthright expression of the views of the *bas peuple*. It may be added that some of the most effective radical propaganda of the Revolution was expressed in *poissard*, notably Hébert's grisly and loud-mouthed *Le Père Duchesne*. It seems that in moments of far-reaching upheaval, illiterate and vulgar speech is apt to be exploited in this manner. At the time of the Reformation, for example, a somewhat analogous patois in corrupt Latin was used in the *Letters of Obscure Men*, an engine of Protestant propaganda.

At the various libraries of Paris, one may bring to light a large number of Revolutionary songs written in *poissard*. A few of these pieces antedate the fall of the Bastille.[47] There is in them, along with a rough equalitarian flavor, an atmosphere of boastfulness, as if the language of the streets and even of the back alleys were quite as good as, if not a little superior to, that of the Court. There is, besides, in the *poissard* writings of this period an atmosphere of realism and a note of skepticism that is often entirely lacking in pieces that were written in good French.

A typical *chanson poissarde* is that which purports to be written by a "Master Fisherman of Gros-Caillou."[48] In this song one is brusquely reminded that "before the State has been made over, they [the deputies] will have eaten more than one egg."[49] The same song treats ironically the report that the great (among whom are included the deputies of the Third Estate), laden down with ornaments of honor, are in fact moved by friendship for the poor. Even though it is said that "we [the poor] can drink with them, can go to see them and talk as much as we please," such a prospect appears to the Master Fisherman of Gros-Caillou as "mighty strange." The fishermen will reserve their right to be optimistic until the

[47] The *poissard* songs for the period covered in the present chapter are numbers 5, 6, 15, and 21 in Bibliography 1.

The first of these, *Arrêté des Habitans de la Grenouillère . . .* (5), closes with an epilogue in French which betrays its learned origin. On the other hand, it should be noted that the songs which the market people of Paris sang were by no means always in *poissard*. For example, *Le Tiers Etat . . .* (11), written in good French, is described as expressing "the Compliments of the Fishwives to their Confreres of the Third Estate," and as "Stanzas Sung May 18 at the Archbishop's Palace, by a Deputation of Fishwives of la Halle." See Bibliography 1 (11), edition "b" and note.

[48] *R'quête en magnier' d'écrit . . .* (6). Gros-Caillou was a Paris river port on the Seine, located between the present Pont des Invalides and the Pont de l'Alma.

[49] *Ibid.*, stanza 2.

affairs of the state are left to a single person. They will be convinced only if some much stouter fellow than the deputies says: "It shall be so, I will it."[50] They believed in salvation through a dictator, and chose for that role the King's minister, Necker.[51]

Another of these *poissard* songs, while sharing the prevalent optimism, decidedly lacks the tolerance and good will which are generally expressed in the songs of this period. This piece, the *Motion of the Herring Women of la Halle*,[52] concerns the popular impatience with the higher orders at the time when they were blamed by the patriots for not cooperating with the Third Estate. The author asserts that the greatest riffraff is to be found not among the ordinary people, but in "these dogs of Parlement, in the Nobility and their hangers-on . . . it isn't their King, so loyal, whom they love, it's the Royal treasury."[53]

The song concludes as follows:

> Si les Grands, troublent encor
> Que le Diable les confonde
> Et puisqu'ils aiment tant l'Or
> Que dans leux gueule on en fonde
> Voilà les sinceres voeux
> Qu'les Harangères font pour eux.

This is indeed a brutal wish, but there is a saving grace in the "if." The fishwives, exasperated though they were, linked their anathema to a continuation of evils, and thus extended to the "Great" a final chance to mend their ways.

Equally vigorous in tone is *Chanson poissarde*.[54] This song, presented in the vaudeville manner of the time, consists of a prose narrative interspersed with lyrics.[55] After the narrator has proudly

---

[50] *Ibid.*, stanzas 4 and 5.   [51] *Ibid.*, stanza 6.
[52] *Motion des Harangères* [*sic*] . . . (15).   [53] *Ibid.*, stanza 3.
[54] *Chanson poissarde* (21). The text used is the *Edition nouvelle avec additions*, 12 pp., this being, so far as is known, the only edition extant.
[55] *Vaudevilles*, which date from fifteenth-century France, were originally popular songs consisting of catchy new words put to familiar airs. The word *vaudeville* long retained its original meaning, and is defined in the *Encyclopédie*, vol. xxxv (Berne and Lausanne, 1781) only in this sense.
In the eighteenth century, songs of this character were interpolated in plays—the plays themselves being called at first *comédies avec vaudevilles*, and later simply *vaudevilles*. As time went on, the songs were frequently given original musical settings. In these plays the dialogue was spoken, which distinguishes them from light opera of the early Italian type wherein the whole libretto was sung.

proclaimed himself a member of the Third, and has denounced the envious nobles,[56] he ominously suggests that there is strength in numbers and that might is right:

> En nombre quand z'on est l'pus fort,
> On finit par n'avoir pas l'tort.[57]

These lines are followed by prose: "In truth, this calls for vengeance. A handful of nobles and shaveling priests wish to dominate millions of men!" Deep conflict, however, was not foreseen, and the concluding stanza of the song contains this expression of devotion to Louis:

> Mais d'tous nos voeux, le plus ardent,
> C'est que not' bon Roi soit content.

Thus, there appear in the many songs of this period—and especially in the songs of the *genre poissard*—lengthy references to specific grievances. Such expressions of discontent, however, are not the dominant feature of these pieces, and thus do not belie the spirit of optimism that pervaded the songs as a whole. Even the coarsest of these effusions is stamped with that faith in the golden age which prevailed in the spring of 1789.

[56] This song was written toward the end of June. The allusion is to the protracted opposition of the nobles to the merging of the three orders.
[57] *Chanson poissarde* (21), p. 7.

AFTER the first meetings of the Estates General on May 4 and 5, all did not go so well as the commoners had hoped. Obliged to sit separately, the members of the Third Estate refused to verify their credentials—or to take any other step which might seem to concede that their own order was to have a separate corporate existence. It was thus by a masterful program of inaction that they hoped to force a merging of the estates. But only with difficulty could they maintain their cherished illusion that their tactics had the support of certain private wishes of the King; for when the nobility and the clergy, separately convoked, each turned down the proposal of the Third that the three orders should merge, Louis gave no encouragement to the commoners.

The commoners, however, would not give in. As the representatives of the people, they were determined to dislodge the upper orders from their position of predominance. They elected their commissioners to negotiate with the privileged bodies, but otherwise refused for three solid weeks to transact any business. At the end of this time, May 28, Louis proposed royal mediation— a move inspired by reactionary influences, and quite properly suspected by the Third Estate.[1] The commoners acceded, at least formally, to the proposal of the King, but in effect they disregarded his wish by attempting still to win over the upper orders. One good possibility seemed to remain: would not the clergy (in whom the Third had more hope than in the nobles) voluntarily merge with the unprivileged class? Another fortnight passed in intense bickering. Popular opinion grew impatient. Finally, on June 12, the commoners took matters into their own hands. Proclaiming that they were the "representatives of the nation," they proceeded to the verification of the powers of the deputies of all three orders. The delegates of the nobility and the clergy were simply to be counted absent until they should take their places with the Third Estate.

---

[1] For reasons eloquently set forth by Mirabeau in the eighth of his *Lettres . . . à ses commettans*.

Here was a daring move—the beginning, indeed, of a parliamentary revolution. On June 17, the excited commoners, their number augmented by the presence of nearly twenty priests, dropped the title "Estates General," and, in the course of inflammatory speeches, proclaimed themselves a "National Assembly." It was an assumption of power which might, according to the old pattern of absolutism, have resulted in the dissolution of the Estates General, but instead it was destined to change the course of French history. Two days later, the clergy, whose membership included a large proportion of humble priests, voted for partial cooperation with the Third Estate, and failed only by a narrow margin to approve complete participation in this new creation, the National Assembly.

Almost daily, fresh landmarks were being made in the parliamentary struggle. On June 20, the commoners, having been denied admittance to their regular meeting place, repaired in a mood of desperation and defiance to the palace tennis court, or *Jeu de Paume*. Here they pledged an end to absolutism by swearing—in the so-called Tennis Court Oath—never to separate until they had established a Constitution for France.

This brave commitment was made at the suggestion of Jean Joseph Mounier, already famous for his leadership the year before in the uprising in Dauphiné. Although a pedestrian parliamentarian compared to Count Mirabeau, whose commanding personality tended increasingly to dominate the Assembly, Mounier was at this time one of the chief architects of the new order. So, too, was the Abbé Sieyès, whose writings—especially *Qu'est-ce que le tiers-état?*—had lifted him to fame early in 1789. The presiding officer at the time of the Tennis Court Oath was Jean Sylvain Bailly, distinguished Parisian scientist, who, at fifty-three, appeared aged in comparison with most of his colleagues. The other deputies of the Third Estate who enjoyed some degree of prominence did so by virtue of their successful careers as administrators, lawyers, journalists, etc., either in Paris or in the provinces. They were almost all substantial citizens—members of the upper bourgeoisie. Only a handful were primarily concerned with the lot of the lower classes. Perhaps the most radical of this group, although as yet by no means well known, was Maximilien Robespierre, a lawyer from Arras. It should be added that among the members of the emergent National Assembly it was not a commoner at all, but—as will presently appear—a liberal noble, the Marquis de La Fayette, who came to be regarded by the people as the truest exemplar of the popular cause.

Everything had been going contrary to the King's wishes. It was not that he was unsympathetic to reform or that he was unwilling to give something resembling "constitutional" guarantees. But he could not countenance as a means of attaining these ends a revolutionary procedure, which, although gratuitously attributed to his leadership, in effect reduced him to naught. Besides, after the death of the Dauphin[2] on June 4, Louis had retired to the relative seclusion of Marly, and there he had been subjected to the influence of a small Court clique. His ear was caught especially by his brother the Count of Artois,[3] and by the Duchess of Polignac, both scheming reactionaries who acted on principle only in the matter of opposing reform.

Whether as a result of this influence, or through prompting of his own, Louis forced a crisis. He summoned the representatives of all three orders to appear at a Royal Session, June 23. The preparations were somewhat ominous, the King having surrounded the gathering place with four thousand troops, a precaution which, as Arthur Young observed at the time, seemed to admit "the impropriety and unpopularity of the intended measures."[4] Though proposing some specific reforms, Louis took the side of the upper classes. He commanded the orders to sit separately,[5] to turn to financial affairs only, and to leave aside constitutional matters as not within their province. At this session Necker was not in his appointed place—as the deputies were amazed to discover. This was not so significant as it appeared, since Necker had planned to at-

[2] Louis-Joseph-François-Xavier, in his eighth year at the time of his death. He was succeeded by four-year-old Louis-Charles, the Dauphin of Revolutionary fame, who in 1792 was imprisoned in the Temple, where he died three years later.

[3] The younger of the King's two brothers, who was destined to emigrate within a few weeks, and who himself eventually became King of France as Charles X (1824-30).

[4] *Travels in France During the Years 1787, 1788, 1789*, Betham-Edwards, ed., London, 1900, p. 175.

[5] On the previous day, 149 members of the clergy and two nobles had joined the Third Estate.

tend and was dissuaded only at the last moment by his wife and his daughter, Madame de Staël.[6] His failure to attend, however, did his reputation as a champion of the popular cause much good, for it was generally supposed that by his absence the Minister was giving the signal for a revolt against the King's measures.

Before the Royal Session was over, the commoners were given a chance to register their own disapproval. At the conclusion of his speech, Louis ordered all the deputies to leave the hall. He himself withdrew, followed by the nobles and the upper clergy. The deputies of the Third Estate, and the lower clergy as well, would not leave. An emissary of the King appeared on the dais to repeat the royal order. Mirabeau, who had moments of lionesque grandeur, replied that nothing but force would move them. He then proposed a resolution, which was passed by an overwhelming majority, to the effect that the person of each deputy was inviolable.

Although troops were stationed about Versailles, there was the possibility that they would not support the Court against the people.[7] It may be that Louis felt powerless to enforce his edict. In any case, he liked matters simple, and this disobedience had complicated them. When he was told that the Third Estate would not obey except by force, he shook himself out of the role of king— which he could do rather easily—and remarked, like an ordinary tired human being, "They mean to stay! . . . Well then . . . let them stay!"[8] Thus the Royal Session, which was to have quashed the popular unrest, ended in a victory for the intractable reformers, and June 23 became a day of patriotic rejoicing.

While Louis slumped in this way, the so-called National Assembly continued to gain strength; for, on the following day, it was joined by a majority of the clergy, and on the day after by a delegation of forty-seven nobles led by the Duke of Orleans[9]—left wing

[6] They insisted that it would not become his dignity to attend, as several of the proposals which he had made in anticipation of the Royal Session had been overruled by the King and the Court.

[7] This applies particularly to the French Guards, who were regularly stationed at Versailles and Paris and who had been much influenced by radical propaganda. For consideration of a song which relates to this time, *Remerciemens aux Gardes Françaises* . . . (17), see pages 207-09.

[8] The quotation is borrowed from Madelin, *The French Revolution*, p. 65.

[9] Louis-Philippe Joseph, Duc d'Orléans, a cousin of Louis XVI, had long been a bold, though somewhat erratic, proponent of the new ideas, and was a great idol of the masses. In times of famine he made lavish gifts to the poor—which, as the richest

of a nobility that was either blandly to proceed, or ruthlessly to be dragged, into a maelstrom.

If Louis had been at heart a revolutionist, he might now have yielded certain of his prerogatives and made room for the new movement. Having been born and nurtured a monarch, he acknowledged no impairment of his sovereignty, but instead presented himself as the patron of the insurgent forces then ruling the state. This newfangled thing, this illegal creation of the popular will, the National Assembly, was now a *fait accompli*, something that, for the time being at least, could not be dislodged.

Accordingly, Louis—abandoning the stand he had taken but a few days before—announced on June 27 his desire that the three orders should sit together and vote as a single body.

This procedure had previously been revolutionary, because it had been followed against the King's will. But now, by commanding in a matter where the royal prestige was threatened, Louis had transformed a revolutionary triumph into an expression of continued despotism, of a despotism that was helplessly—and, therefore, pathetically—benevolent. In compliance with the King's request, the nobility joined the other orders. The National Assembly, at last complete, proceeded to deliberate on matters that concerned the New Day, without being further distracted by the question of its own composition, an issue which should have been settled by the Court at least as early as December of the preceding year.

The stability of any society depends upon a fundamental continuity of institutions. Despite the last-minute surrender of the King, this affair of the three orders, and its outcome, had marked a rupture. Broken (and only precariously mended) were habits in regard to sovereignty that had been built up in the course of centuries of French history. We can see this today. From the vantage point of the present, "June 23, 1789" appears clearly to have inaugurated a period of uncertainty, turmoil, and strife. But had we

---

man in France, he was well able to do—and, as a general practice, he threw open the gardens of his Palais Royal to the people of Paris. In January, 1793, he voted for the death of the King; but later in the same year he himself fell under suspicion and was guillotined.

As a result of the Revolution of 1830, his son Louis-Philippe was made King, thus at least for a time establishing the House of Orleans on the throne of France.

been living at the time—and had we not happened to be of that small band of sober-eyed critics who so often see something wrong just as things seem to be going well—we would have known that peace had come to France. This would have been our interpretation of the news of June 27, that the King had taken the side of the people and that the three orders, after so much deplorable contention, were now united.

The struggle over the orders had caused bitter disappointment. But patriotic resentment was reserved for the Court and for those nobles and clergy who had refused until the last moment to join the Third Estate. It did not touch the King. Even his attempt, at the Royal Session of June 23, to quash the ambitions of the Third Estate, had not turned the patriots against him.

The popular reaction is expressed in a song entitled *New Potpourri on the Affairs of the Times*,[10] which lampooned many illustrious persons who had tried to thwart the popular cause. The most scathing of the denunciations in this piece is reserved for Madame de Polignac, who "has exhaled the poison which corrupts the entire Nation."[11] Certain of the higher clergy, especially De Juigny, Archbishop of Paris, also came in for castigation. De Juigny was a generous donor to the poor, but had supposedly influenced the King against the cause of the Third Estate. Two days after the Royal Session, De Juigny was mobbed and barely escaped death. The author of the *New Potpourri*, having reviewed the charges that were currently made against the Archbishop, boasts that "the People," at their own good pleasure, made him repent.[12] But the King is given no rebuke. Indeed, despite the fact that on June 23 he had opposed the whole constitutional trend, he receives an encomium.[13] The poet accords praise also to Necker, and warns that a clique opposes the Minister at the very moment when he is "undertaking by his skill to bring us the golden age."[14]

The King, having tried to stop the onrush of the patriotic move-

---

[10] *Nouveau pot-pourri sur les affaires du temps* (18). Appearing in the same brochure with this piece are two other songs—*Chanson: "Notre S. [Saint] Père est un dindon . . .* (19) and *O filii national* (20) both of them acrimonious, though somewhat frivolous, attacks on the upper clergy. These pieces are considered in a discussion of anticlerical writings. See pages 200-1.

[11] *Nouveau pot-pourri . . .* (18), stanza 19.   [12] *Ibid.*, stanzas 12 and 13.

[13] *Ibid.*, stanza 2.   [14] *Ibid.*, stanza 11.

ment, approved the merging of the three orders, as we have seen, only as a last resort. None but a few intimates understood that Louis was suffering from grave misgivings, or could know that on June 26 he had secretly sent out an order summoning twenty thousand troops to the vicinity of Versailles and Paris.

Three songs are extant which celebrate the King's sanction of the so-called "reunion" of the three orders, June 27. One, written by Minier,[15] an obscure author, is a rare item, the copy in the Library of the French Senate being the only one known to exist. Another was by Déduit,[16] whose *Le moment désiré* has already been mentioned. The third of these pieces was anonymous and was published some weeks later in the brochure *La France régénérée.*[17] These songs express immense satisfaction with all three classes of French society. The mere fact that all representatives, regardless of class, were to vote in a common body, seemed to the lyrists a token that the members of the hitherto separate orders would from now on be united in spirit. It is true that under the new arrangement, the Third, outvoted in earlier days, could now hold its own, and, indeed—with the aid of its many supporters from the other two orders—could command a considerable majority; but it remained to be seen what effect this fact would have on the nobles as a whole and on high churchmen who had been forced to surrender the favored position that their classes had enjoyed for centuries. Regardless of the uncertainties of the situation, the lyrists found only one conclusion possible—that an all-encompassing spirit of fellowship would result from the triumph of the Third Estate.

Such, evidently, was the view of Minier, who assumes that with the merging of the three orders, "discord has taken flight." He praises with impartiality the Bourbon Princes of the blood, the clergy, the worthy nobility, and the Third Estate, all of whom he pictures as having a common concern for the public weal.

Against the background of a pastoral setting, the author then suggests the disappearance of class distinctions:

> Les Pasteurs et leur Troupeaux,
> Sont en paix et vivent en frère;

15 *Les trois ordres réunis, par Mr Minier* (22).
16 *La réunion des trois ordres . . . par M. Déduit* (23).
17 *Les trois ordres réunis* (24).

On verra dessous l'Ormeaux,
La joie renaitre au bruit des verres.

It was indeed a new day for France! Not only would all classes now hold council together, but they could drink together, without discrimination. The "flock"—that is to say, the citizens—could safely relax their efforts. This we may assume not only from the bucolic imagery of the song, but also from Minier's assurance that, a just balance having been attained among the three orders, "each one [of the deputies] fulfills his duty."[18]

Déduit was no less sanguine. He readily forgot class distinctions and the animosities which they had engendered.[19] The "reunion" having been achieved, the patriots would find loyal leaders in all the representatives, regardless of class. "Each of you," wrote this hopeful patriot (who later became a follower of the intractable Marat), "is a great man. Thanks to you, all the evils are going to end."[20] Déduit was sharing a supposition widely held in the first stages of the Revolution, that the leaders experienced the same feelings as the people. It was a part of this faith that no one adopted the patriotic cause as a matter of self-interest. In this connection, Déduit's apostrophe to the Duke of Orleans, "what a noble sentiment inspires thee," was characteristic of the time.[21]

Somewhat the same spirit is expressed in a song by the Marquis de C - - - P - - - -. Here the disappearance of class barriers and the emergence of equality are pictured as on the verge of attainment:

Le siècle d'or va reparoître,
Les laboureurs, les artisans,
Le clergé, les petits, les grands,
Tous sujets d'un seul et bon maître,
L'égalité verront renaître;

[18] Les trois ordres réunis, par Mr Minier (22); reference is made above to stanza 4 (quoted in part) and to stanzas 3 and 6.

[19] La réunion des trois ordres . . . par M. Déduit (23).

[20] Ibid., stanza 4.

[21] Ibid., stanza 3. This particular tribute, however, may be regarded with some misgivings. The Duke of Orleans is known to have lavished gifts for propaganda in his own behalf, and Déduit may have been within the orbit of this influence. In any case, he was author of Couplets sur la bienfaisance . . . (26), written in praise of the Duke and Duchess of Orleans and printed "with permission." But, regardless of whatever inferences may be drawn, the sentiment quoted above is precisely such as could have had a spontaneous origin at the time when it appeared.

Nobles, seigneurs, abbés, prélats, [bis]
Vous serez tous, [bis] membres du tiers-état. [bis][22]

The key to so felicitous and sudden a change in human nature is given in the final stanza—it is man's new and better way of looking at things, the "enlightenment," which has transformed France:

> Une saine philosophie,
> Qu'un vieux tems ne connoissoit pas,
> Eclaire aujourd'hui nos climats;
> On n'est plus dans la barbarie,
> Si funeste pour la patrie. . . .

In this exhibition of fine motives, Louis, of course, held first place. It would have been inconsistent with the patriotic outlook to have pictured a Louis acting in despair when, on June 27, he requested the merging of the upper orders with the Third. To be sure, such a disillusioning view might have resulted naturally from Louis' effort a few days previously to prevent this very thing. On June 23, in commanding the orders to sit separately, he had said, "If . . . you abandon me . . . , I alone will attend to the welfare of my people; alone, I shall consider myself their true representative."[23] But now he was following in the train of events.

How might a patriot interpret Louis' belated acquiescence in the popular demands? To the patriots, the answer was easy, for they already had a suitable formula which had only to be applied to the new situation. Déduit sensed this. He queried, in the opening stanza of his *Reunion of the Three Orders*: "Is not a king whom tenderness inspires worth a hundred conquering kings?" and added, "Louis seeks only to know the truth in its fullest clarity."[24] The anonymous author of another song which appeared at this time placed Louis in the same light, declaring that "He wishes only our happiness."[25] Minier's conclusion in regard to Louis' motives on the occasion of the *réunion* was in the same strain:

> L'amour et la bonne foi,
> Au Monarque dictent les loix.[26]

22 *Chanson sur les affaires du temps* (27), stanza 4.
23 *Archives parlementaires . . . , première série (1787 à 1799)*, vol. viii, p. 145.
24 *La réunion des trois ordres . . . par M. Déduit* (23), stanzas 1 and 3.
25 *Chanson poissarde* (21), p. 12.
26 *Les trois ordres réunis, par Mr Minier* (22), stanza 2. See also stanza 5.

Thus, in all respects, unity was supposedly attained. The disquieting possibility that conflicting opinions would be represented in the same assembly—and perhaps with increasing bitterness now that men of different class backgrounds were face to face—was rejected in favor of the view that there would be a merging of spirits in one common purpose. It is true that many of the patriots felt a deep hatred toward the Court clique, which they frankly avowed, and that there were denunciations of privileged groups—especially the upper clergy. But, in general, the patriots seem to have been moved by an inner compulsion to attribute to important personages the type of leadership that popular hopes called for.

Events, as it turned out, were to put such assumptions to a severe test. In *Où le bas nous blesse*[27]—written in July, but before the Bastille uprising—the author complains of factionalism, observing that "already parties are being formed." The verses of this song, and the several pages of notes which expound their meaning, delineate the weaknesses of the old order and the dangers of reaction. Finally, in addressing the "worthy representatives of the Nation," the author puts on record a prophetic warning:

If the Estates-General does not support the people, if strength should fail the people, their last breath will be a cry of rage. Despair will replace all else for a moment, and in that moment will occur the total collapse of the social structure: a building which is faulty at the foundations does not last long. For great evils, great remedies. Think well on that, Fathers of *la Patrie*![28]

The author of this dire warning had heard the news, recently come to Paris, that troops were converging on the city. Attributing their advance to the aristocrats, he offered this consolation: "The King, M. Necker, Monsieur,[29] the Duke of Orleans, and Twelve million brave Frenchmen, they are the Hero-Patriot-Soldiers who will oppose these Aristocrats, these friends of despotism."[30] The summoning of the troops and the various alarms which resulted

---

[27] *Où le bas nous blesse* . . . (28), *Paris, juillet 1789.*

[28] *Ibid.*, pp. 28-29, from note on stanza 17.

[29] The Count of Provence, the elder of the King's brothers. This cold, self-interested person, supposed friend of the popular cause, fled in 1791 to join the *émigrés* and the foreign enemies of France. Finally, on the restoration of Bourbon rule in 1814, he reigned as Louis XVIII (1814-24).

[30] *Où le bas nous blesse* . . . (28), p. 12, from note on stanza 1.

appertain, however, to the general subject of the Bastille uprising, which is considered in a later chapter. For the moment the Third Estate had gained a sweeping strategic victory, and it was generally hoped by the patriots that this parliamentary success might in itself be sufficient to secure the much desired reforms.

THE hopes of the patriots in the spring of 1789 were obviously excessive, and it is amazing that they were so universally sustained.
One is left with the feeling that he must go behind events and such
enthusiasms as are readily apparent, if he would discover how a
mood which was in many respects unrelated to facts could thrive
so vigorously. Because in the quest for hidden motives and obscure
beliefs, informal and spontaneous writings are particularly revealing, I have examined the popular literature of 1789 to determine,
if possible, by what pattern of thought—or even of faulty rationali-
zation—the patriots were able to sustain their faith in a golden age.
That faith, of course, released great stores of vital energy, but at
the same time it gave the Revolutionary movement an orientation
that was out of line with certain inexorable trends. By making the
patriots unduly sanguine, it exposed them to dangers which were
unseen but none the less real, and to disasters by which many of
them were later destroyed.

The impression that I have gathered from the songs and from
other writings of the period is that the patriots were able to sustain
their excessively sanguine hopes by a faith in leadership that was
akin to superstition. The role of the hero, with all that it had implied through primitive and classical times, was revived in eighteenth-century dress. Accordingly, one may note in the people a
deep sense of dependence, despite the feelings of self-reliance
which they professed and the talk of self-government in which they
indulged. This dependence they expressed in terms of abject deference for leaders, without realizing that a contrary, or at least modified, view is an indispensable condition of government by the
people.

In many ways, to be sure, the profound attachment of the French
to a King whose authority might well be a determining factor in
the success of the popular cause, and to a Minister whose devotion
to reform had long been demonstrated, may seem so natural as not
to require discussion. But actually that attachment was highly
complex and is worthy of study. In the first place, it was charged
with emotion bordering on religious ecstacy. The devotion of the

people to their leaders was not a matter of measured loyalty—it became a cult. In the second place, that attachment was not simple and direct; on the contrary, it involved several crosscurrents, as we shall presently see. Of course, we are not dealing here with the King and his Minister as they now appear to the detached student of history—as mere historical personages. We are concerned rather with their idolization in 1789, and from this standpoint one is justified in considering them frankly as gods created by the people in their own image. Indeed, in this phase of the French Revolution man's myth-making proclivities are clearly revealed.

For the purposes of the present analysis, the King provides the obvious point of departure. Revolutionary hopes, as we have seen, were centered in Louis, who as a magnet seems to have attracted and given common direction to the various elements of the popular cause. It is not enough to say, as so many have done, that Frenchmen on the eve of the Revolution believed in monarchy. The people placed their confidence, not primarily in the institutional form of government which they had inherited, nor even in the reform of it which they contemplated, but rather in its flesh and blood embodiment—Louis XVI. There is no use seeking justification of this confidence in the records of his person, or of his performance. What the people trusted was the Louis XVI they had created. They made of their ruler a symbolic figure. The symbol served many purposes. As we shall later see, it enabled the patriots to bear toward the King strangely contradictory sentiments: to feel in one way or another the loyalty of good sons and subjects; to experience, at the same time, the new equalitarian sense of partnership in a common task; and, on occasion, to express the defiance of "free" citizens who might later dictate their own terms.

A careful analysis reveals that three main superstitions had grown up around the person of Louis XVI:

First, that he was a good man, generous and true, whose acts would bear witness to his goodness.

Second, that he was in sympathy with democratic impulses, and spontaneously approved any changes which the popular cause demanded.

Third, that august though the King was,[1] yet he was simple and approachable, with all the attributes of a loving father.

The extent to which gratuitous assumptions were made about Louis' goodness is amazing. The people seem indeed to have been thirsting after righteousness and to have found in their King its source. It is by his "virtues" and his "equity" that Louis is worthy of ruling over France, according to Déduit, in *Le moment désiré*. The author adds that in this happy hour each of the three orders "burns incense" to Louis.[2] One is assured in another song[3] that "the Golden Age resuscitated, will be presented to him as the work of his goodness."[4] In fact, in the prose of parliamentary discourse one finds a similar emphasis; Louis, for example, was praised before the Estates General as "worthy on account of his personal virtues" of the love of his people.[5]

The kingly quality, as popularly conceived, is nicely suggested in Déduit's song, where Louis is pictured as "a sun which shines by the rays of its goodness."[6] This is reminiscent of the sun-king image of Louis XIV; but whereas in the days of *le Grand Monarque* this figure expressed power, it now has the connotation of virtue. There will be later occasions to comment on this particular emphasis, which plays an important part throughout the early phases of the Revolution.

The second superstition in regard to Louis grows out of the first. In the days of the revival of the Estates General, a king could hardly have been regarded as good if it had not also been believed that he was well-disposed to the popular cause. Despite his none-too-consistent record, Louis was pictured, therefore, as being, not merely agreeable to reform, but as having a veritable genius for it. To the people who craved a better society, it seems to have ap-

---

[1] Louis was not infrequently presented in this light; as in *Le moment désiré* (7), which opens:

> Enfin le bonheur va renaitre [*sic*]
> Sous le plus auguste des Rois. . . .

By the final stanza Louis becomes "un père adoré."

[2] *Ibid.*, stanza 3.   [3] *Hymne en l'honneur de la Résurrection* . . . (3), stanza 48.

[4] A year earlier, a lyrist had written of the King that "his great soul acts less on his own behalf than on behalf of you [the people]." *Couplets sur l'Assemblée des Notables*, stanza 6. See *Ibid.*, Bibliography iii, A, and Appendix A, 177.

[5] Speech of the Marquis de Sillery, June 25, 1789, *Archives parlementaires*, vol. viii, p. 154.

[6] *Le moment désiré* (7), stanza 2.

peared as inevitable that the person on whom they most depended
—to wit, the King—was the staunchest reformer of all. His was the
role of "un Roi régénérateur."[7]

This idea was naïvely expressed by "A. L. G." in the opening
lines of his *New "O Filii"* . . . :

> Chantons notre Roi bien-aimé,
> Le Peuple il veut soulager,
> Et de tout temps le soulagea,
> Alleluia.[8]

Hence, the King was supposed to take delight in the changes that
were occurring. There is assurance of this in the same song, several
stanzas of which are devoted to an account of Louis' participation
in the procession of May 4.[9] It is necessary to read the stanzas in
question in order fully to appreciate the naïve enthusiasm of the
author, whose confused joy seems a fair reflection of popular feeling at this time. The song pictures the royal personages in the procession as "surrounded by the entire nation assembled." The enthusiasm for Louis XVI is pictured as immense, and we are told
that it is "impossible to express the *vive le roi* that were reiterated." But whereas we are given some index as to the popular enthusiasm, we are obliged to take the author's word for the assertion
that "never has the King felt so pure a joy" as on this occasion. In
this connection, the historian is bound to recall the well-known
fact that at the gathering which followed the procession of "the
entire nation assembled," the King fell asleep.

In the eulogies of Louis there was an element which might at
first sight be regarded as purely formal. This consisted in the elaborate comparisons of him to the beloved Henry of Navarre, or
Henry IV. As a matter of fact, this comparison had been made at
the young King's coronation in 1774, and was perhaps never entirely lost from sight.[10] It might seem perfunctory throughout had
it not enjoyed such tireless repetition and gained such extraordi-

---

[7] By early summer of 1789 this characterization was widely used. The earliest occurrence of it that I have noted in the songs occurs in *La réunion des trois ordres
. . . par M. Déduit* (23), stanza 4.

[8] *Nouvel "O Filii"* . . . (14).   [9] *Ibid.*, stanzas 8-13.

[10] It was brought to the fore by Barentin, the King's Keeper of the Seals, at the
meeting of the Estates General on May 5. Barentin likened the role of His Majesty
also to that of Louis XII. *Archives parlementaires*, vol. viii, p. 2.

nary emphasis in 1789. The full Revolutionary significance of the comparison can be appreciated only in connection with the role of Necker, presently to be considered. Here it is enough to suggest that the patriots were attracted by the idea that the popular movement was not altogether an innovation, but was grounded in the past. From this standpoint, the King, in his aspect of supposed Revolutionist, was regarded not only as the embodiment of a new day, but also as the expression of a prized tradition. He is referred to as "the worthy scion of Henry,"[11] as having "the great heart of Henry,"[12] or simply as "Henry IV."[13] These citations are from songs previous to the fall of the Bastille; as time went on they became more frequent.

To conclude in regard to the first two popular delusions concerning Louis, one may say that confidence in him had to be maintained at any cost. We are reminded of this in the opening stanza of the *Motion of the Herring Women of la Halle*:

> Ces grands états Généraux
> F'ront-ils du brouet d'andouille
> Ces Messieurs s'ront-ils si sots
> Que d's'en r'tourner chés eux bredouille
> Quand par miracle un bon Roi
> Veut faire l'bien, et d'si bonne foi.[14]

In this and in other *poissard* songs, it appears that certain illiterate groups expected little of the deputies who had been assembled. This is almost a heresy and stands in contrast to the view that one finds expressed in more conventional songs. Rather than put their trust in deputies, the fishwives would put that trust in the beneficence of Louis. However skeptical in other ways, they would believe in the King's goodness—even at the cost of a miracle.

We come now to the third attribute of the popular view of the King, that he was related to his people specifically as a father is to his children.

At this point, it may be suggested that the general enthusiasm, which was far beyond what the facts would justify, might have

---

11 *Les trois ordres réunis, par Mr Minier* (22), stanza 7.
12 *Le Tiers Etat* . . . (11): edition "a," stanza 7; edition "b," stanza 5.
13 *Le moment désiré* (7), stanza 4.   14 *Motion des Harangères* [*sic*] . . . (15).

quickly dissipated had it not been made intelligible to the people through the prevalence of certain homely symbols. The political ferment of the times could have meaning for the masses only if reduced to simple aims and familiar relationships. The patriots at first took refuge in the concept of the "father," which from primitive times had held a place of basic importance in most European societies. Resort to this particular symbol, apart from being in accord with deep natural impulses, is further explained by reference to France's historical development.

The old regime had been built on the principle of hierarchy, wherein the patriarchal concept, implicit from the beginning, was subsequently preserved and exploited. In Funck-Brentano's *L'Ancien Régime* one may find ample evidence of the extent to which the father symbol furnished, down to the eve of the Revolution, the emotional basis for cohesion not only in the family, but also in all the phases of the social hierarchy, and in the monarchical and absolutist aspect of the realm as a whole.[15] The concept originally implied sternness and power, a patriarchal severity.[16] The father symbol thus left little, if any, room for insubordination or sentimentality, and made for authority and order.

But by the end of the eighteenth century, the notion of father, both in the family and in its wider political application, had been sentimentalized. The father in his new role was thought of as pliant and yielding, as one who sought only to anticipate the wishes of his family.[17] Thus, since the age-old dictum that the king is the

---

[15] Funck-Brentano, *L'Ancien Régime*, Paris, 1926.

[16] See *ibid.*, pp. 26-113.

[17] Funck-Brentano goes so far as to declare (*op.cit.*, p. 558) that the real cause of the Revolution was "the transformation of the family" which took place in the course of the eighteenth century. Although this is too exclusive a claim, the exaggeration may perhaps be forgiven, since the author is stressing a matter of fundamental importance, which has on the whole been neglected by others as incidental. And such earlier consideration as the subject has received has not always been felicitous; for instance, in *La puissance paternelle* (1910), Emile Masson writes (p. 51): "Jusqu'à la veille de la Révolution, la famille avait gardé son antique constitution. L'authorité souveraine du père de famille était comparable à la puissance absolue du roi. Mais la ruine de l'authorité royale devait amener une transformation profonde dans le coeur même de la famille, transformation qui se fit sans délai. . . ." But as Funck-Brentano makes clear, the "profound transformation in the heart of the family" began far in advance of the Revolution; and accordingly it must not be pictured as the sudden result of the collapse of royal authority (which, too, was not sudden, there having been a long period of decline). Even so, one need not go so far as Funck-Brentano in picturing the former influence as sole cause. No doubt, the

father of his people no longer implied the traditional submission, it is not surprising that the patriots could be among the first to insist upon the patriarchal role of their king. Far from proving inconvenient, the symbol, in its sentimentalized form, suited their needs in a variety of ways, and, for the time being, afforded them reassurance and comfort.

The possibility of a fascinating study is furnished by the persistence from the old regime of the father symbol, and by its replacement, at a later stage of the Revolution, by the symbol of the mother (expressed in various Revolutionary goddesses; above all, in the incarnate *La Patrie*). In the present chapter, it is enough to demonstrate the extent to which the notion of the king in the role of gentle father pervaded the earliest songs; it is recurrently their main theme. For example, in the second stanza of *Le moment désiré*,[18] Déduit addresses the following line to the King: "Your people are all your family."[19] He then proclaims that the clergy, the nobility, and the Third Estate, reunited, have promised to be "your children, your friends."[20] In concluding, he characterizes Louis as "an adored father of his people."

The idea of the good father is also expressed in the following stanza, which, though written in conventional French, appears at the end of a *poissard* song:

> Après avoir été
> Longtemps dans la misère
> Et près de succomber
> Dans nos pauvres chaumières;
> Louis, notre bon Père,
> Pour guérir tous nos maux,
> Convoque, en cette affaire,
> Les Etats-Généraux.[21]

---

undermining of parental authority in the family—in its relation to the gradual decline of royal authority—acted as both cause *and* result, in one of those long and complicated processes of interaction which so commonly underlie historical change.

[18] (7).

[19] The text reads "ton peuple et toute ta famille," but the sense of the passage as a whole suggests that "et" is a misprint for "est." Typographical errors of this sort occur frequently in the songs.

[20] The text is "D'être les enfants, tes amis." The "les" is presumably a misprint for "tes."

[21] *Arrêté des Habitants de la Grenouillère* . . . (5), p. 11.

It was as "this good father," according to other lyrics, that the King, on June 27, commanded the upper orders to join the Third Estate; and it was incumbent on them to do so, since "all the French are his children."[22]

This filial respect is repeatedly evident during the first two years of the Revolution. And, indeed, it was prevalent somewhat earlier. There is a delightful instance in the *Couplets sur l'Assemblée des Notables*, which presumably appeared in 1788.[23] In this work of M. du Croisi, not only is the father symbol suggested, but the relationship is completely imaged in a picture where sentiment is given full play. As the song opens, the people of the French nation are invited to believe that they see their father, who takes his place amongst them. He asks his children to speak with "a sincere heart," and tells them that their advice, if good, will be followed. "Yes," says the King, "I desire that my family be happy for a long time; especially that gaiety shine on the faces of my children." The children are represented as saying, with true filial devotion: "Each one of us admires you and puts everything into your hands. It is Heaven which inspires you. Ah! my Father, its favor blesses your noble ardor." Here are accents which suggest that the role of the King as father merges with that of God the father.[24] At the end of the song, we leave the "heureux Français" an assembled family en-

22 *Chanson sur les affaires du temps* (27), stanza 2.

23 In addition to the song of 1788 described in the paragraph above, one may cite *L'heureux retour du Parlement, chanson patriotique*, celebrating the uprising in Dauphiné in 1788. In the opening lines of stanza 3, one reads:

> Louis fait notre bonheur,
> Parce qu'il est notre père;
> Il est le consolateur
> D'un peuple qui le révère.

Concerning these two songs, see Bibliography III, C, and Appendix A, 177 and 178*.

24 The theory of rule by "divine right," though a tenet of political orthodoxy that was little stressed at the end of the eighteenth century, was, nevertheless, a venerable survival and one which unquestionably played a part in conditioning the attitude of French subjects. As a result, much of the respect felt for the King was distinctly religious and, in particular, Christian in character. Inversely, the modern ideal of the Christian Deity is not unlike the Revolutionary ideal of the monarch in 1789. For example, the following lines from the *Psaumes et cantiques* (Paris, 1895) of the French Reformed Church,

> Je veux t'aimer, toi mon Dieu, toi mon Père,
> Mon Rédempteur, mon Roi!
> Je veux t'aimer, car la vie est amère
> Pour ton enfant sans toi,

might but for one or two matters of style have been addressed by a patriot to Louis XVI.

joying the parental love of Louis, and are reminded that "this idea is not at all a dream in this day."

The prevalence of a popular conception of Louis as *ce bon père* has not been much emphasized in history. It is either discounted as purely formal or superficial, or is regarded—and even then with too little effort at interpretation—as a picturesque and somewhat fanciful reminder of an antiquated aspect of French monarchy. The revival and vogue of the father symbol at this time, however, reveals a significant feature of the Revolutionary mood. By resorting to this symbol, the patriots were able to reconcile the new freedom which they were demanding as citizens with the traditional sense of childlike dependence which they had inherited as subjects; for, as we have seen, they had abandoned the authoritarian patriarch in favor of the indulgent father who responds to his children's desires. In attributing to Louis qualities which suited their convenience, the people had in part created a monarch out of their own imaginations. It was in this sense that they could love Louis so unreservedly. Recognition of the complex nature of this relationship makes possible an understanding not only of the patriots' initial devotion to Louis, but also of much of their behavior toward him.

One might assume from the foregoing that the King's position as national hero was unchallenged. Such, however, was not the case. By the spring of 1789, Necker, having regained the favor which he had so precipitately lost in the autumn, enjoyed a popularity which rivaled that of the King. The two were almost invariably celebrated together, praise of one seeming to call for praise of the other. This dual leadership introduces in the hero worship of that time an important—and, to be sure, somewhat complicating —element.

The hold which the Minister acquired on the popular imagination is attributable to several factors. First of all, it was generally believed that he stood staunchly for the popular cause. Then, with his great reputation as a financier, he seemed to the patriots to be the indispensable man in matters of economic reform.[25] They

[25] This was the case, by and large, even though in June there was an undercurrent of adverse criticism in connection with the scarcity of bread. Necker was attacked, for example, in *L'Ami de l'humanité* and in *Le Pain du Peuple . . . , le 21 juin, 1789* (Tourneux, *Bibliographie . . . ,* vol. i, no. 1301). In respect to the latter, one may

hailed him as a one-man cure even for the threat of national bankruptcy:

> On n'entendra jamais parler
> De la banqueroute, si redoutée;
> Necker a sçu remédier à cela,
>   Alleluia.[26]

Not only did Necker seem to his followers to be the useful man
par excellence, but he was esteemed by them also as a moral force.
Indeed, on occasion he was represented as the personification of
absolute good:

> Sans doute le grand Necker
> Est vainqueur de l'enfer [*bis*]
> Car il foule aux pieds Lucifer,
> La Discorde et l'Envie
> Ah! c'est un bras de fer
> Qui rompt la Calomnie. [*bis*][27]

An incident on the evening of the Royal Session of June 23—
from which Necker had been so conspicuously absent—illustrates
the reverence of the people for the Minister. Word spread that
Necker had resigned. This caused consternation at Versailles, and
resulted in an ovation to him on the part of a frantic populace.
The King and Queen called the Minister to the palace, and prevailed upon him to remain. The mob, which was first moved by
apprehension, was now overwhelmed with joy. The extraordinary

---

consult at the New York Public Library, *Justification de M. Necker en réponse à un
écrit intitulé, "Le Pain du Peuple"* (not mentioned in Tourneux). This small current of anti-Necker literature was perhaps primarily the work of reactionaries, and
in any case did not betoken any serious defection in the ranks of the patriots.

26 *Nouvel "O Filii"* . . . (14), stanza 6. From the very beginning of his ministry,
Necker had been welcomed as the man who could rescue France from the anarchy
into which it seemed to be slipping. In a song of 1788, one reads, after an excoriation
of Brienne and Calonne, that

> Un brave et Sage étranger
> Soutient l'Etat comme une colonne;
> Necker change le mal en bien
> Et pour tant d'peine i ne prend rien. [*bis*]

Considérations politiques des Notables de la Halle au pain . . . , stanza 8 (III, B).

27 *Le coup heureux de Versailles* . . . (16), stanza 2. This song, celebrating the successful defiance of the Third Estate on the occasion of the Royal Session of June 23,
is known only through its appearance in *La France régénérée*, which was published
after the Bastille uprising. See Appendix A, 187.

demonstration which both preceded and followed this event, and which lasted through much of the night, is perhaps best known from the unsympathetic account of the Marquis of Ferrières.[28] But there were many popular accounts which pictured in a highly favorable light the meeting between Necker and the vast throng of his admirers. A brief quotation from one of these accounts may serve to suggest the sincerity and simplicity of the interview, at least as popularly conceived:

M. Necker a été obligé de sortir pour rassurer ces généreux Français, qui lui criaient: *M. Necker, notre père, notre bon père, ne nous abandonnez pas!*

Non, mes amis, s'est écriée cette âme pure & sensible; non, je resterai avec vous. . . .[29]

The writer adds that during the night the air echoed with cries of "vive M. Necker! vive le père du Peuple."[30]

What does it mean that the people should characterize the Minister in this manner? It was on the afternoon of that same day that Louis, in his address at the Royal Session, had referred to himself as "le père commun de tous mes sujets," and had described the royal proposals as "mes intentions paternelles."[31] This emphasis seemed convincing even to those who resisted His Majesty's program. The Marquis of Sillery—one of the nobles who on June 25 joined the Third Estate, despite an order to the contrary which the King had given at the Royal Session but two days before—spoke in terms of filial respect as he made his initial address to the new and unsanctioned National Assembly: "Let us never lose sight of the respect which we owe to the best of Kings. . . . He calls us his children! Ah! without doubt we [the three estates] should regard ourselves as a reunited family, having different tasks in our paternal mansion."[32]

In seeking to explain the Revolutionary mentality at this time, one is bound to inquire whether Necker was actually rivaling the King in the hearts of the people. The allusion to the Minister as

---

[28] *Mémoires* . . . (M. de Lescure, ed., Paris, 1880), pp. 42-43.
[29] The italics appear in the original. *Suite des nouvelles d'hier, mardi 23 juin 1789,* p. 4. (IV, C)
[30] *Ibid.,* p. 5.   [31] *Archives parlementaires,* vol. viii, pp. 143 and 144.
[32] *Ibid.,* p. 154, and in *Lettre de M. Necker, du 24 Juin 1789; et Discours* . . . , p. 13. (IV, C)

"the Father of the People" is but one bit of evidence, by implication, that such was the case.[33] Evidences may be sought, also, in other directions. Since, for example, the intuition of an enemy is sometimes even more revealing than the protestations of a friend, one may well consider an anonymous satire, *Ma Confession*, directed against Necker and the popular worship of him. Its conclusion, however ironic and bitter, is striking. Necker is supposed to be delivering a long soliloquy, which comes to a close as follows:

> But I hear a thousand voices raised! It's SULLY! it's COLBERT! it's LYCURGUS! it's SOLON! it's a GOD—ALTARS! TEMPLES! STATUES! . . . People wish that I retain the Ministry, they declare me Protector of France. . . . For my part . . . I yield to their too pressing demands; I am touched, I withdraw my resignation & I REIGN.[34]

There was, of course, never any danger that Jacques Necker, essentially timid and inadequate, would "reign." But that, in the thoughts of the people, he should in various indirect ways be identified with the King is a matter of considerable interest. This represents a trend which will presently be illumined by other evidence.

As the reader may already suspect, certain of the feelings of a religious nature which the patriots experienced on the revival of the Estates General found an outlet in the popular worship of the Minister. The *Hymn in Honor of the Resurrection of the Estates General* depicts this adoration in naïve and expressive terms.[35] It is related that against a background of "trouble and fury" (which according to the author, resulted not from general conditions, but from the misrule of an oppressive minister), "Necker appeared as Savior." When the news burst forth it seems that everyone believed it, except those who were most deeply concerned, the Third Estate, whose faith, we are led to presume, could hardly have been expected to grasp such a stupendous fact. But Necker, restored to power, was there to reassure his flock. The simplicity and charm of the narrative—and its religious overtones—will no doubt become clearer as one resumes the foregoing in the original:

---

[33] To be sure, the appellation "Father of the People" was not restricted in French usage to kings; but from the time of Louis XII it was used primarily in that sense, and was uppermost in men's minds in the spring of 1789 as applying to Louis XVI.

[34] *Ma Confession* . . . , pp. 15-16. (IV, C)

[35] *Hymne en l'honneur de la Résurrection* . . . (3).

Parmi le trouble et la fureur,
Effet d'un Ministre oppresseur,
N e c k e r parut comme un Sauveur.
    Alleluia.

Lorsque la nouvelle éclate,
Chacun la crut, la débita,
Hors le Tiers-Etat qui douta.
    Alleluia.

C'est moi, dit-il: n'ayez point peur;
Touchez mes mains, touchez mon coeur:
Je renais pour votre bonheur.
    Alleluia.[36]

The doubts of the Third Estate were accordingly assuaged. The people exclaimed with joy. The lyrist then pauses to express in his song the thought of Christ, that "happy are those who without having seen, shall have believed with constancy to the end!" "Heaven," he concludes, "will bless their virtue."

In lyrics which antedate the gathering of the Estates General, Necker is referred to as "this protecting God of the Third."[37] *Dieu tutélaire*, the heart of the phrase, is a characterization which was much repeated. In another early piece, appreciation and adoration of the Minister are expressed as follows:

Français, Necker est notre appui
Comme le fut, le grand Sulli,
Le Dieu de la France il sera,
    Alleluia. [*bis*][38]

Precisely the same stanza occurs in the New "O Filii" ... except that in it the third line reads "Sauveur de la France...," instead of "Le Dieu de la France il sera."[39] Elsewhere in the songs, similar homage is paid to the Minister, as in the following lines:

Vive le sauveur de la France!
    NECKER, *vivat!*[40]

[36] *Ibid.*, stanzas 8-10.   [37] *L'Alleluia du Tiers-Etat* (1), stanza 13.
[38] *Chanson nouvelle sur l'assemblée* ... (8), stanza 7.
[39] *Nouvel "O Filii"* ... (14), stanza 5.
[40] *Le Tiers Etat* ... (11), edition "b," stanza 4. See also edition "a," stanza 6.

It is not easy to interpret these obeisances, which appear so prominently in the optimism of 1789. One may readily say, however, that they were neither abject flattery nor unsubstantial rhetoric. The patriots were convinced that Necker had performed a great service for his country. The achievement with which they credited the Minister was well summarized in one of the songs written to celebrate the Reunion of the Three Orders, June 27:

> Necker, homme sensible et sage,
> Ne dois-tu pas être content?
> Notre bonheur est ton ouvrage,
> Couronne de gloire, t'attend.
> Reçois-la [bis] des mains de la France,
> Dont tu deviens libérateur:
> Pour prix de sa reconnaissance,
> Sois à jamais son protecteur. [bis][41]

The gifted daughter of Necker, Madame de Staël, pictured her father in this happy light.[42] Perhaps no writer since her time has agreed. Michelet, who bestowed halos so generously on most of the earlier leaders of the Revolution, found Necker worse than undeserving.[43] Historians today consider him to have been moderately able in routine matters, incapable of grasping large ideas, subject to forces he could not control, and complacent in the face of dangers he did not understand. It is true that he had gained deserved renown in 1781 by exposing the state of the royal finances; but the role which he subsequently played was largely ineffectual.[44]

[41] *La réunion des trois ordres . . . par M. Déduit* (23), stanza 2. The same idea persisted for some time; for example, one finds an anonymous pamphleteer writing in August, in a tribute to Necker, "The reunion of the Three Orders is due to you, who have brought all spirits into agreement." *Tribut de reconnoissance de la Nation Françoise au meilleur de ses amis; Août 1789*, p. 6. (IV, C)

[42] See her *Considérations sur les principaux événemens de la Révolution française*, Paris, 1817, which she wrote partly as a defense of Necker. This effort Thiers described as "la perfection de la médiocrité." A somewhat milder criticism would have been more just.

[43] Necker's fondness for moderation and compromise was particularly distasteful to Michelet, who described him as being in June, 1789, "the courtier at one and the same time, of the people and of the enemies of the people." *Histoire de la Révolution française*, Paris, 1879, vol. i, p. 183.

[44] For two contemporary criticisms of Necker—Mirabeau's forecast in August, 1788, of his failure, and Malouet's disdainful opinion expressed some months later—see A. Chérest, *La chute de l'Ancien Régime (1787-1789)*, vol. ii, pp. 163 and 601. For

In view of all this, how may we account for the Revolutionary homage to Necker as "liberator" and "protector," as "god" and "savior"? I would submit that this frenzy of hero worship can by no means be understood exclusively in the light of the optimism of the spring of 1789—that one must recall the circumstances that attended the outbreak of the Revolution. Despite generally improving conditions in France, the people were still heavily burdened with taxes, alarmed at the specter of national bankrupcy, and harassed by the presence everywhere of unjust distinctions and privileges. Those who were prosperous were uncertain of their future and of that of their country. The poor, better off on the whole than the poor elsewhere in Europe, nevertheless often lived in miserable hovels, frequently wore tatters, and at times suffered from food shortage. Many were the groans and tears occasioned by the abuses of the old regime. One bright side of the picture was the influence of the *philosophes*, who had pointed the way, it was generally believed, to national health and happiness. Some of the more radical thinkers assured the people that they could themselves bring into being their own bright new world. However seductive this promise may have been to contemporaries, the fact remains that the French people were almost entirely lacking in the experience of self-government and that any steps which they might take on their own behalf were bound to be tentative. In view of the disturbing conditions of life in the France of that day, of the high hopes that had been aroused, and of the comparative helplessness of the masses, one may ask if there was ever a time when people might be more apt to seek some leader as the means of their salvation. It was into this world that Louis, trying desperately to find a Minister whom his exasperated subjects would approve, invited Necker.

The new Minister was to the people the embodiment of certain symbolic values. As we have seen, his hold on the popular imagination in the spring of 1789 did not grow out of his own strength

---

the views of two historians—Droz's estimate of the demoralizing effect on the Minister of his own popularity, and Chérest's partial justification of him—see *ibid.*, pp. 602 and 603. Particularly to the point is Arthur Young's commentary that when Necker's "great opportunity" arrived (with the assembling of the Estates General) he gave a "speech you would expect from a banker's clerk of some ability." *Travels in France . . .* , Betham-Edwards, ed., p. 161.

or result from ability on his part to meet the needs of the situation then existing in France. In view of the naïve dependence of the people upon Necker, one is forced to the conclusion that he stood to them in an almost primitive relationship, as the archetype of the priest, or redeemer, of early human society.

Of course the uncritical ardor with which the people also accepted Louis, and their unlimited faith in his leadership, sprang from similarly deep roots, kingship itself being an archetype of primitive leadership. Louis' role in this respect remained fundamentally unchanged until his fall—the traditional symbol of kingship continuing naturally to reside in him. It is interesting to observe, however, that the symbol of the popular will was not a similarly constant factor. It was embodied only temporarily in Necker, whose role was assumed, as occasion required, by various successors.

Though to this point we have considered the King and his Minister as separate heroes, Necker did not really have an individual existence as savior of France. He was praised largely in connection with the King. The two were taken to be inseparable, the notion of their indispensability to one another being evident in every aspect of patriotic thought. Necker, the man of the people, was also the support of the King, the "soutien des lys."[45]

A prose passage appended to one of the songs quaintly depicts this relationship as it was popularly conceived. After lamenting that conditions in France had not improved, the author consoled himself with the following thoughts of Necker and Louis:

One may place the highest hopes in the wise and beneficent views of the friend of the people, and the friend of the King . . . ; M. Necker unceasingly conjures away the storms which multiply above his worthy head, is for France a God; the King knows his merit, the King loves

[45] This phrase is taken from the *Cahier du Marquis de Fulvy* (4), stanza 14. The same expressive image appears elsewhere; notably in a song by a patriot of La Rochelle, the first four lines of which indicate, delicately and indirectly, the waning prestige of the monarchy and its dependence upon a popular leader:

> Amis, buvons à la Patrie,
> Au Monarque, aux Ordres unis,
> Au Ministre, dont le génie
> A relevé l'éclat des Lys.

Autres [*couplets*] (53). This song appeared somewhat later, after the capture of the Bastille and the return of Necker.

him, the King esteems him, the King sheds tears on the bosom of this friend who in turn is unable to withhold his own.[46]

This supposedly intimate partnership, which was such a great source of satisfaction to the patriots, was celebrated not only in various obvious ways, but also by indirection. In the latter connection, we must recall the inclination of the patriots to compare Louis XVI to Henry IV. This comparison signifies more than a simple tribute to Louis, and more even than an effort to justify his leadership in terms of the past; for Revolutionary writers, in their allusions to the reign of Henry IV, repeatedly emphasized the alleged parallel between a particular feature of the government in that early age and in their own day—to wit, the collaboration between a good king and his minister. Had not Good King Henry depended on his trusted minister, the great Sully, who had traveled shoulder to shoulder with him in the cause of reform?[47] And did not memories of this epoch in French history serve as a traditional justification for Necker, as well as for Louis? That such was presumed to be the case is suggested by a further examination of the song material.

In one of the preceding quotations, there was reference to Necker as *le grand Sulli*. As a matter of fact, similar comparisons appeared often in the early period, and for many months persisted in the songs. Necker either resembled "the great Sully"[48] or was "a second Sully."[49] These references were as a rule accompanied by the reminder that Louis XVI was the worthy successor, if not the positive image, of *Henri Quatre*.[50] Thus, the recurrent allusions to the age of Henry IV—in addition to affording a happy opportunity for praise or flattery, and to endowing the Revolu-

---

[46] *Où le bas nous blesse* . . . (28), note on stanza 1, p. 12. This brochure appeared in July, less than a fortnight before Louis' dismissal of Necker.

[47] This collaboration the Revolutionists somewhat idealized. Henry and Sully were frequently at odds, especially in matters of policy, the Minister having at heart an agricultural France, while the King's vision encompassed industry and overseas trade. Nevertheless, the two were energetic and loyal partners, and together they introduced many important reforms.

[48] See, for example, *Chanson nouvelle sur l'assemblée* . . . (8), stanza 7; and *Nouvel "O Filii"* . . . (14), stanza 5.

[49] *Les trois ordres réunis, par Mr Minier* (22), stanza 2. The same idea is somewhat differently expressed in *Le moment désiré* (7), stanza 4; and in *Chanson sur les affaires du temps* (27), stanza 3.

[50] *Le moment désiré* (7), stanza 4; *Les trois ordres réunis, par Mr Minier* (22), stanzas 5 and 7.

tionary cause with a certain traditional sanction—served as a subtle means of strengthening, in the popular imagination, the alleged spiritual bond between the King and his Minister.

However greatly Necker was revered by the patriots, he was never pictured by them precisely as a rival to the King. A contrary impression might have been given in one of the preceding pages,[51] where we saw, according to the Master Fisherman of Gros-Caillou, that the people, rather than put their trust in the deputies, would put it in a single strong will, which was said to be the will of Necker. The King would seem to have been relegated to second place. But such a conclusion would be hasty; for at the end of the song the Minister is pictured as "harnessed with *not' bon Sire*, in order to pull out of the ruts of distress an entire poor, dear nation which is dying."[52] This imagery happens to be extremely apt. Perhaps there is no better way of picturing the association of the King and Necker. They were a team. To a considerable extent they both represented sanction: the King, the sanction of tradition (at least, of its benevolent aspects); Necker, the sanction of the popular mood. Together they were pulling "a poor, dear nation" out of the bog. The nation, being thus rescued, was bound to be thankful, and could afford to be passive.[53]

[51] Pages 68-69.   [52] *R'quête en magnier' d'écrit . . .* (6).

[53] After the description given above had been completed on the basis of an independent investigation and on the basis of such sources as are cited, I discovered that Hippolyte Gautier, in preparing his *L'An 1789* (written for the first centennial), had obtained strikingly similar impressions. This monumental work depends on an extensive use of iconography and a variety of literary sources. In order to reinforce what is said above, and thus better establish certain facts concerning popular opinion in 1789, I shall quote, in closing, appropriate remarks of Gautier. But it may first be said that this nineteenth-century scholar, in observing the dominant trends of Revolutionary opinion, had nothing to say of their meaning. He seemed to see them merely as external occurrences, without psychological or other inner significance. His summary, nevertheless, presents with admirable clarity findings which deserve careful analysis, but which, in general, have gained from students of the period only casual notice or no notice at all. The following passage especially deserves to be quoted: "Dans les nuages d'encens par où s'exhale la reconnaissance publique et sur les autels qu'elle dresse, le Roi n'est point séparé de son ministre. L'adoration est commune. On les met sur le même rang. . . . Ce sont deux puissances associées l'une à l'autre. On partage en bons frères l'amour des peuples. On figure à deux dans les apothéoses. Comme pour mieux resserrer ce lien et le rendre indissoluble, il se produit des images qui montrent le portrait du monarque et celui de M. Necker attachés par une chaîne. De même que Louis XVI additionne en son nom Louis XII et Henri IV (XII et IV font XVI), le ministre réunit en sa personne Colbert et Sully. La symétrie est parfaite, la balance bien tenue. Ce serait à croire que les louangeurs ont le mot. Ils ne chantent point d'hymnes d'allégresse, sans

Certain important questions arise in connection with the emotional history of the spring of 1789. Why the extraordinary confidence in Louis? Why the exalted love of him? Such adoration assuredly did not result from the mere fact that he was King. Despite a mystical reverence for the throne, Frenchmen in the past had not hesitated on occasion to deride, or even denounce, their monarchs. When, in 1715, death put an end to the long and exhausting reign of Louis XIV, popular literature was characterized by anathemas rather than eulogies of the Grand Monarch.[54] Furthermore, the defects of the wordly Louis XV, who for a time enjoyed the sobriquet of "Well Beloved," were relentlessly exposed in the lampoons of pamphleteers and song writers.[55] Nor in the early years of his reign was Louis XVI spared similar shafts of derision; and the shameless attacks made on Marie Antoinette are still notorious.[56] Thus the adoration of the King, as we see it in the spring of 1789, can by no means be taken as a matter of course. The people needed his leadership, that is true; it must even have seemed that the success of the popular cause might depend on winning his approval. That the people should have praised and even flattered the King is natural. Yet in considering the person and performance of Louis XVI in the spring of 1789, one finds little to justify the notion of the patriots that His Majesty was unfalteringly devoted to the new order.

The peculiar quality of the popular reverence for Necker is, as we have seen, quite as difficult to account for. Admittedly, he had presented himself, despite some irresolution and ambiguity, as a

---

qu'après la strophe du roi vertueux, n'arrive la strophe du vertueux ministre; et il n'est point d'adresses de corporations, de villes, ou de provinces, qui ne contiennent, avec un hosannah au souverain paternal et juste, un hosannah au 'génie tutélaire' qui le conseille." *Op.cit.*, Paris, 1889, pp. 18-19.

54 Songs were a part of this hostile outburst. A number of them which are interesting in this connection are gathered in E. Raunié, *Chansonnier historique du XVIIIe siècle . . .*, Paris, 1879, vol. i. Note, for example, *Louis XIV aux enfers*, pp. 32-33, and other pieces, pp. 5-31 and 33-45.

55 These were "seditious words and indecent writings, in which the person of the monarch is not spared," according to a letter which Mercy, the Austrian Ambassador, wrote to Maria Theresa, April 16, 1771. Cited in J. B. Perkins, *France under Louis XV*, Boston and New York, 1897, vol. i, p. 329.

56 By and large, Louis XVI was popular during the early years of his reign. He sometimes fared badly, however, in connection with the attacks made on Marie Antoinette. Referring to them, Casimir Stryienski writes that "Songs, calumnies, satires of the most audacious sort fall like rain on Paris, the provinces, and abroad." *Le dix-huitième siècle*, Paris, 1913, p. 257.

leader of the popular program and he filled an office of the first importance. Admittedly, he should have been in high favor. Yet here again we are concerned not with such admiration as might be expected, but with a quasi-mystical cult of hero worship. Still more baffling is the degree to which the King and his Minister were pictured, in the popular mind, as being in complete personal and political accord. As a matter of fact, there had been fairly clear evidences of friction, and Necker, whom we have seen described as "personally odious to the sovereign," could not in any reasonable way have been regarded as particularly dear to Louis, by whom he was dismissed on July 11.

The fact is that many popular beliefs in the spring of '89 baffle understanding unless it be assumed that, in reordering French society as allegedly loyal subjects, the people were experiencing all the excitement that they could comfortably bear and found it impossible to acknowledge the inherently radical nature of the role which they were assuming. About to tear away from conventional moorings, they were distraught and really needed a father, a "protector" and even a "savior." The King became an emotional symbol for this need—but not for all of it. For, though the people were unwilling to face the fact, much of the criticism that was directed against the old regime should have included the King. Even though there was, as we have seen, real need for faith in Louis XVI, there must have existed, at the same time, an underlying contempt for him and for the kingly role, as there was for all similar objects in the old regime. This contempt for Louis was later betrayed in various incidental ways, even before any open break with the throne occurred; and it had, besides, found some outlet in the years preceding the Revolution. But in the hearts of the individuals of France in the spring of 1789, it was suppressed.[57]

This hostility, for want of any direct expression, was sublimated. Praise of the Minister seems to have provided the outlet by

[57] This generalization is subject to scarcely any exceptions. Aulard, in seeking proponents of republicanism at this time, was able to single out only Desmoulins (*Histoire politique* . . . , pp. 50-51); and even Desmoulins for a time thereafter lent his support to the cause of limited monarchy. In this connection mention may be made, too, of Carra, who expressed impatience with monarchy in the following terms: "Changez enfin toute la constitution civile & politique de cet Empire; si vous conservez le Monarque, mettez-le dans l'impossibilité absolue de faire le mal ou de le laisser faire." *L'Orateur des Etats-Généraux*, no. 8, pp. 33-34.

which to defy the King; for Necker symbolized the strongest force then in existence—the will of the people.[58] The new force was stronger even than old loyalties; and it was potentially, and inherently, defiant. Being more than any other person the expression of this popular will, Necker appealed to the patriots not only as an ally of the King, as was gallantly set forth, but also as a potential buffer against him.[59] This latter possibility was for the most part denied conscious recognition—in any case, was assiduously concealed—since admission of it would have been heresy from the standpoint of the new inspiration, and treason from that of the old.[60]

Only in roundabout ways and by a most discreet indirection did the lyrists suggest the potential conflict. Let us consider, for example, the concluding lines of the *Alleluia of the Third Estate*:

> Que tous nos voeux soient pour Louis,
> Nos trésors pour l'éclat des Lys,
> Nos forces pour le Tiers-Etat.
> Alleluia.[61]

One sees here that the people, although apparently devoted to the King, reserved their might for the popular cause. Other indications that the King's position was becoming perilous—or, at least, was bidding fair to lose its Bourbon character—occur in the new terminology that soon made its way into popular writings; already in the summer of 1789 one may find Louis referred to as "Roi-Citoyen"[62] or proclaimed "Roi d'un Peuple Libre."[63]

Just as Louis was becoming a creature of the new forces, so was Necker becoming a guarantor of the old. An article, referring to the Minister as "identified with the popular cause," described him

---

[58] Necker's position was unique. "Of the thirty-six persons who held portfolios between 1774 and 1789, there was only one that was not a noble: Necker." Mathiez, *The French Revolution*, p. 6.

[59] Madelin writes in regard to the gathering of royal troops in early July, that "One fact did somewhat assure those anxious minds 'of the deputies'; as long as Necker was there, nobody would dare to lay a finger on the representatives of the nation." *Op.cit.*, p. 68.

[60] Even when the King dismissed Necker on July 11, the patriots made an effort to conceal the conflict by alleging that the King had been dominated by others and was, therefore, not responsible.

[61] From *L'Alleluia du Tiers-Etat* (1).

[62] In certain of the songs, for example; see page 145.

[63] From the inscription placed on the Hôtel de Ville after the Bastille uprising; quoted in *La France régénérée*, p. 12. (II, C)

as "the guardian angel of the people *and of the throne* [italics
mine]."[64] In a patriotic song, loud in its praise of the King, there is
the following suggestion that loyalty to the sovereign depended
upon the popularity of the Minister:

> D'un grand Roi il est chéri,
> Il rend tous les Sujets fidèle.[65]

In so far as the loyalty of subjects thus depends upon the mediation
of a popular hero, the basis of monarchal rule is already undermined.

There was even a tendency on the part of the patriots actually to
identify Necker as King. We have already seen the Minister sharing a royal attribute when pictured as "Father of the People." He
will emerge in a subsequent chapter as the recipient of other comparable tributes. Even if in the arts and letters of the day the crown
was not actually bestowed upon the Minister, the idea of his coronation was, as we shall see, at least poetically suggested—the identification being made by Necker's admirers apparently without
awareness of its implications.

The implications are there, nevertheless—beneath the surface, to
be sure, since denied conscious recognition. The most telling of the
Revolutionary writings thus become—unwittingly, it would seem
—fabrics of subtlety and nuance. A poem by the "Marquis de C - - -
P - - - ," which echoed the uncertainties and alarms that were current in the days before the Bastille uprising, affords an example.
In this piece, entitled *Avis au peuple* . . . ,[66] the popular cause is
pictured as in grave danger, the French "people" being warned
that they are "about to perish." In the face of the plots which
threaten them, they have but one hope. "A god avenges thee, and
thou knowest him not!" The avenging god, a footnote explains, is
"M. Necker, Father of the People." The people are assured that
the Minister is "already armed" with their power. This statement
might seem to imply an affront, or at least a challenge, to Louis,

---

[64] *Moniteur*, July 29-30, 1789, vol. i, p. 122. The *Moniteur* did not begin to appear
contemporaneously with events until November 24; I am unable to cite a strictly
primary source for the quotation given above.

[65] *Les trois ordres réunis, par Mr Minier* (22), stanza 2.

[66] *Avis au peuple sur les événemens présens et à venir, suivi d'une chanson* . . .
1789 (II, D). For mention of the song (27) which concludes this brochure, see page
201.

but the Marquis de C - - - P - - - does not long permit such a conjecture to stand. Following an admonition to the people to "watch over and shield him [Necker]," the author hastens to add, "Thy king wishes it." Here is pictured that seemingly perfect—but really precarious—partnership which had been conjured up in the popular imagination. As a matter of fact, in a footnote referring to "Necker et ton roi," the lyrist exclaims, *As long as they are together* [italics mine], oh, my friends! fear nothing!" This commentary discloses as succinctly as anything could the provisional character of the dual leadership in which the patriots had put their trust.

The lyrists thus hinted at—but took no frank account of—a smoldering rivalry which, if it flared up, would dispel the golden age by subjecting France to the ravages of open enmity and perhaps of civil war. Not until early July was the admission made that things might go wrong. Blindness to such a possibility was preserved by the triple legend of leadership—consisting of the legend of Louis as a benign reformer, of Necker as a savior, and of the two as united in the service of the popular cause.

The fact that the lavish praise accorded Louis was almost never unaccompanied by comparable praise of his Minister suggests that the national hero at this stage of the Revolution was a sort of Louis-Necker godhead, involving a duality of potentially opposing forces. I am, however, far from suggesting that the Revolutionists deliberately set one leader against the other. It seems likely that the habit of balancing the Minister against the King, which characterized popular writings at this time, operated—if we view the matter from the psychological standpoint—as an "unconscious mechanism" adapted to the attainment of desired ends. Nor was this complex balance of loyalties highly transitory in character and, therefore, incidental; for popular opinion—in so far as it remained buoyant and intact—depended on the same mechanism throughout Louis' reign. This was true even though Necker, as symbol of the popular cause, was replaced by various successors.

These successors appear at first, quite as one would naturally expect, in human embodiment (e.g., alternately Lafayette and Bailly); but before long they emerge, no less forcibly, as abstractions (as *la Loi* in 1790; and *la Constitution* in 1791)—in what may be called a persisting dichotomy.[67] This brings one to the threshold of an interesting subject, which falls largely beyond the scope of the present inquiry. But this much is already clear, that the inclination of the patriots to place Necker and the King in juxtaposition, and to praise them both somewhat indiscriminately, made it possible for the people to assert Revolutionary claims without destroying their traditional habits of thought and the sentimental ties to which they had become accustomed. It also enabled them to suppose that the anticipated reforms would be won in peace. Indeed, by preserving a lively sense that France was no less a monarchy than before, the patriots were able to imagine that their feet were still firmly planted on the bedrock of time-honored sanctions while at the same time they enjoyed the exhilarating atmosphere of a new day for mankind.

[67] No reference can be given, since, so far as I know, nothing has been written along these lines. But I am convinced from my own investigations that this conception corresponds to the facts and can serve to illumine many phases of the Revolution under the monarchy.

V

THE CAPTURE OF THE BASTILLE

ALTHOUGH Louis appeared to have yielded to the popular movement with good grace, his acquiescence, as we have seen, was far
from voluntary. Whether or not he was inclined to use force
against a revolution which thus far had been bloodless,[1] he had
secretly sent for troops. Furthermore, he had summoned several
regiments composed of foreign soldiers, since native units had been
influenced by the spread of Revolutionary ideas and were daily
becoming less reliable.

The military situation of the moment has been well summarized
by Sagnac, as follows: "On June 26, the King caused orders to
march to be dispatched to six regiments, three of infantry, three of
cavalry. The first of July, following undisciplined acts by the
French Guards of Paris, he caused similar orders to be sent to ten
other regiments of infantry and to two battalions of artillery, which
were drawn from the North and East, the majority Swiss or Ger-
mans: six of these were due to arrive between the fifth and tenth.
In the first days of July, a concentration took place around Versailles, and especially around Paris. The Marshal de Broglie was
invested with the general command at the château of Versailles,
and had under his orders Besenval . . . who was charged with over-
seeing Paris."[2]

Exactly what use His Majesty himself intended to make of these
forces no one could say, although it was suspected that some of his
advisers, at least, meant to abolish the National Assembly and to
suppress any uprising on its behalf. This apparent threat aroused
widespread indignation and alarm among the people and their
leaders. In the Assembly, Mirabeau gave repeated warnings. At the
session of July 8, he exclaimed: "When a great number of troops

---

[1] There had indeed been acts of violence and bloodshed, but until the July events
these spontaneous outbursts were not connected in the popular mind with the Revolutionary movement as such. The significance of the turbulence being not properly
understood, the turbulence itself was largely overlooked. As Bainville observed: "No
one seemed even to have noticed the frequent bloody riots which had taken place in
Paris in the winter of 1788-89 and which the famine, or fear of it, had provoked; nor
the violent incidents which in many places had accompanied the electoral cam-
paign." See J. Bainville, *Histoire de France*, vol. ii, pp. 31-32.

[2] P. Sagnac, *La Révolution (1789-1792)*, pp. 36-37—*Histoire de France LAVISSE,
Histoire contemporaine*, Tome I, Librairie Hachette, Editeur.

were already surrounding us, more still arrived; they arrive daily; they pour in from all directions." He proposed that the troops and artillery be sent away, describing their activities as "preparations for war."[3] On the eleventh, the Assembly sent an address to His Majesty, asking why "a king adored by twenty-five million French would gather about the throne, at great expense, several thousand strangers"[4]—the final reference being, of course, to the fact that the incoming troops were largely foreigners. The King replied that the troops were not intended as a threat, but were necessary to maintain order in the capital and its environs.[5] This reply satisfied no one who adhered to the patriotic cause, least of all the general run of Parisians, who were incensed to find themselves so little trusted by the King, and who began to ask one another whether the vast mobilization might in fact be a first stage of warfare against themselves and the things for which they stood.

People in a state of alarm, as were the inhabitants of Versailles and Paris, are especially eager to be shown a sign, that they may judge whether or not their fears are warranted. Finally, after days of suspense, there came a token as telling as any could have been. On July 11, Necker, supposed partner of the King in reform and personification of the national will, was dismissed. This divorce of the King from his Minister—who thereupon withdrew via Brussels to his native Switzerland—tended to rend asunder the fabric of faith which had been built up in the preceding months. The most conspicuous part of this pattern had been, as we have seen, the assumed identity of interests between Louis and Necker. It is perhaps not too much to say that the maintenance of peace depended upon the continuance of this basic assumption. And now this cornerstone of faith appeared to crumble. That the patriots were under the spell of a complex emotional attachment was not generally recognized. It was evident, however, to the counterrevolutionary Rivarol, who wrote that, "It was then as impolitic and dangerous to the court of France to separate itself from M. Necker, as it would have been to the court of Naples to have cast into the sea the vial of St. Janvier."[6]

---

[3] *Le Point du jour . . . , no. xix, du 9 juillet, 1789*; vol. i, p. 140.

[4] *Ibid., no. xxiii, du 13 juillet, 1789*; vol. i, p. 181.   [5] *Ibid.*, p. 183.

[6] Patron saint of Naples, whose blood, preserved in a vial, or ampulla, was supposed to have various mystical qualities of great benefit to the city. The quotation

Thus, in Louis' name, the patron saint of the popular will had been denied and swept from the limelight of France into an intended obscurity, while His Majesty's troops continued to mobilize about Versailles and Paris.

For long, the patriots had been content to live on hopes alone. Having enjoyed a single opportunity to take part in government on the occasion of the elections to the Assembly, they had thereafter entrusted their cause to the representatives, whom they had had at least an indirect share in electing. But now—with Necker gone and the Assembly in a state of alarm—they felt that their first gains were threatened, and that their dearest hopes were at stake, with no means of saving them except by battle. There were patriots, too, who began to fear for their skins. Idealism, which had been sustained by hope, was now strengthened by fear.

By this time, nearly everyone on the patriotic side had fallen prey to that state of anxiety and elation which the prospect of a fight engenders. But the upper bourgeoisie of Paris had special concerns of their own. They were terrified not only by the alleged plots of a reactionary and revengeful Court, but also by the marauding of poor townsmen, who in many cases were starving. They were, besides, alarmed by news that vagrants were pouring into the city from the suburbs and the provinces, and by reports of their pillage and incendiarism. These were the so-called "bandits" who terrorized France in the spring and summer of 1789. The soldiers regularly stationed at Paris, especially the French Guards, contributed to the general excitement by disobeying their orders. They had proved ready converts to the patriotic propaganda. That they would not support the discipline of a scheming court was certain; but whether, in their newly attained sense of freedom, they would support any discipline must have been a consideration of grave concern to sober-minded members of the community.

It was the dismissal of Necker, July 11, which caused all the smoldering unrest to burst into conflagration. When the news of his fall reached Paris on the following day, mobs surged into the open court and colonnades of the Palais Royal, a sort of Hyde Park of the French capital, which attracted the more voluble members

is from the *Journal politique-national des Etats-généraux* . . . , no. 6 (published in 1789, but cited above from ed. of 1790, vol. i, p. 69).

of the Paris citizenry and some of its most radical and energetic leaders. The crowd sensed in the dismissal of Necker a plot of the reactionaries against the people. Many of the indignant citizens protested frantically, others remained sullen; yet all were determined on some form of resistance. It was in the excitement of this moment that Camille Desmoulins, a fiery youth and aspiring journalist, climbed upon a table and cried out the slogan which fixed the purpose of that hitherto aimless mass of men and women.

"Tonight," he said, "all the Swiss and German battalions in the Champs-de-Mars will come out and slaughter us! We have but one chance left—to fly to arms!"

Aux armes! These words and this enthusiasm spread to thousands of Parisians. But they had no arms to fly to—only the nascent determination to fight. Where? Whom? Answers to these questions were not immediately forthcoming.

People surged about the city. One group robbed a store of its wax busts of the Duke of Orleans and of Necker, and paraded through the main thoroughfares in proud possession of these images, which were displayed as the respectable insignia of a growing rebelliousness.

On the site of the present Place de la Concorde, the mob encountered a regiment of the King's dragoons under Lambesc, who had been sent to restore order and who now undertook to clear the square. A fracas ensued, in which civilians hurled garden chairs at the soldiers. Members of the French Guards appeared on the scene; they should have supported Lambesc and his troops. Instead, they took the side of the populace and opened fire on the dragoons, some of whom they killed. Here, on a small scale, was civil war. Lambesc retreated.[7] Besenval, in charge of the royal troops at Paris, had given no support to Lambesc, lest he provoke a general uprising! The populace, aided by mutinous troops, had won the day and, to all appearances, the city.

This was on July 12. It was a prelude. On the thirteenth, a less spectacular, but even more momentous, insurrection against the King's authority occurred at Paris. The group of outstanding citizens who had been chosen as the Paris electors for the Estates Gen-

[7] There is a song in denunciation of Lambesc, entitled *La Trahison du Prince Lorrain*. It seems, however, to be attributable to 1790, rather than to 1789. See Appendix A, 188.

eral had continued to meet, apparently as the self-appointed guard-
ians of the city, after they had done their voting and after there was
no legal justification for their corporate existence. At first
they were not encouraged by the regular municipal officers, appointees of the Crown, the chief of whom was Jacques de Flesselles.[8]
But by June 27, the electors were granted a room in the Hôtel de
Ville, or city hall, for their deliberations. A fortnight later, July
13, when the city mobs seemed to be getting out of control, they
created a "Standing Committee," made up of regular municipal
officers and of electors, with the latter in the majority. Paris thus
suddenly obtained a government that was partially representative,
but it is important to insist that the electors themselves had not
been elected for the functions which they undertook to fulfill.[9]
When on the following day royal authority was challenged by a
popular uprising, the electors assumed complete control. By arro-
gating to themselves the authority which was supposedly invested
in royal appointees, they gave France an impressive example of
municipal revolt. It was a victory of the popular will over the
Crown.

A further undermining of the King's authority occurred at this
time. On the first day of its existence, July 13, the Standing Committee, turning to practical considerations of law and order,
brought into being a *milice bourgeoise*, or civic guard, to be composed of one battalion from each of the sixty municipal districts.[10]
This was done to meet a delicate situation. Many of the King's soldiers could not be counted upon to preserve the peace; whereas
the rest—those who could be relied upon to enforce the royal orders—were feared as enemies of the people. The organization of a
civic guard meant, therefore, repudiation of the army, which, to

---

[8] Flesselles was *prévôt des marchands de Paris*, a position corresponding to that of
mayor. Almost continuously since the sixteenth century, this office and others associated with it had been filled by royal appointees, although the pretense of election
by the notables of Paris was maintained.

[9] The development was perhaps not so fortuitous as it might seem. A few months
before, the Parisians had in their *cahiers* addressed to the King requests for an elec-
tive municipality. Circumstances now enabled the leaders to gain by stratagem what
they had all along wanted.

[10] The formation of such a militia was actually proposed by Ethis de Corny, *pro-
cureur du Roi*. This royal official was an admirer of Voltaire, something of a liberal
—no doubt a fair example of the "repentant nobility." He won the confidence of the
electors at this critical time and served their cause well.

be sure, was stationed within the city itself in insufficient numbers, but which would have been progressively hated in proportion to its sufficiency. It was this new type of soldiery, presently created by alarmed municipalities in the provinces, as well as at Paris, that was destined to become famous in Revolutionary history as the "National Guard."

These were the forces that were later to fight "tyranny" at home and abroad. But it is highly significant that in bringing them into being, the Standing Committee was taking precautions not so much against the encircling forces of the Court, as against the unruly masses of the city. It was not merely that the Parisian mobs were stampeding about, waving pikes and other weapons, and uttering every sort of mad alarm, such as "Victory, or the Hangman's Rope—that must be our motto now"; not merely that the troops known as the French Guards were fraternizing with the disorderly elements of the population and sharing in that spirit of anarchic jubilation which it would ordinarily have been their business to suppress. The situation was gravely complicated by the activities of pillagers, to whom reference has been made, some of them coming in from outside, others emerging from the crowded quarters of the city. Together these groups terrified the more substantial citizens by looting shops and by sacking places which were either inadequately protected or not protected at all, such as the Garde-Meuble, the Lazarist convent, and the house of the Lieutenant of Police. They even attacked a prison, La Force, and set loose some criminals. Though apparently bent on destruction, many of the rioters were striving to anticipate an attack against the people, which they supposed the reactionaries were about to make.

The precaution of the electors in undertaking to form a civic guard had come too late. It is true that some of the more vigorous of the townsmen, transformed hastily into soldiery, did, on the night of July 13, bring tranquillity to the city. But early the next morning at the Invalides (Soldiers Home), a mob which had come to demand arms got completely out of hand. Overrunning the place, they discovered in the cellar thirty-two thousand guns with bayonets and absconded with them.

If we turn our glance to the streets of Paris on the morning of the fourteenth, we see a partly armed populace despairing of all the ordinary means of arbitration and preparing for battle. As always, the martial spirit communicates itself quickly. The nature of the anticipated attack, however, and even the zero hour itself, are regarded as secrets in the camp of the enemy. The thought spreads like a contagion that only by taking the initiative can the worst imaginable disasters be forestalled.

Mirabeau, referring to the King's concentration of troops, had spoken of "preparations for war." Here were countermeasures. The ferment in Paris had a recognizable quality; it resembled the excitement of a people united in a common cause and launched upon a war, civil and defensive to be sure.

The dreaded advance did not, however, crystallize. The patriots had to some extent created the crisis out of their own imaginations. As contemporary documents reveal, in their minds the enemy itself was shadowy and unsubstantial and the object of many and varying suspicions. But although apprehensions may have remained diffuse, objects on which to vent fighting zeal were not wanting, and they gave substance to unreality, or rather made possible a combining of the two.

There were hated objects within easy reach—for example, the Bastille. The Bastille now amounted to little more than an obsolete fortress and a somewhat neglected prison, but it had been used by the Bourbons as an instrument of oppression, and so strong was the impress of tradition that the name connoted to the popular imagination the most tyrannical despotism. There was another circumstance which brought the fortress into the public eye: considerable quantities of powder had recently been deposited there, and this fact was generally known. In order to lay hands on this ammunition and to seize more arms, a crowd began to gather before the Bastille and to surge around its forbidding walls. Enterprising members of the mob broke down the drawbridge. Following exchanges of fire in two successive onslaughts, leaders of the citizen militia and of the three hundred French Guards, who had by this time joined the attack, breached the inner defense of the fortress. Once capture seemed certain, the commander of the Bastille, De Launay, surrendered with his force of slightly over one hundred men, of whom more than a half were pensioners. But already eighty-eight of the besiegers had been wounded and eighty-three killed. Scholars are not in agreement as to whether the King's garrison or the populace was guilty of initiating the bloodshed.[11] All seem to agree, however, that there was nothing sanguinary about De Launay; that he acted with moderation and, if with no show of military sense, at least with good intentions. But the mob, owing to a misunderstanding,[12] was sure that it had been lured on unsuspectingly, that there had been foul play, that De Launay had committed "treason"; and this report gained general credence. One of the patriots felt such indignation on this score that he attacked De Launay and severed his head; whereupon the assailant and other members of the mob paraded the head about the streets of Paris on the end of a pike. The mayor, Flesselles, was likewise decapitated on the same day, and his head similarly paraded.

No doubt jail should have been the least punishment for the civilian besiegers, while the mutinous French Guards should have been court-martialed; but the victors, the street fighters, had one signal and saving distinction from all other of their French compatriots. They alone at a moment when the life of the popular cause was known to be sorely threatened, had resorted to action and had won a victory over the Crown. They had demolished the symbolic citadel of Bourbon tyranny. They had, it was hoped, terrorized Louis and his Court. When the news reached the National Assembly, sitting at Versailles, its members, instead of taking a stand for law and order, were thrilled. As remarks made by many of them at the time sufficiently reveal, they felt that the end of a period of tension had come, that great deeds had been performed, a new freedom gained; we can almost believe, not without smiling,

---

[11] Cf., for example, the conflicting accounts of L. Madelin, *The French Revolution*, p. 77, and A. Mathiez, *The French Revolution*, p. 47.

[12] The misunderstanding arose from the fact that, in the course of the fray, a group which represented itself as a delegation from the Hôtel de Ville sought admittance to the fortress. These individuals displayed the white flag, and De Launay was prepared to receive them. There was, however, a delay of some moments; the delegation withdrew and was lost to sight in the milling crowd that surrounded the Bastille. The fortress was again attacked, and the defenders fired upon the assailants. These rapidly changing circumstances were not visible to the spectators, who supposed that the delegation, still seeking a peaceful entrance, was exposed to murderous gunfire. For contemporary accounts, one expressing the popular view of the "treason," the other, the standpoint of the defenders, see L. G. W. Legg, ed., *Select Documents Illustrative of the History of the French Revolution*, Oxford, 1905, vol. i, pp. 75 and 87-88.

the words of a modern English writer, that they supposed that they had themselves taken part in the attack.[13]

Louis, who but a few days before had perhaps been in a position to arrest the popular movement by a show of force, was suddenly confronted by a quite different situation. The writing on the wall now more clearly than ever spelled "revolution"; and he had no hope of obliterating that lettering in the immediate present. Maladroit at times, Louis was occasionally an opportunist of the first order. Such he proved himself to be in the present crisis. The day following the capture of the Bastille, he appeared before the National Assembly, and by his promise to withdraw the troops whose presence had helped to incite the outbreak, and by his own attitude of general good humor, won a measure of approval from the deputies. But to face Paris and to win it—that was the test. The King had been invited to appear there and to take part in a "reconciliation." On July 17 he proceeded to the capital in his coach, accompanied by a deputation of one hundred members of the Assembly. Once there, he was titular head of the patriotic festivities. He actually led in ceremonies (one of them religious) to celebrate the defeat of a small detachment of his own soldiers and the capture of the royal prison which they had, without success, defended. By his presence and by his pathetic simulation of cordiality, Louis appeared to give royal sanction to the rebellious deeds of subjects who, in establishing the power of the people, had undermined that of the Crown.

We have seen that it was not in the spirit of a riot, but in the spirit of warfare, that the Bastille was seized. Louis' coming to Paris put an end to all this excitement; made it seem that apprehensions had been worse than the reality; that the previously suspected presence of an enemy had proved in a measure illusory; that the fears of an imminent tyranny had been an ugly and unsubstantial dream; and that forbearance and kindliness, in the person of the King, crowned the whole Revolutionary movement.

This movement had been most evident in its garish and spectacular form, in the warlike feats of the mob. But it had gone forward also in a more quiet fashion. The day before, July 16, the Assembly

13 "Very soon the respectabilities [of the States-General] were convinced that they had captured the Bastille themselves." G. Elton, *The Revolutionary Idea in France, 1789-1871*, London, 1923, p. 25.

of Paris Electors had on its own responsibility—one could hardly say "authority"—chosen a mayor to replace the King's appointee, the murdered Flesselles. The Electors had, besides, named Lafayette commander of the newly created *milice bourgeoise*—or *Garde bourgeoise*, as is was popularly called. This force, which boasted its loyalty to the throne, had nevertheless come into existence without royal initiative—composed, we may say, of king's soldiers without the King's knowledge![14]

On the occasion of Louis' visit, the new mayor, Bailly, received him "officially" on behalf of the Parisians. It was Bailly who was the presiding officer of the Assembly when, on the occasion of the Tennis Court Oath, it defied the royal wish. There had been a time in the history of the French monarchy when a Bailly might have been thrust into the Bastille prison, and a Lafayette severely disciplined, for they were both partners in colossal usurpations of the royal prerogative. But Louis was forced by the special circumstances of the hour to honor these popular heroes. He had graciously to receive the welcome of the Revolutionary mayor, Bailly; and he went out of his way to assure Lafayette that he confirmed his appointment as Commander-General of the *Garde bourgeoise*.[15] More remains to be said of this remarkable "reconciliation," but here it should be added that on the day before, the sixteenth, Louis had assented to the recall of Necker.

Such were the main events of the days from July 12 to 17. Having briefly recalled the patriotic excitement which they occasioned, we are now in a position to consider certain of the songs which appeared at this time.

It is necessary to say at the outset that many Revolutionary songs written to celebrate the capture of the Bastille were not strictly contemporaneous—a fact which has not always gained recognition.[16] There are, however, some twenty songs extant which the

[14] Louis, to be sure, was promptly informed; and on July 19 the National Assembly was advised of his authorization of the *milice bourgeoise*. *Archives parlementaires*, vol. viii, p. 239.

[15] The King's statements on this occasion, as recorded in the *Procès-verbal des Electeurs*, are reprinted in Legg, *op.cit.*, vol. i, pp. 93-94, and 95.

[16] For example, in the bibliographical work of Constant Pierre, three songs by T. Rousseau (Pierre's nos. 191, 196, 197) devoted to the July events are listed under the year 1789, though they were not published until 1791 or 1792. Also, *La Gloire immortelle ou la Prise de la Bastille, le 14 juillet 1789*, which Pierre ascribes to 1789, relates to the anniversary celebration of the following year (see Appendix A, 189).

writer feels may safely be regarded as having appeared immediately preceding or shortly following the attack.[17] Several of these clearly were written on the spur of the moment, as is indicated by their titles or by publishers' imprints. One may cite, for example, Callière's *Song on the Capture of the Invalides and the Bastille. . . . At Paris, this Friday, the 17th . . . done at the Hôtel de Tours, after leaving the guard at noon;*[18] and Rousselet's *A Few Verses Written July 17 on the Subject of the Memorable Capture.*[19] One song, devoted to events which preceded the attack, bears the imprint "July, 1789."[20] Another topical piece was sung before the Paris Assembly on July 20;[21] still another is known to have been sung at a theatre, July 26.[22] It is unfortunate that the only known copy of yet another piece which might have been of some importance, and for which the precise date of composition is given in the title, *Potpourri on the Events Occurring in Paris July 13, 14, and 17, 1789,* written by "a patriot, this twentieth day of July, 1789," is reported lost at the Bibliothèque Nationale.[23] Two songs of somewhat uncertain date[24] are mentioned in the text which follows, warning being given in each case that they may not have appeared until the first anniversary of the Bastille. The remaining songs on which I have drawn, though not dated, appear to me, after a searching inquiry on the basis of internal evidence, to be contemporaneous with the summer of 1789, and they are generally attributed to this time.[25]

Pierre's dating of Ligny's song on the capture of the Bastille is also subject to question (see Appendix A, 191*). Likewise, in a collection of French Revolutionary songs published by L. Damade (*Histoire chantée de la Première République, 1789 à 1799,* Paris, 1892, pp. 13-15) the *Hymne sur la journée du 14 juillet ou la Bastille renversée* (Pierre's no. 1828) is attributed to 1789, though its first known date of publication was 1796. It is obviously essential that, in any study of the development of popular opinion, such items be assigned to their appropriate years.

[17] See Bibliography I, 27 to 44, inclusive, and 56. Note that 37† may have appeared a year later (see Appendix A, 190), and in regard to the date of Rousselet's pamphlet, which contains song 30†, see *Détail intéressant . . .* (Bibliography II, D).

[18] *Chanson sur la prise des Invalides . . .* (29).

[19] *Quelques vers faits le 17 Juillet . . .* (30†).   [20] *Où le bas nous blesse . . .* (28).

[21] *Chanson nouvelle chantée par les Dames députées . . .* (34).

[22] *Chanson jettée sur le Théâtre à Brest . . .* (44).

[23] *Pot-pourri sur les événements . . .* (33). This piece, published with music, was put on display at the Revolutionary Exhibition in 1928; since that date the document has disappeared.

[24] See footnote 17.

[25] In addressing the Assembly on July 15, Mirabeau complained that the foreign troops which the King had summoned had "predicted the enslavement of France in

Typical of several songs celebrating the capture of the Bastille is one by the Chevalier de Callières de l'Estang,[26] a former advocate and a patriotic leader of some standing. The author was a relative of Moreau de Saint-Méry, President of the three hundred electors of Paris, to whom the song is dedicated.

Callières commences with an apostrophe to a nascent goddess of the patriotic cause:

> Liberté qui m'es chère,
> Cent fois plus que le jour;
> Toi que mon coeur préfère
> Au bonheur de l'amour. . . .

In view of the sacrifices which the defenders of the Revolution were later called on to make, there is a prophetic quality in the suggestion that the patriot place before all private passions his devotion to Liberty. This goddess, one soon learns, is not so much universal as tribal—or, more precisely, national: it is her "glorious French" that the "radiant eye" of Liberty "both caresses and contemplates."

The next few stanzas are devoted to Necker. After comparing the Minister to Jupiter and Minerva, the author pictures him as having "saved" France "against a scepter of iron." He warns the patriots against the power of evil behind the Minister's dismissal:

> L'audacieuse Envie
> L'enlève à nos climats:
> C'est vous ôter la vie,
> Citoyens et Soldats.

This intervention of evil comes as an assault on the good and the luminous:

> Necker[27] est une lumière,
> Qui brilloit en ces lieux,
> Au haut de sa carrière
> On l'éclipse à nos yeux.

The significance of the dismissal of the Minister is further developed as follows:

---

their impious songs" (*Lettres . . . à ses commettans*, no. 19, p. 28), but apart from this allusion, I have found no trace of anti-Revolutionary songs at this time.

[26] *Chanson sur la prise des Invalides . . .* (29).

[27] Spelled in the original, *Neckre*.

> C'est la Ruche timide
> Qu'on prive de son Roi;
> Et l'Essaim intrépide
> Se ligue en son effroi.

The beehive may be regarded as a conventional image; but to picture the French people as a "timid" beehive is unusual, and may perhaps be taken to suggest that sense of insecurity which from the very beginning was a part of the patriotic mood, its less obvious side.[28] In any case, it is significant that the "King [*sic*] of the Beehive" is not Louis, but Necker—a transposition which suggests that Louis was the beloved king to the patriots only in so far as he seemed to endorse the Revolution. Once he seemed to defy the popular cause, it was apparently natural for a poet-patriot such as Callières to picture Necker, the representative of the popular will, in the kingly role. To be sure, this conception, expressed in terms of practical politics, would have been contradictory and indeed incomprehensible. But at times a flight of fancy exposes the hidden inclinations of the human heart, and, as if by accident, casts a beam of light beneath the conventional surface of opinion.

The following description of the representatives of the nation and of their anguish over Necker's dismissal contains interesting symbols:

> Cette auguste Assemblée
> De Héros, d'Immortels
> Gémit, et désolée,
> Lui dresse des Autels.

However stylized this passage may seem, it reveals that prevailing conceptions of immortality and of the altar—whether Christian or pagan in origin—were already attaching themselves to the patriotic cause as early as July, 1789.

The sixth stanza of Callières' song concerns the royal power:

> La Couronne s'empresse
> De fléchir sous les Loix;

---

[28] The songs confirm in an interesting way the known facts of the period. As Madelin points out, the "Great Fear" of the summer of 1789 was preceded by a lesser fear in the early days of July. In fact, as regards Paris he ascribes the beginnings of this phenomenon to the month of April. *The French Revolution*, p. 69.

> Et la Raison la presse,
> Plus forte que les Rois.

At first sight these lines may appear confusing; but on examination they are seen to be a perfect example of the rationalizing process by which an attempt was made to redefine the powers of the King. One may point first to the assumption of the poet that "the Laws" have an authority separate from that of the King. The particular merit of Louis, it appears, is that he is guided by them and by "reason"—both attributes of the popular will—rather than by his royal prerogative (expressed above as "the Kings"). Thus, Louis is pictured as eagerly discarding the old basis of sovereignty in favor of Revolutionary sanctions which he was not permitted to define, but which were interpreted for him in accordance with the mood of the patriots.

As new trends of Revolutionary opinion emerge, many old ones are sustained—a fact which gives continuity to the patriotic enthusiasm. Among various reminders of attitudes already established, we read of Louis XVI as having "all the conquering traits of the Great Henry," of whom he is the "image."[29]

But elsewhere Callières strikes a new note. He pictures a people acting on their own behalf and no longer waiting on the King, on his Minister, and on the Assembly for a relief which they could have no share in effecting. Inspired by the invasion of the Invalides and by the attack on the Bastille, he writes,

> Achevez votre ouvrage,
> O Peuple de Catons!
> En méritant l'hommage
> Que l'on doit aux Platons.

However naïve this tribute to antiquity and to the men of the hour in France may be, it foreshadows the really imposing prospect that the people may find self-made leaders from among their own number, and that the cult of hero worship, which had long filled the masses with deference, may now provide them an outlet for self-reliance and self-approbation.

[29] In the lines which follow, one learns that the author was a devotee of the Duke of Orleans:

> LOUIS a notre hommage,
> Et d'Orléans nos coeurs.

After lamenting the famine and the hardships of the people, Callières expresses concern over the victories thus far gained by violence. He apparently felt that the glory of the Bastille mood depended upon its not being pursued too far. So he gives a warning:

> Mais la guerre civile
> Respecte nos foyers:
> Citoyen, sois tranquile
> Sous l'abri des lauriers.[30]

The last stanza contrasts the miserable fate of the "evil ones," who have occasioned the uprising, with the happy prospects of the patriots:

> Aux bornes de la Terre
> Chassez nos Ennemis:
> Ne faisons plus la guerre,
> Et soyons tous amis.

The thought—"let us all be friends"—portrays the notion prevalent in July, that the benefits of the new day are to be shared by "all" except a few, "our enemies." On these the comforting light of the *siècle d'or* is not to shine. This minority must somehow, and as expeditiously as possible, be pushed aside. It must not, in any case, be permitted to destroy the unanimity of "all"!

The song of the Chevalier de Callières embodies important new trends that were expressed in other songs celebrating the fall of the Bastille: first, a new sense of conflict; and, second, the note of a new individualism, or at least of a new self-reliance, among the people. Both these new forces will bear further examination. They were critical in determining the direction and future development of certain Revolutionary attitudes that had important consequences for France and the rest of Europe. As a matter of convenience we may disentangle these two trends, which in fact are

---

[30] It would be well to leave good enough alone, as anyone under the spell of the author's mood as he expressed it on July 17 must have agreed; for, following his warning on civil war, he writes:

> Jamais la belle Aurore
> N'annonça plus beau jour,
> Que celui qui décore
> De la Paix le retour.

inherently related, and turn first to the character of the new individualism.

When we contrast the elation of July with the quieter mood depicted in the previous chapters, we realize that the peaceful attitude of the early spring was to be expected. It had not at first occurred to the people that there was anything drastic that they might do to further their exalted hopes. These hopes they placed on Necker and others, while they passively awaited a mysterious salvation. But the sudden threat to the popular cause, resulting from the conspiracy of a reactionary Court, rendered the first hero worship inadequate. Necker, being absent, obviously could not be credited with the leadership of the hour. Besides, faith in the King was severely strained: the best that the patriots could do was to try to distinguish, and somehow disentangle, the Louis whom they idolized from the Louis who had just now dismissed the trusted and beloved Minister. As for the representatives of the people, they were still sufficiently revered, but they had, nevertheless, since the formation of the National Assembly and the Tennis Court Oath, disappointed the patriots by too much discussion and too little vigorous action. This general abandonment—or seeming desertion from above—occasioned the first really dark hours for the exponents of the New Day, and made room for new attitudes which, once and for all, changed its character.[31]

The new attitudes were based on a restlessness—even a desperation—that led to action; and action, in turn, had a formative effect on the outlook of the patriots. The opportunity to riot successfully, to fight in the streets, and to attack and invade strongholds put a premium on physical prowess, which previously had found no outlet, and on a rough and ready leadership that had not until now seemed appropriate to the patriotic cause. Popular writers lavished their praise on the reckless leaders[32] and on the soldiery, and

---

[31] Shortage of food, to which references have been made, continued as a basic cause of unrest. In a song celebrating the capture of the Bastille, *Chanson des bourgeois de Paris* (32), the author includes among the various "scourges" which afflicted the people, the "horrors of the famine."

[32] They were, for the most part, praised as a group. Individuals conspicuous for their feats of daring—Maillard, Hulin, Elie, and others—were not, as a rule, singled out at this time. Only later, especially on the occasion of the first anniversary of the Bastille, did the practice of calling the roll of individual heroes become something of a vogue. This trend is illustrated in *La France régénérée* . . . (36), a revision of

perhaps above all, on the "citizens." In the storming of the Bastille, civilians—ordinary men and women—had shared in accomplishing great deeds for the nation. This was something to contemplate; and the patriots were swept on a wave of self-glorification to a high pitch of enthusiasm. Thus commenced the Revolutionary cult of its own popular heroes—the beginning in modern times of what we may call the democratization of the heroic ideal.

Though of course only a relatively negligible proportion of the Parisians had been participants in the overt conflict, yet all, by identifying themselves with the feats of valor, appear to have felt, in a heightened degree, the same sort of ego-expansion that the sport fan experiences in cheering a winning team with which he has identified himself. This projection of everybody's more or less humble self into the victory extended beyond Paris, and created the impression that the success of the uprising redounded to the credit of all the patriots, to the glory of the nation.[33]

A song bearing the suggestive title *France Regenerated* conveys this idea in its opening lines:

> Chantons la gloire de la victoire,
> Du TIERS-ETAT,
> Qui manifeste comme ils sont lestes
> Dans un combat. [*bis*][34]

Thus all members of the Third Estate were glorified through the victory. As proclaimed in another piece celebrating the capture of the Bastille, "France at last is free, the Third Estate has avenged itself."[35] It was not just the aggregate of half-armed, undisciplined, shrieking, sweating, moiling participants who had "manifested" their skill; it was, apparently, the Third Estate. In particular, it was the bourgeoisie: dignitaries of the marts of commerce, substantial burghers who despised violence and disorder, intellectuals of all sorts, and townsmen who made a living as small proprietors or from wages. It is important to note that "bourgeois" as used by the Revolutionists at this time did not denote primarily such class

---

which carried mention of several heroes, including Hélie (*sic*) and Maillard, while the earlier version had not done so.

[33] "Participation mystique," the phrase of Levy Bruhl, describes from the standpoint of social psychology the phenomenon which I have preferred to consider, from the standpoint of the individual, as identification.

[34] *La France régénérée* . . . (36).   [35] *La lanterne merveilleuse* (38), stanza 1.

lines as the term suggests today; it usually indicated merely such "town dwellers" as did not belong to the privileged orders. The term was thus apt to include wage earners. It was for this reason, and in this contemporary sense, that a song entitled *Chanson des bourgeois de Paris* could picture the whole Bastille uprising as a bourgeois affair.[36]

So far we have considered the Bastille exploit as it affected the participants and the townsmen who vicariously took part. Our observations have not yet taken into account the peasants who, finding the example of the Parisians contagious, actually demolished castles in many parts of the French countryside as their contribution toward effecting a new order in society. The lawlessness which continued in the provinces was an embarrassment to many of the reformers. Yet all patriots, or nearly all, including the most discreet and peace-loving, approved the Bastille insurrection. Having identified themselves with the victors, they seem to have regarded this one outbreak as constituting a proper exception to the general advisability of law and order.

This, too, was the predominant view in the Assembly. Mirabeau, who by the time of his death in 1791 had become as alarmed as anyone at the drift of certain elements of French society into the abyss of mob violence—a descent as inexorable as that of a glacier— was able cheerfully to write in July, 1789, that the capital was in "good order" after the capture. He rejoiced that the *Gardes françaises* (royal troops, to be sure) had not for a moment denied "their noble devotion to the cause of liberty." He appeared to be impressed by "the very character of the People in this singular revolution in which one has seen neither desire for pillage, nor ferocity" (the former may perhaps be granted, but certainly the detached heads of De Launay and Flesselles belie the latter). As for the establishment of the *Garde bourgeoise*, which had played its part in the assault, Mirabeau signalized it as "an example which will soon be copied in the entire Kingdom, and which has done more to advance the restoration of our rights than the labors of

---

[36] *Chanson des bourgeois de Paris* (32). As G. Lefebvre writes of this period, "The famous revolutionary areas of the city . . . had an abundance of small shops in which master craftsmen and their journeymen employees fraternized on the great insurrectionary 'days.' On the whole the wage workers had no clear consciousness of class." *The Coming of the French Revolution*, Princeton, 1947 (translation by R. R. Palmer of *Quatre-vingt-neuf*, Paris, 1939), p. 99.

the National Assembly would have accomplished in years." Nothing—as this great leader then saw it—had fallen out of control as a result of the abandonment of the deliberative process for the method of direct action.[37]

Now that the orthodox conventions of hero worship were undermined, salvation itself had to be sought from new quarters. Mention has been made of the soldiery. From this time on it assumed a new importance, owing to various factors, including both the emergence of citizen volunteers and the altered status of the regulars. Under the old regime, the ordinary soldier had not been popular with the common man; if not, as was often the case, despised, he at any rate belonged to a class that was looked down on. Revolutionary events, however, made possible a new view of the military. It was recognized that there was no need to hold the soldier separate from the general run of people, and that once he was touched by the spirit of the times he became an especially effective patriot. The professional soldiers had indeed done much to save the popular cause; certain of them, as we have seen, had attacked the Bastille when their duty was to support the Crown. But in the excitement at Paris, such distinctions were easily overlooked; and the popular reaction was that of approval and gratitude:

> Braves gardes françoises
> Vous nous aves sauvés.[38]

From now on the soldier's common bond with the people often proved more compelling than his sense of responsibility to officers, who were usually of the noble class. This rapprochement of the citizen and the soldier suited the needs of the moment, and therefore seemed sufficiently innocent. But innocence of this sort was paving the way for an anarchic trend which, after it had helped to demolish the old regime, persisted to imperil the work and

---

[37] *Lettres . . . à ses commettans*, no. 19, p. 31. It may be added that the patriots were perhaps obliged to resort to direct action. The provocations and dangers to which they were exposed have already been considered; and, in view of them, it is often argued that it was the King who, under Court influence, first abandoned the deliberative process. Be that as it may, our concern in the discussion above is not with the causes, but rather with the effects, of the abandonment of the deliberative process—and in particular with those effects as conceived by the patriots.

[38] *Prise de la Bastille* (31), stanza 7.

exhaust the tolerance of those whose task it was to establish a new order.

More novel, and even more portentous, was the role of the citizen volunteers who had taken part in the capture. They, too, had won the plaudits of all patriots; they, too, had proved responsive to the needs of the people:

> NOBLE MILICE, toujours propice
> A nos malheurs.[39]

It would in itself have been a bold stroke if the reformers had been content to wrest from royal control the allegiance of the regular army, and to retain as a further support of representative government such bands of militiamen as were first called into being. But even so great a shift of authority was only a part of the new arrangement of military affairs. Inherent in the transformations of the time was the dawning conception of a vast citizen-soldiery. It was already widely assumed that Frenchmen—for so long a time subjects—were now citizens. This view, coupled with the idea popularly expressed in the summer of 1789, that "each citizen is a warrior,"[40] seemed to imply the militarization of an entire people. Here was an early portent of a change that was vitally to affect, not only the history of France, but also that of the other great powers.[41]

The assertion by the patriot of his right to be a soldier, as we see it first occurring at the dawn of the French Revolution, was one aspect of his mood of liberation, and was essentially an individualistic outburst. But for better or for worse, this discovery of a new and exciting right involved the present disclosure of a corresponding duty. For it soon became apparent that the new conception of the *citoyen-soldat* implied a regimentation extending to each and every citizen. A collectivism of this military character would necessarily control many phases of private life, and, to a corresponding extent, would prove the undoing of personal liberty. Thus the new individualism on its militaristic side was not the purely lib-

[39] *La France régénérée* . . . (36, ed. "a"), *Suite*, last stanza. In the original the use of capital letters for important words and phrases is fairly frequent.

[40] *La Cocarde nationale* . . . (56), stanza 3. This quotation is from a piece which did not directly concern the attack on the Bastille, but which, having appeared in August, 1789, was practically contemporaneous with the songs celebrating the event. For fuller consideration of this item, see pages 141-42.

[41] For further consideration of the origins of this transformation see Chapter x.

erating force that it first seemed, with no obstacle to overcome except in the environmental obstructions of the past. Around the corner were new disciplines, perhaps less arbitrary, but no less rigorous than those of the old regime. These new disciplines the patriots heartily embraced, their wish to be "free" being directed against known restrictions, and being attended by the desire to be bound in some new way. This twofold aspect of the new liberation was generally unobserved at the time. But looking back, we can see that it was more than a chance coincidence that close upon the heels of man's discovery of "liberty" and of the citizen's right to be a soldier, was his discovery of military duty, his establishment of the conscripted armies of a "free" people, and his totally new recognition of the strength that resides in numbers when properly regimented.

A second aspect of the influence exerted on the patriots by the Bastille uprising was the birth of a new sense of conflict. Bitter enmities accompanied the impulses of liberation and the nascent self-reliance which we have just been considering.

Those who seek to popularize the findings of modern psychology as to the thought processes of human beings have coined the phrase "black-white thinking." It is used to describe an attitude of mind which characterizes most people some of the time, and many people most of the time. According to this way of seeing life, all the good resides on one side of a question and all the bad on the other. This attitude, the mark of a mentality governed by impatience and intolerance, is often prevalent because it satisfies the primitive emotional needs for simplicity, for absolute certainty, and for the unqualified justification of self. When men and women are put under a great strain, as in time of revolution or war, black-white thinking wins adherents with lightning-like rapidity.

It was thinking of this sort that came to the fore as the result of the unsettled conditions in France in July, 1789. The complex issues of the hour were resolved into a simple conflict between good and evil. The "much to be said on both sides" attitude of a Sir Roger de Coverley was almost nonexistent. The patriots enjoyed that thrill which comes to men when they can dramatize their own interests in such a way as to make them seem one-hundred-percent right. In this atmosphere any obstructor of the cause, any member of the opposition, seemed to them the incarnation of evil.

Let the song writers be heard. They knew how to quicken the sense of conflict with just the notes that the patriots were now ready to hear. Who are the opponents of the popular cause? They are the "gentlemen of the cabal," a "haute et basse canaille," or merely "our illustrious vermin."[42] They are, we learn from a song which appeared on a woodcut printed in color and published at Orleans, "the infamous ones who wished to betray us."[43] To the writer P. Rousselet,[44] they are "the odious group," the existence of which "is to the heavens what crime is to the sage." The same author further expresses the spirit of the time when he writes of De Launay as "that perfidious Governor, despising the agreements of honor."[45] In the actual conflict, as we have seen, De Launay and his company who defended the Bastille wished to act with moderation. The mass of spectators jumped to the opposite conclusion. Thinking that the entrance of the mob was peaceable and not forced, they had shouted, "Treason!" when they saw the defenders open fire on those who were invading the prison. The misunderstanding was made the most of in the frenzied excitement of the hour, and was emphasized by popular writers until this supposed "treason" came in the annals of the Revolution to have all the force of fact. Certainly it appeared in this light to the author of the sprightly piece, *France Regenerated and the Traitors Punished*, who wrote that "the traitorous Governor" had a "cowardly heart," and that "the citadel, though cruel" could not withstand the attack.[46] The author's glee over the punishment meted out to the enemy on ac-

---

[42] *Prise de la Bastille* (31), stanzas 1, 2 and 5.

[43] *La Prise de la Bastille* (Déduit) . . . (35), stanza 5.

[44] *Quelques vers faits le 17 Juillet* . . . (30†), stanza 1. This song appears at the conclusion of the prose text of Rousselet's undated pamphlet entitled *Détail intéressant, et jusqu'à présent ignoré, sur la prise de la Bastille, et la suite des révolutions, faite par un Assaillant de la Bastille, à un de ses Amis, blessé au même siége.* Concerning uncertainty as to the date of publication of this brochure (1789 or 1790), see *ibid.*, Bibliography II, D. The prose text specifies that the verses were written "July 17." Although the year is not identified, one may presume that it was 1789, at the same time allowing for the possibility that the verses may have been touched up subsequently. In fact, some of the language is characterized by a type of dramatization and vehemence which, though not unknown at the time of the attack on the Bastille, became more general later.

[45] *Ibid.*, stanzas 1 and 7.   [46] *La France régénérée* . . . (36), stanzas 6 and 9.

count of his "atrocious soul" and "ferocious heart," is best expressed in the original text:

> Cette âme atroce, ce coeur féroce
> En est puni, [*bis*]
> L'on fait la fête, coupant la tête
> De l'ennemi. [*bis*][47]

Here, as in several of the songs at this time, righteous indignation is badly discolored by what is apparently intended as a light touch, a sort of macabre gaiety.

"Twenty thousand criminals" is the phrase applied to the anti-Revolutionary forces in the *Song of the Bourgeois of Paris*.[48] Their program is "secret and inexorable treason" and the defenders of the Bastille are "perfidious assassins . . . covered with shame." In a song which may have appeared considerably later,[49] due notice is taken of the treachery of De Launay, and of how the "bourgeoisie," when they entered the Bastille, were "suddenly massacred." Reference is made to the decapitation of the traitorous governor, and to his head having been "marched about, with great strides, on the end of a pike." This deed is explained as "the public vengeance." We are reminded, too, that the people also cut off the head of the Prévôt des Marchands. Clearly, enemies as black as those of the popular cause were made to appear deserved no mercy.

In the language of the songs, then, unqualified evil characterized the opposition. But there was always a happier side to the picture —the contrast of white against black. Each of the excerpts cited has as its counterpart a eulogy of the inspired patriots and of the popular cause. In the song in which the courtiers were "illustrious vermin," the French Guards displayed "valiance, honor and liberty."[50] In the verses of Rousselet the contrast is between the ignominy and cowardice of De Launay and the "courage" and "intrepidity" of

[47] *Ibid., Suite*, stanza 2.

[48] *Chanson des bourgeois de Paris* (32). The two quotations which follow are from stanzas 2 and 4.

[49] *Récit historique* . . . (37†). The quotations which follow are from stanzas 10, 16, and 17.

This song, ascribed by Pierre to 1789, may have been written the following year to celebrate the first anniversary of the capture of the Bastille. See Appendix A, 190.

[50] *Prise de la Bastille* (31), stanza 11.

the patriots.[51] In the *Song of the Bourgois of Paris* we read of the glory of the conquerors, whose arms "heaven blesses."[52] They had "no project or concerted plan"; yet "what good sense, what courage" they displayed! There follows an allusion to antiquity. In the so-called classical era of French history, classical virtues had been reserved for the illustrious; but now, by 1789, the common man could boast of a stature comparable to that of the ancients:

> Croit-on, qu'à Rome ou dans la Grèce,
> En pareil cas, on s'y fut pris,
> Mieux que les Bourgeois de Paris.   [*bis*][53]

The author hastens to point out that the patriot—who to us today appears as an insurrectionist—is "loyal" to Louis, whom he "loves and reveres" and for whom he is ready to "shed all his blood."[54]

When the story of the Bastille was retold, as frequently happened during the Revolution, it was in various ways revised. An illuminating study could be made of the changing views on the significance of the capture which developed from year to year in connection with the anniversary celebrations of July 14. To some extent, interpretations of that event were kept up to date by a series of falsifications to correspond to changing ideals. Some, though not all, of the themes suggested in the present chapter persisted—at the heart, as it were, of the legend. This legend of the Bastille, and what came later to be its almost mythological significance, were made possible in the first instance by such exaggerations and distortions as have been revealed in the preceding pages. It may be that whenever a popular cause entails bloodshed, it is apt similarly to be projected against the background of man's spiritual struggle throughout the ages. In these circumstances, a sort of moral night or blanket of evil is thought to envelop the enemy; while the faithful—finding whatever they do good by comparison—occupy a battleground flooded with light. No sympathy can cross the line. Whatever tolerance may once have seemed natural is suddenly discovered to imply an intolerable concession, for it robs the elect of that sense of absolute right which they find necessary for

---

[51] *Quelques vers faits le 17 Juillet* . . . (30†). Cf. stanzas 4 and 7. Concerning uncertainty in regard to the date of publication of this piece, see footnote 44.
[52] *Chanson des bourgeois de Paris* (32), stanza 1.
[53] *Ibid.*, stanza 3; "à" is without accent in the original.   [54] *Ibid.*, stanza 6.

the release of a maximum of moral energy. In this process of over-simplification, primitive concepts clearly influence—and doubtless unbalance—man's hopes and plans for a better world.

In the drama of July, we may regard as the first act the conspiracy of the Court, ending in the dismissal of Necker; and as the second, the uprising of the Parisian populace. The third and last act was the coming of the King to Paris on July 17, his rather painful acceptance of a *fait accompli*, and his reconciliation with the people. In the excitement and joy of this occasion there were moments when the pretense that the King had somehow been on the side of the patriots frankly broke down. People could admit that a situation akin to war between Louis and his children had temporarily existed, now that it seemed no longer to threaten. It is furthermore true that peace prevailed not as the outcome of compromise, but only because a great victory, a revolutionary change in the structure of French monarchy, was assumed by the patriots to have been permanently achieved.

It is against the background of this fact that one can understand why Bailly, in offering a mayor's welcome to Louis at the gates of Paris and in presenting him with the keys to the city, was able to remark with no apparent intention of giving offense: "These same keys were presented to Henry IV: he had reconquered his people: now the people has reconquered its King!" The mayor's tribute has become famous in the annals of the Revolution for being maladroit. It was no doubt a momentary indiscretion, and an amusing one; because thereby the venerable Bailly gave overt recognition to a breach between the King and the popular will that was supposed not to exist, and especially because he did so by means of the Henry IV analogy, which had hitherto been used to conceal any conflict.

The "reconquered" King proceeded to the Hôtel de Ville, where he sat through ceremonies to celebrate his sublime leadership of a cause which he had, of course, tried by several maneuvers to obstruct. There followed a great ovation. An official presented Louis with the new Revolutionary cockade of red, blue, and white. The King, heir to two centuries of Bourbon tradition, placed it in his hat.[55] He acceded to so much that was extravagant that the part

---

[55] The Paris Electors had decided that the newly created Paris guards should have a cockade of the colors of the city, blue and red. It was presently observed that these

which he played on this occasion appears utterly ambiguous, and it is usually described as pathetically confused and contradictory. And, indeed, so it was, from the standpoint of logical consistency. But the King's behavior is at least partially explicable from quite another standpoint, as will appear in the following chapter.

Less obvious, but equally important, was an ambiguity in the role of the Revolutionists themselves. The patriots, in their new self-confidence born of the Bastille uprising, were in a measure proclaiming a new order in which their own sovereign power transcended that of the King. In the light of certain events, and of many of their pretensions, theirs was clearly an attitude of insurrection. But this cannot be described as the prevailing mood; it was only one phase of a total mood. A contrasting element was the continuance of that spirit of dependence which had characterized the patriotic mentality from the outset. One might expect that either one of these two attitudes, defiance or subservience, would have absorbed the personality of the patriots to the exclusion—or at least to the apparent exclusion—of the other. But at this epoch of the Revolution, these attitudes seem to have made room for one another. Neither in the possession of self-confidence, nor in the lack of it, did the patriots display any consistency; on the contrary, their emotions appear to have been attracted first in one direction, then in the other. Perhaps no patriot resented such a contradiction, which we may suppose corresponded to his own inner feelings of traditional loyalty on the one hand, and of ill-defined resolution on the other. Illustrations of this ineluctable dilemma could be cited in abundance. An example is furnished in the song of Rousselet,[56] where we find lines such as these directed to Louis:

> Cesse de t'éloigner de lui [le Peuple];
> Reçois sa plainte et le rassure,
> Puisque toi seul est son appui.

---

were also the colors of the house of Orleans, and, as a distinguishing touch, white, the venerable color of the French monarchy, was added. Thus was born the famous tricolor of the Revolution. Lafayette, who took a leading part in the final decision, proclaimed, either in the folly of exaggeration or with a fair degree of foresight, "I give you a cockade which will go around the world." See his *Mémoires*, Paris, 1837, vol. ii, p. 267.

[56] *Quelques vers faits le 17 Juillet* . . . (30†), stanza 11. Concerning uncertainty in regard to the date of publication of this piece, see footnote 44.

Here seems to be a continuance of the spirit of traditional dependence. But in the same song Louis receives the following warning
that his scepter may be lost:

> O Roi! sa perte est infaillible
> Si tu n'écoute la vertu.

France Regenerated and the Traitors Punished is also of interest
in this connection. We are concerned here with the last three
stanzas. They open with an invocation to the "Roi débonnaire,"
who is characterized as "worthy Bourbon," and who is invited to
be "the father" and to render the nation prosperous. Likewise, it
is confidently hoped that the Duke of Orleans, and of course
Necker, will be helpful to "the good children." These expressions
suggest a continued sense of insecurity and submissiveness; but the
song ends on a contrasting note. The closing lines recall the self-
reliance of the people, by paying a tribute to "these conquerors,"
the Paris militia.[57]

There was, in short, something equivocal both about the protestations of submission and about those of apparent defiance.
There was here an ambivalence of feeling, of which we shall see
further instances in other connections. But in any case, whether
inspired primarily by self-confidence or by reliance on the leadership of the King, the dominant theme after the Paris uprising was
peace. Peace was supposedly attained on July 17, when Louis and
the Parisians were to all appearances reconciled. As a poet sensing
the spirit of the moment exclaimed, "Neither history nor fiction
furnishes anything approaching this ineffable day . . . this forever
tender and touching day."[58] Thus the third act of the Bastille
drama ended with faith and optimism well sustained.

Peace was won. But in gaining it, the National Assembly and the
King had acknowledged acts of popular violence out of which a
new self-reliance of the people had sprung, and out of which had
emerged a sense of conflict, with its balanced pattern of unmeas-
ured condemnation on the one hand and of exaggerated self-justifi-

---

[57] *La France régénérée* . . . (36, ed. "a"), *Suite*, stanzas 9-11.

[58] *Chanson des bourgeois de Paris* (32), stanza 7. Similar rejoicing characterizes
several of the songs at this time, among them the *Chanson des dames des Marchés
S. Paul* . . . (42) and *La Cocarde du Roi* (43), which are described in the next chapter.

cation on the other. These attitudes, amply expressed at the time of the Bastille, were capable of great intensification and elaboration, as future events were to prove; and the drama, which seemed to be at an end, had only begun.

VI

IN THE summer of 1789 a wave of disturbances swept over France. Many municipalities, threatened by anarchy, organized impromptu governments to replace the ineffectual representatives of the Crown. In country areas the peasants ransacked or demolished châteaux and committed other acts of violence. It was difficult, frequently impossible, to collect taxes; food was badly distributed; an acute currency situation was arising. The repressive instruments of law and order were lacking, for the discipline of the regular army was demoralized, and the loyalty of the new forces, the volunteers of the nation, was to an equalitarian cause which encouraged every sort of military irregularity. There were black clouds not only in the offing but directly overhead.

Still the ideas of revolution and reform were thought to be just as good as ever: a conspiracy of the Court had been overthrown and a great popular victory won. The representatives of France were credited with making new efforts on behalf of the nation; the leaders of the patriots seemed, for most practical purposes, to be pulling together; a Declaration of Rights was in process of being prepared by the National Assembly, and a new Constitution was promised. The patriots were already in a mood to reap the benefits of a revolution which they believed they had thus secured by a twofold success. On the high level of parliamentary struggle they had emerged triumphant; while at the street level, so to speak, of blows and bloodshed they had also confounded their enemies. The political and moral atmosphere which resulted was in large measure one of good feeling. Ready at hand for the expression of this good feeling was the tradition of *sensibilité*, a literary and artistic mode which had been developed in France and elsewhere earlier in the eighteenth century. By and large, the patriots adopted this tradition as a medium for the expression of their feelings.

But at the same time there were other currents of feeling which could not be accommodated within the general trend. Something must be said of these at the outset. If, by way of example, we turn again to lyrics, we find various songs embodying moods quite different from the *sensibilité* that generally prevailed. One of these songs, *The Marvelous Lantern*,[1] gave expression to the sadistic impulses that asserted themselves in the Bastille and post-Bastille excitement. It should be said here that on July 22 Paris mobs assailed the aged and arrogant former Minister of Finance, Foulon, and his wealthy son-in-law, Bertier, and decapitated them, Foulon having first been hanged. The heads of both were paraded around Paris, a reminder of the revenge taken the week before on De Launay and Flesselles.

The Marvelous Lantern derives its name from the lantern posts to which victims were hanged by the populace. The song abounds in ghoulish details and gruesome hints, but purports above all to be merry. There are allusions to the parading of De Launay's head upon a pike, to that of Foulon similarly displayed, to the hay stuffed in the dead mouth of the latter, and so forth, each of the allusions being followed by the gay sounds of a rippling chorus,

> La faridondaine
> La faridondon,

to the air of *A la façon de Barbari*.

The opening lines of all five stanzas express what are assumed to be reasons for popular rejoicing. The second commences:

> De la tete du Gouverneur
> On a fait un éxemple
> Pour que chaque traitre aye peur
> Sitôt qu'il la contemple. . . . [2]

The "Gouverneur," as a note explains, is De Launay. The third stanza, which singles out Foulon, opens by supposing that with his death the profiteers are routed:

> De bleds cruels Accapareurs
> Adieu votre espérance
> Adieu vôtre Or, et vos grandeurs
> En proye à la vengeance. . . .

---

[1] *La lanterne merveilleuse* (38). This song, which is undated, presumably appeared soon after the events of July 14 and 22, which it celebrates.

[2] In the original, "tête" and "traître" appear without accent. On the other hand, the adjective "vôtre" appears once with, and once without, accent, as shown in the next stanza quoted above. The products of the Revolutionary press, especially many of the *feuilles volantes* and small brochures, are full of such irregularities in spelling. Punctuation is often largely neglected, as in the song above.

The final stanza is representative of the general tenor of this song, which neatly combines the dual motifs of vengeance and glee:

> Traîtres qui vouliés nous périr
> Tremblés de ce supplice
> Le ciel qui veut nous secourir
> Punit votre injustice
> A la lanterne sans façon
> La faridondaine
> La faridondon
> On vous accroche dieu merci
> Beribi
> A la façon de Barbari
> Mon ami.[3]

Such stanzas illustrate an important point—that a revolution which is to gain the support of the populace must strike the masses not only as a worthy cause but also as an exciting game. In revolution as in war, there is an element of sport. From this standpoint, even atrocities serve as a source of merriment to those who can stomach them.[4]

It is safe to say that no book on the French Revolution has yet taken notice of a pamphlet called *The Citizen in Good Humor*, which is to be found at the Bibliothèque Nationale. This work, according to a legend on the title page, "has carried off the prize, not of the French Academy, but of the Bacchic Academy, in the presence of forty renowned drinkers." The brochure is dated 1789. Its sixteen pages contain prose and two songs. The foreword is a well-turned exposition of the phlegmatic attitude in human nature.

---

[3] Another song of this type is the *Chanson des Dames de la Place Maubert* (39). In stanza 5, the deaths of De Launay and Flesselles are celebrated as follows:

> Mais, grace à nos bons François,
> Tous deux ont fait la grimace.
> Pour couronner leur succès,
> Ils ont vu l'gibet face à face,
> Comme ils vont s'targuer là-bas,
> Parmi nos fiers Aristocrats.

In stanza 10, gratitude is expressed to "Not' bon Roi" for having promised to recall Necker.

[4] This happily is but part of the picture. As Sagnac assures us, "Peaceful folk withdrew in order not to be witnesses of these savage scenes." *La Révolution (1789-1792)*, p. 52.

The studied complacency of the citizen in good humor suggests the turmoil which confronted a man of detachment in those days. The foreword says in part:

But if I do not possess any of those merits, at least I remain calm; I don't go at all to societies to proclaim against the Estates-General; I don't undertake to appall citizens with terrifying pictures; I go to the Palais Royal, but only to enjoy the air or cold drinks: when a commotion starts on one side, I betake myself to the other; I'm nothing; I don't want to be anything, in anything; I restrict myself to making wishes for the prosperity of the country; I ask God that he bring into agreement, if he can, the Nation and the King, and that he send his holy spirit into the midst of the National Assembly.

I allow myself, however, from time to time, some few amusements, which do no harm to anyone; I received a few cases of excellent Bordeaux wine; while awaiting the arrangement of affairs; waiting to know on which foot to dance; waiting to know whether we are to have peace or civil war; waiting to know whether there will be a King in France or whether there will not be one; waiting to see whether people are to have bread and money; while awaiting finally, this famous Constitution . . . , we drink our wine, my friends and I, and we are none the less gay from it. We go so far as to compose Songs. . . .

I believe that at a moment when people have read moral and political discussions in such abundance, when they are certain of having so many more still to read, they might enjoy hearing the Estates-General, the capture of the Bastille, and the befallen Heads spoken of in a slightly gayer language and tone; and I made up my mind to offer to the Public three songs[5] stolen yesterday from my three Companions; they will perhaps be annoyed by this infidelity; but I promise them anonymity. . . .

Actually events were too critical for this mood of gentle mockery, bordering on indifference, to have any vogue. Such an attitude prevailed in no small measure under the Directory—a period of reaction after years of overstrain. But in July, 1789, the tempo was different, and he was a rare person who was not swept along with the rush of events. As a matter of fact, if ridicule had been in order, the humor of the "renowned drinkers" might have served as effective satire. In one of their songs, the *Estates-General of Bacchus*,[6] jibes are directed at the most honored practices of the patriots, which already included invocations to the deity, Latin hymns, oaths of loyalty, fraternal kisses, etc. When the Estates General of

5 The brochure, *Le citoyen en bonne humeur* (II, D), contains only two.
6 *Etats généraux de Bacchus* (40).

Bacchus assembles, it is under the tutelage of the Deity ("of rev-
elry," to be sure). In this atmosphere of mock gravity it is necessary
to swear an oath, "which ought to establish confidence." Then a
prayer to the skies is in order. The *Te Deum* is dispensed with; is,
indeed, more than amply replaced, the song alleges, by the clink-
ing of glasses. Then is exchanged the kiss of peace, "as custom pre-
scribes." Thus was an effort made to deride the nascent ritual of
the Revolution. The author and his companions were not interested in seeing politics become some sort of cult, wrapped up in
quasi-religious sanctions. The only thing about which the Estates
General of Bacchus seemed to be really serious was the wisdom of
the minister Necker,

> A qui Sulli légua son coeur,
> Et son génie, et son courage.[7]

In the second song, called *The Peaceful Drinker*,[8] the title character is too peaceful to have his composure disturbed by all the
plotting factions, or by a little violence here and there. But the
limelight of history is seldom turned on peaceful drinkers. They
are entirely lost to sight in the turmoil of 1789 and of the following
years. It was for those capable of becoming fired with indignation
at the aristocrats, and even, if not especially, for those who could
sing gleefully about death at the lamp post, that the foreground of
the Revolutionary scene is reserved in the annals of history.

The optimism that prevailed at the time of the gathering of the
Estates General had a certain character which was delineated in
Chapter II. It was suggested that many of the views which became
popular were the result not of rational analysis, but of wishing, and
that this wishing, far from being haphazard, grew out of related
hopes and impulses and created a definite climate of opinion. The
optimism was shot through with inconsistencies, as we have seen;
but it enabled the patriots to feel at home in an environment of
political and social unrest, and thereby served a useful purpose.
That there was need for this sort of consolation is further revealed
by the fact that even after events in July had changed the external
situation, the illusions of the spring either persisted or were re-

---

[7] *Ibid.*, last stanza.   [8] *Le buveur paisible* (41).

vived.[9] It goes without saying that this aspect of the patriotic mood was fraught with danger. The possibility that the King, recalcitrant on so many occasions, might try to undo the work of reform, or that the most unruly elements of the populace might try to seize control of the Revolutionary movement, aroused misgivings in many leaders, but failed to have a sobering effect on public opinion. Nor, despite scattered rumors of reactionary conspiracies, was it generally admitted that there were any further cards that the aristocrats could play. Their spirit had presumably been crushed, once and for all, by the Bastille demonstration.

The tendency to revive an earlier optimism was reflected in nearly all of the songs which came out between the celebration of the capture of the Bastille and the recurrence in September of disillusion and anxiety. A few examples may serve to suggest the atmosphere of unbounded confidence. On July 20, the Paris General Assembly of Electors received a delegation of market women who came to express their loyalty and gratitude. This they did, in part, by singing a patriotic song.[10] The Assembly voted that the song, along with a prose tribute that preceded it, be printed in the *Journal de Paris*, where it appeared two days later. The tribute, "composed by six fishwives," after praising the King, concluded by announcing to the Assembly, "vous êtes tous des Necker." The song embodied the various phases of hero worship characteristic of the Revolution at this time, and expressed the prevailing confidence that past miseries were now banished.

The same spirit extended to the provinces. Patriotic verses, entitled *The Cockade of the King*, were sung at a theatre in Bordeaux to celebrate His Majesty's reconciliation, on July 17, with the Parisians.[11] To the lilt of music, the spectators were told that the King, far from being offended by the Bastille uprising, had been touched by the occurrence:

[9] I am far from suggesting that the spirit of the time was in this respect abnormal. On the contrary, there is much evidence to suggest that people in their group relationships normally tend to appraise existing conditions through roseate glasses, and to find acceptable only such views as strengthen their faith in present undertakings and flatter their hopes for the future. Emotion of this sort provides the basis of much so-called public "opinion."

[10] *Chanson nouvelle chantée par les Dames députées* . . . (34).

[11] *La Cocarde du Roi* (43).

> Son coeur fait pour la vérité
> De douleur étoit pénétré
>   Le passé le désole . . . [bis]
> Au Tiers-états alors il vient. . . . [12]

In the next stanza, his innocence is contrasted to the villainy of the Court reactionaries:

> Fuyez hommes vains et méchans
> C'est un père avec ses enfans. . . .

With the opening of the final stanza, the Bordeaux audience was assured that

> *Louis* la Cocarde au chapeau
> N'aura jamais d'instant plus beau. . . .

The allusion was to the sufficiently humiliating ceremony at Paris, July 17. Finer for whom, one may ask? The remainder of this stanza is revealing if one bears in mind the dual character of hero worship that has been explained in a previous chapter:

> Pour mettre le comble à cela
> Oui par nous *Necker* restera
>   C'est ce qui nous console. [bis]

Thus, it is with praise of Necker that this tribute to Louis is brought to a close. Contained in this one song are several of the emotional trends of an earlier period, made topical and current, to be sure, but nevertheless recurring with significant tenacity.

The cockade of red, blue, and white quickly became the distinctive emblem of the Revolution. As we have seen, Louis disported it on the occasion of his visit to Paris after the Bastille uprising. This was an incongruous gesture, even though white, the Bourbon color, had been added at the last moment to the red and blue of insurrectionary Paris. But it all seemed sufficiently appropriate to the author of a song which was launched by an actress at a theatre in Brest, July 26.[13] The Breton audience, hearing the news of Paris in this agreeable way, was assured that

> Cette Cocarde est le modele
> Des vertus de notre bon Roi:

---

[12] *Ibid.*, stanza 3.
[13] *Chanson jettée sur le Théâtre à Brest . . .* (44).

> Le Blanc sans tache nous rappelle
> Sa douceur et sa bonne foi. . . . [14]

The red, she went on in explanation of Louis' role, is "the image of his love for his subjects," the "celestial Blue . . . the presage of Happiness." In the next stanza, one sees Louis as the father of the new era—

> Et le Protecteur de la France
> De ses enfans marche entourné . . . ,

but by a curious inversion of the natural order he seems to arouse in his children a semblance of paternal solicitude:

> Plus de Gardes, plus de contrainte,
> Le Camp cruel n'existe plus;
> Mais Louis, droit être sans crainte
> Il est gardé par ses vertus.

Another song to celebrate the new Revolutionary emblem, *The National Cockade or Patriotic Equality*, appeared in August.[15] This piece, written by Mercier de Compiègne, presented the patriotic outlook in such vigorous terms that it enjoyed reprintings— in revised editions, to be sure—under the Republic.[16] It is interesting to note that the cockade is described in the first stanza as the "emblem of equality"; and in the second, as "the standard of liberty" and as "this fraternal cockade." These three phrases together foreshadow the great slogan of the Republic, "Liberté, Egalité, Fraternité," which was formally adopted in 1793.[17] The cockade of 1789 is viewed by Mercier as the badge of militant citizenship: "Each citizen is a warrior," he writes, and "each displays the laurel as the avenger of *la patrie*." As a consequence of the Bastille insurgency, the author alleges that peace is won:

> Tous, sont frères, tous, sont égaux;
> *Necker* revient, un astre brille;
> Et la france oubliant ses maux,
> Ne forme plus qu'une famille. [*bis*][18]

[14] *Ibid.*, stanza 2.   [15] *La Cocarde nationale* . . . (56)
[16] In *Le Chansonnier de la Montagne, l'an 2*, p. 104, and in *Le Temple de la Liberté. . .* , *3e Année Républ.*, p. 55. (II, F)
[17] Aulard writes, "I do not recall having seen the words *Liberté, Egalité, Fraternité*, on any official or public act before the year 1793." *Etudes et leçons sur la Révolution française, Sixième série*, Paris, 1910, p. 16.
[18] *La Cocarde nationale* (56), stanza 3.

The National Cockade or Patriotic Equality ends with lines to the "Sexe charmant." Mercier invites the members of the fair sex to "grant a vow dictated by patriotism," namely, to "share our heroism"—an opportunity which presently came to the women of the Revolution and which they avidly welcomed.

The sentimentalism which is such a marked characteristic of many of the patriotic songs affected most of the literature of this time and was, in a measure, representative of an epoch. We have already seen how often it has been said that the Revolutionists, influenced by the eighteenth-century philosophers, relied upon reason as a primary force by which to change human affairs. Indeed, it must be admitted that members of the Revolutionary assemblies and publicists of that day are properly famous for the extraordinary extent to which they emphasized in their speeches and writings the principles of "reason." But it may not be amiss to repeat a word of warning on this subject, for reason today is taken in contrast to feeling, and there is a tendency to regard the two as opposing faculties; whereas at the end of the eighteenth century, reason and feeling were supposed to be closely allied through the unifying force of Nature, from which they both sprang. Though people talked much about reason, they consulted their hearts as much as their minds; in fact, an appeal to the emotions was considered quite "reasonable." It was in such an atmosphere that the patriots lived. Thus to them, the triumph of reason involved, among other things, a triumph of good feeling—of the most sublime, delicate, and exquisite emanations of the human heart. Such an outlook accounts in part for the devotion of the patriots to this faculty, which as the Revolution progressed was personified as *la déesse Raison* and became the nominal basis of a cult.

In its mid-eighteenth-century setting, this outbreak of sentiment —of *sensibilité*—served as a corrective to formalism and, on the whole, contributed to a more abundant life. But *sensibilité* immediately led to extremes of sentimentalism, such as one finds expressed in parts of Rousseau's life and writing, in Diderot's dramas, and in Greuze's paintings. By the time of the Revolution, the vogue of sentimentalism served not merely as a literary and artistic inspiration, but had caught the imagination of the average man.

Frequent references to *le coeur*, to *la tendresse*, to *les sentiments*, suggest the extent to which the patriots were influenced by *sensibilité*.[19] This awakening of feeling was neither vague nor undirected, but found expression in timely applications to new events. In the early summer of 1789, the patriots waxed mawkish over the "surrender" of Louis; interpreted in a light favorable to monarchy the rise of the masses to power in the onslaught on the Bastille; rationalized other immediate causes of uneasiness; and, finally, began to bring into the foreground of contemporary thought the phenomenon of death, not as a perhaps necessary evil in the struggle for liberty, but as a seductive ideal about which the human imagination might profitably revolve. In short, death was pictured as a welcome consummation.

A brief examination of three songs will serve to convey the atmosphere of Revolutionary sentimentalism and to indicate its timely and topical elements. First, let us glance at a piece by one Madame Dupray.[20] Here we are far from the salon and its fastidious expression of thought and sentiment; for this song was written on behalf of the women of four of the markets of Paris, and the authoress was herself a market woman. According to the announcement following the title, her humble words were "Approved by M. le Maire de Paris." In the course of effusive praise to Louis, nothing is said of the Monarch's mind or thoughts, but his heart, we are told, is all right: "Il a le coeur en bon état." A tribute is paid to the representatives who are diligently working for "the happiness of all France." The name of the Mayor, Madame Dupray "loves to pronounce." Lafayette, who is "the model of great warriors," is "our friend." "Our father, our friends, our brothers"—thus are characterized the King, the citizens, and the soldiers in their relation to the market women. In the closing lines, the author apologizes for not having the proper words to express her sincere wishes, but she pleads that her heart is in the song, "which is all that matters."

Such sentiments need not be discounted as the emotional excesses of an ignorant woman. Consider along with them the views

[19] Emphasis in the present discussion is placed upon but a few aspects of *sensibilité*. The subject as a whole is reviewed by Pierre Trahard in his book *La sensibilité révolutionnaire (1789-1794)*, Paris, 1936.

[20] *Chanson des dames des Marchés S. Paul . . .* (42).

of M. Dugazon, an educated man, pensionary of the King, as expressed in a song by his hand,[21] which appeared, August 1, in the journal *Affiches, Annonces et Avis divers.* Here we read of the "tenderness" of Louis, of "the public happiness" which has "just dawned," of "no more cares!" and of "the golden age." The author, expressing a pretense that was widely used by the patriots, finds the King triumphant rather than abashed as a result of the Bastille uprising:

> . . . nos Soldats,
> Avec leur appareil de guerre,
> Sont moins puissans
> Qu'un bon Roi qui commande en Père,
> A ses enfans.[22]

August 25 was the fete day of Saint Louis.[23] This occasion brought forth a song entitled *Verses for the Saint Louis 1789*, by M. de la Boessière, Master at Arms.[24] One is prepared by the subtitle, "Bouquet to the King," for the florid quality of this tribute to Louis. There is at the outset reference to "his tenderness," and, later, to his "tender efforts." Presently it appears, in connection with the scarcity of food, that he "sheds tears on account of our needs." His solicitude for the people is further pictured as follows:

> Sur nos sentiments l'imposture
> Crut en vain l'induire en erreur,
> D'un bon Père le tendre coeur
> Sait le pouvoir de la nature;
> Il se livre à nous dans Paris,
> Plein d'une noble confiance,
> Nous trouve armés pour sa défense,
> En dignes enfants de *Louis*.[25]

---

[21] *Chanson, par Dugazon* (49).

[22] *Ibid.*, stanza 2. The song ends with an accent on virtue that anticipates the abolition of titles:

> Les trois Ordres, dans leur sagesse,
> Ne voudront plus
> Compter pour titres de noblesse,
> Que les vertus.

[23] The leading part in this annual festival was played by the Carmelites. Details concerning its observance are given in H. Monin, *L'Etat de Paris en 1789*, Paris, 1889, p. 629.

[24] *Couplets pour la Saint-Louis 1789* (54).

[25] *Ibid.*, stanza 7. The three quotations which immediately precede are from stanzas 1, 5, and 2, respectively.

So it was for "his defense" that the Parisians were armed! As in the preceding song, the author would make it appear that the King's position was strengthened rather than weakened by the Bastille uprising.

In the next stanza, M. de la Boessière sets forth the claim that "all the French"—"defenders of the fleur-de-lis . . . proud sons of *la patrie*"—

> Préférant l'honneur à la vie,
> Sont prêts à mourir pour Louis.

It is fair to point out that, so far, the sons of *la patrie* had died, if anything, *against* Louis; and that, furthermore, if the union were as perfect as pictured, there was no imminent prospect of their having to die *for* him. On the surface, therefore, this tragic emphasis was inappropriate. Is it not a sign of uncertainty, when along with professions that everything is going surpassingly well, there appear forebodings that sacrifice unto death may be necessary? And these forebodings occur with noticeable frequency. For instance, in lyrics written for a patriotic gathering on August 13,[26] the following lines bring to a solemn ending an otherwise cheerful song:

> Ciel, à L o u i s prête un bras tutélaire;
> D'un Peuple libre il est le digne appui;
> Roi-Citoyen,[27] pour nous qu'il vive en père:
> Chacun de nous saura mourir pour lui.

Without disparaging the strength which goes with willingness to sacrifice to the utmost for a cause, one may say that "death" at this stage of the Revolution was a sentimental rather than a profound theme. The atmosphere of *sensibilité* endowed it, as well as life, with an easy charm. In the patriots' glib welcome to death there is an element of danger, the character of which becomes increasingly clear as the Revolution progresses.

As one encounters in the lyrics of the time a sentimentalism which may seem too extravagant to reflect the outlook of everyday life, the question arises whether the songs that were in vogue were

[26] *Couplets à M. le Marquis de la Fayette* . . . (50).
[27] The use of the slogan "Roi-Citoyen" at this early stage of the Revolution is interesting. The term appears also in *Chanson sur l'Assemblée nationale* . . . (25), stanza 7.

unduly exuberant and hence not representative of general trends. Recourse to the prose of the period is obviously indicated; and here one encounters almost an embarrassment of riches, for the output of pamphlets, so voluminous in the spring, continued strong throughout the summer. A few citations, confined to a single historical episode, must serve to represent a very considerable literature.

The episode in question is the return of Necker—nothing so caught the popular imagination in late July and early August as that event. As we have seen, on July 16 Louis announced the Minister's recall. When the word reached Necker, he was already in Bâle, Switzerland. His return across France was triumphal. He arrived at Versailles on July 28, and for two days was the recipient of a tremendous public welcome. He then went to Paris, where, on July 30, he was given a similar and even greater ovation.

Indicative of the anticipations of the people is a *Letter of the Parisians to M. Necker, to Invite Him to Resume His Place*, by a patriot who signed himself "M. F. R."[28] According to this "invitation," the whole Revolutionary movement revolved around Necker. A brief quotation will suffice:

> Your removal, Sir, has been the cause of a great revolution in Paris, and in all France. . . . Now that the efforts of the intriguers are forestalled . . . we have need of you for the regeneration of France, we do not wish in this matter any other; and you, Sir, will again be the beloved one of the Estates General.[29]

Among tributes to the Minister upon his return to Versailles was a welcome by members of the French Guard. The occasion is described in an account by one of the company, a lawyer, Vialla.[30] It appears that upon news of the arrival of M. Necker, the French Guards "assembled of their own accord, and hastened to his house." They were well received. Their spokesman is quoted as follows:

> Ah! Sir, we shall not tell you what a thunderbolt struck us all upon the news of your sudden disappearance; no expression could convey other than imperfectly our common solicitude and the horrors of the painful situation into which it had cast France. . . .

[28] *Lettre des Parisiens à M. Necker. . . , par Leb . . s* (Lebois). (IV, C)
[29] *Ibid.*, pp. 2-3.
[30] *Compliment à M. Necker, fait et prononcé par un Garde-Françoise . . . , 1789.* (IV, C)

He then assured the Minister that "spirited cries—'A Father is restored to us, long live the able architect, the sublime pillar of French liberty'—will be uttered by all, and will fill the void that your absence has left in all hearts."[31] Thereupon, one of the Guards presented Necker with a bouquet bearing the legend, *Au régénérateur de la Liberté*.

. . . All Frenchmen [the speaker continued] burn with the desire to cry out, as we do on seeing you, "May the Regenerator of liberty and of the first People of the Universe live forever."

The Guards, we are told, exclaimed at this point, "Long live the Restorer of France"; whereupon the spokesman concluded his remarks by assuring the Minister that the memory of him would "live eternally in all hearts."[32]

At Paris the climax of the welcome to Necker was his reception, July 30, at the Hôtel de Ville—an event which inspired many prose accounts, not a few of them being published separately as pamphlets. Some of these works were apostrophes addressed to the hero —rather than mere descriptions—and they suggest that the people felt their bond with the Minister to be highly personal. There are many touching documents of this character. One must not be deceived by the observation of so many learned critics of the period, that the Revolutionists were disposed unduly to indulge in rhetoric —"mere rhetoric," as is often said. As a matter of fact, every generation currently has its own rhetoric, which, as long as it is current, goes unobserved as such and passes for effective speech. From this point of view one may regard the following tribute to Necker as once having had vital significance; and since the compliment derives much of its warmth from the tone of the French, it is best given as found:

[31] *Ibid.*, pp. 2-3. This passage contains literary flourishes which I have been unable to preserve in translation: "Ces cris animés . . . vont orner toutes les bouches, et remplir le vuide que votre présence ravie avoir laissé dans tous les coeurs."

[32] Mention may be made in passing of a song written to celebrate Necker's return to Versailles—*Couplets en l'honneur de M. Necker . . .* (45), which opens, "Necker, notre dieu tutélaire. . . . " The text of this song is unfortunately not available. This item and a piece entitled *Le retour de M. Necker, dédié à la nation par MM. C . . . et T.* (48), issued by the music publisher Coulubrier, which existed in unique copies at the Bibliothèque Nationale, were shown in the Revolutionary Exhibition of 1928, and were reported at the Library as having disappeared at that time. Titles, airs, and first lines of these two pieces are given in Pierre, *Catalogue . . .* , nos. 204 and 203, respectively.

Vous avez dû voir, lorsque vous avez été à l'Hôtel-de-Ville de Paris, le coeur du François par les bénédictions dont il vous combloit sur la route: chacun vous appelloit son Père, son Bienfaiteur, son Ami, vous regardant avec raison comme le Sauveur de la France; chacun vous admiroit, & faisoit retentir le Ciel de cris d'allégresse, d'avoir au milieu d'eux un homme de votre mérite & de votre savoir.[33]

This is from the *Tribute of Gratitude of the French Nation to Its Best Friend*. One might similarly consider another anonymous Paris publication, a leaflet entitled *The Joy of the French, the Arrival of M. Necker*. This time the author chooses to characterize, rather than to address, his hero:

At last has arrived that adorable Minister, that Sully of Henry IV. . . . All France must rejoice; for her the return of this Minister is a re-generation. . . . Everything will be put to order; it is indeed a happy day which sees the return of this demi-God.[34]

Among the lines omitted in the passage quoted above is a reference to Necker as "this friend of the French, this wise and discreet counselor of Kings!" This counselor, recalled and reinstated, could now serve again as a personification of the power of the people against the King, in the dual relationship of which much has already been said. It is amusing, in this connection, that a group of Parisians actually presented a crown to Necker, albeit innocently, as is revealed by the title of verses that appeared in the *Affiches, Annonces* . . . of August 19: "The Lyrical Tribute, or Verses Accompanied by a Crown of Flowers, and Presented to M. Necker, on his Arrival at the Hôtel de Ville, Thursday, July 30, 1789."[35] The author of the piece was one Bavouz, "citizen of the district of the Oratoire." His apostrophe to Necker commenced as follows:

O toi dont les vertus brillent de tant d'éclat!
Permet que sur ton front je pose une couronne;
Elle n'est que de fleurs: mais c'est le Tiers-Etat,
Le Peuple ton ami, c'est lui qui te la donne.

Thus, in the ceremony of welcome, we see charmingly revealed the

[33] *Tribut de reconnoissance de la Nation Françoise au meilleur de ses amis, Août, 1789*, pp. 4-5. (IV, C)

[34] *La joie des Français, L'Arrivée de M. Necker*, pp. 1-2. (IV, C)

[35] *Tribut lyrique* . . . (47). This piece was originally published as a poem, but was subsequently put to music, as announced in the *Affiches, Annonces* . . . , April 27, 1790.

desire of the patriots to dignify their own cause and, in so far as delicacy permitted, to crown it in the person of Necker.[36]

It must be admitted that poetry at this point is an intrusion, inasmuch as a brief survey of prose writings had been promised, but, at the celebration to Necker, it was the participants who decided in favor of verse. As a matter of fact, so elated was the Revolutionary spirit that those who sought to express it were often drawn in this direction. There is, for instance, the *Bouquet Presented to M. Necker, on His Entrance to Paris, 30 July, 1789*, a leaflet by the Abbé de Courchon.[37] The Abbé felt constrained to relegate a prose telling of "this happy revolution" to "History," since "her peaceful and calm style does not lend itself to our rapture." "Only poetry," he avers, "can convey the expression of our gratitude and homage to the beneficent Beings, who alone on this earth are the veritable image of the Divinity." After these disclosures (in prose), the Abbé expresses gratitude and homage in a song, in the course of which it appears that the "beneficent Beings" are Louis and Necker.[38]

Clearly, some at least of the prose writings of this period are more rhapsodical even than the lyrics. This is obviously true of a pamphlet entitled *The Triumphal Entry of M. Necker to the Hôtel-de-Ville*, as illustrated by a few quotations. "Let us rejoice," it is written, "the father of the people has arrived. O ineffable hap-

[36] I had concluded that Necker was a hero not simply in the ordinary sense, but that there existed in the popular imagination a tendency to identify his role as leader with that of the King—a matter of some psychological significance—when I came across the following by Augustin Challamel in his description of Necker's return: "Finally when he came to the Hôtel de Ville, at Paris, he was received there like the king himself. A crown was placed upon his head, a cockade in his hat, laurel branches in his hands. There were illuminations. People wrote on the door of his house: 'Au Ministre adoré.' They made an address to him; they said to him: 'May the people never be able to forget that it is thanks to Necker that they exist.' In a song he was called the 'vrai père du peuple,' as if this appellation, given previously to Louis XVI at the time of his visit to the capital, had been only a derision." *Histoire-Musée de la République Française*, 3rd ed., Paris (1857-58), vol. i, p. 68.

[37] *Bouquet présenté à M. Necker . . .* (46).

[38] In the second stanza, the Abbé gives a strange turn to the Henri-Louis analogy:

> Ce Monarque, cet Henri quatre,
> Devenu notre bon ami,
> Contre l'erreur a su se battre,
> Et reconquérir son Sully.

The song ends with praise to Necker, "the object of whose happiness is to make a Nation happy."

piness!" A paragraph on the Minister's return opens, "O divine man!" To the author of this prose tribute, the familiar Necker-Sully comparison is utterly inadequate: "The glory of Sully," he ventures to assure Necker, "is but a puff of smoke dissipated by your glory."[39]

Of course, in the reactionaries Necker had enemies, but they were cowed by the successful onrush of the Revolutionary movement. Although we have noted some criticism of Necker in June even on the part of the reformers,[40] it is safe to say that by the time of his recall in July few, if any, of the patriots regarded him critically, and none thought of damning him, which most of them were destined later to do.[41] Necker's pre-eminence in the summer of 1789 would thus seem even greater than ever, were it not that new luminaries were appearing on the horizon.

It was the Paris uprising which brought to the fore other popular leaders. As long as interest was limited to such matters as voting for the Estates General, overcoming the deficit, and so on, Necker could serve as the man of the hour. But when in July the Revolution became militant, worship of the soldier-leader was bound to obtain its share of emphasis. As a result, Lafayette began more and more to attract that sort of tribute which previously had been reserved almost exclusively for Necker.

It is also noteworthy that in the course of the July events, Paris had assumed the effective leadership of the Revolutionary cause. The result of this Parisian predominance, from the standpoint of hero worship, was that Bailly, mayor of the city and symbol of its leadership, came also to be regarded, to some extent, as a personification of the Revolutionary, or popular, will. But Bailly was overshadowed by Lafayette, and references to the mayor, therefore, will be somewhat incidental.

[39] *Entrée triomphante de M. Necker à l'Hôtel-de-Ville* . . . , pp. 1 and 3. (IV, C)
[40] In connection with the food shortage. See page 90, footnote 25.
[41] Concerning Necker's fall from grace at a later time, see page 242, footnote 4. The reaction may be dated from March, 1790, although in October, 1789, there was the isolated and abortive attack launched by Marat in No. 27 of his *Ami du Peuple* (for an interesting extract see *Actes de la Commune de Paris* . . . , vol. ii, p. 243). Earlier in the year even Marat, as revealed in his *Offrande à la Patrie*, had shared the prevailing admiration of Necker.

The sudden vogue of Lafayette[42] introduces interesting new elements (including a potential threat to Necker), without, however, fundamentally changing the ideological pattern of the initial phase of the Revolution; for, as an object of hero worship, Lafayette symbolized, just as did Necker, two opposing forces—the will of the King and that of the people. In short, one may still see persisting the dichotomy described in an earlier chapter. This twofold relationship is suggested in lyrics which appear in *The Gazette of the Markets*.[43]

One reads, in reference to Lafayette:

> François, partagez son courage,
> Et vous redevenez heureux;
> Votre bonheur est son ouvrage,
> Il est l'objet de tous ses voeux.[44]

Thus is Lafayette identified with the patriotic cause; while in another stanza he is similarly identified with Louis when it is alleged that he "has the confidence of the King," that he was in fact chosen by him, whereas he was chosen at first without royal authorization by the Paris Committee of Electors. The fiction of Lafayette's closeness to Louis is further emphasized in the following verses:

> Sage, courageux, Populaire,
> Et toujours l'ami de son Roi.[45]

Let us note, in passing, the capitalization of the word "Popular," which perhaps represents a quasi-personification of Lafayette as symbol of "the people," and has the effect of balancing the capitalization of the word "King." It may, therefore, not be taking too

[42] This vogue found expression in several patriotic songs. One of them, *Couplets à M. le Marquis de la Fayette, présent à la bénédiction des Drapeaux du District des Cordeliers, le 13 Août 1789* (50), pays tribute to Lafayette's part in the American Revolution, and pictures him as "the hero . . . of Liberty."

[43] *La Gazette des Halles, Dialogue, mêlé de chansons, pour ceux qui les aiment. No. 1er* (II, D). This brochure was printed at the expense of "les dames de la Place Maubert." The text suggests that women and children, as well as men, are ready to fight under the leadership of Lafayette. This curious document is, among other things, a rough and ready expression of feminism.

[44] *Ibid.*, p. 10, from *Chanson sur le brave La Fayette* (51). In *La Gazette des Halles . . .*, this song is divided in two parts, which are put to different airs. Though the *Gazette* as a whole is of the *genre poissard*, this piece is written in good French. The song was also published separately and intact in a *feuille volante*. Concerning these two editions see Bibliography I, 51.

[45] *Ibid.*, p. 11.

great a liberty to conclude that even in orthography, as in other slight and apparently accidental ways, are revealed the pretensions of the sovereignty of the people as against that of the Crown.

But we do not have to go to such lengths to discover that the joint worship of Lafayette and Louis represented a delicate balance of loyalties. This fact is explained by the actual situation. Lafayette, as commander of the Parisian troops, and Bailly, as mayor of the city, professed to be devoted supporters of the Crown, which, in a certain Revolutionary sense, they were. But, above all, they, like Necker, were props against any reactionary moves by the King, and in this sense were potentially his rivals.[46] A song by M. de la Boessière, already mentioned,[47] eloquently expresses this rivalry. Whereas the piece carries the subtitle, "Bouquet to the King," it opens with a dedication not to Louis, but to "M. Bailly, Mayor of the City of Paris, and to M. le Marquis de la Fayette, Commander General of the Parisian National Guard." The piece, as we have seen, is marked by expressions of excessive confidence in Louis and of sentimental devotion to him. But, like the Player Queen in *Hamlet*, M. de la Boessière doth protest too much. When such overemphasis occurs in expressions of Revolutionary enthusiasm, there is usually some accompanying theme to serve as a corrective. The song in question has its corrective in the final stanza, wherein Bailly and Lafayette are described as *auprès de Louis* and are hailed as being "the voices of the subjects of Paris and of all the Empire." It is these voices—in short, the voice of the nation—which share the ovation to the King. In fact, the "Bouquet to the King" ends just as it began, in being dedicated to the popular leaders.

Another song, which also celebrates the increasing popularity of Lafayette, is of interest in a more general connection. It consists of *Verses Sung to Madame la Marquise de La Fayette*, on September 22, 1789, "the day of the benediction of the Flag of the District of St.-Etienne-du-Mont,[48] following a dinner given by Monsieur the

---

[46] Mathiez, referring to this period, wrote that "Louis XVI was afraid of him [Lafayette], and treated him with respect." *The French Revolution*, p. 59.

[47] *Couplets pour la Saint-Louis 1789* (54). See pages 144-45.

[48] The reference is to the custom, which commenced in August, 1789, of blessing the colors of each new battalion in the church of its district. For a brief description of these ceremonies, in which religious and patriotic elements merged, see J. Tiersot, *Les fêtes et les chants de la Révolution française*, Paris, 1908, pp. 15-16.

Commander of the Battalion of this District," to which the Lafayettes had been invited as guests of honor.[49] This piece bears interesting testimony to the hold which the family relationship had on the French mind. Further evidence on this topic is perhaps not superfluous, for it is difficult for the modern reader, who is familiar with democratic forms and practices, to realize that the idea of popular sovereignty must at one time have seemed to entail a rather cold and forbidding concept. In a political democracy made up of individuals, each member of the body politic is a relatively independent and isolated unit; while in olden France, the unit tended to be not smaller than the family, which with all its extensions and retainers was often a considerable group. It was through the cooperation of heads of families, rather than individuals as such, that political cohesion was attained. Furthermore, social and political institutions, including the state, were built upon a patriarchal principle, and were, in a measure, projections of the family relationship. There was warmth in these ties, and something to lose in departing from them. Of course there was something to gain, too: new freedom, and indeed a new warmth, for the human heart found a way to emotionalize even so vast a concept as that of popular sovereignty. But in the first striving for a new political orientation the family concept frequently recurs, to lend to the patriotic cause the comfort of its intimacy and charm.

In the song addressed to Madame de Lafayette at the St.-Etienne-du-Mont reception, one may find a delightful instance of how this intimate sense of the family could be projected into the whole realm of human relationships—as a summary of each of the five stanzas of the song, together with the quotation of significant lines, may serve to suggest:[50]

First stanza: It is implied that all the guests are regarded as the family of Lafayette, and it appears accordingly that "his wife, in our midst, is with her family."

---

[49] The Marquis was absent, but his wife and son attended.

[50] *Couplets chantés à Madame la Marquise de la Fayette . . .* (58). The leaflet which contains this song was consulted at the British Museum. No copy of it is known to exist elsewhere. The piece is by Ducray du Minil, who signed himself "a member of several literary societies," and who was a corporal in the battalion of St.-Etienne-du-Mont.

Second stanza: Lafayette's family consists of all humanity—

> Toujours embrâzé par l'honneur,
> Quand le crime ravage ou pille,
> S'il entend le cri du malheur,
> Par-tout est sa famille!

Third stanza: Lafayette has inherited the shining virtues of the great generals of France, of Saxe, Turenne, Villars—in that sense he is of the same family as they.

Fourth stanza: Madame de Lafayette is to be adored, it would seem, as a universal mother—

> Près d'elle le pauvre est joyeux,
> L'orpheline est soudain sa fille!
> Protectrice des malheureux,
> Ils sont tous sa famille!

Fifth stanza: This concluding stanza contains a tribute to the sons of the general and to his wife, that is, to the Lafayette family itself.

Such sentiments clearly illustrate the adaptation of the family ideal of the old regime to the philosophic humanitarianism of the eighteenth century and to the Revolution itself. The replacement of the traditional sense of solidarity through family ties by the new notion of relatedness through common citizenship was evidently gradual. The stresses and strains of this transition—which no doubt played an important part in the evolution of political democracy— have apparently not been made the subject of a systematic study.[51]

In lines which serve as a sort of epilogue of the song considered above, the author declares that upon seeing the sons of Lafayette, the new generation will exclaim,

> "Voilà ses Enfans précieux,
> Dont le père a sauvé la France!"

As we have observed in the case of Necker, homage of this extravagant sort reflected the patriots' sense of utter dependence on leaders. Lafayette perhaps had no intention of assuming the role of "savior." But once he begins to fulfill this function in popular ex-

[51] A background for such a study has been provided by Funck-Brentano in his *L'Ancien Régime*, Paris, 1926.

pectations, he promises to become *the* man of the Revolution; and, thereby, is presaged the eclipse of Necker, who had amply served the first purposes of the popular movement as *dieu tutélaire*.

By a sympathetic approach we have attempted to understand the patriots, not only in respect to their outward acts, but also from the standpoint of their inner motivations. In this way one may appreciate to a certain extent the attitude of individuals, as distinguished from the mere outward forms of mass behavior. Similarly one could make a meticulous analysis of the attitude of any of the leaders concerning whom there is abundant knowledge. This in general would take us beyond the scope of the present work, but at least something may be said here concerning the character of the King, who served as a symbol of the old order and in a measure as a guarantor of the new. The purpose of the brief commentary which follows will be to consider Louis as the creature of his environment, and especially to examine the effect on him of the Enlightenment.

Historians have found no difficulty in demonstrating that in the pre-Revolutionary period of his reign Louis XVI experimented with "enlightened despotism." His prompt appointment of the physiocrat Turgot as Minister (1774) is obviously a case in point. Other evidences appear in such undertakings or designs as were mentioned early in the present work in connection with the royal program.[52] But Turgot lasted only two years, and Louis' abandonment of that staunch reformer clearly signified a faltering attachment to the ideas of rational reform. Eventually—so conventional accounts would have it—Louis succumbed to old-regime influences, to a reactionary Court, and to his own personal traits of character. Notable among these last were kindness, indolence, and an allegedly congenital inability to decide or to act. These traits, it is said, became glaring defects under the critical stresses and strains of 1789-1792. Every chronicler of the period seems to dwell on Louis' incapacity; as if to seal the matter, his most recent biographer adduces the phrase "as helpless as a paralytic."[53] But when

[52] See pages 38-40.
[53] S. K. Padover in *The Life and Death of Louis XVI* (New York, 1939), which is based in part on new material.

such personal qualities or attributes are offered as first causes in Louis' tragic career—as the *given* data—they serve only to describe, but hardly to explain, Louis' character.

What remains to be shown—and to be shown systematically—is that while Louis partially abandoned the Enlightenment on its analytical, or more rational, side, he became progressively a product of the emotional or sentimental impulses of that movement. Indeed, certain of his traits which are traditionally pictured as personal—and hence purely individual—may, it seems to me, be understood as an expression of that vast system of feeling that undermined the intellectual and social conventions of the old regime.

Here one thinks of the movement associated with the name of Rousseau, and the question arises as to its influence on one who wore the crown. That there ever was such a positive influence may at first glance seem unlikely; for how obvious it is that the external defenses of the Bourbon monarchy were assailed and finally destroyed by the inflamed disciples of a part of Rousseau's political doctrine! Yet, at the same time, one may contend that in a definitely personal way Louis' resistance was undermined in advance—that His Majesty's resolution was deflected, if not captivated, by certain other aspects of the doctrine of that vagabond philosopher.

The precise role of Rousseau, however, is immaterial. If not influenced directly by his preachments, was not Louis then conditioned by the larger climate of opinion which was conducive to Rousseau's own growth and to the wide acceptance of his work? Such was the experience of the Queen, who plainly exhibited her own susceptibility. But Marie Antoinette externalized her love of Nature, of peasant things, of simple, honest ways, in a place apart and as a pastime. Her revolt against the formalism of Versailles, however conspicuous, was superficial. The rustic retreat which she created, the Petit Trianon, charmed her transiently with new opportunities of expression, but left her no more a peasant and no less a Hapsburg than before.

Her husband seems to have felt deeply the influences which touched her only lightly. Less robust, less capricious, and less outgiving, he continued to engage in solitary hobbies or conventional pleasures, and dully to act what he conceived to be the role of king. But he was no less inconvenienced by the restraints of a moribund tradition than Marie Antoinette. For him, too, the prevailing cult of Nature offered an escape; but whereas the Queen found in that cult aesthetic satisfaction, Louis' response was essentially in the moral sphere. He, too, it would seem, devised a retreat—not, however, in outward form, but hidden in the heart—a wondrous world of Nature, in which affections rule mankind and find their consummation in devotion to the ruler. Here was the bright new world of eighteenth-century sentimentalism: society a single family requiring only gentle guidance; its ruler a father whose divine right it was not so much to command as to be loved.

This was the prevalent faith, and it seems that even royalty could not resist it. There are many evidences that such was the case; some have been mentioned in preceding pages. The evidences, to be sure, are mostly circumstantial, because, as a rule, there is no way to demonstrate that official words or acts correspond to inner convictions. But even circumstantial evidence gathers weight when sufficiently recurrent. Besides, there are moments of spontaneous behavior which are particularly revealing.

In this connection an anecdote is worth recalling. It relates to Louis' reception at the Hôtel de Ville on July 17. One may remark in passing that Louis' anomalous position was disclosed on a placard newly hung above the portals; it proclaimed him "King of a Free People."[54] In the course of this visit of "reconciliation," when all was expected to go exceedingly well, the King suddenly found himself in disagreement with the Paris electors. A moment of embarrassment followed. Louis, given a chance to improve the situation, could only blurt out, "You can count upon my affection."[55]

At the same gathering, Count Lally-Tollendal had made a congratulatory speech to the King. Contained therein was the following passage, which may be regarded as a notable exposition of the new statescraft:

And since, surpassing the virtues of his predecessors, he [Louis] has wished to entrust his power and his majesty to our love, to be obeyed only by love, to be protected only by love, let us be neither less sensitive nor less generous than our King, and let us prove to him that even

[54] The inscription read, "Louis XVI, le Père des Français, le Roi d'un Peuple libre."

[55] As the author of an excellent recent work ventures to observe, "The words were sincerely meant." J. M. Thompson, in *The French Revolution*, New York, 1945, p. 69.

his power, even his majesty, have gained more, by a thousand times, than they have sacrificed.[56]

It is not to be thought that Louis was unaffected by reiterations of this view, which indeed created a pervasive atmosphere. To the very considerable extent that Louis was susceptible to the new ideals, he actually was the Louis that the patriots embodied in their praise. There was thus in what I have called the popular myth of his leadership, a considerable element of reality. No student of ideas will be surprised that such was the case, for myths are never what they so often seem—products of pure imagination, but are always derived from human experience, which, in turn, they tend to shape. While, on occasion, outwardly fulfilling the expectations of the patriots, Louis appears in a measure to have been satisfying the demands of his own reformed nature. Accordingly, we may presume that he shared to some extent the inner conflict of the patriots, who welcomed the new, but could not altogether depart from the old.

No doubt a certain weakness of character accounts in the first instance for Louis' having succumbed to the widely prevalent and seductive atmosphere of sentimentalism. The result in his case was bound to be fatal, because eighteenth-century sentimentalism was anti-authoritarian in spirit and feeling. It was suited in a measure to saints, but not at all to monarchs. It is quite understandable that such an involvement should appear to have had paralyzing effects.

This characterization is confirmed when we look beyond 1789. Throughout the trials of the Revolution, the King recurrently trusted to sentiment. In so far as he wished to make secure his leadership of the Revolutionary forces (and this possibility ever strongly attracted him), sentiment was his primary recourse; whenever it seemed to fail, as increasingly it did, he plotted treasonably against the patriots and even against France.[57] But one can sense

<hr />

[56] *Moniteur*, vol. i, p. 87; and *Archives parlementaires*, vol. viii, p. 247.

[57] As early as October, 1789, Louis began to plot against the Revolution, while promising it his support. At that time he sent a secret agent to his cousin the King of Spain, advising him in advance that he (Louis) would regard as null and void any steps which he might take under pressure. On the basis of this and subsequent evidences of duplicity, it can of course be argued that Louis was at no time sincere, but was simply pretending to approve the popular cause by way of playing for time. This view, though perhaps plausible, seems to me superficial. Certainly such derelictions must be considered as part of a much larger picture, which, for one thing, reveals Louis as halfhearted or inhibited in almost all of his anti-Revolutionary moves.

at the basis of this duplicity a great measure of confusion (Louis was ever being advised from all quarters) and of desperation. It is difficult to tell where Louis placed the greater faith: in the paternalism of *sensibilité,* or in the old patriarchal authority which the reactionaries wished him to uphold. There was much vacillation between the two. His devious efforts to preserve the old order are now obvious—the record having been exposed—but quite as striking is the attachment which he showed to the popular cause. No matter how trying the circumstances of the antimonarchal movement or how unruly the mob, Louis seems to have gained comfort from the crowd (his children) if they showed any evidence of good will, and he displayed remarkable forbearance on occasions when they scorned or imperiled him. At the time of his trial and in the hour of his death, he exhibited no enmity.

Perhaps such circumstances explain why many French to this day, though renouncing Louis as a traitor, remember him as a martyr. Without acknowledging the paradox, they sense the sorry situation. Neither the King nor his "free People" could be steadfast to the love they had proclaimed, and in the important field of the emotions they had created no other basis for the survival of the monarchy.

VII

WHILE in the summer of 1789 the Revolutionary leaders at Versailles and Paris were announcing that France had been saved, uprisings in the provinces continued. In some instances they were vigorously suppressed. One reads of 20 persons killed and 60 held prisoner in one locality; of 100 killed and 170 taken prisoner in another rural area.[1] In the towns, too, there were outbreaks and retaliation; in Mâcon, for example, twenty rioters were condemned to death. Violence was sometimes directed against members of the upper middle class as well as against the nobility; Mathiez goes so far as to describe the disturbances in Dauphiné as "class war."[2] There were thus some early indications that the Revolutionary party might itself split according to divergent economic interests.

To some extent, these uprisings throughout France represented a concerted reaction to the example which Paris had given; but they were in a measure sporadic. Such disorders—together with various rumors of reactionary conspiracies, of possible foreign intervention, and of ill-defined dangers—created the almost nation-wide panic known as "the Great Fear."

The National Assembly had done nothing to meet the situation, but by midsummer many of its members, especially those of the Third Estate, were ready for measures of repression. The lead, however, was suddenly taken—and taken in a quite different direction—by a group of liberal nobles. One of them, the Vicomte de Noailles,[3] proposed, on the night of August 4, that the Assembly abolish tax exemptions enjoyed by privileged groups, put an end to feudal dues on land (subject to compensation), and wipe away all feudal survivals of personal servitude. These were amazing proposals. The nobles were being asked to give away privileges that had existed in their families for centuries. Although feudal dues on property were to be redeemed in cash, and thus much of the burden of the feudal system would remain in a modified form, Noailles' sweeping offer involved great concessions in the way of justice and freedom for the peasants. Liberal nobles, including the

---

[1] Cited in Mathiez, *The French Revolution*, p. 51.   [2] *Loc.cit.*
[3] He was Lafayette's brother-in-law.

Duc d'Aiguillon and the Duc de Châtelet, approved the proposals; and then there followed an outburst of unprecedented generosity. Landowners rose to surrender their hunting rights and their exemption from taxation; members of the clergy clamored for the opportunity to yield tithes and fees; spokesmen for cities surrendered ancient charter rights; and favored provinces abandoned ancient privileges. In all, some thirty resolutions were passed. The session, which had commenced at eight in the evening, lasted into the following morning. Ordinary restraints were abandoned. Some members embraced one another; some wept. The business of that night promised to transform much of the economic and social structure of France. The members of the Assembly, however, were not ready to accept full responsibility. After taking the initiative in matters of the most far-reaching importance—and doing so without at all waiting upon the King—they brought their session to a close by passing a resolution which proclaimed Louis XVI the "Restorer of French liberty."[4]

The decisions so hastily taken were reconsidered at subsequent sessions and were largely embodied in the famous decree of August 11. Many of the far-reaching changes were not to take effect at once (for example, although tithes were abolished in principle, payment of them was to be continued until some other means of support for the Church could be found); and what promised to be the most important gain of all—the liberation of the land from feudal dues—was bound to be illusory for most peasants as long as they were confronted by the requirement of cash compensation.

Such qualifications, which soon enough seemed inappropriate and irksome, were not at first heeded, because the decree of August 11 included a statement that the Assembly "completely abolishes the feudal system."[5] This sweeping claim caught the imagination of most Frenchmen and was taken by them as the key to the whole matter.

[4] This appellation was literally "wished on" the King. He had no enthusiasm for the decrees, presented for his approval on August 13. It was not until September 20, and then only reluctantly, that he appeared to give them his sanction, and it was considerably later, November 3, when he finally promulgated them.

[5] Actually, the decrees destroyed only a part (reckoned by Elton, *The Revolutionary Idea* . . . , p. 32, at about a third) of the burden of the feudal dues, and the peasants were not entirely relieved of them until 1793. For a survey of the subject, see A. Aulard, *La Révolution français et la régime féodal*, Paris, 1919, p. 106 to end.

One would think that the session of August 4 would have occasioned patriotic songs to celebrate what appeared at first as the veritable end of the old order. But such, so far as one can determine, was not the case. At least, no one of the songs of 1789 that have come to my attention bears evidence of having been directly inspired by the event. Whereas there may have been such pieces of which all record has been lost in the course of time, it is not likely that many songs of considerable popularity would have altogether disappeared. It is, therefore, perhaps safe to assume that the lyrists did not generally celebrate the August decrees. No doubt, one reason for this apparent dearth of material was that popular expectations had already anticipated official procedure. Before its action on August 4, the Assembly had been advised that revolution in the provinces was already a *fait accompli*: "The taxes, the feudal dues, are all extinct; the laws are without force, the magistrates without authority."[6] Even if allowance is made for exaggeration in this report, it is clear that French subjects had rejected the feudal basis of society before the legislators turned dramatically, but belatedly, to their great reform.

Another event of epoch-making importance in the summer of 1789 was the passage by the National Assembly of the Declaration of the Rights of Man. This was a declaration of principles which was to precede the Constitution that the Assembly had promised France and that was just then in the making. As time went on, the Assembly passed separate provisions for the new plan of government, but the work on the Constitution itself progressed slowly, and over two years elapsed before the task was completed. The Declaration of Rights, however, was subjected to no such delay. Various committees prepared drafts, and by August 20 the Assembly turned to the plans that had been submitted. The final product, which was something of a composite, was completed on August 26.

When the Declaration appeared it was heralded by its sponsors as "the Catechism of the Nation."[7] It expressed the main political tenets of eighteenth-century philosophy: "Men are born and re-

---

[6] From the statement of Salomon, on behalf of the *Comité des rapports*, evening session of August 3. *Moniteur*, vol. i, p. 135.

[7] Credit for devising this slogan belongs to Barnave, according to Louis Blanc. *Histoire de la Révolution française*, Paris, ed. 1878, vol. iii, p. 311.

main free and equal in rights." "The essence of all sovereignty resides in the nation." "Law is the expression of the general will." Property was listed as one of several "natural and inalienable rights of man." Various past wrongs, such as arbitrary imprisonment and excessive punishment, were prohibited. Liberty of speech and liberty of the press, subject to definition by law, were proclaimed. Freedom of religion was granted in rather qualified terms. Aside from a few definite prohibitions, the document consists mostly of generalities, which, as seen by a modern historian, were at the time "little more than revolutionary propaganda."[8] Possibly the ringing phrases of the Declaration constituted all-too-effective propaganda. In any case, some of them became an embarrassment to the members of the Assembly, who by and large had no intention that all the words of the Declaration be taken too literally. As Madelin says, the legislators put the "catechism" in a tabernacle and drew a curtain over it.[9] But they could not suppress it. According to Challamel, the Declaration was reprinted in forty successive editions.[10]

This publicizing, however, did not begin at once, and again the lyrists seem to have been strangely silent. Although the Declaration of Rights was presently to serve as a charter of liberties and to have great educational influence, only one of the songs of 1789, as far as I have been able to determine, was written to celebrate its passage: *The French Constitution and the Rights of Man, Patriotic Song*, by M. S., National Guard of the Saint-Gervais District,[11] published in Paris, in "the First Year of Liberty."[12] The text con-

[8] L. R. Gottschalk, *The Era of the French Revolution*, Boston, 1929, p. 144.

[9] Madelin, *The French Revolution*, p. 98.

[10] Challamel, *Histoire-musée* . . . , vol. i, p. 77. There were, besides, many expositions of the significance of the Declaration. Some of these patriotic writings were naïve and even fatuous, and provided anti-Revolutionary writers ample opportunity for travesty. The best known of their satires is Marchant's *La Constitution en vaudeville, suivie des Droits de l'homme, de la femme et de plusieurs autres vaudevilles constitutionnels, Paris . . . 1792*. (III, F)

[11] *La Constitution française* . . . (55). Two other pieces concerning the Declaration of Rights are attributed by Constant Pierre to 1789, but apparently they did not appear until 1792, or 1791 at the earliest. For consideration of these songs, see Appendix A, 214 and 215.

[12] 1789. Some writers dated the "first year" of liberty from July 14, while others regarded it as having commenced at the outset of 1789. This conception of the Revolution, as marking the dawn of a new era, at first caught the fancy of only the more ardent patriots. It is an interesting presage of the *calendrier républicain*, which offi-

sists of paraphrases of some of the more important principles of the Declaration, to which were added patriotic reflections presumably inspired by the document.

Two stanzas are of particular interest. In the first of these the author suggests—it is difficult to say how deliberately—the paradox that was inherent in the principle of liberty:

> L'homme est né libre,
> Tous sont égaux en droits;
> Tous peuvent suivre
> Leurs penchans et leurs choix,
> Mais doivent vivre
> Sous l'empire des lois.[13]

The problem implied in these verses is the reconciliation of liberty and law. Out of the Revolutionary doctrine of equality arose conflicting claims of individual self-expression and of submission to collective authority. The claims in both these directions tended to be absolute; and it was often in this doctrinaire sense that the Revolutionists were encouraged to follow "leurs penchans et leurs choix" and at the same time to live under an "empire des lois." Many patriots at this time envisaged freedom in both liberty and law,[14] without foreseeing that through an excess of one or the other, either liberty or law, or both, might be lost. The author of *The French Constitution and the Rights of Man* was thus pointing to a fundamental dilemma, which necessitated unforeseen compromises as the Revolution progressed.

Toward the end of the song there is a stanza which relates significantly to the growing spirit of militarism:

> De la Patrie
> Chacun est le soldat,
> Et de sa vie,
> Pour soutenir l'Etat,

---

cially replaced the Christian calendar in 1793. According to it, the new era commenced with the establishment of the Republic, September 22, 1792.

[13] *La Constitution française* . . . (55), stanza 2.

[14] In the passage quoted above, law appears as a check on liberty. In patriotic writings, the law is more frequently contrasted with the arbitrariness of the Court or with other abuses of the old regime, and, as such, represents a positive aspect of liberty.

Avec furie,
Va courir au combat.[15]

This prospect of battle is followed by assurances of peace, and the
final emphasis of the song is on the "happiness of the French" that
is to be attained by future decrees.[16] The text thus embodies a
confusion of ideas which appears as an important and integral part
of the Revolutionary enthusiasm. The patriots were comforted by
the joyous sense of peace on earth and good will to all men, while
at the same time their blood tingled at the not-altogether-disagree-
able prospect of a call to arms.

A matter of interest may be mentioned in connection with the
third article of the Declaration, which asserted that "the essence of
all sovereignty resides in the nation." This claim had been an impressive part of Rousseau's political doctrine, and implicit in it
was a threat—largely unrecognized at first—to every throne. There
soon developed in connection with this principle a Revolutionary
conception of high treason. Traditionally, criminal disloyalty to
the state had gone under the appellation of *lèse-majesté*, an attack
on the public safety being considered an attack against the King,
in whom all sovereignty resided. Since kingship was conceived
of as divine in its origin, such an offense was sacrilege. On the eve
of the Revolution, proponents of popular government appro-
priated this historic conception to their own use by coining
the word *lèse-nation*.[17] A few days after the capture of the Bastille,
the Assembly removed treason from the jurisdiction of the King,
and took official cognizance of the new term by decreeing that
crimes of *lèse-nation* were the concern of the representatives.[18] By

---

[15] *La Constitution française* . . . (55), stanza 16. These lines were presumably
prompted by Article XII of the Declaration, which states that: "The security of the
rights of man and of the citizen requires public military forces. These forces are,
therefore, established for the good of all. . . ."

[16] *Ibid.*, last stanza.

[17] It is clear that contemporaries were at first uncertain how best to suggest the
sanctity of the new nation. Such terms as *lèse-patrie*, *lèse-liberté*, and *lèse-humanité*
—as well as *lèse-nation*—appear in the *cahiers*. (Hyslop, *French Nationalism in 1789*
. . . , pp. 159-60.) These alternative terms did not at once disappear. One may come
across *lèse-humanité* in the second number of the *Révolutions de Paris*, (*du 18 au 25
juillet, 1789*), p. 30. *Lèse-patrie* was more common; for use of this term at two of the
federations in the summer of 1789, see quoted matter in Aulard, *Le patriotisme français*, pp. 138 and 152.

[18] July 23, 1789. By decrees passed on October 14 and 20 of the same year, the
Assembly transferred jurisdiction over "crimes of *lèse-nation*" provisionally to the
court of the Chatelet.

implication, this hybrid term seemed to enthrone the nation in place of His Majesty. Here is another interesting instance of how the patriots sought to sanctify the new order in terms of the old. At the same time, they had coined a word which served as a challenge to the King. In this respect, *lèse-nation* was a slogan. It served a useful purpose only so long as the rivalry between royal sovereignty and popular sovereignty remained acute. Once the conflict was decided in favor of the people—that is, by 1792—the term disappeared, so far as I am able to discover, from the French language.[19]

If it is true that the lyrists largely ignored the Declaration of Rights at the time of its passage—as appears to have been the case—then their indifference may be explained, at least in part, by the general situation. Here again, as with the abolition of feudalism, the legislators were in the train, not in the vanguard, of the most articulate and aggressive Revolutionary opinion. As for the mass of the people—especially the peasants—it was only gradually, and as a result of systematic indoctrination in subsequent months, and even years, that they came to realize the substance and full implications of the Declaration.

It may be that such a document was prematurely delivered; that the flame of popular enthusiasm needed to be dampened, rather than fanned, by the leaders of France. Mirabeau, at any rate, thought so. When the Declaration first came up for consideration, he favored postponement. "It is a veil," he said, "which it is imprudent to raise all at once."[20] Other leaders, alarmed by the disorders throughout France, had suggested that it might be well to have a Declaration of Duties. Malouet correctly prophesied a conservative reaction in the Assembly (without, however, foreseeing its failure) when, in counseling against the Declaration, he asked this question: "Why transport a man to the summit of a mountain, there to show him all the kingdom of his rights, when we are obliged, afterwards, to make him descend, to assign him bound-

---

[19] Though *lèse-nation* is a term of definite historical interest, little or no notice appears to have been taken of it. The word is not included in P. Larousse, *Grand dictionnaire universel du XIXᵉ siècle*, or in *La grande encyclopédie*, nor do I find mention of it in any similar works of reference that I have consulted.

[20] This quotation and the one from Malouet which follows are taken from C. D. Hazen, *The French Revolution*, vol. i, p. 277.

aries, and to cast him back into the real world where he will find restrictions at every step?"

The National Assembly itself, as we shall see in a later chapter, was quick to assign "boundaries" in certain all-important matters— such as those pertaining to the suffrage and eligibility for office.

In general, however, the representatives concentrated on the demolition of the old barriers, and gave their encouragement to the program of creating—overnight, as it were—a new France. There was need, first of all, to put into practice the great principle of equality before the law. Not long after passing the Declaration, the Assembly enacted the beginnings of an enlightened criminal code.[21] Somewhat later, November 3, it swept away the upper structure of the old judiciary—which had become a particular object of patriotic scorn[22]—by suspending the *Parlements*, or higher courts of the realm.[23] The representatives thus cleared the way for eventual reform, but their elimination of the *Parlements* left in the judicial area a void which it took some time to fill.[24]

In the administrative area an even more crucial void developed. The principal royal agents throughout France, the *intendants*, at once hampered by local assemblies and on occasion intimidated, for the most part ceased to function—if not in July, at least by August. The Assembly had no effective remedy to offer for the disintegration which inevitably resulted.[25] The effects of this disintegration were serious indeed, even if one considers only the matter of

[21] "Décret de l'Assemblée Nationale sur la réformation de quelques points de la Jurisprudence criminelle," in *Procès-verbal . . . , des 8 & 9 octobre 1789*, vol. v.

[22] Several of the songs reflect this view, for example: *Hymne en l'honneur de la Résurrection . . .* (3), stanza 37; *Cahier du Marquis de Fulvy* (4), stanza 9; *Motion des Harangères [sic] . . .* (15), stanza 3; *Nouveau pot-pourri . . .* (18), stanzas 7 and 8; *Le voile leve* (59), stanzas 9 and 10.

[23] In legal language, they were ordered to remain *en vacances*. The *Parlement* of Paris was abolished in May, 1790; the *parlements* of the provinces, in September of the following year.

[24] A report projecting a new system of courts was read to the Assembly before the close of 1789 (by Thouret, on behalf of the Committee on the Constitution, December 22), but the work was not completed until 1791.

[25] On November 11, 1789, the National Assembly promised a "new division of the kingdom," and on December 22 it voted the first of measures which, in the following year, replaced the irregular and overlapping jurisdictions of the old regime with new and relatively uniform *departments* and with similarly uniform subdivisions. The scheme encouraged a vast amount of activity in local government, but it did not provide for centralized control. In short, it afforded no corrective for the disintegration of national authority which took place in the summer of 1789.

revenue—for tax collection, as will presently appear, was practically impossible almost from the beginning of the new regime. All in all, we see the representatives abandoning (in effect, if not always by intention) the old controls—judicial, financial, administrative—without establishing for the new order any equivalent authority.

VIII CAPTURE OF THE KING

A PRESAGE of a famous event in the history of the French Revolution occurred in the last two days of August, 1789, when two radical leaders, Saint-Huruge and Desmoulins, tried to lead fellow Parisians to Versailles to enforce certain popular demands and to bring the King and the Assembly back to Paris. The proposed march to Versailles found many advocates, and was thwarted only with great difficulty by the soldiers of the National Guard. One thing which had aroused the radicals was the King's failure to approve the August decrees abolishing the feudal system. Louis, apparently, had not been flattered into acquiescence by being proclaimed the "Restorer of French Liberty." He was more concerned with restoring some measure of his own authority. Another provocation was the proposal of certain members of the Assembly to give to the King the power of an absolute veto over legislation. The radicals at Paris were convinced that both the King and the Assembly were falling under the influence of the aristocrats; and they believed that, lest they lose their newly won liberties, they must resort to direct action.

Not only the extremists, but all Frenchmen, were disturbed by the political uncertainty which continued to confront them. The new Constitution, promised in June, was only beginning to come into being two months later, and the future course that France was to follow remained still to be determined. It was at first supposed that the creation of a just frame of government, to replace the arbitrary regime of old, would serve to unite all citizens. When, however, the National Assembly turned in August and September to the task of formulating definite provisions of the Constitution, the rivalry between the aristocrats and the commoners became increasingly intense, and—what is even more significant—the Revolutionary party itself split into two camps. There were now the "moderates," led by Jean-Joseph Mounier, and the so-called "patriots" (or enragés, as their enemies called them) led by Duport, Barnave, and the brothers Lameth. The extreme left—represented by Robespierre, Pétion, and others—for the time being adhered to the party which was opposing Mounier, who, in addition to being leader of the "moderates," was prominent as chairman of the Committee on the Constitution. Mounier, though a sincere reformer, believed in preserving a strong measure of monarchical power and gave many evidences of distrusting popular government.

The question of ultimate sovereignty surpassed all other matters in importance.[1] Was the King to have a veto over legislation, or were laws of the new National Assembly to stand, regardless of the King's wish? If the former—if the King were to be put in a position to block reform by his veto—what had been gained by the uprising? What of the Revolution? If the latter—if there were to be no check on the ill-advised measures that a popular body might approve— what of the restraints of tradition and experience? What of the King? Mounier, in this matter as in others, was on the conservative side. He proposed that the King be given the power of an absolute veto. It is an interesting fact that Mirabeau, at times a radical leader, sided with him. But not so the great majority of patriots. The Paris populace, especially, was alarmed at the prospect of a strong monarchy. The agitators of the Palais Royal denounced the veto and all who favored it. The journalist Loustallot warned his readers that the granting of such power by the Assembly would "hurl us all back into the chains of slavery."[2] He later expressed his alarm in the form of a question: "What! shall a single man be able to suspend and enchain the will of the nation?"[3]

At the same time there was scarcely a patriot—even among the radicals—who would have dispensed with the King;[4] in fact, most of them still had a mystic reverence for the throne. The Assembly appeared to agree with the words spoken on September 1 by Rabaut Saint-Etienne: "They [the French] revere the benevolent prince whom they have proclaimed the restorer of French liberty. It is to the consolation of the throne [vers le trône consolateur] that the eyes of afflicted people always turn; and whatever may be the evils under which they groan, a word, a single word, the magic

[1] Also of great importance was the question whether the new legislature should be composed of one or two chambers. The Committee favored the bicameral system. But on September 10, 1789, an overwhelming majority of the Assembly voted against it. There were many reasons for this decision, chief of which was the belief that an upper chamber might become the stronghold of privilege.

[2] Révolutions de Paris, September 6, 1789, no. viii, p. 8.   [3] Ibid., p. 29.

[4] Concerning isolated evidences of antimonarchial sentiment, see p. 101, note 57.

charm of which can be explained only by their love—the paternal name of king—suffices to restore their hope."[5] It is perhaps literally, as well as symbolically, true that only the blade of the guillotine, which on January 21, 1793, sent Louis to his death, severed the hold which monarchial sovereignty had on the imagination of living Frenchmen. Arrogation to themselves of ultimate sovereignty was the one thing of which the Revolutionists of this period stood in awe, and which they consistently evaded.

Their inhibition in this regard was rooted in the depths of man's inner being, as a brief comment on the larger implications of the subject may suggest. Ultimate sovereignty, involving final responsibility for decisions of life and death, is historically a godlike attribute. In its origin, sovereign power was associated with magic, in historic times with the divine right of the king.[6] In the "universal" order of Medieval Catholicism, we find an interesting application of the same principle. The absolute power over life and death claimed by the Church was attributed to its divine mission and to the possession by the pope of "the keys of Saint Peter." Who was Man—countless ages would have asked—that he should assume the awesome responsibility of ultimate sovereignty? It was in the realm of the Church that the first great daring to do so occurred in modern times. The Protestant Reformation, with its attack upon the

[5] Cited in Aulard, *Histoire politique de la Révolution française*, Paris, 1921, p. 53.

[6] The subject is summarized by R. M. MacIver, in *The Modern State*, Oxford, 1926, pp. 8-9: "The nature of sovereignty . . . is surrounded by a halo that dates back to the tribal reverence which alone, in primitive ages, could sanction the obedience it must command. It is said that men died of shock on hearing of the execution of Charles I and of Louis XVI, just as savage man perished when they unwittingly broke the taboo surrounding the chief and his belongings [footnote, p. 9: "Striking examples of this savage reverence are given in Lang's *Magic and Religion*, as also in Frazer's *Golden Bough*"]. This magic of sovereignty became transformed into legal prerogative, divine origin passing into divine right. When that proud title fell in turn from the relaxing grasp of monarchism, it was transferred from the person to *the incarnate state*. The mystic name that had exalted the obvious reality of the king now crowned a being as mystic as itself, *the omnipotent majesty of the state*." The author adds that "the new sovereign dwelt apart in the shadowy realm of abstraction."

The italics are mine, for I wish to enlarge on the significance of these two phrases as they relate to the French Revolution. Thinking in terms of this particular era of transition, one might say that sovereignty was transferred from the person (of the King) not merely to an "incarnate state," but to *the people* who composed it; and that the mystic name (of divine right) now crowned "the omnipotent majesty" of *the individual*. Furthermore, from the standpoint of what the Revolutionists themselves thought and felt, the new sovereign dwelt not "apart in the shadowy realm of abstraction," but in the flesh-and-blood citizenry of France.

hierarchy of the priesthood and the absolutism of the Renaissance popes, tended, at least at the outset, to place the ultimate moral responsibility on the individual, and marked the rediscovery of God in man. Something analogous happened in the era of the French Revolution; and this leads us to its deepest significance. *The transition from royal sovereignty by divine right to popular sovereignty by innate right* was the core of the Revolution in France and the gist of its message to the peoples of other nations in Europe.

When in August and September, 1789, the French patriots faced the question of the veto power of the King, they were in varying degrees aware of this fundamental issue of sovereignty. But the issue was bound for the time being to remain unresolved, for among the zealous reformers who rejected France's traditional reliance on kingship, there were few who could accept without inhibitions the alternative of popular sovereignty.[7] Under the circumstances a compromise over the veto was inevitable. After heated argument—which was echoed and intensified in the press— the Assembly voted, on September 11, that the King could veto any piece of legislation of which he disapproved; that if the same measure were passed by a subsequent session of the legislature, he could still disallow it by his veto; but that if the measure were passed by a third session of the legislature, it would then become law, regardless of the King's approval or disapproval. This ingenious compromise, adopted as a provision of the new Constitution by 673 to 325 votes,[8] was called the "suspensive veto."

The measure applied obviously to simple legislative acts. Did it apply, also, to the fundamental laws then in the process of enactment—that is, to the Constitution itself? Was the King to have a

[7] At least in practice. We know that the Assembly had avowed in the Declaration of Rights that "the principle of all sovereignty resides essentially in the nation." A month later, September 23, it passed as an article of the Constitution a similar aphorism: "All powers emanate from the nation, and can emanate only from it." These were brave words; they were triumphs of the intellect, but did not have sufficient tap roots in the soil of popular conviction to make the revolution which they implied immediately real. It should be added, too, that such professions were not as democratic as they sounded. The National Assembly, which contained no representatives of the lower classes, understood by "the nation" not the people as a whole, but, in the words of Aulard (*op.cit.*, p. 55), "a new privileged class, which we call the bourgeoisie."

[8] Those who opposed were partly conservatives, who would have given the King an absolute veto; partly radicals, who objected to his having any veto power at all.

suspensive veto over its provisions? An unforgettable event in June had been the Tennis Court Oath, by which the Assembly had sworn to give a Constitution to France. In the light of this resolve, it was unthinkable that the King would now be permitted to sweep aside the promised Constitution by his veto, or that he would be allowed even suspensively to delay it. And yet the Assembly refrained from making a precise declaration on the subject. The Committee on the Constitution was the first to hedge. Mounier, its spokesman, advised against raising the question. Mirabeau, sharing the view held by most of his colleagues (that enactment of the fundamental law did not depend upon the King's approval), nevertheless felt that this truth was "dangerous to enunciate." One may detect in the high-flown language which Mirabeau used at the moment an indication of his embarrassment; he remarked that the Assembly (in refraining from declaring that the King had no power in the matter) had cast *un voile religieux* over "the great truth that a constitution has no need of being sanctioned."[9] What the Assembly actually did was to decree, October 1, that the articles of the Constitution, when voted, and the Declaration of Rights as well, would be "presented for the acceptance of the King." This meant, as Aulard was at pains to point out, that in the matter of fundamental law the King could not apply a veto, that the Constitution would be imposed upon him.[10] Aulard might have added that the legislators found their alleged power to override the King not only dangerous to enunciate, but difficult even to contemplate; for by presupposing Louis' acquiescence—for which the record gave no warrant[11]—they had evaded the issue of sovereignty, conjured away disillusioning strife, and preserved temporarily the guiltless atmosphere of universal accord. In short, they had devised a means

[9] Session of September 14. *Point du Jour*, September 15, 1789, vol. ii, p. 375. For similar views of Mirabeau see *ibid.*, p. 373.

[10] *Op.cit.*, p. 57.

[11] There was already ample evidence that, in fact, Louis was prepared to oppose what was "presented." As was all too well known to the reformers, His Majesty had steadfastly refrained from promulgating the Declaration and such constitutional laws as had been passed. It was only later, on October 5—when the uncertain prestige of the Assembly was fortified by the incalculable power of an unpredictable Paris mob—that Louis, in utter vexation and under circumstances of extreme danger, helplessly signed his acceptance of the articles presented by the National Assembly.

of keeping over their own eyes the "religious veil" of which Mirabeau had spoken.[12]

Over and over again, one sees that the majority of Revolutionary leaders were not unabashed innovators. Exponents of a new future, they were, also, products of a past; and their past held them enmeshed by many ties which they could not deliberately break. Though they eagerly looked forward to establishing new social and political relationships, they were at the same time disinclined to abandon the old; it was as if they feared irrevocably to fling themselves across the chasm which separated the new world of their imagination from the old world of habit. This commentary is not intended to disparage the courage of the French Revolutionary leaders, for they belonged to a notably daring generation; but it does cast light on the revolutionary impulse itself, which, contrary to a general impression, often has its own timidity to overcome and its own conservatism with which to effect compromises.

A case in point may be cited. When the Assembly took note of the fact that the King's title, "Louis, by the grace of God King of France and Navarre," had feudal connotations, it sought an appellation that would be in the spirit of the Revolution. Accordingly, in October it voted that the King should henceforth rule as "Louis, by the grace of God and the Constitution of the State." A victory for popular sovereignty is expressed in the final phrase, but in the traditional allusion to God's grace the connotation of divine right remained. Here was but one of the many compromises by which the question as to where ultimate sovereignty resided was left unanswered.

The debates and decisions of the Assembly were eagerly followed by an aroused citizenry. The legislators, as it happened, were lagging behind public opinion. True, many representatives of the Third Estate seemed to espouse democratic doctrines in their attack on upper-class privilege; but, with few exceptions, the mem-

---

[12] The tenor of the entire discussion at this time seems to bear out this assumption, as does the body's subsequent disinclination to recognize any defection on the part of the King—even such as took place on June 21, 1791, when Louis tried to escape from France and jettison the Constitution. On this distressing occasion, it was not only for ulterior motives, but for inner psychological reasons as well, that the members of the Assembly—in the very act of suspending the King—decreed that he had been kidnaped (*enlevé*), and thus proclaimed him innocent and, by implication, loyal to the cause for which they stood.

bers of the Assembly were men of property and social standing, who did not anticipate that their egalitarian preachments might be taken altogether seriously and applied in practice by the masses. But there was in France, and especially at Paris, a different type of leader, who wished for a swift and radical application of the doctrine of popular government. This was the attitude of many journalists and of many young and aspiring political leaders. Such persons began with increasing shrillness to remind the common man that he had little to lose and much to gain by fulfillment of the more extreme promises of the Revolution. By September, 1789, the most relentless of all critics of reaction, Jean-Paul Marat, was already bringing out his inflammatory *L'Ami du Peuple*. This is but one indication that the work of the radical press had begun. Paris offered a good field for men like Marat; for Desmoulins, pamphleteer and rabble rouser; for Loustallot, editor of the *Révolutions de Paris*. In their writings and speeches, these leaders and others of the same temper could daily remind men of their miseries—for the lot of the poorer elements in the city was deplorable. Money was scarce and prices were rising. Harvests had been bad, and food, including bread, was hard to get. Owing, in part, to the emigration of wealthy aristocrats, unemployment in France had greatly increased. Thousands of people, in Paris especially, were hungry and wretched.

Not understanding the causes of their distress, the Parisians were angry and suspicious. In this atmosphere, agitators were readily believed when they explained the economic dislocation in terms of political causes that were sometimes quite unrelated. They aroused indignation against the Assembly for having adopted the suspensive veto. So strange did the term "veto" sound to an uneducated citizenry that there were those who supposed it to be some hidden evil—and no doubt a cause of existing miseries.[13]

Although the Assembly no longer enjoyed the unanimous approval of the people, it was chiefly the King who aroused the resentment of the radicals. Not until September 20 did he express even partial approval of the August decrees limiting feudalism; and even then he was unwilling to sanction the Declaration of

[13] For popular misconceptions of the veto, see G. G. Andrews, *The Constitution in the Early French Revolution (June to September, 1789)*, New York, 1927, pp. 30-33.

Rights and such constitutional provisions as the Assembly had passed. Clearly Louis was obstructing the Revolution itself. No doubt—according to the popular interpretation—he had fallen a prey to the sinister influences of the Court and the aristocrats.

In this atmosphere of explosive resentment, Louis embarked upon a strange course of action, which showed that he had not learned from previous experience how grim and relentless was the patriotic mood once it was openly challenged. The patriots had regarded the King's reliance on foreign troops in July as such a challenge, and had answered with the Bastille uprising. Now in September reactionary Royalists were urging the King to take measures to assure his own safety and to stem the revolutionary tide. Louis did not go to the extreme lengths that some of his advisers advocated, but he took at least the precautionary step of summoning troops to Versailles. Among these was a foreign unit, the Flanders regiment, which arrived at the capital on September 23. When news of this action reached Paris it caused widespread alarm. Lafayette, who had not been consulted in the matter, demanded that the troops be sent away, as did, also, the Paris Commune. These protests apparently made no impression on Louis.

At this juncture an incident occurred at Versailles which overcame the inertia of the watchful and resentful Parisians, and again set the Revolution off on a course of direct action and violence. On October 1, the officers of the King's bodyguard gave a banquet of welcome to the officers of the Flanders regiment. In the gaiety of the occasion the specter of the Revolution was ignored. When Louis, accompanied by Marie Antoinette, with the Dauphin in her arms, entered to greet the guests, the band of the Flanders regiment struck up an air from Grétry's opera *Richard Coeur de Lion*.[14] The theme of the piece was Richard's imprisonment upon his return from the Crusades. The sentimental refrain, "O Richard, O my king! the universe abandons thee!" came to new life and was greeted with enthusiastic applause, for it served to convey the distress of Royalist sympathizers over the encroachments which had been made on Louis' authority. There followed spirited toasts to Louis and Marie Antoinette. Guests disported the royal cockades

[14] Music by A.-E.-M. Grétry, words by M.-J. Sedaine; first produced in 1784.

of white or black. A toast to the nation was deliberately omitted, while the new national cockade was said to have been trampled underfoot.

The affair, reported to Paris on October 3, became suddenly infamous. Many Parisians regarded it as evidence of a plot to overthrow the Constitution before it was completed. Meetings of protest were held, at which counter measures were proposed, including a call to arms and a march to Versailles. At first, it was French women, rather than men, who sprang to action.[15] On October 5, a crowd of "women of all classes"[16] found their way into the City Hall and armed themselves with weapons which were stored there. Then, led by Maillard, one of the heroes of the Bastille, they proceeded, armed and dragging cannon with them, toward Versailles. The women, 6,000 to start with, were joined by others, and by men, some of them masquerading in women's attire. This motley army left Paris at noon and arrived at Versailles four and a half hours later. It turned out to be only a vanguard. In the meantime, the National Guardsmen of Paris had assembled—they, too, were determined to proceed to Versailles. Lafayette, their commander, did all in his power to dissuade them. He was able to delay their departure, but, seeing that he could not prevent it, he decided to lead the march. The National Guard of Paris set out, 15,000 strong, followed by a band of many thousand unorganized volunteers. Lafayette and his followers reached Versailles shortly before midnight. In the meantime, the King had been frightened by the first arrivals into an unwilling acceptance of the Declaration of Rights and of the articles of the Constitution. He had, besides, promised bread and provisions to the clamorous and hungry mob of Parisian women. But none of them returned home; women, National Guardsmen, and Paris volunteers camped around the palace for the night.

At six in the morning, a mob forced an entrance to the palace, massacred several of the sentries,[17] and revived the excitement of the Bastille uprising by displaying the heads of their victims on

[15] A continuing shortage of bread at the Paris bakeries helps to explain this circumstance.

[16] This is the phrase of Mathiez, *The French Revolution*, p. 64.

[17] The gallant Varicour among them. The song *Le beau Varicour, garde du corps*, which Pierre attributes to 1789, is presumably of later date. See Appendix A, 239.

pikes. They then proceeded to the apartment of the Queen, who made a narrow escape. A detachment of the National Guards arrived in time to prevent further violence. There followed a great demonstration outside the palace, in which the King and his family were ordered to move to Paris. The mounting disorder was ominous, and the tide seemed irresistible. Finally Louis agreed.

At noon began the famous march back. Its bizarre elements are strikingly brought together in the brief account of a modern historian: "At the head of the procession were the National Guards carrying loaves of bread or sausages on the points of their bayonets. Then came carts of wheat and flour covered with foliage, surrounded by women and marketmen, armed with pikes and carrying branches of poplar; then women on horseback or astride cannon, carrying branches of trees ornamented with ribbons. 'One would have thought it,' says an eyewitness, 'an ambulating forest, through which flashed the iron of pikes and gun-barrels.' More guards, Parisian grenadiers, bodyguards without arms and wearing cockades. Then came the King, in a coach, with the Queen, the Dauphin, the King's daughter, Madame Royale, his brother, Monsieur, his sister, Madame Elizabeth, the royal governess, Madame de Tourzel. Lafayette, on horseback, rode along beside the royal coach. Then, in carriages, a hundred members of the Assembly, and behind them a miscellaneous crowd of men and women, and a mass of National Guards. This interminable, monstrous, bizarre procession moved slowly on, hour after hour, in the mud, stopping from time to time to fire off salvos of musketry, as a sign of joy, and shouting, 'We are bringing back the baker, the baker's wife and the baker's little boy!' "[18]

After this humiliating experience, the royal family was installed in the neglected and dreary apartments of the Tuileries, which Louis XIV had abandoned a hundred and twenty years before. Within a few days the National Assembly transferred the seat of its deliberations from Versailles to Paris.

The insurrection of October 5-6 seemed the last straw to many of the aristocrats. The nobles as a class were already alarmed by the growing strength of the popular cause, some of their number

[18] C. D. Hazen, *The French Revolution*, vol. i, p. 302.

having left France at the time of the Bastille uprising. This second, and in certain ways more threatening, outbreak of mob rule prompted a new wave of emigration. Even some of the "moderates" who had hitherto befriended the Revolution were now alienated. Among those who retired from the Assembly at this time were Mounier and Lally-Tollendal. Through violence and threats the Parisians had worked their will on the King and the Assembly, with an inestimable loss of prestige to both. Lafayette, actually reluctant and faltering, appeared as the hero of the occasion. Thanks to circumstances, rather than to his own initiative, he had been raised to a new level of popularity. But most of all the uprising was a victory for Paris, long the greatest city of the world in outward glory, and now acclaimed by its inhabitants as the mother city of man's emancipation, the protectress of France's future.

The October insurrection was so full of incongruities, rash violence, and unhappy forebodings that it has seemed a dread affair to many writers on the French Revolution. To a long line of critics of conservative or Royalist leaning, it has stood as one of the most shocking chapters in French history. Even to the detached student, it serves as a sobering reminder of the primitive and wanton forces that can suddenly burst through the surface of civilized habit and tradition. Such views, however, are not at all characteristic of Revolutionary opinion at Paris in 1789. We get a picture of what one of the patriots supposed to be the significance of that October drama in a song entitled *The Journey of the King from Versailles to Paris, Where He Makes His Residence*, "by a Companion of the Journey, Soldier of the Parisian National Guard," written to the air of *Vive Henri IV*.[19] The verses of this narrative are sufficiently expressive to be quoted at length:

> Jour mémorable
> Ou le Peuple François,
> Ferme, immuable,
> Pour assurer ses droits,
> Vole, infatigable
> Au séjour de nos Rois!

[19] *Le Voyage du Roi* . . . (61). There are thirteen stanzas in the original; the nine reproduced in the text are stanzas 1-5 and 7-10.

De ce voyage,
Rien n'arrête l'instant;
Le vent, l'orage
Conspirent vainement;
Contre le courage
Que peut le firmament?

Vives alarmes
Saisissent tous les coeurs,
Séchez vos larmes,
Femmes, filles en pleurs;
Un jour plein de charmes
Va calmer nos douleurs.

Brisant la chaine
Qui nous separoit d'eux,
L'amour entraine
Deux Epoux glorieux
Aux bords de la Seine,
Pour resserrer nos noeuds.

Un Peuple immense
Sur leurs pas s'est porté;
De leur présence
Paris est enchanté;
Quelle jouissance!
Quelle félicité!

. . . .

Dans votre enceinte,
Trop heureuse Cité!
Brille l'empreinte
De la Divinité,[20]
Sans aucune atteinte
A votre liberté.

[20] "Brille l'empreinte/ De la Divinité"—it is worth noting that the allusion here is to Louis.

Toujours prospère
A nos voeux prevoyans,
O tendre Père,
Daigne vivre céans!
Peut-on mieux se plaire
Qu'an sein de ses enfans?

Je vois éclore
Au gré de nos soupire,
La douce aurore
Du bien et des plaisirs;
Un Roi qu'on adore
Va combler nos désirs.

Plus de rebelles,
Plus d'effroi, plus d'ennuis;
Sujets fidèles
Au même Roi soumis,
Vuidons nos querelles,
Et soyons tous amis.

There follow further homilies on fraternal happiness, and an apostrophe to the National Assembly. The final stanza closes with lines to the royal family:

Vive Louis seize,
La Reine et le Dauphin!

What is most remarkable in the atmosphere of this song is the pretense that Louis had not been forced to change his residence owing to the popular distrust of his motives. His abandonment of Versailles is somehow made to appear a natural consequence of his devotion to the people, and of their devotion to him. Furthermore, Louis' continuing sojourn in Paris is pictured as an expression of his own pleasure. That the Parisians set out to Versailles "pour assurer ses droits" is proclaimed in the first stanza, but there is otherwise no hint of their purpose to wrest the King from the hands of the reactionaries and keep him under surveillance. Finally —as in previous crises—disorder and violence, such as characterized the days of October 5 and 6, are not seen as an ominous presage of further violence, but are extolled as the culmination and end of popular restlessness, and as the beginning of a brave new world of freedom and abundance, of fatherly love and fraternal felicity.

On the same subject, there is a *Chanson poissarde*, with the subtitle, "Their Arrival at Versailles, and Their Return to Paris with the King and the Royal Family."[21] This song of the marketwomen[22] opens on a note of gratification over Louis' presence in Paris:

> Nous n'irons plus si loin, ma foi,
> Quand nous voudrons voir notre Roi;
> J'l'aimons d'une amour sans égale,
> Puisqu'il d'meur' dans notr' Capitale.[23]

It closes with a vivid account of an early phase of the feminism of the French Revolution:

> A Versail' comme des fanfarons,
> J'avions amené nos canons: [*bis*]
> Falloit voir, quoi qu'j'étions qu'des femmes
> Un courage qui n'faut pas qu'l'on blâme.
>
> Nous faisions voir aux homm' de coeur,
> Que tout comme eux j'n'avions pas peur; [*bis*]
> Fusil, mousqueton sur l'épaule,
> J'allions comme Amadis de Gaule.
>
> L'on a bien voulu nous r'pousser,
> Mais j'n'avons point voulu r'culer: [*bis*]
> Tout' prêtes avec nos fierr' Cocardes,
> D'agir d'espontons d'hallebardes.

---

[21] *Chanson poissarde: Leur arrivée à Versailles . . .* (64), published in a brochure which has as its title piece, *Le Voyage du Roi . . .* (61), mentioned above. This pamphlet, which contains also the *Départ des poissardes . . .* (63) subsequently mentioned, and *Autre Chanson* (62), is preserved at the Bibliothèque Nationale, but is not known to exist elsewhere.

[22] The marketwomen, as we have seen, were a conspicuous element of the Parisian populace. They came to the fore on every occasion of patriotic excitement. Mathiez notes, *op.cit.*, p. 66, that "On October 7 the Patriot Gonchon, an agent of Lafayette, organized a demonstration of marketwomen, who marched to the Tuileries to cheer the King and Queen and ask them to take up their permanent abode in Paris. Marie Antoinette had become so unaccustomed to hearing shouts of 'Vive la Reine!' that she was moved to tears."

[23] *Chanson poissarde: Leur arrivée à Versailles . . .* (64), first stanza.

Trotout, tout d'mêm' que des guerriers,
J'avons remporté les lauriers, [*bis*]
Et la gloir', la bonne espérance
De fair' le bonheur de la France.[24]

Indeed, the entire pamphlet in which this song appears is a curious document in the literature of what has been called French Revolutionary Amazonism. The same brochure includes another *poissard* song, *The Departure of the Fishwives of Paris for Versailles*,[25] in which it is alleged that "each woman here has the heart of a dragoon." The King is referred to as "notr' Papa l'Roi d'France." We can only guess as to the authorship of these colorful declarations, but they appear as a fresh and convincing expression of the naïve faith of the fishwives and of the spirit of their exploits.[26]

At the markets there were brawny fellows who did the heavy lifting and who had long been known from their occupation—as they still are—as "les forts de la Halle." A song, the title of which bears their name, seems to have enjoyed some popularity in Paris. No printed copy is known except that in the *Chronique de Paris* of December 7, 1789: *Song of Messieurs the Porters of the Market and of the Port-aux-Bleds*.[27] "We have been astonished," wrote the editor, "to hear the following song sung in the streets, and we have believed that we might give pleasure to our readers in making it known to them." The ideas expressed in this piece are as follows:

[24] *Ibid.*, stanzas 4-7. The gusto of this passage is not altogether lost in translation: "To Versailles, like braggarts, we dragged our cannon; had to show, although we were only women, a courage beyond reproach. We showed men of spirit that just like them we weren't afraid; gun, musketoon across the shoulder, we went like Amadis of Gaul. They would have liked to repel us; but we had no mind to draw back—all ready, with our proud Cockades, to act with pikes and halberds. Everywhere, just like warriors, we carried off the laurels and the glory—the good hope of making the happiness of France."

[25] *Départ des poissardes . . .* (63). Concerning the brochure, see footnote 21, above, and *Le Voyage du Roi . . .* (II, C). A title of interest at this point appears in Bibliography I, *Courage patriotique des Dames de la Halle, dans l'affaire du 5 et 6 oct. 1789, par Labré* (65).

[26] In this connection, I have rejected the amusing *Chanson nouvelle de deux dames de la Halle qui ont eu l'honneur de voir le Roi, la Reine, Monseigneur le Dauphin et toute la famille royale au château des Tuileries en 1789* by Barré (Pierre's 249) as expressing a retrospective point of view. This piece, which Pierre attributes to 1789 and which Damade in his *Histoire chantée . . .* (p. 40) reprints under the same year, is not known to have been published until 1790. See Appendix A, 249.

[27] *Chanson de MM. les Forts de la Halle . . .* (75).

the King is enjoying himself at Paris, a fact which delights the hearts of the people; after all, Paris is the King's native city and the Parisian populace will see that he lives well there, just as they did in the case of the good Henry. But should there be any reactionaries who would take advantage of the King—who would "arouse their brigands"—the "forts de la Halle" will know how to use strong-arm methods. They will restore order. "It's only in tranquillity that one enjoys liberty," a condition which, after all, seems assured, as a rhetorical question suggests—

> Not'roi qu'est l'meyeur des pères,
> Aura ti d'mauvais enfans?

The famine no longer threatens, the aristocracy is humiliated, there is no longer any reason not to rejoice; the price of liberty wasn't great—only a "few heads" (which reminds the author that "there are no good banquets without a few broken glasses"); drinking and singing are in order, since we have the brave Lafayette, the wise Necker, and the good Bailly, who in time will straighten things out.

Rough though this *poissard* song may be in form, it has a moralistic tone, and was possibly intended to propagate moderation. In any case, the journal which presented it was by no means radical. The sentiments which we have reviewed seem at first glance sufficiently reassuring, and no doubt they did give pleasure to a considerable number of readers. Nevertheless, there must have been patriots who found in the song disturbing elements: that its spirit, like that of most of the *chansons poissardes*, was of a rough-and-ready egalitarianism; that it was patronizing to the monarch whom it seemed to honor; that in justifying direct action and strong-arm methods, it exalted brawn above brain; and that, in effect, it put the porters of the market place on a parity with the representatives of the nation as the saviors and protectors of France. It was all meant in the spirit of good humor, and was so received. As Bernard Shaw has suggested, the first successful attack on social institutions is often made through the paths of humor; and the unthinking laughter of those who are threatened is frequently the first breach in their defense. In any case, just as certain aristocrats endorsed the demands of the upper middle class against their own apparent interest, so many bourgeois leaders, delighted by the phraseology of revolution and democracy, tolerated, and even encouraged, the inflammatory claims of the poor and the lowly, whom for the time being they regarded as allies.

Factional strife, evident in the Assembly toward the end of August and intensified by the October insurrection, was reflected in songs after the King's removal to Paris. Until then, practically all the lyrics which have come to light were in the spirit of reformation and change, if not, strictly speaking, of revolution. By the middle of October that homogeneity of a general sort was lost. In the first place, the aristocrats, now increasingly disaffected, at last fully recognized the propaganda value of songs and availed themselves of it. Furthermore, songs came to be used for all sorts of special pleading, and to advance factional interests.[28] Although we are concerned primarily with popular—as opposed to aristocratic—opinion, note must be taken of anti-Revolutionary compositions, for they were provocative and had a direct effect on the tenor of patriotic writing.

A song called *The Parisian Troubadour*,[29] which was published separately and also in the Royalist journal *Les actes des apôtres*,[30] is interesting as expressing a somewhat guarded irony. The author, Gabriel-Joseph d'Eaubonne, pretends to have sympathy for the Revolutionary cause and some faith in it; such feelings he professes to reconcile with his deep loyalty to the Royalist cause. His opening tributes to the King and to the Queen are lavish, though his comparison of the former to Marcus Aurelius and of the latter to

[28] An example is the *Justification des Messieurs et des Dames de la Halle . . .* (66), written in the *poissard* manner. The lengthy title may be rendered in English as follows: "Justification of the Men and Women of the Market of Paris, in regard to the crimes of the execrable French Revolution, notably those of October 5 and 6, 1789, committed at Versailles, in which they are accused of having taken part." The argument is that the events in question were "the crimes of brigands," of which the men and women of the market were innocent. The marchers to Versailles were "rabble . . . paid by this rascal of an Orleans." The Duc d'Aiguillon, branded as a traitor, is accused in a footnote of having been "disguised as a fishwife in the crowd that demanded the head of the Queen." This song exaggerates the role of the agitators, incorrectly denies any degree of spontaneous participation on the part of those whom it seeks to justify, and represents primarily special pleading to discredit Orleans, Mirabeau, and Aiguillon.

[29] *Le troubadour parisien . . .* (70†, ed. "b").

[30] No. 61, pp. 14-16. This issue of *Les actes des apôtres* appeared approximately March 1, 1790. However, the song itself seems to have appeared considerably earlier (concerning other editions, see Bibliography I, 70†, and Appendix A, 243).

Venus suggests an ill-assorted pair. The song, written in the style of a troubadour lament, is a recital of the events of October 5-6. It recounts how at the day's end, to the sound of drums, "many a perfidious Amazon" approaches. The results are sad to contemplate:

> Ah que de mal on a fait!
> La nuit voilait le forfait.

So goes the chorus for several stanzas. Over the cruelty of "this horrible night," the author's heart still groans. But presently he professes to see in the havoc which was wrought, a joyous outcome:

> Dans la Ville de Paris,
> Secondés par La Fayette
> Louis, la Reine et le Fils
> On[t] trouvé douce retraite.
> Ne pensons plus au forfait
> Ne voyons que le bienfait.

> Ils sont comme citoyens
> Au milieu de tous leurs freres. . . .[31]

Although this thought may have been less than consoling, d'Eaubonne ventures to appropriate a patriotic argument and ends with an appeal to liberty: inasmuch as liberty is to be a general good, royalty should share it. May Louis be free to enjoy his chateaux and visit "all his France!" The final chorus consists of this injunction:

> D'être libre est votre Loi
> Libre doit être le Roi.

A franker expression of anti-Revolutionary sentiment occurs in the famous Royalist lament, *Le troubadour béarnais*,[32] published in *Les actes des apôtres*,[33] January, 1790, and reprinted some two years later in *L'Ami du Roi, Almanach des honnêtes gens*. The troubadour is distressed by the "crimes" committed at Versailles and by the misfortunes of the royal family. Their removal to Paris

---

[31] *Le troubadour parisien* . . . (70†, ed. "b"), stanza 8 and the first two lines of stanza 9.

[32] (69†).Two manuscript editions of this song, with musical score, are preserved at the Bibliothèque Nationale. Concerning various editions, see Bibliography I, 69†, and Appendix A, 218.

[33] No. 28, pp. 13-15, under title *Chœur béarnais*.

he sees as a heartless captivity. The following sad refrain is developed with variations:

> Louis, le fils de Henri,
> Est prisonnier dans Paris.

The troubadour is struck by the ingratitude of the people:

> Chez vous, l'homme a de ses droits
> Recouvré le noble usage,
> Et vous opprimez vos rois!
> Ah! quel injuste partage!
> Le peuple est libre, & Louis
> Est prisonnier dans Paris.[34]

This lament, which dramatizes the plight of Louis and his family, discloses a Royalist sentimentalism that corresponds to the sentimentalism of much patriotic writing. It is unusual in this respect, for—as soon appeared—the preference of the poets of reaction was for satire and invective; and their language was frequently as violent and vulgar as that used by the most disreputable journalists in the popular camp.

Mention may be made of a piece entitled *The National Assembly or France Abused*.[35] Though by no means an example of the coarsest strain in Royalist writing, it pleads the aristocratic cause in the slang of the streets, in contrast to the genteel language of the two pieces just cited. After referring to the "good king" as a "prisoner at the palace of the Tuileries," the song continues bluntly:

> Jusqu'à quand, braves guerriers
> Souffrirez-vous tant d'avanies?
> Voulez-vous qu'à votre roi
> Un tas de gueux fasse la loi?[36]

This piece was accompanied by a virulent song written in denunciation of the Duke of Orleans,[37] the two appearing in a brochure entitled *Etrennes à la Nation*, dated 1789.

A consideration of the lyrics occasioned by the October insurrection reveals that the Royalist picture of events, at least in so far

---

[34] *Le troubadour béarnais* (69†), stanza 8.
[35] *L'Assemblée nationale* . . . (67).   [36] *Ibid.*, stanza 5.
[37] *Chanson: "Le duc d'Orléans reviendra* . . . " (68).

as it concerned Louis' position, was on the whole truthful, whereas
the patriotic accounts were full of distortions. Louis had not
wanted to come to Paris, and, although he experienced fleeting
moments of satisfaction, he did not wish to remain there. A
hint as to Louis' distress emerges, inadvertently no doubt, in a
song which otherwise follows the patriotic formula. The hint
comes almost as an afterthought:

> Laissons-le dans son tranquille;
> N'affligeons plus son bon coeur:
> Que c'bon roi, dans sa bonn'ville,
> N'ait pu d'sabat ni d'horreur.[38]

Just as the capture of the Bastille had given patriots the feeling
of ascendancy over the Court, now, after the October days, they
had the same feeling of ascendancy in respect to the King.

As one patriotic song put it, "We possess Louis."[39]

What greater check could there be on the Royalist enemies of
the Revolution than to hold the King hostage? This was the reality,
but the thought of it was kept in the background. Furthermore,
the patriots at Paris felt in some primitive way that, since they
possessed the body of Louis, they controlled the spirit as well. He
was expected to show pleasure and relief at being delivered from
the machinations of the court at Versailles. Heartened by the devotion of his subjects at Paris, he would presumably wish to remain
in their midst. Of interest in connection with this analysis, based
on lyrical expression, is an incident which relates to the press.
We have it on the authority of Mathiez that "word was sent round
to the newspapers to repeat that the King was staying in Paris voluntarily, of his own free will."[40] This was apparently at Lafayette's

---

[38] *Chanson de MM. les Forts de la Halle . . .* (75), stanza 6. For consideration of
the song from which this quotation is taken, see pages 183-84.

[39] *Les nouveaux apôtres aristocrates* (71), last stanza.

[40] Mathiez, *The French Revolution*, p. 66. The General Council of the Paris Commune advised the provinces that "it was only the absolutely free and unconstrained
love of His Majesty for his capital that had secured it the happiness of having him
in its midst" (see P. Gaxotte, *The French Revolution*, p. 120). As a matter of fact,
Louis, without confirming this view of the matter, gave it some support. In describing his future intentions, he said on October 9, "I shall willingly make my habitual
residence in my good City of Paris, in the confidence that I shall see peace and
tranquillity prevail there." These remarks occur in the reply of the King to Bailly,
on the occasion of the latter's visit to the Tuileries as head of a delegation from the
Paris Commune. *Actes de la Commune de Paris . . .* , S. Lacroix, ed., vol. ii, p. 232.

instigation—a good example of official propaganda. But no measure of this kind in itself explains a situation. The student of public opinion is bound to ask: why was a particular line of propaganda adopted? And, if successful, why did it succeed? What we may call the "voluntary theory" of the King's stay at Paris was adopted in the first place as a matter of convenience, to placate personages who might be offended and to satisfy certain external demands of the situation. But it was adopted, also, because the common people carried in their hearts many hopes that could thrive on such a fiction. And it was for this reason, especially, that the theory made good propaganda. The Parisians willingly denied that the King was captive, because implicit in the idea of capture was conflict and an open break. Although they had defied and overwhelmed Louis, they were still bound by a deep-seated attachment to the throne, which they regarded as voluntary, and for which, as we have seen, they found the catchword "love." Love was to be the *deus ex machina*: it would make possible the reconciliation of the principle of royal sovereignty and that of government where "all sovereignty resides essentially in the nation."[41] This new panacea— the great force not of authority and obedience, but of love—would preclude any grievous conflict between the King and his people.

These hopes might have been short-lived, of course, if Louis had been recalcitrant or unable to act his part of the relationship. But, as we have seen, he himself was affected by the currents of feeling which were so profoundly moving to the heirs of the enlightenment, and was from this standpoint a child of the Revolution, as well as its alleged father. There is always renewed evidence of this, as his reaction to the critical events of October 6 may suggest. Toward eight that evening, Louis, having at last arrived at Paris, was received at the Hôtel de Ville. A welcoming address to His Majesty by one of the Presidents of the Assembly of the Paris Commune, Moreau de Saint-Méry, ended thus: "When an adored father is summoned by the desires of an immense family, he must naturally prefer the place where his children are gathered in the greatest number." Whatever Louis' feelings may have been, the minutes declare that the King appeared to listen to "this truly patriotic dis-

41 "Le principe de toute souveraineté réside dans la nation." *La Déclaration des droits de l'homme,* article III.

course with the greatest interest."[42] The King said little on that historic day, and no historian is justified in speaking for him. But one may still judge by outward appearances, and I note that Madelin, in picturing the arrival of the royal family at their final destination, the Tuileries—at nine thirty, by torchlight—gives top emphasis to a contemporary impression: "The King looked radiant."[43]

Thus the chief problem of the Revolution—the issue of sovereign authority—was relegated to the field of the emotions, and resolved for the time being in terms of *sensibilité*.

Now that obstruction by the King was for the moment no longer feared, the Revolutionary leaders could turn their attention to other matters: to the complaints of a people distraught by economic depression, and to the various measures which remained to be taken for the security and advancement of the new order in France.

[42] *Actes de la Commune de Paris* . . . , vol. ii, p. 192.
[43] *The French Revolution*, p. 111.

THE framers of the Constitution of the United States, who gathered at Philadelphia in 1787 in a constituent assembly, were free to devote their entire attention to the creation of a new form of government. The members of the French National Assembly were not so favored. Being members of a national parliament, as well as of a constituent assembly, they were obliged to devise legislation to tide France over during the period in which they were framing the new constitution. They had, besides, to attend to the mass of routine matters which beset any legislative body. Accordingly, their contemplation of inalienable rights and long-range principles was constantly being interrupted.

Of all the immediate problems which confronted the Assembly, the most irksome was that of the finances.[1] The government was burdened with a huge debt, which by this time approached four billion livres, and the credit of the state was practically exhausted. Necker launched two loans in August, but they were only in small part successful. To make matters worse, it was almost impossible to collect taxes, owing to the condition of anarchy which spread over France in the summer of 1789. The economic historian Marion has well pictured certain of the disastrous effects which the newly acquired sense of liberty produced: "All tax-gathering was completely destroyed. It was not only the collection of the *tailles, capitation* and *vingtièmes* which ceased: by an irresistible impulse, the people rose up against the local customs gates, which they overturned; against the granaries, which they pillaged; against the collectors' offices, which they plundered; against the government agents, whom they put to flight."[2]

This was clearly a protest against the hated institutions of the old regime. It remained to be seen what response there would be to the revenue-raising efforts of the new government. In September, Necker himself proposed to the Assembly a twenty-five percent

---

[1] The National Assembly had assumed control of taxation early in its existence—July 19, 1789.

[2] Interesting illustrative material follows. See M. Marion, *Histoire financiere de la France depuis 1715*, Paris, 1919, vol. ii, pp. 7ff.

tax on all incomes. A "patriotic tax," it was called: each taxpayer would declare his income and pay a quarter of it to the treasury—there was to be no inspection and no compulsion. The measure, passed on October 6, contained no exemptions at lower levels—a fact which appears strange today; but what must have seemed even more strange to contemporaries brought up in a society of privilege was the absence of any exemptions for the rich. This was proportional taxation—what the reformers had been clamoring for. But once approved by the government, this new and heavy tax was ignored by the people. They apparently did not see that they were thereby threatening with ruin a state that was nearly bank-rupt. And even if they sensed the danger, they resented and re-sisted taxation—not only that of the old regime, but also that spon-sored by their own representatives. It is characteristic of the Revo-lutionary psychology that the patriots, having defied the govern-ment in its efforts to raise money, undertook to fill the depleted treasury by voluntary gifts.

The *dons patriotiques*, as these gifts were called, were initiated by a group of Parisian women, who visited the Assembly on Sep-tember 7, in order to donate their jewels to the nation. The desk on which the youngest of these "citoyennes vertueuses" placed the offering, became in that moment, as one contemporary put it, "the veritable altar of *la patrie*."[3] This example of patriotic devotion was contagious. Soon thereafter, nearly every session of the As-sembly opened with the reception of gifts which patriots placed at the bar, or with the reading of letters from the provinces, which announced that money or various objects of value were being con-tributed to the government. On September 22, the Assembly was informed that the King had donated his silver plate to the cause. Even Necker hoped for the success of this recourse, and himself made a patriotic gift of one hundred thousand livres. People no doubt made sacrifices and accepted inconveniences in thus coming to the rescue of the state. They seemed to be proving that the com-pulsion of taxation was an adjunct of despotism, that a free people would find a way to sustain government through acts of spontane-ous generosity. However, their voluntary offerings, though occa-sionally substantial, were, by and large, nothing more than sym-

[3] *Journal des Etats-Généraux*, vol. iii, no. 23, p. 337.

bolic gestures. That the people had no conception of the immense sacrifices which the requirements of the state called for is suggested by the figures which follow. At the end of the first six months (March, 1790) the *dons patriotiques* amounted to something over one million livres collected and two million promised. This was not one-tenth of one percent of the national debt. It was little more, pledges included, than the amount that Necker had been able to borrow in August, which was in fact less than one-tenth of the sum that he desired to raise at that time. Accordingly, the new regime was unable to meet even the ordinary expenses of government. Something drastic had to be done.

The Church was rich. Its lands are estimated to have comprised from about six to ten percent of the surface of France;[4] but from the standpoint of value these lands and the buildings thereon constituted a considerably greater proportion of the nation's wealth in real estate.[5] The benefits of these vast holdings, which had been built up for centuries, accrued largely to privileged members of the higher clergy. It is true that the Church supported public worship, schools, hospitals, and poorhouses; but it neglected much of its landed estate, and it had by means of various revenues accumulated incomes far greater than the sums which were spent for religious and charitable purposes. As a matter of fact, the ecclesiastical revenues had been curtailed by passage on August 11 of a decree to abolish the tithe.[6] But the physical properties of the Church were as imposing as ever, and its lavish expenses were still a subject of criticism. By way of correcting this situation, and by way of acquiring revenue at the same time, the state might conceivably possess itself of the ecclesiastical lands, and in turn provide for the churches, schools, hospitals, and other charitable institutions. Any funds which remained could be devoted to the needs of the nation. The versatile Talleyrand, later to enjoy fame as a diplomat, but

4 The lower and the higher figures are taken, respectively, from H. Sée, *La France économique et sociale au XVIIIᵉ siècle*, pp. 10-11, and G. Lefebvre, *The Coming of the French Revolution*, p. 7.

5 Probably not as much as a fifth, but J. M. Thompson indicates (in *The French Revolution*, p. 154) that contemporary estimates went from that to as high as a half.

6 At least in principle, and for the future. For the time being—and until some corresponding means of income for the Church could be found—the tithe was supposed to be paid; but actually, after passage of the decree of August 11, it was largely uncollectible.

then prominent in the Assembly as the Bishop of Autun, proposed this on October 10 as a solution of the financial problem.[7]

Talleyrand was right in saying that palliatives would not work. "Large measures are required to meet the situation," he declared. "Ordinary means are exhausted."[8] Nevertheless, the government could not seize Church property and take over the support of the clergy and of various ecclesiastical functions without undermining the position which Catholicism had enjoyed in France for centuries. The Church had been a cornerstone not only of French society, but to some extent of the government as well. It had its own administrative controls, its own revenues, its own juridical areas. In spiritual matters it had a sort of sovereignty, challenged from time to time by the French kings, and progressively reduced, but still real. It is important to note that Talleyrand's proposal did not contain the modern element of separation of church and state; it involved the subordination of the one to the other. His motion aroused a storm of protest among the devout and among conservatives generally.

Included in Talleyrand's plan was a provision that the parish priests, who often fared rather badly, be assured a minimum salary of 1,200 livres per annum—more than twice the amount that many of them were getting. This provision was cleverly calculated to divide the clergy, it being likely that the priests who were to benefit by this extra consideration would discover merit in the plan as a whole.

Almost everyone recognized that the seizure of Church property by the state was a radical step, for which moral justification would have to be found. It is a noteworthy fact that men seldom abandon old institutions in favor of new ones on the promise of practical benefits alone. In the awesome matter of achieving social change, they seek to plant their feet on moral ground. If possible, the sanctity that attaches to the old institution must be made to seem implicit in the new. Talleyrand had the perspicacity to introduce his proposal, with all its material benefits, as a means, not of weakening religion, but of putting it on a higher plane. His plan to de-

[7] The idea in a less drastic form had already been suggested by Dupont de Nemours at the session of September 24.

[8] *Motion de M. L'Evêque d'Autun sur les Biens ecclésiastiques, 10 Octobre 1789*, p. 1. (*Procès-verbal de l'Assemblée nationale*, vol. vi.)

prive the Church of its lands would, he said, restore the Church to its primitive state of purity.

As it happened, the bill which Talleyrand introduced to the Assembly was long and complicated. On October 13, Mirabeau made a far simpler motion, calling merely for a declaration that the lands of the Church were the property of the nation, on condition that the state provide for public worship and the support of the ministers, and guarantee to parish priests the minimum salary of 1,200 livres. In the light of our present-day conception of religious freedom, the outlook of Mirabeau, though he spoke in the name of "liberty," is apt to seem strange and disturbing. "I would observe," he explained, "that all the members of the clergy are officers of the State; that the service of the altars is a public function, and that religion belongs to all. It follows necessarily that the ministers should be in the pay of the Nation, as the magistrate who judges in the name of the law, as the soldier who defends the commonwealth in the name of all."[9] Thus, Mirabeau hoped, would certain traditional abuses be overcome; and thus would all man's energies, spiritual as well as social and political, be embodied in the new Nation.[10]

Mirabeau, long notorious as a debauchee, found it prudent, as had Talleyrand, to present the proposed change in a sanctimonious light. He argued that "a more just distribution of the goods of the Church would put a check on luxury and licence," and that the expropriation of the Church lands would accordingly "serve the interest of religion itself."[11]

Mirabeau's motion became the center of an acrimonious debate in the Assembly. Legalists, both ecclesiastical and lay, led the arguments on either side. When distinctions became too fine-spun, practical-minded advocates of the measure, reminding their colleagues of the great wealth of the Church and of the economic plight of the country, held before the Assembly the specter of bankruptcy. Against the pressure of expediency, it was of no avail for

[9] *Moniteur, du 29 au 30 octobre 1789,* vol. i, p. 328 (session of October 30).

[10] French Revolutionary doctrine, which contributed so much to present-day democracy, contributed a share also to the totalitarian ideologies of modern Europe. Mirabeau's interpretation of the function of religion—which soon became the accepted Revolutionary view—is a case in point.

[11] *Moniteur, loc.cit.*

leading churchmen, including such Revolutionaries as Sieyès and Camus, to argue that in the Declaration of Rights "property" had been declared inalienable. Advocates of the bill were of course aware that "property" had not been defined in the Declaration, and it was easy to say that only the property of the individual was intended, and not the collective property of a corporation such as the Church.

Finally, on November 2, 1789, Mirabeau's motion was passed by the Assembly.[12] The ecclesiastical estates were now "at the disposal of the Nation." This did not mean that the state actually took the lands or that anything could be done about them without further legislation. The representatives had, however, at least established title. The proponents of the measure could console themselves with the knowledge that a victory in principle is often half the battle won. It is indeed possible that some of them, in venturing to invade the highly sensitive area of religious conviction, had been troubled in their own minds. In any case, they were content to take one step at a time.

It was not enough, though, to come to theoretical conclusions about the Church lands. The plight of the treasury continued to cause the gravest concern. On November 14, Necker was urgently reminding the legislators that they must do something. He himself proposed an elaborate financial scheme, involving the establishment of a national bank and a gradual sale of the lands of the Church.[13]

While rejecting the Minister's plea for a national bank, the Assembly finally voted, December 19, that Church lands to the value of 400 million livres be offered for sale, and authorized the issue of bonds for the total amount, at five percent. The somewhat complicated refunding arrangements need not detain us, the primary fact being that the state had found a source of new wealth. The scheme seemed to involve no undue risk, for the 400 million was but a modest part of the total value of the ecclesiastical lands, which, roughly speaking, were worth three billion livres.

The reference which I have made to "bonds" is not the customary way of putting the matter, the debentures being described by

---

[12] By a vote of 568 to 346.

[13] *Mémoire lu par le premier Ministre des Finances à L'Assemblée nationale, le 14 Novembre 1789, et imprimé, par ses ordres. (Procès-verbal . . . , vol. vii.)*

the law as *assignats*, or "assignments." But to call them *assignats*, as is ordinarily done, is misleading, for by the following year *assignats* were issued which were a form of paper money, rivaling the existing currency. They became the paper money which drove out the coin, the bad money which drove out the good. Issued in increasing amounts, they helped to plunge Revolutionary France into the miseries of inflation,[14] and finally, in 1797, they were repudiated. In contrast to such issues of paper currency, the original *assignats*, as Mathiez makes clear,[15] were treasury bonds, which were to be retired (actually destroyed by the state) as the Church lands were disposed of.

The scheme broke down in practice, because the ecclesiastical lands would not sell. Prospective buyers were frightened away by complications arising over titles (which were disputed by the Church), by previous indebtedness, and by other encumbrances. It was in an effort to promote the sale of the lands that the Assembly, in April, 1790, entered on its venturesome course of making the *assignats* a form of currency. This was not the only recourse at hand, and certainly the rather cautious use which the legislators had made of *assignats* in December, 1789, cannot be blamed for the inflation which resulted from the ill-advised steps of the following spring. Nevertheless, in appraising the work of 1789, it should be pointed out that the members of the National Assembly, owing partly to their own lack of courage and partly to their suspicion of the administrative branch of government, failed to find any effective means of checking the anarchy to which reference has been made, and of collecting the revenues of the state. By this neglect, they contributed to the prevailing irresponsibility about finances, and made reckless and even desperate measures almost inevitable at some later date.

One feature of the economic dislocation which particularly affected the man in the street was the actual scarcity of coins. In the fall of 1789 this was a source of frequent complaint. Although ob-

14 Actually, the immediate, though transient, effect of the use of *assignats* as currency was to stimulate business, and to confirm the patriots' belief in the arrival of the Golden Age. But it was a matter only of weeks before the stimulating effect of the inflation was spent.

15 *The French Revolution*, p. 98.

scure factors contributed to the situation, certain causes were obvious. For one thing, the aristocrats who had emigrated had taken
with them stores of money, as was well known. Then again, many
capitalists and others who distrusted the success of the Revolution
had begun to hoard money. It is true that the food shortage, which
had been acute in September, was somewhat relieved later in the
fall; but the fact that there continued to be an insufficiency of
money for ordinary transactions struck the average man as a clear
indication that the government was falling down on the job. It was
no longer altogether easy to cherish such hopes as had been expressed by a song writer in the spring:

> Le déficit disparoitra,
> Et le Trésor se remplira,
> Pour lors l'argent circulera,
> Alleluia.[16]

By the end of the year a pensive quality had replaced the first
exuberance. A song entitled *The Scarcity of Coin* appeared at this
time. The author's theme is proclaimed in the opening lines:

> L'an mil sept cent quatre vingt dix
> Sera t'il heureux pour la france[?]
> Oui Messieurs je vous le prédis
> Si vous arrangez la finance[.]
> Occupez-vous de ce soin la
> Pour voir un peu [*bis*] comment ça f'ra. [*bis*][17]

It is revealed in a footnote that the "Gentlemen" thus addressed
are members of the Committee of Finance.[18]

The lyrist complains that "our enemies taking refuge abroad"
have carried off all the currency through "the desire of avenging
themselves." The need of a remedy is then pictured as urgent.
Everyone, "animated by an entirely pure motive," the author explains, is convinced that it is necessary to begin with the Church:
"Let us seize its possessions." But in spite of the plan to do so, and

---

16 *Nouvel "O Filii"* . . . (14), stanza 7.

17 *La rareté du numéraire* (87†). The original is largely without punctuation, as
indicated in the stanzas above.

18 This Committee, established July 11, consisted of sixty-two members of the National Assembly.

in spite of the *dons patriotique*, one does not, judging by the poet's complaint, find more money in circulation.

Despairing of the work of the Committee, the author proposes, in conclusion, a simple way out:

> Maint capitalistes dit-on
> Pour nous oter toute espérance
> Cachent au fond de leur maison
> Tout l'or et l'argent de la france[:]
> Pendons d'abord ces coquins la
> Pour voir un peu [*bis*] comment ça f'ra. [*bis*]

To be sure, monopolists and hoarders had become active, as they do in any time of uncertainty. But to hang those at hand and curse the *émigrés* could not alone restore the public credit and revive prosperity. The patriots had inherited a bad economic condition and, besides, lacked the self-denial which would have made possible the introduction of sound policies. They could not see this. The enemies of their well-being must be tangible, destructible. "Citizens," the ardent patriot Loustallot had pleaded somewhat earlier under similar circumstances, "can our misfortunes result only from endlessly recurrent crimes? Shall we attribute nothing to chance or to the succession of a multitude of little causes that are difficult or impossible to foresee? Shall we never acknowledge our own faults?"[19]

Mention has been made in earlier chapters of attacks on the clergy.[20] More must be added here of this anticlerical movement, which continued throughout the year, and became one of the great issues of the Revolution. To be sure, it was the financial situation, as we have seen, which prompted the first drastic measures against the Church, but economic necessity merely intensified a rivalry that had long been developing in the eighteenth century between the so-called "rational" critics of Catholicism and its adherents. Finally, by 1789, when the architects of a new order began to strike out the foundations of absolutism, the traditional structure of religion was by no means spared. Many patriots were convinced that

[19] Written concerning the popular clamor over the shortage of flour in August. *Révolutions de Paris (du 22 août, 1789)* no. 6, p. 30.

[20] See especially pages 65-66.

a new era of morality had dawned, and it was in the name of virtue, as well as of reason, that they assailed the Church.

The battle was waged on a broad front, involving the regular, as well as the secular, clergy. Popular writers accused both groups of unbecoming worldliness and gross immorality. It was in this spirit that the author of one of the earliest of the songs of 1789 proposed liberating the monks from their vows and abolishing the monasteries,[21]

> Qui nourrissent tant de faignans:
> Et en se mariant,
> I zaurions des enfans
> Dont on connoîtroit du moins les pères.[22]

This mordant critic called also for the suppression of papal annates,[23] sums paid on certain occasions to Rome, in accordance with a practice dating from the Middle Ages. Frenchmen had long resented these payments,[24] and on August 11, 1789, the National Assembly abolished them.

A song that was not only anticlerical, but sacrilegious as well,[25] appeared in June, as an expression of popular resentment against De Juigny, Archbishop of Paris, who was then counseling Louis to preserve intact the order of the clergy. This piece, a parody on *O Filii*, opens with a lively defamation of the highest officers of the Church:

> Notre S. Père est un dindon,
> Le calotin est un fripon,
> Notre Archevêque un scélérat.
> Alleleuia.

In a subsequent stanza,[26] the poetaster accuses the clergy of hiding their treasure—wealth which he hastens to add the people will soon

---

[21] Writing of an earlier period, Beatrice Hyslop reports that, "Whereas 235 cahiers spoke for maintenance or reform of the monastic orders . . . , only 22 cahiers asked for outright suppression." (*French Nationalism in 1789 . . .* , p. 105). Thus the movement for suppression did not originate in the era of the National Assembly; but it was then that it suddenly prevailed. Indeed, by February 13, 1790—in a matter of but months—the Assembly had passed its famous decree which forbade perpetual vows and largely broke up the monasteries.

[22] *Arrêté des Habitans de la Grenouillère . . .* (5), stanza 19.   [23] *Ibid.*, stanza 22.

[24] By the eve of the Revolution denunciation of payments to the papacy was widespread. See B. Hyslop, *French Nationalism in 1789 . . .* , pp. 102-3.

[25] *Chanson: "Notre S. Père . . . "* (19).   [26] *Ibid.*, stanza 5.

find (the recurrent "alleluia" having by this stage of the song ceased to be ironic).

A companion piece[27] in the same brochure warned the people of the nefarious designs of the higher clergy:

> Jouant Dieu, vos hauts Calotins
> De leurs plus perfides venins
> Croyoient empoisonner l'Etat.
> Alleluia.

In directing their gibes at the clergy, the song writers usually made a distinction between the ecclesiastics of great wealth and noble background, whose sympathies inclined to be aristocratic and reactionary, and the priests, who lived with the people and, by and large, sided with the Third Estate. As one lyrist, writing in the summer, explained:

> Du clergé, l'ordre nécessaire,
> C'est celui de nos bons curés,
> A la patrie sont dévoués;
> Ils instruisent le monde en chaire,
> Le soulage dans sa misère:
> Sages curés, plus que prélat, [bis]
> Vous instruisez et soulagez le pauvre tiers-état. [bis][28]

The Veil Lifted—consisting of no less than fifty-six stanzas—is a veritable compendium of ecclesiastical abuses.[29] Here again the religious air *O Filii* is used, not only for the purpose of parody, in which the song abounds, but also as a medium by which reverently to express hopes for a new day when the purity of the Revolution shall prevail and the Church be purged of its corruption. The opening stanzas proclaim, along with the spirit of parody, the irony and indignation of the author:

27 *O filii national* (20). This piece and the one above are included in the *Nouveau pot-pourri sur les affaires du temps, Versailles . . . , 1789.* (II, C)

28 *Chanson sur les affaires du temps* (27), stanza 8. According to the author of a patriotic song which appeared in May, "the villages which have no *curé* at all, hope that they will be given one" (14, stanza 25).

29 *Le voile levé* (59) is by one who signed himself M. L. C. D. V. It is followed by *Chanson: "Les Français sont des diables . . . "* (60), by the same author. In this short humorous piece, two characters, a jurist and L'Abbé Coco, are made to sing boastfully of their successes in fooling and exploiting the people.

> Défiez-vous d'un Calotin,
> Qui veut vos femmes et votre bien:
> C'est un fourbe, un mauvais Chrétien
>   Et un gredin.
>
> Son but est de vous enchaîner,
> Les maris de cocufier,
> S'il réussit il s'écriera
>   Alléluia.

The songster goes on to say that in all times past, the poor have been robbed and despoiled by the Church. In the present state of affairs—wherein the deputies are honest and beneficent—the higher clergy and the members of the *Parlements* are malcontents who plot "the counter-Revolution."[30] The nuns in the convents are their agents and confidantes.[31] A warning is given against abbots, who, according to this song, would arm their followers in order to massacre the citizens, or to place them in prison, there to die.[32] After grim premonitions of this kind, the author implores the God of goodness to be "the protector and the avenger of the People."[33] His denunciation of churchmen and jurists is not, however, without some qualification: "everywhere," he concedes, "are honest folk, in the Church and in the *Parlements*."[34]

Many of the complaints in *The Veil Lifted* remind one of the observations which Erasmus made in his *In Praise of Folly*, on the eve of the Reformation. The Revolutionary satirist, resembling the Dutch humanist, gleefully exposes the relish of high churchmen for "good food and good wine," "fine carriages," and so forth. No doubt going further than his predecessor, he finds many ways to say that the *moeurs* of the land would be improved if the clergy were to marry "as good Citizens." They would then no longer lavish their wealth on prostitutes, or seduce the wives and daughters of the people.[35] A few Christian precepts are expressed toward the end of the song: "Let us worship God, love the good, and help our neighbor."[36] Regeneration is just a matter of getting in step with the Revolution: "the ecclesiastic [*l'abbé*] who is not a *citoyen* is a

---

[30] *Le voile levé* (59), stanzas 9-10.   [31] *Ibid.*, stanza 13.
[32] *Ibid.*, stanzas 18-20.   [33] *Ibid.*, stanzas 28-29.   [34] *Ibid.*, stanza 30.
[35] For these allusions, see *ibid.*, stanzas 33-38.   [36] *Ibid.*, stanza 53.

vaurien."[37] The final stanzas include an apostrophe to Louis, "tender and adored father," endowed with "great virtues" and "an excellent heart," who is happy only when blessings are bestowed upon "his children."

Patriots who were clamoring for a reformation of the Church of course rejoiced when in November the National Assembly declared that the ecclesiastical lands were at the disposal of the state.[38] Members of the Assembly who supported this measure were at pains to point out that no "spoliation" (the ugly word of the opposition) was intended or committed. The popular writers were far less discreet. They had no scruples about spoliation. One gathers from contemporary literature that they regarded the rich clergy as the original plunderers. Any measure to shear them of their wealth was a matter of plain justice to the people. As for tact in handling the disconsolate clergy! well, the tables were turned and now the churchmen could take all the lampooning that was due them.

"Rich canons . . . proud friars, you are deceived in your hopes: no longer will you tell us that these fat revenues are your patrimony." Such are the sentiments expressed in the opening stanza of *Les nouveaux apôtres aristocrates,* which according to the subtitle was written "on the occasion of the decree of the National Assembly that the goods possessed by the Clergy belong to the Nation."[39] The author, rejoicing over the plight of the churchmen, chides them with reminders of Scripture and admonishes them from now on to mend their ways:

> Faites de courts repas,
> Soyez sages en ville;
> La licence n'est pas
> Dans l'évangile.[40]

The third stanza, written in the same spirit as the quotation above,

---

[37] *Loc.cit.*

[38] A curious expression of this delight is the *Requiem aeternam of the Clergy of France* (72), a song written "by M. P. on leaving the National Assembly of November 2nd, 1789." The only extant copy, as far as I know, is at the Cleveland, Ohio, Public Library. The author's naïve enthusiasm—he assumes in connection with the passage of the decrees against the Church that famine and war are banished and that men may now live in peace—is an indication of the extent to which overzealous patriots attached symbolic significance to each new triumph of the Revolution.

[39] (71).   [40] *Ibid.,* stanza 2.

was published separately some months later in the *Chronique de Paris*.[41] According to an editorial comment, this mordant rebuke to the so-called "aristocrats" of the Church was sung in the streets to the great satisfaction of bystanders:

> Du sacerdoce
> Prenez l'humilité,
> Dans un carosse
> Dieu n'a jamais monté;
> Saint Pierre nous l'apprit;
> Et dans Rome en crédit,
> Monté sur une rosse,
> Avait-il moins l'esprit
> Du sacerdoce?

It appears in subsequent lines that from now on the pastors will remain "in residence"—a gibe at the upper clergy who were frequently absentee—and will henceforth "lead their flocks in innocence." The King has prepared the path of "gentle virtue" by coming to reside "with his people."[42]

The final stanza expresses a conviction—recurrently held by patriots after every crisis—that the Revolution is over: "peace is in our midst. . . , prudence reigns."[43]

Déduit, the author of another song celebrating the November decrees, made no attempt to placate the clergy. In the opening lines of his *Ni vu ni connu* . . . ,[44] he no doubt expressed what many a patriot felt:

> Ah! quel plaisir j'ai
> Messieurs du Clergé
> De voir comme on vous dépouille . . .

In a jingle of rapid-fire slang, the author makes it appear that the "too proud" ecclesiastics are losing their lofty tones and their airs. In the final stanza, he joyfully exclaims, "As good citizens, let us pool all our possessions."[45]

---

[41] May 18, 1790, vol. iii, pp. 549-50.

[42] *Les nouveaux apôtres aristocrates* (71), stanza 4.

[43] Though the air of *Les nouveaux apôtres aristocrates* is given as *La Lanterne*, the usual significance of the "lantern" (or lamp post to which the victims of popular disapproval were hanged) is reversed. This song, which heralds peace, has as its theme, "*plus de lanterne!*"

[44] (73).

[45] "En bons citoyens/ Mellons [*sic*] tous nos biens." *Ibid.*, ed. "b," stanza 4.

In the religious sphere, the claims of the Revolutionary party tended to be absolute. Rabaut Saint-Etienne boasted on the day after the passage of the November decrees that "the priests will have to keep in step with the State now." Mirabeau, as we have seen, pictured the clergy as "officials"—adjuncts, as it were, of the new national state. Members of the National Assembly refrained in the first months of the Revolution from acting on the full implications of this view. But the atmosphere of some of their debates and the trend of popular opinion in 1789 suggest that the Church might later be called upon to surrender not only its possessions, but also much of the spiritual integrity for which Christianity had stood.

Nevertheless, not all of the impulse of religious reform was subordinated to the exigencies of national unity. In the religious field, as elsewhere, the Revolutionary devotion to liberty had its effect. A considerable degree of freedom of worship was promised in the Declaration of Rights, and there were, in the course of the Revolution, certain applications of this principle. Its influence was a factor in the separation of church and state which Revolutionary France for a time achieved (1795-1802).

Thus, the spiritual impulse of the French Revolution contributed its share to two outstanding, and potentially divergent, aspects of modern life: on the one hand, to the tradition of liberalism which defends the right of the individual to worship God in his own way; and, on the other, to the tradition of nationalism which discourages or denies any worship that conflicts with the national interest.

As early as 1789, Mirabeau and Rabaut Saint-Etienne, among many others, went far, as we have seen, in projecting the latter development. It may appear at first glance that they were merely carrying on the age-old struggle of the temporal power to check, or control, the Church; but, actually, they were initiators of a movement that would itself absorb, rather than confine, man's religious instincts. Had they foreseen the full implications of this trend— such as were realized in the patriotic religion of the French Revolution at its climax and such as are manifest in much of the nationalism of our own day—they might have predicted that "Not only the priests, but also the gods, will have to keep in step with the state."

WHILE the impulse of religious reform, with its far-reaching implications, was sweeping over France in 1789, transformations of
comparable importance were taking place in quite a different field.

The French Revolution marks a turning point in the military
history of modern man. Before that democratic upheaval, wars
were carried on by the kings' armies. The honors of warfare were
reserved for the officers, who, except in the lower grades, were
exclusively of the noble class. The common soldier was supposed
to be more interested in subsistence than glory and was not as a
rule esteemed by civilians, to whom life in the barracks epitomized
a rough, lowly, and separate existence.[1] But with the Revolution,
military service became one of the most highly prized rights of
citizenship. The army of the future could thus be a people's army,
inspired by the new notions of liberty and patriotism.[2] How
quickly it became so! In the autumn of 1792, when France had
been at war but a few months, citizen volunteers, who were animated by the new patriotic faith of the Revolution, won a victory
at Valmy over the mercenary troops of Austria and Prussia. Goethe,
who was present at the battle, recognized the nascent force of
democratic nationalism, and correctly prophesied the commencement from that day of "a new era."

The transformation in France which made possible this new
era embodied two trends: first, the demoralization of the regular

[1] The composition of the army on the eve of the Revolution is described by
Spenser Wilkinson as follows: "The ranks of the French regiments were filled by
voluntary enlistment, that is by the wiles of the recruiting sergeant and the tempta-
tions of bounty. The recruits . . . were drawn from among the less fortunate of the
poorer class, the idlers of the towns, and the unemployed of town and country. The
bourgeoisie remained outside the army." *The French Army before Napoleon*, Oxford, 1915, p. 85.

[2] Here, at least, was the beginning of the practical application of such a view.
Nearly twenty years before, Count Guibert, in his *Essai de tactique général* (London,
1770; Paris, 1772), had pointed to the advantage which "a national army" would
have over the traditional professional armies. An outstanding authority on military
matters, Guibert was concerned with the inculcation of "manly virtues" and the
achievement of "great and decisive results in war." More in the spirit of popular
government was Rousseau's advocacy of a citizen-army, which he set forth in Chapter XII of his *Considérations sur le gouvernement de Pologne et sur sa réformation
projetée*, 1772.

army of the *ancien régime*; and, second, the creation of a new type of army of citizen enthusiasts. Both these trends progressed far in the course of 1789. Though something has been said in an earlier chapter concerning this military revolution, its importance warrants the introduction at this point of additional data and of a general summary.

The defection of the royal military establishment commenced with the French Guards, who were stationed habitually at Versailles and Paris, and who, unlike most of the regulars, fraternized freely with the people. This regiment—composed at this time of forty-eight hundred men—had been created by Catherine de Medici as a special bodyguard. Although the Guards owed a particular duty to the monarch, we have seen that some of them sided with the Parisian populace on July 12 and in fact fired on the King's dragoons under Lambesc, and that many of them played a leading part in the attack on the Bastille. In the preceding weeks they had already been converted—or corrupted, according to one's view—by the patriotic propaganda.

Of interest in this connection is a song entitled *Grateful Acknowledgment to the French Guards and to the Swiss Guards, on the patriotic manner in which they behaved after the Royal Session of June 23.*[3] This song was published "in the name of the Citizens of the Palais Royal." The troops, according to the author, were ordered to fire on the people, but refused to do so. There is even today much historical uncertainty concerning this alleged crisis, which is mentioned in but few contemporary records, and then only in general terms.[4] There seems to be little doubt, however, that the habitués of the Palais Royal believed that such a mutinous incident had occurred.

[3] *Remerciemens aux Gardes Françaises . . .* (17).

[4] The song refers to the circumstances surrounding Louis' return to the palace after the Royal Session. The King was followed by a vast throng of persons who were alarmed because of Necker's absence on that occasion. The crowd poured into the Court of the Ministers. Then, according to some testimony, two companies (not identified) were ordered to fire on the people; by the same accounts, the soldiers refused to obey. In marshaling the evidence that bears on the incident, Victor Fournel, in his *Les hommes du 14 juillet* (pp. 27-29), was able to point to only three sources: a passage in the *Moniteur*; brief statements in a letter of Camille Desmoulins to his father (Desmoulins was not an eyewitness—see *Oeuvres . . .* , J. Claretie, ed., vol. ii, pp. 320-21); and the song referred to above.

The *Grateful Acknowledgment* . . . consists in part of a dialogue between a citizen and one of the Guards.

"Do they take us for fools," the Guard exclaims, "when they call upon us to shoot at you all! . . . We are men, and, besides, Citizens."[5]

Subsequent lines reveal how stale and unimaginative mere discipline by now appears, in contrast to good common sense:

> L'ordre est raisonable,
> Nous obéissons:
> Est-il à la diable
> Nous nous en moquons.[6]

The Guard then explains to the Citizen how this way of looking at the matter has come about:

> Autrefois machine,
> Le pauvre Soldat,
> Sous la discipline,
> Etoit un forçat:
> Depuis qu'il sait lire,
> Il n'est plus oison;
> Il tient à l'Empire,
> Mais par la raison.[7]

Here seems to emerge a new variant of the Platonic scheme—the philosopher-soldier! But, after all, this novel and challenging attitude is only the Enlightenment carried to a logical conclusion—the triumph of reason, in the ranks.

The disobedience of the soldiers could be interpreted—as were all Revolutionary acts at this time—as a supreme form of loyalty to the sovereign. The disingenuous Guard, referring to the refusal of the soldiers to fire, raises this question:

> Qu'eût dit Louis seize
> Si sur ses enfans,
> Sa Garde Française
> Eût fait feux roulans?

The Guard then assures the Citizen that "our good King" would have been "too greatly saddened" had such an incident occurred.[8]

---

[5] *Remerciemens aux Gardes Françaises* . . . (17), stanza 2.   [6] *Ibid.*, stanza 6.
[7] *Ibid.*, stanza 7.   [8] *Ibid.*, stanza 4.

At the end of the dialogue the lyrist of the Palais Royal exclaims, "What great good the wise soldier can do!"[9]

Despite historical uncertainty as to the actual occurrences to which this song alludes, the *Grateful Acknowledgment of the French Guards . . .* well reflects a growing tendency on the part of the patriots to condone, and even glorify, military disobedience as a civic duty. Four days later, June 27, the French Guards at Versailles refused to patrol the streets when ordered to do so. Even more serious derelictions occurred at Paris. There the French Guards fraternized with the citizens, especially with the more ardent patriots of the Palais Royal. Two companies disobeyed orders on June 24. Some days later a mass of Parisians—four thousand, or more—forced the release of several French Guards who had been imprisoned for disobedience. Not only were the Guards out of control; other troops sent to restore order, shouted *Vive la Nation!* and sided with the people. The prisoners who were released by the mob were promptly pardoned by the King, at the urgent request of the Assembly.[10] The defection of the royal army was thus accompanied by a certain degree of official approval.

There was now no doubt, as the Parisians said, that the Guards were "on the side of the nation." "Already the most astonishing miracle has taken place," wrote Camille Desmoulins in his pamphlet *La France libre.* "Our soldiers have cast down their arms. The example which the French Guards have set will be by no means lost on the army."[11] This was an entirely correct estimate.[12]

---

[9] The rapprochement of soldier and citizen is pictured as follows in *La Constitution française . . .* (55):

> Le militaire
> N'a plus le coeur d'airain,
> De l'arbitraire
> Il n'est plus le soutain,
> Et comme un frère
> Il voit le citoyen.

(Stanza 16 in editions indicated "a" and "c" in Bibliography 1: stanza 15 in edition "b.")

[10] The strange theories of military duty which were current at this stage of the Revolution are eloquently expressed in two contemporary brochures: *Adresse des Gardes-françoises enlevés des Prisons de l'abbaye, au Roi. Au Palais Royal . . . 2 juillet, 1789;* and *Lettre des Gardes-françoises au Roi pour remercier sa Majesté de la grâce qu'elle vient de leur accorder* (n.p.), *le 2 juillet.* Both these items are in the Talleyrand Collection of the New York Public Library.

[11] *La France libre, par M. Desmoulins . . . , troisième édition, 1789,* p. 68. This work was written in June, according to Aulard, and first published July 17, 1789.

[12] Royal troops mutinied at Caen, Strasbourg, and many other places during the

"Brave soldiers," continued the ardent young Desmoulins, "mingle with your brothers, receive their embraces. . . . You are no longer the satellites of the despot, the jailers of your brothers. You are our friends, our fellows, citizens, and soldiers of *la patrie*."[13]

The author pictured the creation of "a national army" composed of a bourgeois militia "like the magistracy, like the priesthood, where virtue, the voice of the people, and proper esteem will lead to everything, and birth, wealth, favor of the prince to nothing." Here was the new gospel of careers open to talent, with all that it implies. "Yes, this fortunate revolution, this regeneration is going to be accomplished; no power on earth can prevent it. Sublime effect of philosophy, of liberty and of patriotism! we have become invincible. I myself, I frankly confess it, I who was timid now feel myself to be a new man." Desmoulins then compared himself to the Spartan Otriades: "My body pierced with blows, I also would write with my life's blood, *France is free!*"[14]

While this demoralization of the regular army was taking place, the citizen-soldiery was gaining in strength. The "bourgeois guards"—created at Paris in July and shortly thereafter in the other municipalities of France—were officially recognized by the Assembly on August 10 as a "national" reserve force.[15] The representatives did not, however, make of them an agency of the centralized government; instead, they left the new volunteers subject to the various municipalities. The scattered units of the National Guard, however, tended to coalesce through a spontaneous popular movement, of which more will be said presently.

From the very beginning, the citizen-soldiers were inclined to make a cult of the patriotic cause. In time, they developed a ritual of their own, but at first they depended heavily on that of the Catholic Church, which to some extent they were able to appropriate

---

summer. In a letter written on September 3, 1789, the Count of Fersen described how the garrison at Valenciennes got completely out of hand, rioted, and pillaged. It was suppressed only with the aid of the bourgeois militia. "What is extraordinary," he continued, "is that the same thing has occurred in nearly all the garrisons and that in all the Kingdom there have been comparable revolts." Cited in H. Gautier, *L'an 1789* . . . , Paris (1889), p. 653.

13 *La France libre* . . . , pp. 73-74.   14 *Ibid.*, p. 75.

15 They were described in the decree as "milices nationales," but were to be generally known as "Gardes nationales." The long-established militia of the old regime was abolished in principle on August 4, 1789, and by law on June 1, 1790.

to Revolutionary ends. For example, during August, services were held in several churches to honor citizens who died in the attack on the Bastille. At one of these, the preacher, Claude Fauchet, by implication at least, compared the sacrifice made by the departed heroes to the immolation of Jesus. Fauchet's text, taken from Paul's Epistle to the Galatians, contained a timely message: "For, brethren, ye have been called unto liberty." The preacher, an ardent Revolutionist, described the will of the public as "the voice of God"; and he pictured even Calvary in terms of the new patriotism when he held that "Jesus Christ died for the human race by dying for his country." "O my brothers," Fauchet said in bringing this theme to a climax, "IT IS THE ARISTOCRACY WHO CRUCIFIED THE SON OF GOD."[16] As Louis Blanc truly says, such expressions coming from the lips of a priest were "a great and striking novelty."[17] After the service Fauchet was escorted by two companies of soldiers in a triumphal procession, with drums beating, to the city hall. The fact that this priest had himself been an assailant of the Bastille—together with his penchant for blending Revolutionary doctrines with those of Holy Writ—brought him great prominence. To Fauchet's mind, the Revolution was the realization anew of that for which primitive Christianity had stood. Many of the patriots already held this view, and they were flattered to find that it had an energetic and fearless sponsor in the Church itself.

Each battalion of the National Guard at Paris had its standard blessed at a service in the church of its district. Many such services —bénédictions des drapeaux, as they were called—were performed during August and September, 1789.[18] The atmosphere of these ceremonies was an interesting blend of religious reverence and patriotic excitement. A general benediction of all the flags of the Paris National Guard was held on September 27 at Notre Dame. On this occasion, the Archbishop blessed individually the battalion

---

[16] *Discours, sur la liberté françoise, prononcé le Mercredi 5 Août 1789, dans l'Eglise Paroissiale de S.-Jacques & des SS. Innocens . . . , par M. l'Abbé Fauchet, Paris, 1789*, p. 1 and pp. 7-8. There is also a contemporary version in English, *A Discourse by M. L'Abbé Fauchet . . .* , translated from the French by William Harvest, London, 1790. (IV, C)

[17] *Histoire de la Révolution française*, vol. iii, p. 297.

[18] Two songs which relate to such occasions have already been mentioned—*Couplets à M. le Marquis de La Fayette . . .* (50), and *Couplets chantés à Madame la Marquise de La Fayette . . .* (58). See pages 151-52, including notes 42 and 48.

flags, and the Abbé Fauchet delivered to the vast assemblage in the cathedral another of his addresses on French liberty.[19]

An important feature of the nascent ritual of the citizen-soldier was the cementing of various loyalties by solemn "oaths." This procedure, on many occasions spontaneous, was at other times prescribed. For example, the National Assembly decreed, August 10, that all soldiers of the regular forces be required to swear in the presence of their officers an oath to be "faithful to the Nation, to the King, and to the Law"; and that the officers, in turn, swear such an oath in the presence of the municipal officials. This practice was extended, with some modifications, to the National Guard. It was in accord with the same trend that Bailly, heading a Paris delegation, went to Versailles, August 25, to swear to His Majesty an oath of loyalty that had been dictated by the Assembly of the Paris Commune.[20] More will be said presently of such commitments. It will suffice to remark at this point that by their oaths of loyalty to the nation and to one another—which were taken on almost every possible occasion—the patriots were creating an integral and, in a sense, sacred society of their own.[21]

The fraternal movement had, of course, its lighter side. Convivial celebrations were held by National Guardsmen at Paris and in the provinces. It was customary to sing patriotic songs at these gatherings, and some of the pieces written for special occasions have been preserved. For instance, there is at the Bibliothèque

[19] According to Tiersot, "military symphonies" by Gossec supplemented the regular church music. See J. Tiersot, *Les fêtes et les chants de la Révolution française*, p. 16.

[20] This oath, as a matter of fact, had the same ambivalent quality that has been described in an earlier chapter: "Je jure à Dieu, entre les mains de Votre Majesté, de faire respecter votre authorité légitime, *de conserver les droits sacrés de la Commune de Paris* [italics mine], et de rendre la justice à tous." *Actes de la Commune de Paris . . .* , vol. i, p. 341. And obviously the oath of the soldiers, given above, reveals the same potential implication of divided loyalty.

[21] Mathiez, one of the few writers who has considered the psychological significance of this subject, observes that the "social origin of the civic oath unmistakably stamps the revolutionary faith with the character of religious faith." *Les origines des cultes révolutionnaires (1789-1792)*, Paris, 1904, p. 26. The religious impulses in this case were, of course, not derived from traditional Christianity. It is likely that they owed much to the influence of Freemasonry, which, it may be said in passing, served its adherents as an avenue of religious expression. This point has been made by Gaston Martin, who writes in the course of a well-documented work that "The Freemasonry of the eighteenth century was in certain respects a church," and who refers to the movement as a religion. See his *La Franc-Maçonnerie française et la préparation de la Révolution*, 2nd ed., Paris, 1926, pp. 82ff.

Nationale the unique copy of a leaflet containing "Stanzas sung by a citizen soldier of the National Guard of Compiègne at the fete given on September 13, 1789, by the citizens of that town, to the detachment of the Paris National Guard sent to escort the convoy of arms coming from Maubeuge."[22] This patriotic song is of interest particularly as affording evidence that both Bailly and Lafayette enjoyed the same high regard in Compiègne that they did in Paris. Also extant is the text of a song printed at Bordeaux, which was composed by "a volunteer of the army" for a patriotic fete in November.[23]

A similar use of the patriotic song is revealed in "Stanzas sung at the Assembly of the Companies of Grenadiers and of Chasseurs of the Battalion of Bonne-Nouvelle . . . ; and repeated to those of the Battalion of the Oratoire . . . December 20, 1789," by Charon, former officer of the National Guard.[24] The opening lines, which suggest the pride taken by the volunteers not only in the success, but also in the cosmic significance, of the popular movement, may be translated somewhat freely as follows: "What more sublime example than that offered to the universe by a magnanimous people which has just broken its chains!"[25] According to Charon, this liberated people, though obliged to "track its enemies to the very steps of the Throne," has made "the Crown more secure on the head of Louis."[26] In this piece, as in most of the patriotic songs which appeared at this time, lavish praise is accorded to Lafayette. The new note of comradeship is struck in the final stanza, in which the soldiers are admonished to see "a relative, a brother, in each Fellow-citizen."

About this time, National Guardsmen of the District of the Cordeliers celebrated what one of their number announced in the press as the first patriotic festival of the Revolution. The circumstances which occasioned the gathering are of considerable interest. One Brichard, captain of the Battalion of the Cordeliers, in the course of travels to the south of France, received an ovation at

---

22 *Couplets, chantés par un soldat citoyen . . . , par M. Mounier, cit de Compiègne* (57).

23 *Couplets, chantés chez le sr [sic] Bardineau . . .* (74).

24 *Couplets chantés en l'Assemblée des Compagnies de Grenadiers . . .* (79).

25 The original reads: "Quel exemple plus sublime/ Qu'aux regards de l'univers,/ Offre un peuple magnanime/ Qui vient de briser ses fers."

26 *Ibid.*, stanza 2.

Montpellier, where he was elected a member of the local National Guard. Brichard thereupon proposed that "a close union" be established between that city and the capital. Delegates from Montpellier accompanied him on his return to Paris. The visitors were presented by Lafayette to the Assembly of the Commune, which enthusiastically approved "an affiliation of the National Guard of Montpellier with the Paris National Guard."[27] This was on December 19. The following day the District of the Cordeliers extended special courtesies to the deputies of Montpellier, culminating in a banquet in their honor. There were eighty-four covers, and the table, according to a contemporary report, "offered the touching spectacle of one and the same family." The last of many toasts was "to the liberty of the universe," or, as one would say today, to freedom everywhere. M. Dugazon, "former officer and now a soldier of the Paris National Guard," sang verses of his own composition, to celebrate the union of Montpellier and Paris.[28] These details are derived from a letter written by one of the diners, and published in the *Moniteur*.[29] The contributor ended with the wish that other patriots would imitate the occasion, "as one of the best means of cementing the formal engagement of all good citizens to defend liberty and her happy children." His fondest hopes must have been more than fulfilled by the subsequent popularity of similar festivals.

Shortly after taking up his residence in Paris, the King put Lafayette, Commander-General of the Paris National Guard, in command of all the troops, including the regulars, within the area of the capital. This was but one step in the amalgamation of the regular and volunteer forces.

One may remark in passing that despite the immense popularity which Lafayette enjoyed at this time and the assurances of loyalty which were expressed by all the patriots, he had difficulty in holding together his command. That such was the case is revealed in remarks which the General addressed toward the end of October "to

[27] For a full account, see *Actes de la Commune de Paris*, S. Lacroix, ed., vol. iii, pp. 219-22.

[28] *Couplets chantés par M. Dugazon* . . . (80). Although the circumstances which occasioned this composition are reported with unusual fullness, the lyrics of only one stanza are preserved.

[29] December 22, 1789, vol. i, p. 495.

the officers of the National Guard assembled at his home."[30] He begged ("je vous le demande à genoux") that they take an oath to sacrifice their personal interests "for four months more," which he regarded as the time required for "the solid establishment of the constitution." Lafayette then referred to his experiences in America, where, he said, the soldiers underwent every kind of privation for seven years without complaint.[31] He thereupon rebuked his officers who, though enjoying the comforts of life at home, were complaining of "seven months sacrificed in order to be free forever."

Insight into the sensibilities of the new type of soldier is amply furnished in *The Great Noel of the National Guards, formerly the French Guards.*[32] This long song, separately published as 1789 drew to a close, is worth quoting in some detail. The author, referring to Voltaire as his authority, declares that soldiers formerly were mere automatons directed by the aristocrats. The Revolution, it appears in a remarkable passage (each part of which is deserving of scrutiny), has brought about an awakening:

> Nous sentons qui nous sommes;
> Nos coeurs règlent nos bras,
> Et nous jurons d'être Hommes,
> Avant d'être Soldats.[33]

France now undertakes to have in the army "only true Citizens!"[34]

The song presently discloses the new relation of the soldiers to their officers. It is well at this point to mention a change wrought by the Revolution. According to the Declaration of Rights, there was to be no distinction between citizens "except that of their virtues and talents," and this meant, in theory at least, that the higher positions in the army would no longer be reserved exclusively for members of the noble class. The regular army was not at once reformed in this respect; but from the beginning the soldiers

[30] *Extrait d'un Discours adressé par M. le Marquis de la Fayette, vers la fin d'Octobre, aux Officiers de la Garde Nationale, assemblés chez lui,* Paris (1789), 8 pp. (IV, C)

[31] Such, at least, was the general's testimony: "Je jure sur mon honneur que pendant sept ans de misère je n'ai pas reçu une plainte réelle d'un Américain . . . ." *Ibid.,* p. 5.

[32] *Le grand Noël des Gardes Nationales . . .* (81).   [33] *Ibid.,* stanza 2.

[34] *Ibid.,* stanza 3.

of the National Guard elected a certain portion of their officers, who, by and large, were members of the bourgeois class.[35] This fact pleased the author of *The Great Noel*, who compares the officer of the present, "chosen amongst our own," to the "severe, and often contemptuous, officer" of the past.[36] Under the old regime—the song goes on to say—the ambitious soldier could become an adjutant at best, and that only with difficulty, whereas now he can readily attain any of the higher ranks. Although the author was describing a development that had hardly begun, from his day commenced the theory in Europe, and to some extent the practice, of freeing military leadership of caste restrictions, of building the army of the future on the basis of "careers open to talent."

Three of the twenty-four stanzas of *The Great Noel* are devoted to praise of Lafayette. In one of these, gratitude is expressed that the harsh treatment of former days has been replaced by his "gentle discipline [*discipline douce*]."[37]

The song then pictures the new freedom of a National Guardsman. In earlier times the military force was segregated,

> Mais le soldat moderne
> N'est plus dorénavant
> Cloître dans sa caserne
> Comme dans un Couvent:
> Il boit à la taverne. . . .
>
> Si nous aimons les filles,
> Si nous aimons le vin,
> Ce sont des Peccadilles
> Qu'on blâmeroit en vain.
> Notre ami Henri-Quatre,
> Fier de ces deux besoins,
> Quand il falloit se battre,
> Ne s'en battoit pas moins.[38]

It is interesting that, in this analogy, the soldiers of 1789 are compared, not to those in the time of Henry IV, but to the King himself.

---

[35] There were various restrictions: only persons with previous military experience could be elected officers; and a considerable proportion of the higher positions were filled by vote of fellow officers, rather than by that of the enlisted men.

[36] *Ibid.*, stanza 9.   [37] *Ibid.*, stanza 13.   [38] *Ibid.*, stanza 18, in part, and stanza 19.

Would not this general disruption of the old discipline—the modern reader wonders—weaken France, and endanger Louis? No such doubt entered the mind of the patriotic author of *The Great Noel*. France, as he saw it, was transformed and made stronger by new values. Supposing, for example, Louis should be urged to break his promise to remain in Paris—

> Si par un plan contraire
> Quelque jour les méchans,
> Engageoient ce bon Père
> A quitter ses enfans,
> A force de prières,
> Fixons-le dans Paris,
> Les coeurs sont des barrières
> Dont ce Roi sent le prix.[39]

Here again we see, as has been evident in so many other instances, that the "new day"—in which love binds men more strongly than any external power—was regarded by the patriot not as a promise for the future, but as already achieved.

In the concluding stanza, the hopes of the Guards are summarized as follows:

> Sur nos Drapeaux, d'avance,
> Tous nos voeux sont portés. . . .
> Combattre pour, la France,
> Ou pour ses Députés;
> Servir la Capitale,
> Louis le Bienfaisant,
> La Famille Royale,
> Et notre Commandant.

These wishes implied the unity of France. Everywhere such hopes were expressed. But they were the product of an optimism which was made possible only by blindness to the fundamental conflicts existing between the capital, the deputies, and the King.

In revising most of the institutions of the old regime, the men of 1789 were bound to consider what role, if any, the royal army should continue to play. Might it be replaced by a citizen-soldier

---

[39] *Ibid.*, stanza 22.

force similar to that which had already come into being? What, after all, was the appropriate military establishment for a people who had gained their liberty? These questions came before the National Assembly on December 12.

The Military Committee, following the advice of La Tour du Pin, Minister of War, favored the maintenance of a regular professional army recruited on a volunteer basis, and, in addition, a militia drawn by the sort of lottery to which Frenchmen were well accustomed.[40]

Dubois de Crancé, later a member of the Committee of Public Safety and one of the master architects of the warfare which France waged under the Republic, rose to object on principle to an army of professional soldiers. He ventured to say—amid calls for order—that a man armed to defend liberty could not march with one (the professional soldier) who had sold his. Dubois de Crancé then proposed that all men entitled to vote compose the National Guard, and that of this number those between the ages of eighteen and forty form the "active army." Only thus—and not by an army of mercenaries—could liberty be preserved.[41] Dubois de Crancé's plan meant conscription.

Bureau de Puzy, another prominent member of the Assembly, three times elected its President, had a regard for liberty which led him to an entirely different conclusion. Conscription, he argued, would result in coercive and punitive measures to force men into the army. It was, he said, worse than absurd, in setting men free, to require of them military duties for which they might not be fitted. To illustrate his point, he continued in the following manner:

A citizen might say: "I was born weak and timid; do you require that I be strong and courageous? Leave me by my fireside to consecrate to my country the faculties that nature has given me, and by means of which I can make myself useful." Will you reply by confronting him with ruin, grief or infamy! No—legislators who have given evidence of

[40] The militia, an institution of long standing, was made a permanent reserve force by a royal ordinance in 1726. Members of the Third Estate, who, with certain exceptions, were liable for service, were chosen by an annual lottery. Beatrice Hyslop (*French Nationalism in 1789* . . . , p. 120) writes, "The majority of the *cahiers* opposed the form of compulsory service which the militia represented, and therefore evinced approval of voluntary service."

[41] According to the *Moniteur*, December 14, 1789 (session of December 12), vol. i, p. 463.

the most profound respect for the inalienable rights of man will not attack liberty. They do not need to be unjust. The French have not fallen from their antique prowess to such an extent that it is necessary to constrain them, by a rigorous law, to serve their country.[42]

The future, as later generations were to discover, was on the side of total war, and in matters of defense concern for individual liberty was destined to give way to concern for the security of the group. But somewhere in the consciousness of liberty-loving peoples must still lurk the sense of paradox inherent in this question which Bureau de Puzy put to the Assembly: "Whereas he who voluntarily signs away his liberty for a few years takes the step of a free man, will not a person who shall have been forced to obey the law be taking the action of a slave?" Bureau de Puzy held that the support of liberty is "an army composed of free men."[43] This insistence on the freedom of the individual was the spirit of 1789. But it was also the spirit of that time—and here is the entering wedge of total war—to magnify the importance of the people of a free state by proclaiming that "every citizen is a soldier."[44]

It was thus the paradoxical achievement of the men of 1789 to create an atmosphere of liberty which made conscription seem reprehensible, and, at the same time, to arouse a sense of civic responsibility that made it inevitable. Both of these trends are expressed in the songs of that year.

The citizen-soldiers of 1789 and 1790 played an important part in the integration of Revolutionary France. This they did primarily through the remarkable "federative movement," to which Aulard, in his important history of French patriotism from the Renaissance to the Revolution,[45] devoted as much as a third of his attention.[46] We have seen that in some respects France, under the impact of the Revolution, was falling apart—the Assembly, as well

---

[42] Ibid., December 16, 1789 (session of the same day), p. 472.

[43] Loc.cit. The only immediate result of the debate was the passage of a decree, December 16, 1789, retaining the system of voluntary enlistment for the army.

[44] The times were soon to catch up with Dubois de Crancé. On August 23, 1793, the Convention voted its famous levée en masse. A few years later (1798) the Directory instituted a regular system of compulsory military service. France thereby created a pattern of incalculable importance in the history of modern times—that of "the nation in arms."

[45] Le patriotisme français de la Renaissance à la Révolution, Paris, 1921.

[46] Ibid., pp. 136-240.

as the people, having destroyed many of the most fundamental ties of the old regime without being able at once to substitute adequate institutions. In addition to such immediate causes of disunity, the traditional separatism in France militated against patriotism in the modern sense. The various French provinces were very old—many of them having at one time or another enjoyed independence, virtual or complete—and the sentiment of provincialism, whether Norman, Burgundian, or Provençal, was naturally deep-rooted. Besides, there were many *pays*, smaller than the provinces, to which Frenchmen here and there had become deeply attached.

There was thus the possibility—quite apart from any harm that the reactionaries might do by their dreaded "plots"—that the Revolutionary ideal of national solidarity would be lost. To offset this danger, there developed a spontaneous movement of thousands of brothers-in-arms—citizen-soldiers of the new National Guard—who, together with enterprising municipal officials, created the organizational means of implementing that ideal. The initiative was taken in scattered communities throughout France. At meetings—usually held outdoors—delegates of neighboring communities gathered to form local federations. By means of such bonds, they hoped to check banditry, to repel possible attacks by aristocrats, and, in general, to take by united action measures to make secure the achievements and promises of the Revolution.

The federations, the first of which date from August, 1789,[47] became numerous and widespread as the months passed. Aggregations of increasing size were built up, until sometimes the communities of an entire province, or those of parts of two or more provinces, would federate. The interesting feature of these gatherings and unions is that the transcendent theme of their spokesmen was not local security, but the welfare of *la Patrie*.

Here, for example, is the message of a colonel speaking on behalf of the National Guards of Vivarais, to delegates who had come from towns of Dauphiné, across the Rhône, to form a federation:

We offer you, all of you, National Guards, our fellow-citizens, our brothers freely consecrated to the defense of the restored *patrie*, the

[47] Aulard calls attention to certain preliminaries undertaken in Franche-Comté as early as July. *Op.cit.*, pp. 151-52.

oath to aid you in your dangers, to correspond uninterruptedly with you, to remain united to you by a sacred trust, to regard you as members of the same corps, for the defense of which we have sworn to sacrifice our lives, and we ask you in return to join with us in the same engagement, to extend it to your neighbors, to communicate it, from place to place, to the remotest parts of the Empire, in order that, from one end of France to the other, fraternal friendship, watchfulness and mutual support may become for us, forever, the absolute guarantees of happiness and liberty.[48]

Clearly, this was an elaborately developed movement, in which people were acting as the creators of a new order, rather than as subjects. Something of the spirit of democratic nationalism, which is a commonplace today, was thus appearing for the first time in modern Europe. It had been centuries in coming. Certainly it could not develop so long as the "subject-master" mentality engendered by despotic government, remained.

A brief glance at one area of France, the southeast, where the federative movement was especially strong, may serve to emphasize some of the outstanding characteristics of this new sense of national solidarity, and to indicate the rapidity with which it spread. The proposal of the Vivarais colonel, quoted above, led to an "act of union" which was sworn to by National Guard delegates from twenty communities, some in Languedoc, some in Dauphiné. On December 13, a federation took place at Montélimart which drew together delegations from seventy-five communities, scattered in three different provinces (Languedoc, Dauphiné, and Provence).[49] According to the oath taken at the time, "We French swear to God and to la Patrie to defend, unto death, the enforcement of the decrees of the National Assembly, and for that purpose, to bear one another all necessary aid."[50] Mention may be made of yet another federation, held at Tournon, a fortnight later, which was attended by the National Guards of eighty-six parishes of Dauphiné and

[48] Federation at La Voulte, November 29, 1789. Aulard, op.cit., pp. 143-46.

[49] An item of bibliographical interest may be added here, since Aulard remarks in a footnote (op.cit., p. 147): "Nous ne connaissons cette fédération de Montélimart que par la mention que fait M. Gustave Vallier, ouvrage cité." In the collection of the New York Public Library (DFD, p. v. 17, no. 2) is the Fédération de Montélimart, en Dauphiné, n.p.n.d., 14 pp. This brochure contains speeches made on the occasion, details of the federation, and other interesting data. It was decreed that copies of the record be sent to the National Guard of Paris and to the municipalities of the Kingdom.

[50] Fédération de Montélimart, en Dauphiné, p. 8. (IV, C)

Vivarais. "Gentlemen and fellow citizens," said one of the spokes-men on this occasion, "we have from now on only one common *patrie*, and the name of fellow-citizen belongs henceforth to all Frenchmen who inhabit this great kingdom."[51]

The same impulses were at work in widely scattered parts of France—notably in Brittany and Franche-Comté. In the former province there was an interesting resort to correspondence,[52] re-sembling in a measure the circular letters which the American colonists had used some twenty years earlier as an effective means of propaganda. Something of a youth movement, too, developed in this area. It was sponsored by the young people of Quimper, who sent out a proposal of union to "all the young citizens of Brit-tany."[53] In Franche-Comté, delegates of fourteen towns, meeting at Besançon, are reported to have sworn a solemn oath at the "altar of *la patrie*"[54]—the new altar of modern nationalism, which was to receive such prominence later in the Revolution. These are but a few indications of the vigor of a movement which the patriots un-dertook to spread, in the terms of one memorandum, to "all the towns and villages and communities of France entire."[55]

The greatest triumph in this remarkable development was achieved at the Festival of Federation, held on the first anniversary of the capture of the Bastille. Here was the culmination of the whole federative idea. On a proposal made by the Commune of Paris and approved by the National Assembly, delegates—one for every two hundred National Guardsmen in France—were invited to converge at the capital to join the Parisians in taking an oath of loyalty to the new nation which the Revolution had created.[56] It is estimated that three hundred thousand people attended the cere-

[51] Aulard, *op.cit.*, pp. 146-47.   [52] *Ibid.*, p. 176.

[53] *Loc.cit.* Gaston Martin writes that young people's societies, which from the eve of the Revolution exerted considerable political influence in Brittany, were of Ma-sonic origin. *La Franc-Maçonnerie française et la préparation de la Révolution*, 2nd ed., Paris, 1926, p. 133.

[54] Aulard, *op.cit.*, p. 154. Aulard does not give the date, but it appears from his discussion (pp. 153-55) to have been between September 27, 1789, and February 21, 1790.

[55] *Ibid.*, p. 153.

[56] Wilkinson states (*The French Army before Napoleon*, p. 106) that "14,000 deputies of the National Guard and deputies of every regiment in the army" gath-ered at Paris to join in taking the oath of loyalty at the Champs de Mars. According to the same writer, no less than two and a half million National Guards had been enrolled by that time.

mony of July 14, 1790, which a modern historian has called "the first public translation of the Revolution into a national religion."[57] Political songs came into especial prominence on this occasion,[58] and from this time dates the interest of the patriots in the new sacred literature of Revolutionary hymns.[59]

Particular mention has been made of the local federations of 1789, because the citizens who brought them into being deliberately aimed at such an extensive national unity as that which was celebrated at Paris in July, 1790, and because they did much to create that spirit of fervent brotherhood which gave to the Festival of Federation its religious character, and which remained an integral part of the Revolutionary faith thereafter.

It was this mood which animated the new citizen armies. Born, as we have seen, not only of common affections but also of common dangers, it embodied, along with elements of supreme devotion, an implacable hatred toward enemies. This spirit of intense fraternalism became, as it were, a weapon which, put to the service of the Revolutionary cause in the first instance, has ever since been exploited in the nationalism of modern times.

[57] L. R. Gottschalk, *The Era of the French Revolution*, p. 181.

[58] As already suggested in the Introduction; see pages 8-9. In his *Catalogue* Pierre lists over eighty songs that were occasioned either directly or indirectly by the Festival of Federation (see especially his 307-365*; 367; 369-382*; and 389-390). By far the greater part of these are songs of the citizen-soldiers. Many of them are lengthy. Together they give a vivid and informative portrayal of the new Revolutionary patriotism, as I can testify from a careful analysis of over seventy texts.

[59] The scores of important hymns are reproduced in Pierre's *Musique des fêtes et cérémonies de la Révolution française*, Paris, 1899.

ALTHOUGH it was feared by many of the patriots that the aristocrats
were ever on the point of launching a violent counterattack against
the Revolution, the reaction of the nobles was at first primarily
one of scorn, or of retreat. In July, 1789, disaffected nobles began
to leave the country. This exodus, following the capture of the
Bastille, had as its most distinguished member the Count of Artois,
the younger of the King's two brothers. The disturbances in the
provinces during the summer occasioned a second wave of emigration, and a third followed the October insurrection. Having escaped the Revolution, these refugees—or *émigrés*, as they were
called—gathered at points near the borders of France (at Brussels,
Coblentz, Turin, and a number of other important centers), where
they were free to plot—frequently in conjunction with foreigners—
the overthrow of the Revolution and the restoration of the old
regime. But by no means all of the disaffected aristocrats left
France; many remained to fight openly against the Revolution, or
to undermine it by boring from within. By the fall of 1789 rumors
of plots were rife. Nothing, however, of a desperate character was
brought to light until the very end of the year, when, as we shall
see, a conspiracy of the aristocrats was exposed.

On November 2, the first number of the famous anti-Revolutionary journal, *Les actes des apôtres*, appeared. The ironic vein
which characterizes this work is heralded in the title, the "Apostles"
being none other than the members of the National Assembly.
This journal, to which reference has already been made,[1] is described by Marius Sepet as "the most reactionary" of that time, as
"the most feared and most hated by the patriots." As the same critic
remarks, "There reigns therein an infinity of wit, but an almost
complete lack of taste."[2] One need not go so far, however, as an
Irish historian who declared that the paper's founder, Peltier, and
his associates hoped to "poison their opponents with the stench
arising from the pages of their journal."[3] As a matter of fact, the

[1] See pages 185 and 186.
[2] *La chute de l'Ancienne France—La Fédération*, Paris, 1895, pp. 309-10.
[3] J. H. McCarthy, *The French Revolution*, London, 1890-97, vol. iv, p. 104.

ribaldries of Peltier were no ruder than those of many patriotic writers, and his vicious attacks on individuals and groups were part of an atmosphere of mean and frantic quarreling in which both sides participated and which became worse as the Revolution progressed.

Issues of *Les actes des apôtres* customarily ran to sixteen pages of octavo size. Songs, which at first appeared only occasionally in this journal, were later published in it with increasing frequency. By the time *Les actes des apôtres* came to an end (August 10, 1792) it had printed over eighty anti-Revolutionary songs. The first of these was a short item which circumstances have made justly famous. This *Chanson nouvelle*, as a facetious editor set forth, was written to "the solemn air of the minuet of *Exaudet*."[4] It centered about proposals made in the National Assembly by Dr. Joseph-Ignace Guillotin, a leading physician of his day and one of the many truly kind and philanthropic spirits which that age produced. Dr. Guillotin had argued that in matters of capital punishment there should be no distinction based on the status of the victim (hitherto nobles condemned to death had been beheaded; commoners, hanged) and that the death penalty should be expeditiously administered.[5] The speaker then explained the nature of a certain invention which he had perfected. It appears that he inadvertently caused his hearers to laugh by assuring them that his death-dealing machine would not hurt one in the least;[6] and for some time the doctor's proposal was disregarded by the Assembly.[7] However, *Les actes des apôtres*, which seldom missed the chance of putting a deputy in a ridiculous light, seized upon the incident and published a song which commenced:

[4] *Chanson nouvelle. "Guillotin, Médecin, Politique . . . "* (76), in *Les actes des apôtres*, no. 10, pp. 15-16.

[5] The same proposal, which stemmed from eighteenth-century philosophy on penal reform, had been advanced in some of the *cahiers*: "For egalitarian as well as humanitarian reasons, several cahiers would substitute beheading, in cases of the death penalty, for hanging." B. Hyslop, *French Nationalism in 1789 . . .* , p. 141.

[6] This incident is not mentioned in the *Moniteur* in accounts of Dr. Guillotin's remarks to the Assembly on October 10 and December 1, 1789. I have borrowed from C. D. Hazen, *The French Revolution*, vol. i, p. 384.

[7] Although the Assembly postponed consideration of Guillotin's invention, it decreed on December 1 the first of the articles which he proposed, viz., "Offenses of the same sort shall be punished by the same kind of penalty, whatever may be the rank and condition of the guilty one." *Moniteur*, December 1, 1789, p. 412.

Guillotin,
Médecin,
Politique,
Imagine un beau matin
Que pendre est inhumain
Et peu patriotique.

Part of the lampoon may be omitted; suffice it to say that the versatile doctor seeks a punishment which will eliminate the hangman's office. Finally, after consulting "people of the trade," including the radical leaders Barnave and Chapelier, he succeeds:

Et sa main
Fait soudain
La machine
Qui simplement nous tuera,
Et que l'on nommera
Guillotine.

This appears to be the earliest suggestion that the invention which
was to play such a sanguinary part in the later stages of the Revolution be called the *guillotine*. As a matter of fact, the new instrument was not adopted until 1792. On March 25 of that year, the
Legislative Assembly approved the device at the suggestion of a
certain Dr. Louis—and for a brief time it was dubbed *la louisette*.
But as it turned out, people were partial to the term which had first
been coined; *guillotine*, accordingly, prevailed—to the distress of
its original sponsor, who until his death in 1814 was tortured by
remorse over the bloody associations destined forever to stain his
name.

The second and only other song which appeared in *Les actes des
apôtres* in 1789 was the *National Noel*,[8] a sarcastic attack on the
"wonderful decrees" of the "great senate of France." The song expresses mock approval of the "sacred fury" of the radicals and of
their various achievements, the expropriation of Church property
being particularly derided. Tributes of barbed irony are paid to
a mixed company of patriotic leaders—Barnave, Chapelier, Robespierre, and Talleyrand, among many others. The King, it appears,
"has given way to the hero La Fayette." In the last three stanzas

[8] *Noël national* (82), in *Les actes des apôtres*, no. 15, pp. 12-15.

the author, abandoning irony and indirection, bluntly charges that "a blind and cruel people" have become the laughingstock of other countries; that they are leading France to economic ruin and a state of defenselessness; and that all the efforts of the legislators will accomplish nothing.

No doubt the only effect of such ill-tempered attacks was to strengthen the resolve of the patriots. A sustained, more balanced, and really trenchant satire of the whole patriotic cause appeared in a song that was published somewhat later in *Les actes des apôtres*.[9] Consideration of this piece would take us beyond 1789 into March of the following year. It is enough to remark that not until then did the editors of this famous journal discover that their best means of discomforting the patriots and discrediting their cause was ridicule, expressed in the disarming atmosphere of sustained gaiety. As time went on, certain pieces written in this vein brilliantly exposed the idiosyncrasies of the patriotic fervor.

An effort to present the chief personalities and undertakings of the National Assembly *en vaudeville* was made toward the end of the year 1789 in a pamphlet entitled *Prospectus of a New Journal*.[10] The *vaudeville* form (consisting, as we have seen, of prose narrative with songs interpolated[11]) was used by the patriots with increasing frequency to present in an engaging manner the aims and achievements of the Revolution. It was also employed by the anti-Revolutionists, as in the *Prospectus* mentioned above, as a means of heaping ridicule on the patriotic cause. Satirists frequently expressed confidence that the spirit of Frenchmen was too gay long to tolerate what were alleged to be the dreary solemnities of the reformers. A few songs and a little laughter would, it was hoped, restore France to a happier mood. The *Prospectus of a New Journal* consists of a running account of certain memorable sessions of the National Assembly, the remarks on each session being followed by lyrics written in a light and irreverent manner.[12] The

[9] *Chanson. "Enfin les beaux jours de la France . . . "* (Pierre's 276), in *Les actes des apôtres*, no. 65, pp. 5-8.

[10] *Prospectus d'un nouveau journal, par les auteurs de la Prise des Annonciades, 1789.* (II, D)

[11] For a fuller explanation of the meaning of *vaudeville* at the end of the eighteenth century, see page 69, footnote 55.

[12] There are six items of this character. Pierre lists separately only two, apparently regarding the group as constituting a potpourri. Though this procedure is not

last of the topics concerns the famous proposal of Dr. Guillotin. "The motion has already been celebrated," the editor explains, "by a muse far superior to ours"—a reference, no doubt, to the piece in *Les actes des apôtres* with which the reader is already familiar. There is no need to quote from the *Prospectus* at length; perhaps the following stanza, inspired by the speech of Dr. Guillotin, will suffice to convey the atmosphere of inconsequential mockery which pervades the pamphlet:

> Il propose
> Peu de choses,
> Qu'il expose
> En peu de mots;
> Mais l'emphase
> De sa phrase
> Obtient les *bravos*
> De cinq ou six sots.[13]

Not all anti-Revolutionary ridicule was so gentle. The lampoon of future years—intolerant, vituperous, and tasteless—had already made its appearance by the end of 1789. A pamphlet bearing the disarming title *Noel*[14] contains three songs devoted to attacks against the Assembly as a whole and against certain of its members. In the first of these songs[15] the representatives are pictured as "beasts" grazing in the "Isle of Fools." All sorts of indignities, as one may expect, are heaped upon the Revolutionary leaders who appear in this fantasy. Evidently tiring of his own imagery, the author finally expresses his animosity in forthright language, concluding that "soon we shall see all these thieves hung." The next piece,[16] if less fanciful, is equally virulent. Its personal invective includes an attack on Barnave, whom citizens are told to recog-

---

strictly correct, I have followed it, owing to the slight, if not negligible, political context of several of the items. The opening lyrics in the sequence are *Couplets—"Voyant la féodalité . . . "* (77), concerning the session of the National Assembly on August 4-5. The other item of significance is the last, concerning Guillotin (see footnote following). While deploring the tenor of this piece, Desmoulins printed the text, to suggest how the medium of the song might be used to popularize Revolutionary subjects. See *Révolutions de France et Brabant*, vol. i, no. 8, pp. 371-74.

[13] *Guillotin.* "*Monsieur Guillotin, Ce grand médecin . . .* " (78), stanza 2.
[14] *Noël*, n.p.n.d. (II, D)   [15] *Noël.* "*Menons paître nos bêtes . . .* " (83).
[16] *La lunette* (84). The allusion which follows is to stanza 5.

nize as "the father of lies."[17] The third of the songs[18] denounces various Revolutionary acts, including the "pillage" of the Church, and execrates many of the patriotic leaders, especially "vile Mirabeau."

At the end of the second of these songs it is disclosed that the author is himself "a patriot," who dedicates his life to "the good party." This, it then appears, is the party óf Mounier. Thus does this bitter song celebrate the beginning of the break-up of the Revolutionary movement into factions. It was Mounier who had proposed the Tennis Court Oath in the spring of 1789; by the autumn he had already broken with the Revolution. As we have seen, he believed in constitutional government, but under a strong monarchy. The preponderance of opinion in the Assembly was less conservative. Mounier, who was distressed at the liberal trend, was altogether alienated when the Parisians captured the King in October. The offended Mounier forthwith quit the Assembly, returned to Grenoble, and tried, fruitlessly, to organize a party uprising. By May, 1790, he felt obliged to leave France, one of the first of the initiators of the Revolution to be disillusioned by the radical and lawless forces which he unwittingly had helped to release.

In addition to such political divisions as have been indicated, there were soon to be serious rivalries in the economic sphere. As long as the battle against the privileged classes was the thing of paramount importance, even the humblest Frenchman could suppose that his interests were upheld by the Assembly. We have seen that this was the case in the spring of 1789 and at the time of the Bastille uprising. Furthermore, in August, the Declaration of the Rights of Man promised—or seemed to promise—a democratic regime.

"Men are born free and remain free and equal in rights." So stated the Declaration. Yet how little the representatives were guided by their dictum when in October they took up consideration of the question of the suffrage under the new Constitution! We know the names of only five individuals—among them Adrien

[17] Namely, Satan. Barnave was at this time an outstanding leader of the left. See page 169.

[18] *Complainte.* "*O vous, amis de notre reine . . .*" (85). The allusion which follows is to stanza 13.

du Port, Grégoire and Robespierre—who demanded universal suffrage.[19] To a vast majority of the representatives, Sieyès had expressed the common sense of his day when he wrote that "citizens" fall naturally into two classes: the poor and incompetent, on the one hand; and, on the other, the relatively educated and prosperous. The former would enjoy various civil rights, but not the right to vote. These privileges would belong only to the latter group, whom Sieyès proposed to treat as "active" citizens.[20] This was the basis of legislation which the Assembly adopted over the protests of the very small minority to which reference has been made. The line between "active" and "passive" was drawn according to wealth —that is, Frenchmen of established residence who were over twenty-five years of age and who were not domestic servants were permitted to vote if in the course of a year they paid a tax equal to the value of three days' labor. In practice, this provision qualified four and a quarter million men for the vote, and disqualified over three million who did not pay sufficient tax.

This was not all. The Declaration had stated that "All citizens, being equal in the eyes of the law, are equally eligible to all dignities and to all public positions and occupations, according to their abilities and without distinction, except that of their virtues and talents." Yet, according to the new constitutional decrees,[21] there were to be, in addition to a system of indirect elections, special qualifications for holding office. "Active" citizens were themselves divided into three classes. Those who paid the tax already mentioned had the rather unsatisfactory privilege of voting for candi-

[19] None of the legislators favored extending the suffrage to women. One of the great exponents of Revolutionary thought, however, did favor woman suffrage—the philosopher Condorcet. See L. Cahen, *Condorcet et la Révolution française*, Paris, 1904, pp. 31-32.

[20] Sieyès developed these views in his *Quelques idées de Constitution applicables à la ville de Paris en juillet, 1789*, Versailles, n.d., pp. 19-22. Though Sieyès seems to have been the first of the Revolutionary leaders to formulate the distinction between the two types of citizenship, he did not suggest the provision that active status should depend upon a minimum tax payment. He had proposed that it result from the citizen's ability and willingness to make a small voluntary offering. This basis of distinction was obviously more liberal than that adopted by the Assembly.

[21] Several measures passed separately in the autumn of 1789 were drawn together in the *Décret sur la constitution des Assemblées primaires et des Assemblées administratives* of December 22, 1789 (*Collection complète des lois . . .* , Paris, 1791, pp. 127-80).

dates for "electoral assemblies" from among citizens who paid a considerably larger tax. Persons who paid this larger tax were entitled to elect various local officials and to vote for members of the national legislature. Still wealthier persons alone were eligible to serve in the Assembly as the representatives of the nation. To belong to the third group, one was obliged to pay the equivalent of a *marc d'argent* in taxes—a very considerable sum which restricted future membership in the national legislature to but a few thousand Frenchmen.

However restricted the electoral system of 1789 may seem today, it appears against its eighteenth-century background as a great victory for popular government. Frenchmen were now to enjoy, in varying degrees, privileges of citizenship to be made secure by constitutional guarantees. To be sure, the system was not democratic, but neither was the government of England nor that of the new republic of the United States. Both of these countries were ruled by a propertied class; in America, the members of the Philadelphia Convention found the matter of the suffrage so delicate that they purposely avoided making any mention of it in the Constitution which they drew up. As for Europe, the peoples of the countries other than France were, generally speaking, still under the autocratic control of their rulers. Thus, despite such electoral restrictions as the Assembly imposed, France, long a stronghold of absolutism, was by 1789 in the vanguard of liberal progress.

This does not mean, though, that all Frenchmen were satisfied. The patriots, by and large, had taken seriously the promises of the new day for mankind as proclaimed by the National Assembly. Many had hoped for a freer and more general participation in government than that which was to be allowed them. Thus, the seeds of discontent were sown in 1789. But it was only in later years that disillusionment became sufficiently acute and widespread to precipitate a conflict between such diverse economic groups as together comprised the Third Estate—in simplest terms, between the rich and the moderately well-to-do, and between both these groups and the poor.

A broadside was circulated in Paris on Christmas day, 1789, bearing a sensational and alarming report. According to its brief message, a plot to remove the King to Metz, to abolish the National Assembly, and to murder Bailly and Lafayette, had been exposed. Allegedly involved in this conspiracy were thirty thousand aristocrats. At its head, so went the report, was the Count of Provence. There was no prospect of immediate confirmation, since the announcement bore an entirely unknown signature. But regardless of its source, the broadside caused a great stir. Provence, it will be remembered, was the King's brother.

As a matter of fact, an arrest had been made the night before. A certain Marquis de Favras had been seized by a detail of the Paris National Guard, on charges brought by two informers that he was an agent in such a vast design against the Revolution.[22] The Count of Provence hurried before the General Assembly of the Paris Commune to disclaim any connection with Favras. He appeared shocked and offended that his own lofty devotion to the welfare of the state could have fallen under suspicion. His declaration was accorded frequent and hearty applause.[23] Lafayette and Bailly were present. All seemed convinced of the innocence of the King's brother.

But both Lafayette and Bailly knew that a letter compromising Provence had been found on Favras when the latter was arrested.[24] These popular leaders apparently did not dare trust this intelli-

[22] The Royalist plot may have been less sensational than the broadside of December 25 claimed, but it did involve a plan first of all to take the King away from Paris (Mirabeau shared in this part of the intrigue), and, finally, it would seem, to bring him back at the head of a foreign army.

[23] *Actes de la Commune de Paris pendant la Révolution*, S. Lacroix, ed., vol. iii, p. 284. For the complete account of Monsieur's visit to the General Assembly, see *ibid.*, pp. 283-86.

[24] Lafayette's part is described by Mathiez (*The French Revolution*, p. 68): "When Favras was arrested, a letter compromising Monsieur was found on him. Lafayette chivalrously returned it to its writer and did not divulge its existence."

An exceedingly interesting passage in the diary of Gouverneur Morris indicates that Bailly, also, knew that Provence was implicated and joined Lafayette in concealing the evidence. Morris wrote, December 27, 1789: "Go to Monsr. de La Fayette's. . . . After dinner I speak to La Fayette about Monsieur's speech to the Commons. He takes Short and me into his closet. Tells us that for a long time he has had information of a plot. That he has followed the track and at length took up Mr. de Faveras [*sic*]. That on Mr. de Faveras was found a letter from Monsieur which seemed to show that he was but too deeply concerned in it. That he had immediately waited upon him with that letter, which he delivered, telling Monsieur that it was known only to him and Monsr. Bailli, consequently that he was not compromised. That Monsieur was very much rejoiced at this intelligence." *A Diary of the French Revolution by Gouverneur Morris*, B. C. Davenport, ed., vol. i, p. 346.

gence to the people. In any case, they shared the profound conviction of most of the Revolutionists that the monarchic idea was
inseparable from the cause of reform; no doubt for this reason, and
perhaps, too, because of their deep-seated regard for the majesty of
the throne, they would not expose a member of the royal family.
Accordingly, they permitted Favras, an accessory, to bear the entire
onus of the conspirators' guilt. There is no doubt that great affairs
of state were involved, and that the pressure of expediency was
considerable. From this standpoint, the general and the mayor
were justified—indeed justified far in advance by Machiavelli. But
in withholding the evidence from the people and in providing protection to an enemy of the popular cause, they appear momentarily
to have lost sight of the ideals of the new day.

Favras, gallantly shielding the count, protested his own innocence, but otherwise was uncommunicative when tried by the
Châtelet for the crime of *lèse-nation*. He was condemned to death,
and on February 19, 1790, was hanged in a public square. The
gallows had been made especially tall so that the mass of spectators
could enjoy an unobstructed view, for the occasion was important
in more ways than one. Not only was an enemy of the Revolution
being brought to a deserved end; but here was an aristocrat denied
the age-old right of a less ignoble death by beheading, and subjected, for the sake of equality, to the fate of the common criminal.

The exposure of the so-called Favras conspiracy had varied
effects. Though it confirmed the suspicion of certain radicals that
the aristocrats were dangerous and should be vigilantly watched,
the general reaction in Paris was one of relief and reassurance
that a plot, such as had been dreaded for some time, had been exposed, and its originator—as most people thought—promptly
brought to justice. Another result was an increase in the prominence of Lafayette, whose life, having been endangered, now
seemed all the dearer. Besides, it was his National Guard which
had quashed the conspiracy.

There was still another effect of the Favras incident, which followed somewhat later. The King, advised by Lafayette to show by
a definite gesture that he had no sympathy with the plotting of the
aristocrats, went before the Assembly on February 4, 1790, to pro-

claim his devotion to the Constitution. The manner of the visit was engagingly informal, and the address (prepared by Necker) apparently spontaneous. This step—or *démarche*, as it was called— caught the popular imagination, and was regarded by nearly everyone as an indication that the King and the "nation" were in accord, and that the reform of France could be completed in peace.

A song to celebrate the collapse of the Favras conspiracy was written by the Chevalier de Callières. The reader may recall lyrics by the same author on the capture of the Bastille.[25] It may be mentioned in passing that since that event Callières had founded the Battalion of Veterans. Having himself attained an advanced age, he recruited only men over sixty.[26] Members of his battalion were required to wear beards—and it is even recorded that some, to present a suitable appearance, were obliged to wear false ones. This "venerable battalion," as its founder called it, was a picturesque part of the Paris defense for years to come.

The heading of Callières' new composition was a narrative in itself: "Second National Song. On the Salvation of the Mayor; of the General; of the Minister of Finance; of all the City of Paris. Composed at the Corps-de-Garde, December 28, 1789; and presented to Monsieur [the Count of Provence] the same day, after having relieved the sentinels at his Palace."[27] The song opens with an expression of confidence in Provence, friend of France and "her first Citizen."[28] The piece abounds in grandiloquent phrases, as when the author narrates that, "A barbarous horde concocts a detestable plan." Monsieur himself is pictured as having somehow

---

[25] *Chanson sur la prise des Invalides . . .* (29).

[26] As an instance of the activity of the various local units of Paris, it is interesting to note that on November 24, 1789, the general assembly of the District of the Cordeliers endorsed Callières' proposal and voted that it be sent to the other fifty-nine districts of Paris and to "the august National Assembly." The decree of the Cordeliers was signed by Danton, president. Part of this information and remarks by Callières appear in the *Révolutions de France et Brabant,* vol. i, no. 3, pp. 101-2. See also the *Moniteur* of December 31, 1789 (vol. i, p. 531). For an assemblage of documents on the origin and formation of the "Bataillon des Vieillards" see *Actes de la Commune de Paris . . . ,* vol. iv, pp. 534-43.

[27] *Chanson Nationale, IIe . . .* (86).

[28] Bailly had used this phrase to describe the King's brother on the occasion of the latter's visit to the Assembly of the Paris Commune. "Monsieur," the Mayor declared, "s'est montré le premier citoyen du royaume." *Actes de la Commune de Paris . . . ,* vol. iii, p. 285.

been in danger, and as having been saved from "this criminal conspiracy." As for the "monstrous Marquis" (Favras), haste is being
made to bring about his just end.

Several lines celebrate the escape of Lafayette, "our dear Defender," from death at the hands of the conspirators:

> De ce brave La Fayette
> Tout l'enfer est jaloux. . . .
> Monstres! Sa gloire est complète ⎱ [*bis.*]
> Vous tombez à ses genoux.[29] ⎰

After eulogies of the "immortal Bailly" and of the "great Necker,"
there follows more rejoicing over the exposure of the plot:

> Le sanglant despotisme
> Est enfin désarçonné,
> Et le patriotisme
> Pour jamais enraciné. . . .
>
> La Liberté, triomphante
> Par ses Régénérateurs,
> Chante la Ligue expirante ⎱ [*bis.*]
> Sous nos purs Législateurs. ⎰
>
> Luisez, ô jours prospères,
> Depuis mille ans attendus,
> Loin, gothiques chimères,
> Loin, privilèges, abus.
>
> Il est tems que la nature
> Recouvre ses justes droits;
> Et que chacun sans murmure, ⎱ [*bis.*]
> Souscrive aux communes loix.[30] ⎰

This piece, composed on the spur of the moment, is clearly packed
with feelings characteristic of the time. In conclusion, there is an
exhortation to the King of France to live in perfect assurance "in
the bosom of his Paris." Evidently there is no coercion back of
Louis' rule, other than the gentle suasion of the human heart:

29 *Chanson Nationale, IIe* . . . (86), stanza 5, in part. The suspension points here
and those in the next stanza quoted, appear in the original.
30 *Ibid.*, stanzas 10 and 11.

C'est son âme, forte et grande,
Qui l'a fait Roi de nos coeurs:
Son amour, qui nous commande
N'a que des soldats vainqueurs.   } [bis.]

What, in conclusion, can be said of the aristocrats themselves, who in a time of crisis might have been expected to rally to the support of the King, and to show whatever strength was theirs? In this matter it will be well to defer to the judgment of a Frenchman, for perhaps few Americans, reared in a land which from the time of its founding has outlawed titles of nobility, are in a position to evaluate the aristocratic tradition of Europe. These circumstances explain the introduction at this point of a quotation of more than usual length, from Louis Madelin's *La Révolution française*. Madelin has gathered in succinct and penetrating passages many evidences of the mentality of the aristocrats at the moment when their position was challenged.

"Nothing," he writes, "seemed to move the threatened caste. The winter of 1789-1790 was particularly gay. 'We have had some delightful tea-parties the last few days. We are all amusing ourselves,' writes one doomed aristocrat. On December 31 they bade the old year a joyous farewell; as midnight struck, the gentlemen gaily kissed the ladies of the company. And not a head there but was shaking on its owner's shoulders! They made fun of the Revolution. When Mme. de Simiane was struck by an apple thrown from the upper gallery of the Théâtre Français, crowded with people of the humbler class, she sent it to her brother-in-law, La Fayette, and wrote, 'Here, my dear General, is the first fruit of the Revolution that has reached my hands!' And what amusement was caused by the expression used by the market-women of the Halles, when they went to wish the Assembly a Happy New Year: 'Our children, when they see you, will call you their fathers!' There was much joking, too, over La Fayette and his National Guard. But that was the only vengeance taken. . . .

"When it [aristocratic society] did not treat the Revolution as a subject for scornful mirth, it turned it into a fashionable toy. There were patriotic trinkets, trinkets *à la Constitution*, tricolour snuff-boxes, dresses *à la Constitution*, hats *à la Révolution*. How was anybody to complain of events that had brought in the taste for the antique and driven out the late fashions, thus enabling 'the dealers in frivolities' to change the wares they showed? Those dealers in 'frivolities'! They were ubiquitous all through that winter of 1789-1790, while the picks of the Assembly were tearing down the old kingdom of France, her Parlements, her Provinces, her Corporations, her Clergy, and her Army!"[31]

Since in this book I have had occasion to dwell on political crises, constitutional changes, and other worrisome matters, I may have given the reader an unduly solemn impression of the spirit of France as the year 1789 drew to a close. Perhaps the passages just quoted will serve as a corrective with respect to the aristocrats.

The patriots, for their part—if we except some of the more devoted leaders and fervent propagandists—had amusements of their own. By and large, they felt that laughter, along with prayer (or even without it), must usher in the "golden age."

Certainly public opinion was largely unaffected by such premonitions as occurred to Gouverneur Morris. This detached American visitor, having arrived in Paris in February, 1789, had observed the Revolution from the time of its outbreak. By October 17, 1789, he was convinced that the conservative forces of France, which were badly divided, would soon gain the ascendancy.

"A very little time," he wrote, "must unite the opposition and when united they will of course place themselves under the banners of royal authority, and then farewell democracy."[32]

This prophecy did not altogether miss the mark. Morris was wrong, however, in his estimate of the time element, inasmuch as two years were to elapse before the conservative forces had united and become dangerously strong. Furthermore, the distinguished American had no conception of the strength of the nascent "democracy," which he despised, and was wrong in supposing that the Revolution would not afford it an hour of triumph. But however great the limitations of his foresight, Frenchmen would themselves have occasion to discover what Morris suspected all along: that the conservative elements of France included some of the most enduring strains in the culture of that nation; and that they would per-

[31] Translation by F. S. Barr, of Madelin, *The French Revolution*, pp. 131-32.
[32] *A Diary of the French Revolution by Gouverneur Morris*, B. C. Davenport, ed., vol. i, p. 314.

sist, unite, and, for a time at least, determine as much as any other group the future course of French history.

The patriots, dedicated to a cause which they dearly wished to win, willingly ignored the potential strength of the opposition. Although alarmed on certain occasions, they were inclined, as we have seen, to be sanguine, and were frequently elated. As the year 1790 commenced, the Revolution was supposedly over,[33] and millions of Frenchmen enjoyed for a time a spirit of carefree assurance. Perhaps a single anecdote will serve to illustrate the point, and it may, besides, furnish a fitting end to the present chapter.

The scene of what follows is Perpignan, capital of Roussillon, where Louis' declaration of loyalty to the Constitution, on February 4, 1790, was celebrated by a carnival. The account is from the *Révolutions de Paris*,[34] a few omissions being made for brevity:

On the last day of the carnival, a little lesson was given to the aristocrats of the town, of which the details are as follows:

At the head of a company of one hundred and twenty men of the National Guard marched the commanding officers, with a banner inscribed, "Long live Liberty!" The soldiers carried wreaths of flowers and of laurels, all the while singing, in a martial spirit, a song suitable to the occasion. Then came a wagon covered with inscriptions and garlands. . . . A cask carried thereon provided wine for the people; one could read on the front of the cask, "It flows only for good patriots." A hundred volunteers of various companies of the citizen guard of Perpignan marched next. They were followed by a second wagon, on which there was a staved-in barrel, bearing the inscription, "Repository of privileges," and a broken trunk on which one read, "Repository of feudal rights" addressed to the princes of Germany.

After this second wagon walked an elegantly dressed man, supported by a pair of enchained slaves; he represented an aristocrat, and wore as an emblem a two-faced mask. Following him was a numerous court. When all this throng had arrived at the most popular square in the town, the order to halt was given, and a toast was proposed to the

[33] The turn of the year perhaps accentuated this notion. But Desmoulins was representative of many of his compatriots in supposing the Revolution over well before the old year was out. See, for example, the "Consummatum est" paragraph which opens the first number of his *Révolutions de France et de Brabant* (November 28, 1789).

[34] No. 35 (March 13, 1790), pp. 36-38. The account takes the form of a letter to the editor, "De Perpignan, le 19 février 1790." In translating, I have conventionalized the punctuation, there being almost no periods in the French text, and have introduced "National Assembly," "King," and "President" with capital letters, though they do not appear so in the original.

health of the good king Louis XVI, father of the people, and restorer of French liberty. A unanimous cry of "Long live the good King!" was heard, and thirty musicians sounded a fanfare. The aristocrat gnashed his teeth, and made an effort to disturb this solemn moment. . . . A royal courier, perfectly garbed, appeared on the scene and delivered a dispatch to the commander: it contained the speech which the King had given at the memorable session of the 4th, and a letter supposedly written by the President of the National Assembly to the good people of Roussillon. These the second in command read in a loud voice. At each comforting word for the people, the aristocrat grew pale, and at the moment when he heard these words [of the King], "Let us all profess . . . attachment to the Constitution," he fell over backwards. People rushed to his aid. A doctor having examined him, cried *"He is dead!* It is the effect of sudden grief." Immediately he was placed on the second wagon, and a great number of people of every description, dressed in black and wearing mourning ruffles, came forward to follow the body. The commander thereupon cried out, "Since no more enemies exist, let us drink to union, peace, and concord!" People drank lustily, and the band played an air suitable to the occasion.

"More than ten thousand persons," the writer declares, "were present at this truly comic scene."

 CONCLUSION

SINCE this book is concerned primarily with the *spirit* of 1789, it seems hardly necessary to summarize at length the political reforms of that year, or even the principles from which they sprang. These matters have already been treated in preceding chapters, and moreover they have long attracted the attention of historians.[1]

Deserving further consideration, however, are such underlying attitudes as seem to have been at the basis of formal institutional change. In short, an effort must be made at last to appraise the spirit of 1789.

There are historians who maintain that whereas the climax of the French Revolution was wasteful and oppressive, the first phase was predominantly, if not entirely, coherent and constructive. This view, associated especially with the name of Edgar Quinet,[2] has always made a certain appeal to moderate, peace-loving liberals.

To be sure, if one considers primarily official acts and institutions, rather than such undercurrents of feeling as shape future events, one may find many evidences to support this claim. For example, one may conclude that the suppressions and cruelties of the Terror were in no way the outgrowth, but were rather the denial, of everything for which the men of 1789 had stood.

One may likewise suppose that the regimentation and chauvinism of the Napoleonic era were quite unrelated to the first impulses of the Revolution.

Finally one may assume, as have a number of modern writers, that if succeeding generations had held to the supposedly clear-cut doctrines of the first proponents of popular government in France, there would be less confusion in thought and fewer compromises in practice to plague modern society.

In a sense, all this is true. Viewed in the light of institutional

[1] One may cite as a survey of some length Sagnac's "L'oeuvre de l'Assemblée constituante" (Book II of *La Révolution, 1789-1792*), and as an example of brief interpretative writing James Harvey Robinson's "The Principles of 1789" (Chapter VII in *The New History*, New York, 1912). The Declaration of the Rights of Man is analyzed by Lefebvre in *The Coming of the French Revolution* (translation by R. R. Palmer, Princeton, 1947, pp. 169-81 and 214-20).

[2] *La Révolution*, Paris, 1865, 2 vols.

change, the Terror was a distinct novelty; Napoleon, the creator of a new order; while modern man may be seen as but a halfhearted exponent of the fundamental "rights" to which he willingly gives lip service.

Such a conception of the development and influence of the French Revolution fails, however, to take into account the emotional continuity which persists in human attitudes—with some modifications, to be sure—from day to day and year to year, and even from epoch to epoch.

If we look beneath the brilliant flowering of the first phase of the Revolution, we find that in the soil of 1789 were the seeds of forthcoming disasters, as well as of long-term benefits. At least, as a result of the present investigation, I am convinced that from the beginning there was a profound confusion in the Revolutionary mood, which entailed distress at the time, and which remains a part of the continuing influence of that movement.

In seeking to understand this mood, as expressed in popular opinion, the investigator is bound to be impressed by the extent to which the initiators of the Revolution were torn by conflicting feelings and attracted by essentially incompatible views. A psychologist of our own day has described such an unsettled condition of personality as involving an interplay of "opposites."[3] The term "opposites" affords a convenient means of identifying many trends of thought and feeling that were operative in 1789, as a few examples may serve to suggest.

The first of these concerns the inner struggle of Frenchmen to reconcile their traditional sense of dependence on leaders—which appeared in 1789 in exaggerated form—with contrary feelings inspired by a new conception of human "equality."

Certainly in the annals of modern civilization there is no period when men were more respectful toward leaders—more consciously dependent on the superior talents of certain individuals—than

[3] C. J. Jung. The so-called "pairs of opposites" are discussed in several of his works, notably in *Two Essays on Analytical Psychology* (translated by H. G. and C. F. Baynes), London, 1928. In borrowing this terminology, I do not stress a "Jungian" interpretation. Psychologists since Freud recognize that much emotional life depends upon a polarity of forces, and it is this fundamental conception which is of importance in the discussion above.

were Frenchmen at the time of the gathering of the Estates General and of Necker's prodigious popularity in the weeks preceding and following the capture of the Bastille. It seemed well to stress this point in the opening chapters of the present work, because it is rare that a writer on the Revolution gives it the emphasis that it deserves, although long ago the essence of the matter was emphasized by Fournel in the following passage: "Necker, who was destined to fall so quickly into obscurity,[4] was then the Palladium of France, the providential man, the awaited savior. . . . No other man, neither Mirabeau, nor Petion, nor Marat, attained, in the course of future events, the popularity of this Genevese banker."[5] As for the regard in which the members of the Assembly were held, Mathiez, referring even to the earliest phase of the Revolution, apparently felt that only religious terminology could convey the exalted nature of their role: to the men of that day, the representatives were "the priests of social happiness."[6] The time came when the people supposed that virtue might emerge from the garments of their chosen leaders. It is in this sense that Mathiez repeats from the records of the Committee of Public Safety the following testi-

---

[4] "Obscurity" is too mild. There is nothing more bitter than the disappointed hopes of idealists; and a popular hero fallen from grace either pays with his life—as did Louis XVI—or is subjected to all manner of obloquy before he can derive comfort from an enshrouding obscurity. When Necker's efforts to bring prosperity to France failed, the popular writers did not simply expose the inadequacies and incompetence of the well-meaning Minister, but wrote of him with an unjust and unreasoning bitterness which was the natural concomitant of their once too high hopes. The reaction—begun in earnest by March, 1790, and continued until Necker's resignation in September of that year—reveals the negative and sinister side of hero worship. Such pamphlet titles as the following suggest the trend: *Le géant devenu pygmée, ou Necker au grand jour; Necker jugé par le tribunal de la lanterne*; and *La confession de M. Necker, au moment de son agonie* (with the epigram, "Ces heureux intrigants, qu'adore l'ignorance,/ Quand le masque est tombé, méritent la potence"). Jean-Jacques Rutledge, long a calumniator of Necker, now came into his own with *L'astuce dévoilée, ou origine des maux de la France, perdue par les manoeuvres du Ministre Necker.* . . . (For fuller data concerning these items, see Bibliography IV, C.)

[5] V. Fournel, *Les Hommes du 14 juillet* . . . , Paris, 1890, p. 41.

[6] *Les origines des cultes révolutionnaires (1789-1792)*, p. 20. It was with desperate seriousness that the publicists undertook to maintain this high popular regard for the legislators. Such an outlook became, for various reasons, an essential part of Revolutionary orthodoxy. The journalist Garat, in describing his efforts to sustain this atmosphere, wrote somewhat later (1792): "I was convinced that all was lost, both our liberty and the better hopes of the human race, if, for one moment, the National Assembly ceased to be in the eyes of the nation an object worthy of its respect, of its love and of its hopes." Cited in *Memoirs . . . of Mallet du Pan*, A. Sayous, ed., vol. 1, pp. 174-75.

mony of a member of the Convention: "Women cast themselves about me in order to touch my dress, and withdrew satisfied."[7]

Yet out of this atmosphere of deference and self-abnegation was born the Revolutionary spirit of "equality." This spirit, far from including deference to leaders, would seem almost to have precluded the sense of any need of them. For though the doctrine of equality was soon construed as "equality of opportunity," at first it was widely supposed to mean that there were no fundamental variations in man's endowments and abilities. As one popular writer explained,

> Quand notre créateur suprême
> Tira le monde du chaos,
> Il fit tous les hommes égaux
> Chez tous nature fut la même. . . .[8]

The common experience of birth was evidence enough of man's equality, as suggested in the following passage from a *poissard* song:

> Sarvons-nous enfin d'not'raison,
> Et ne fesons pu d'distinction:
> C'est un artic' ben nécessaire.
> J'n'ons eu qu'un pèr'; j'n'avons qu'un Roi:
> J'somm' tout sortis du même endroit,
> Pourquoi donc tous ces droits,[9]
> Que ne sont, au not'foi,
> Le pu souvent que ceus' ed' mal faire?[10]

In a song of later date (1790) the implications of natural equality were reduced to an aphorism, which aptly reveals this aspect of the Revolutionary mood:

> Tous les hommes sont égaux,
> Mêmes vertus, mêmes défauts.[11]

Such an attitude led inevitably to derision of the most honored and even of the most sacred titles of the old regime, save that of King, which for some time was spared direct attack. However,

---

[7] Mathiez, *op.cit.*, p. 21.   [8] *Chanson sur les affaires du temps* (27), stanza 1.
[9] *"Droits"*—as used here, "privileges."
[10] *Arrêté des Habitans de la Grenouillère* . . . (5), stanza 14.
[11] *L'épouvantail patriotique ou le tombeau des aristocrates* (Pierre, *Catalogue*, no. 450), stanza 12.

there was a leveling tendency in the new conception of Louis as "roi-citoyen."[12] This appellation, which according to the patriotic view implied a tribute to the monarch, in reality presaged his fall.

Concerning the rise of the modern democratic nation, it is often said that the new state assumed not only the prerogatives, but also the sanctity, of the monarchy which it either curtailed or displaced. No doubt, one should go further and inquire whether the citizens of the new nation did not arrogate to themselves as individuals a measure of this fallen majesty.[13] Mallet du Pan warned that an address which the Assembly published in October, 1789, reminding the people "in every paragraph" that "they are absolutely sovereign," would result in "a volcano" which later councils of moderation could do nothing to prevent.[14] Mallet du Pan, though a man of liberal views, nevertheless felt that an overdose of the doctrine of popular sovereignty would unbalance the judgment of his contemporaries. Some weeks later a satirist touched the quick of the matter in the following extravaganza:

Louis XVI, only six months ago, was master of 24 million subjects; today he is the only subject of 24 million kings. It remains to be seen how this nation of potentates will fix the limits of so many empires, and how the subject will ever be able to obey all his sovereigns.[15]

As if to belie this pretentiousness—though actually related to it as a complementary tendency—was that excessive dependence on the leader as "savior" that continued to characterize popular feeling in 1789. So subtle was the interplay of these two tendencies that a critic, judging in haste, might be tempted to describe the Revolutionary mood at this time either as arrogance or as self-abasement; but to do either would be wrong. The mood of the patriots should rather be seen as resulting, in part, from a tension between these two polarites, the former (arrogance) implying the isolation of the "free" individual, the latter (self-abasement) implying his mergence in the democratic mass. Absolute liberty

[12] This conception, which, as we have seen, dates from 1789, was expressed in various forms. To cite a striking example, the frontispiece of the first number of the *Révolutions de France et de Brabant*, November 28, 1789, discloses a portrait of the King, over the legend "LOUIS SEIZE, Premier Citoyen Actif."

[13] For a brief consideration of this question, see page 171, footnote 6.

[14] *Memoirs and Correspondence of Mallet du Pan*, A. Sayous, ed., London, 1852, vol. i, pp. 194-95.

[15] *Les actes des apôtres*, vol. i, no. 28, p. 13.

(according to these tendencies) would mean, in the former case, an autonomous, individual will for everyone; and in the latter, the absence of any will apart from the will of all. Humanly speaking, both these extremes are attractive; but both, of course, are delusive.

The tendencies of arrogance and self-abasement could preserve a precarious equilibrium for the time being, but an eventual upset of the balance in either direction would favor dictatorship. On the one side, it would do so through the outbreak, or threat, of anarchy; on the other, through the breakdown of political initiative, resulting in the dependence of the mass on the archetypal hero.[16]

Another striking antithesis at the outset of the Revolution was between the exalted hope and apparent confidence of the patriots in the success of their ventures, and fear of the most acute and distressing sort. Although the latter mood may be explained to a considerable extent by the alarm of the patriots over what the aristocrats might do and by the threat (often imaginary) of "bandits," it was a fear which in large measure was undifferentiated.

"The whole country," Madelin writes, "was in the grip of that mysterious fear, a sort of national hysteria, which historians will never be able to explain. In Paris that mighty fear dated not from June, but from the month of April."[17]

And yet, as we have seen, the vast majority of speeches and writings in the spring and summer of 1789 expressed the opposite attitude. They echoed a confidence which could seem unduly sanguine even in the best and most secure of times. France, on the contrary, was drifting away from old moorings—a vessel that might either end upon the rocks, or be thrust into uncharted and dangerous seas. Foreign observers—and among them many whose estimates were uninfluenced by prejudice against the Revolutionary cause—saw this.[18] It may be that Frenchmen, too, sensed the dangers, without

[16] Tocqueville, influenced by American democracy as well as by the French Revolution, had many interesting things to say concerning the risks of the leveling process. His observations date from the 1850's. In the twentieth century, one can see even more clearly the interplay between equalitarian trends, on the one hand, and, on the other, the role of the hero, whether as demagogue, "leader," or dictator.

[17] *The French Revolution*, p. 69.

[18] For example, Washington, writing in 1789 of Revolutionary France, predicted that "rocks and shelves, not visible at present, may wreck the vessel, and give a higher toned despotism than the one which existed before." From a letter to Gouver-

being able consciously to recognize them. In any case, their expressions of unqualified optimism and unbounded hope are not easily accounted for.

It has seemed to me that such unwarranted self-assurance should be considered in conjunction with the "mysterious fear" of which Madelin writes. It may well be—to paraphrase Madelin's words—that the whole country was in the grip not only of a mysterious fear, but also of a mysterious elation, and that the latter, as well as the former, was "a sort of national hysteria." Psychologically it would be quite understandable for two such seemingly incompatible trends to run parallel, each acting to some extent as a stimulus to the other. From this standpoint the excessive optimism of 1789 is explainable as the counterpart and, in a measure, the corrective of the Great Fear. Correspondingly, the fear itself may be understood as being in part a negative, or "guilt," reaction to the hopeful and creative impulses of the time.[19]

It is interesting to consider to what extent the Revolutionists lived without regard for tradition, and to what extent they looked back to earlier times to gain sanction for the present and courage for the future. From a standpoint which is often taken, the men of 1789 seem to have turned their thoughts away from the past and to have attempted to create a new order with reason, rather than experience, as their guide. In any case, perhaps no writer has argued that the Revolutionists excelled in what we today call a "historical sense"; and several critics have gone out of their way to say that the Revolutionists lacked this sense completely.

While one is bound to share this view up to a certain point, the matter may be considered, as well, from quite a different angle. If for a brief space I emphasize relatively neglected trends in the Revolutionary outlook, it is not to deny the prevailing tendencies, on which there is general agreement. Surely the early chapters of this book sufficiently exposed the belief of popular writers that the Estates General, and later the Assembly, were creating an

---

neur Morris, in the latter's *Diary of the French Revolution*, B. C. Davenport, ed., vol. i, p. 374.

[19] The principle involved here has been considered by many writers, and with particular relevance to the present discussion by Otto Rank in *Art and Artist*, New York, 1932.

entirely new political and social order; that the past played small part in this achievement, except as an object lesson on evils which had supposedly been left behind; that men were living, as one lyrist wrote, on "a new earth" and under "new skies." Not only publicists, but also the legislators themselves, who described the Revolution as "perhaps the first conflict that has ever been fought by every right principle against every form of error,"[20] appear to have viewed the popular cause as a new and daring creation, an achievement made possible "by enlightenment," and so far beyond anything that had ever occurred before that precedent was useless. In this mood, the men of 1789 seem to have ignored the past.

And yet these apparently dauntless innovators were at times governed by contrary sentiments. Along with the Revolutionary idea that mankind was free for the first time, existed the notion that mankind had been free before. Along with the faith of the patriots that man was now wise and virtuous for the first time—had at last discovered "every right principle"—existed the belief that he had in some earlier day been virtuous. Accompanying the notion that the entire history of France was an unedifying record of despotism, was the thought that various institutions of the country, though long corrupt, had at certain earlier times been exemplary.[21] This outlook, which to some extent had been encouraged by the *philosophes*,[22] was firmly implanted in the imagination of men of 1789, as revealed in the whole tenor of their language. Many words charged with Revolutionary ardor began significantly with the prefix "re." The French people, it was said, had "reconquered" their liberty. Louis was praised not as the begetter of French liberty, but as its "restorer." It was commonly held that by virtue of the patriotic cause, society was "regenerated," or "reborn," as if

[20] From the *Addresse de l'Assemblée nationale au Peuple Français* proclaimed on February 11, 1790. See *Moniteur*, vol. ii, p. 177.

[21] In addition to phases of French history already mentioned, the age of Charlemagne was also idealized, owing to the influence of Mably, who in his *Observations sur l'histoire de France* (1765) had popularized the notion that under their great Carolingian emperor the French had possessed the elements of a constitution. This notion of a golden day, and in particular the idealization of Charlemagne's reign, had been developed—although for quite different purposes—by Boulainvilliers early in the eighteenth century. See Jacques Barzun, *The French Race: Theories of Its Origins . . .* , New York, 1932, esp. pp. 141-45 and 233-35.

[22] For an interesting discussion of the approach of the *philosophes* to history, see Carl Becker, *The Heavenly City of the Eighteenth Century Philosophers*, New Haven, 1932, pp. 106-16.

people were again enjoying benefits which had flourished in some earlier time. To be sure, there had been an Estates General in the background of French history, but the tireless insistence of the patriots on this fact is of more than passing interest. While living in a changed world and faced with the need of devising new parliamentary forms, everyone talked of the "resurrection" of the old. Somewhat in the same spirit was the harking back to the age of Henry IV, of which much has already been said.

Revolutionary inspiration was derived not only from the records of French history, but also from the annals of antiquity. Many writers of the eighteenth century had taught that classical civilization marked the most dignified and, from the civic standpoint, the most moral epoch in man's existence. It was therefore the highest praise to call the deputies "senators of ancient Rome,"[23] or the captors of the Bastille "a people of Catos."[24] Classical allusions occur frequently in the popular writings of 1789. Before the Revolution had run its course, they set the tone of public discussion and of every sort of writing. Besides, the special ceremonial of the Revolution—and of this there was much—was based on the precedents of antiquity.[25]

Thus, although, as is often said, the Revolutionists were in many ways heedless of tradition, they were in an elementary sense, at least, historically minded—that is, they had the historian's gift of seeing human experience as a long-term affair. They professed to cherish in the present certain features of the past, and they insisted that the memory of their own achievements would live in the future.

Their ideas seemed to acquire added weight by virtue of this long-range view; but in reviving only such parts of the record as

[23] *La réunion des trois ordres . . . par M. Déduit* (23), stanza 4.
[24] *Chanson sur la prise des Invalides . . .* (29), stanza 6.
[25] The historical elements of the subject are fully treated in Harold T. Parker's *The Cult of Antiquity and the French Revolutionaries*, Chicago, 1937. In the brief discussion above, emphasis is centered on a single psychological element: the need of men who face an uncertain present to borrow from the past some assurance that they are not altogether innovators. For there are occasions, it would seem, when men seek self-justification in the past through history just as earlier peoples sought it in mythology. From this standpoint, the Revolutionists would have found precedents elsewhere had they not found them conveniently in Greece and Rome. Parker does not enter into such speculations, but the idea presented here is perhaps implicit in his title, which describes as a "cult" what would normally be simply an interest.

pleased them, the men of the eighteenth century escaped the discipline of history. Thanks to their eclecticism, they could look to past experience without having their minds sobered or their wills tamed. On the contrary, by adapting selected fragments of history to their own advantage, they were able to feel ever more self-assured and to become increasingly willful. This perversion of the study of the past to serve present needs may be conceived as a sort of "dynamic history." It is easy to condemn such a dangerous preoccupation; but one should perhaps remark that the problem did not expire with the French Revolution, or, for that matter, with the later introduction of "scientific" methods of research. In our own times, with great issues at stake, an impartial study of the past is in some areas suspect, and is everywhere threatened by a growing tendency to exploit history in the interests of class or nation— to make it once more "dynamic."

The perennial struggle of individuals to reconcile conflicting moods of love and hate appears in accentuated form during the Revolution. In this book are many evidences that love was regarded by the patriots as a principal, if not the prime, moving force of the Revolution. Its influence was to have a regenerating effect on all classes of society. As a result, peace would prevail, it being supposed, according to one strong current of feeling, that the vexatious problems of the past could not persist in a society dedicated to the spirit of brotherhood.

It is notable, however, that from the outbreak of the Revolution undercurrents of extreme cruelty accompanied the insistence of the patriots on the prevalence and efficacy of love. Witness, for example, the murders of Foulon and Bertier, which by and large the popular writers condoned, though these acts were outrages not directly connected with the capture of the Bastille or with any other glorious exploit. It is true that the widespread enjoyment of lawless hangings—expressed in the abundance of witticisms on *la lanterne* —was not approved by all citizens; but the fact remains that many of the popular writers who condoned this sadism were at the same time capable of employing the most exalted language of the Revolution.

There were other indications—equally revealing, though less

violent—that whatever triumphs the Revolutionary spirit of love might achieve, it could not obliterate hate. In the first place, the patriots were perplexed by the problem of how to accommodate their ideal of brotherly love to the presence in the body politic of a large number of unrepentant aristocrats. This situation provoked two modes of reaction, which alternated and even intermingled: all-embracing love—or at least forbearance—based on the sentimental notion that the aristocrats would presently be "converted,"[26] and fanatical intolerance which led later to blind persecution. Accompanying the fraternal spirit of the Revolution were other hatreds of a more insidious nature. By the late summer of 1789 the division of the patriots themselves into factions produced bitter rivalries. "Opinions," wrote Mallet du Pan as early as September, "are distorted; motives attributed on suspicion; those who cannot be confounded are held up to odium; and perhaps at the present time there is not a single truly free and independent mind not groaning under this species of oppression."[27] And by the end of the year there arose, as another deterrent to domestic tranquillity, the disconcerting prospect that a bitter class consciousness might result from the distinction made by the Assembly between "active" and "passive" citizens.

Enough has been said to suggest that brotherly love, which the Revolutionists presently epitomized in the word *fraternité*—though everywhere given lip service and practiced at times with fervent application—was already in 1789 having a precarious existence.

At the same time, the atmosphere of a specious unanimity served partly to conceal the various crosscurrents of distrust which had arisen. We have seen in the present work that the patriots evolved ways of suppressing any doubts which might disturb their Revolutionary faith. It is necessary only to add a comment on the service performed by certain tag words, which were used ostensibly in their literal and ingratiating sense, but which were in reality ex-

[26] As an example of the abundant literature which this view inspired, mention may be made of Vidaillet's *Confession de tous ceux qui ont cherché à trahir la Nation Françoise* (IV, C), which appeared in two editions in the summer of 1789. In this pamphlet the *émigrés* are represented as saying, "Remorse follows us everywhere. . . . Should not this humiliating and sincere confession, accompanied by a repentance comparable to that of King David, obtain pardon for all our crimes?" *Ibid., seconde édition*, pp. 7-8.

[27] *Memoirs and Correspondence of Mallet du Pan*, A. Sayous, ed., vol. i, p. 184.

ploited as weapons. Such a term was "the people." This seemed to imply everybody or, in any case, all the common people of France. However, the patriots—who constantly reiterated the word by way of paying tribute to an expressed ideal of the Revolution—almost immediately gave it a special connotation. They restricted its application to those who had been touched by "enlightenment" and who supported the Revolutionary cause. One can usually detect this particular intent when the word "people" appears in the songs or other popular writings of 1789.[28] Another word which was used from the beginning of the Revolution with constant repetition and particular emphasis, was "citizen." According to current dogma, citizenship was a boon which the Revolution had brought to all His Majesty's subjects. It was therefore a simple matter to suggest the unity of the patriotic cause—and indeed of France—by proclaiming any outbreak of the mob a triumph of *les citoyens*, and any act of the Assembly a matter for common rejoicing by *les citoyens*. The fact remains that *citoyen* came to have increasingly esoteric connotations, which were already apparent in 1789. To the mind of the patriot, a "citizen" was one who embraced the Revolutionary cause. This fact was usually implied in the context surrounding the word, or in the accent given it, but, lest there be any doubt, popular writers soon began to clarify the term by referring to *les vrais citoyens*. As the Revolution progressed, the citizenship proclaimed in the Declaration of Rights and in constitutional decrees offered no protection to the greater part of the populace, whereas a fellowship of "true" citizens dominated France.

Likewise, "fraternity" was itself a tag word with twofold implications. It suggested not only brotherhood in the primary sense as preached by the philosophers, but also the more restricted brotherhood of what is known today, in an exclusive sense, as a fraternal movement. It is significant that by 1793 the whole effective leadership of the Revolution was encompassed in a Jacobin "society." This development was not so completely a denial of the first impulses of the Revolution as some writers would lead one to believe.

[28] Later the Jacobins, ruling as a minority and forced to distinguish their friends from their foes, revised the old catchword to read, "the people in Revolution," which became the current phrase. This was simply a frank avowal, occasioned by necessity, of what "the people" had meant all along. Godfrey Elton has made a searching analysis of the Jacobin conception of "the people" and of the then current use of the term. See his *The Revolutionary Idea in France, 1789-1871*, pp. 41-49.

Although the fraternalism preached by the philosophers was as wide as the universe, the principal experience in practical brotherhood which guided the initiators of the Revolution was that of the highly influential Order of Free Masons. As recent scholarship has shown, Freemasonry, taking strong root in eighteenth-century France, had spread in advance many of the new ideas, practices, and loyalties which emerged so prominently in 1789. This society was dedicated to universal brotherhood and equality, but restricted the application of its principles to an exclusive membership of "enlightened" men. In short, Freemasonry encouraged an enlargement of views, but the narrowing of social and political acquaintance to a "brotherhood" of like-minded persons. This was the fraternity not of a "golden age," but of a club. It was, besides, the precursor of that Jacobin fraternity to which reference has been made.

Before turning from "fraternity" within France itself to the application of this ideal to foreign relations, it may be well to add a word concerning the Revolutionary leadership in 1789. It would be a mistake, it seems to me, to place the entire onus of criticism on the less educated or apparently irresponsible elements of the population. For in a very direct way the members of the National Assembly contributed to the excess of human misery which France subsequently endured.

Theirs was an offense not unknown to other ages, and one which usually escapes opprobrium—the profession by leaders of a moral ardor beyond their everyday convictions. It is indeed strange that such pretension should so often be regarded as beneficial, since misguidance of this sort is apt to end in the disillusionment of the people, with resultant confusion and strife.

The reckless humanitarianism of the leaders of 1789 has already been suggested by reference to the Declaration of the Rights of Man. To be sure, many of its memorable "principles" were a forthright answer to past abuses, an answer inspired by a new sense of human dignity and moral order. Such precepts—those which concern equal taxation, fair trial, the sanctity of property, and so forth —expressed the convictions and the practical purposes of the Revolutionary leaders. But there were other provisions in the Declaration—tremendous in import, though few in number—which lacked this justification. These provisions embodied promises of political democracy which the legislators were not prepared to fulfill. We have seen how, in spite of the hopes which they aroused in the Declaration, the legislators restricted the suffrage according to the amount of tax paid; how they created an electoral system that was indirect, with distinctions of wealth the determining factor; and how they made eligibility for office dependent on an elaborate scheme of property qualifications. As Sagnac says, "Electoral right was thus based on the good fortune of the citizens."[29] Furthermore, before 1789 had come to a close, the Assembly decreed that only "active" citizens could serve in the National Guard, thus excluding from this high honor of citizenship three-sevenths of the manpower of France. These distinctions and others of a similar nature were in line with the determination of the legislators to build a society controlled by the prosperous and educated middle class, a purpose which was not concealed by certain of the leading advocates of the cause of reform.

Historically considered, the real convictions of the men of 1789 —that is, their practical aims—were, on the whole, salutary.[30] On this point faithful students of the old regime, and of the Revolutionary attack upon it, are largely agreed. It seems to be easy, nevertheless, for reformers of a later day, concerned with new needs and favored by new opportunities, to disparage those aims as "bourgeois." Such at least is a Marxian—or, rather, pseudo-Marxian—criticism.[31] But the very note of disparagement in the use of this term is not historical. At least in so far as one can determine from popular writings, in the France of 1789 the term "bourgeois"—

[29] *La Révolution (1789-1792)*, p. 165.

[30] This, of course, is not to disparage the democratic principle, which in the first hour of French Revolutionary enthusiasm was rather wantonly exposed to outrageous fortune. If we may judge by the experience of countries where revolution has been gradual, it appears that political democracy (as distinguished from a somewhat limited participation in representative government) may follow not only as a violent negation, but also as the natural outgrowth, of successful bourgeois government.

[31] Among writers who show the effects of Marx influence, there are some who seem to resent the "bourgeois" (middle-class) character of the Revolution and to blame its leadership for not having been of a more leftist character. This carping tone, which is historically questionable on several counts, is not even Marxian; for Marx, in describing the French Revolution as a "bourgeois" affair, gave it matter-of-fact acceptance in what he deemed to be the historic process.

although it might on occasion suggest class difference—meant primarily "town dweller" and had somewhat the original connotation of "citizen." At the time of the Bastille uprising, we saw the patriotic volunteers described as *Garde bourgeoise,* and found the attack itself, which included the poorest of the people, encompassed in the *Chanson des bourgeois de Paris.* Accordingly, in those days, the word "bourgeois" often appeared in the fighting phrases of freedom, and, like "liberty," implied progress. But quite apart from this matter of terminology, no defender of the Revolution should permit himself to be jostled into the position of apologist for the fact that the movement—or at least its leadership—was middle class. One must not be distracted by the preoccupations of an industrial age if he would see the historical picture. In a country largely illiterate, such as eighteenth-century France, what is now conceived of as a "bourgeois" revolution was alone possible if any considerable degree of liberty were to survive. In an effort to gain more, considerably less was attained, as is obvious when we consider the dictatorships and reaction that followed. If dogmatic categories of a later day must be brought to bear on a historical problem, let us object that the initiators of the Revolution did not remain consistently "bourgeois"—that on occasion they attempted to be prematurely "proletarian." In so doing, they dispensed powers they could not well spare and an equality that was not yet even in sight, and became the guarantors of a future which they themselves made entirely unpredictable.

In the present study it is possible to suggest only in this passing way that many of the extreme measures and forlorn hopes of the later phases of the Revolution were induced in part by the false promises of the legislators.

The cost to France of the violent phases of the Revolution has been reckoned time and again by historians, and one often reads that the suppressions and barbarities of the Terror were not too great a price to pay for the impulses of democratic government which the Revolution gave to modern society. But assuredly the matter does not rest here. The spirit of 1789—or certain phases of it—was a contributing factor not only to the confusion which resulted in dictatorship at home, but also to the impulses which led to conquest abroad, with all its momentous results. As is well known, in the Revolutionary and Napoleonic era the major military exploits of France stretched from Denmark to Dalmatia (even to Egypt and Syria), and from Madrid to Moscow; and lasted, with slight interruption, over twenty years. It was the most extended, most exciting, and most exhausting warfare which had until then engulfed the peoples of Europe.

That France should have drifted into such a conflict and in time become its prime agent, leads us to a consideration of Revolutionary "fraternity" in the larger or universal sense, and indeed recalls our attention to that interplay of opposites of which much has already been said. A strong current of feeling, evident from the beginning of the Revolution, was directed toward the widest possible humanitarianism. Something of this spirit was expressed by the author of the *Resurrection of the Estates General*, who in apostrophizing *précieuse Liberté*, wrote:

> A ta voix, les fers vont tomber,
> Tous les Despotes succomber,
> Et l'Univers te bénira,
> Alleluia.[32]

Other naïve expressions of similar intent could be cited. We have seen that in December, 1789, a company of patriots made the last of several toasts, "To the liberty of the universe!"[33] As a token of this goodwill, the National Assembly voted in May, 1790, France's renunciation of the idea of conquest. A few weeks later, Danton aroused the enthusiasm of a gathering of prominent Revolutionists by proposing his memorable toast to "the health, the liberty, the happiness of the entire world."[34] This vision of universal well-being withstood many vicissitudes, including war. At the opening session of the National Convention, on September 21, 1792, when the struggle against Austria and Prussia had been going on for some months, Manuel announced to the members that they were "an assembly of philosophers engaged in preparing the happiness of the world."[35] Under the Jacobin supremacy, "Liberty of the Universe" appeared as a festival in the Worship of the Supreme

---

[32] *Hymne en l'honneur de la Résurrection* . . . (3), stanza 43.   [33] See page 214.
[34] Cited in A. Aulard, *Le patriotisme selon la Révolution française*, Paris, 1904, p. 9.
[35] *Moniteur*, vol. vii, p. 1129.

Being, which Robespierre proposed and the Convention adopted in May, 1794.

On closer examination, one finds that the humanitarianism of the Revolutionists, apparently so unlimited, contained a strong admixture of national pride. This was true from the beginning. The "Liberty" whom Callières invoked in July, 1789, was, as we have seen, no universal goddess, but rather a patron saint of the French.[36] In his *Second National Song*, composed as the year 1789 came to a close, Callières boasted on behalf of certain National Guardsmen that

> Tout l'Univers nous regarde
> Sous l'Uniforme François. . . .[37]

The Abbé Fauchet had said somewhat earlier, "Frenchmen! . . . we shall be . . . the freest and the gentlest, the most courageous and the most lovable of all peoples." "France," he continued, would become "the model of nations, and the establisher of true liberty in the universe."[38] Something more than a casual compliment to the Assembly was intended when in his speech of December 12, 1789, Dubois de Crancé explained the high honor of being a French soldier by the allegation that "this title is that of defender of the most sublime constitution in the entire world."[39] The same day a spokesman at a federation in Dauphiné, in the course of a reverent tribute to the work of the representatives, described the constitution as "fit to serve all peoples as a model."[40] Interestingly enough, this mood of self-approbation was accompanied by a certain deference. In reading the debates of the Convention, one's eye may be caught by such lines as this: "Once more the French people . . . have proven to the universe that they are worthy of liberty."[41] "Digne de" is one of the strikingly recurrent phrases in the writings of the time. How concerned the Revolutionists were, not only to liberate the universe, but also to be worthy of it!

To be sure, much of the new patriotism of 1789 was a vigorous and healthy movement for national unity and betterment. And yet, as many of the expressions which have been quoted in the preced-

---

[36] See page 117.   [37] *Chanson Nationale, IIe* . . . (86), stanza 12.
[38] *Discours, sur la liberté françoise* . . . , p. 15. (IV, C)
[39] *Moniteur*, vol. i, p. 460.
[40] *Fédération de Montélimart, en Dauphiné*, n.p.n.d., p. 6. (IV, C)
[41] *Procès-verbal* (session of July 4, 1793), vol. xv, p. 104.

ing pages suggest, the first triumphs of liberty stimulated a racial
and national pride which might soon undermine the sympathy of
Frenchmen for the peoples of foreign lands. Furthermore, the language of the times—even that which had to do with the coming of
prosperity and peace—was interlarded with expressions of the martial spirit. Much of this enthusiasm was the inevitable concomitant
of the events of the day; a share of it, however, appears in the light
of vainglory, which in time led to chauvinism. This resurgence of
warrior instincts, so characteristic of man's earlier history, was by
now a matter of unprecedented importance; for under the new dis-
pensation, as we have seen, military prowess no longer remained
the affair of a special caste, but had become the concern of an entire
nation.[42]

Of comparable influence was the belief that the Revolution was
a way of life applicable to all peoples, and that France therefore had
a world-wide mission. We have only to recall the Crusades, and
similar phases in the history of non-Christian faiths, to realize that
although a universal mission inspires certain noble individuals to
attempt conversion through kindly ministrations, it is apt to instill
in the mass of men an impatient and intolerant ardor, and to
prompt them to move in battle array. Accordingly, the Revolutionists, who were surprised and offended to find that not all peoples
had risen in the name of liberty, invaded the territory of their
neighbors to undertake their forcible conversion. As J. Holland
Rose justly observes, "The national impulse in France, which up
to 1791 promised to link all free peoples in a friendly federation,
soon degenerated into a warlike and aggressive impulse, the parent
of rapine abroad and of Caesarism in France itself."[43]

Without trying fully to account for this profound transition, one
may discover in it the interesting interplay of opposing tendencies.
On the one hand, the men of the Revolution compensated for their
sentimentalized—and, therefore, not altogether satisfying—concern
over the welfare of the universe by an intensification of national
interests. In turn—as they undertook to "liberate" the peoples of
Europe by invasion and the sword rather than by enlightenment—
they were impelled, through the need of self-justification, to stress

[42] See pages 124-26 and Chapter xx.
[43] *Nationality in Modern History*, New York, 1916, p. 33.

with greater emphasis than before the humanitarian nature of their undertakings.

This development relates to the whole problem of "fraternity," the implications of which have been considered in connection with the domestic policy of France. It is observable that in foreign, as well as in domestic, affairs, the more restricted *fraternité* became in actual application, the more fervently did the Revolutionists look to its saving grace as an abstract ideal—with the result that, by the height of the Terror, the Jacobins had evolved a cult which perhaps no other religion excels for precepts of gentle humanitarianism.

Contrasting motifs of life and death constitute still another polarity in the emotional excitement of the Revolution. In considering the influence of *sensibilité*, I had occasion to observe that certain songs written to celebrate the advent of brotherhood and peace ended with sudden and emphatic assurances of the willingness of the patriots to die for their cause. This emphasis, which corresponds to the realities of the later war period, seems out of place and almost accidental in certain of the writings of 1789.[44] Yet, just as with some individuals dread of death results from, and in turn augments, fear of life, so apparently is the contrary mood—a ready and eager acceptance of the prospect of death—a concomitant of certain types of exaltation. Whereas there is nothing nobler in the annals of any country than the willingness with which the soldiers of the Revolution sacrificed themselves for the defense of France while the country was in danger, it is notable that after the danger had passed, and when the French armies were engaged in the rapine to which J. H. Rose refers, death for *la patrie* was still regarded as a consummation devoutly to be wished.[45] Certainly then, the concern with this subject in 1789 was not, as one might suppose, merely

[44] In those which celebrate the return of peace or the "new day"; for examples, see page 145. In other writings of 1789, such as those which concern the attack on the Bastille, a grim or tragic note is often entirely appropriate.

[45] While France was still at peace, Bonneville had written in his *De l'esprit des religions*, 1791 (quoted by Becker, *The Heavenly City* . . . , p. 156) that "to die for the fatherland would be to achieve eternal glory, eternal happiness." Many French soldiers of the Revolutionary and Napoleonic era maintained to the end such an ideal, which suggests the faith of the Mohammedan conquerors, or that of the Crusaders.

superficial, but was inherent in the Revolutionary mood. In the light of subsequent developments, it seems a striking premonition.

One may be sure, on the basis of what has become the psychological knowledge of our time, that if the inner conflicts which were inherent in the ideals of 1789 had remained unresolved, patriotic enthusiasms would have ended in a weak sentimentalism. It was equally inevitable—in view of the apparently great energy of the Frenchmen of that epoch[46] and of the remarkable intensity of their convictions—that if a reconciliation of divergent elements of thought and feeling could be achieved, an emotional and spiritual drive of tremendous force would follow.

The spirit of 1789, it thus appears, was bound to terminate either in frustration or in fanaticism. Its development in the latter direction is revealed in innumerable ways, the more violent and sensational of which have been made memorable by much of the fiction and indeed by a considerable part of the history which the Revolutionary period has inspired. The fact remains, however, that the most cogent evidence of the fanaticism of the Revolutionists may be found in their religious faith, expressed successively in the Worship of Reason, the Worship of the Supreme Being, the Decadal Cult, and Theophilanthropy. Aulard pointed out in one of his works that the dominant theme common to these cults was an elated patriotism.[47] Mathiez, in the course of a profounder analysis, has demonstrated that through these cults the Revolution itself became a religion.[48]

Our attention finally must be focused on this religion—especially on such of its origins as appeared in 1789. It should, however, be said at once that Catholicism continued very definitely to be the acknowledged worship of the patriots, not only in 1789, but for some time thereafter. Acting in a manner which unquestionably met the approval of most Frenchmen, the National Assembly, on

[46] Madelin, who does not find in the Revolution many of the qualities he admires, characterizes its outbreak as the explosion and vindication of "the noblest feeling, to my mind, of humanity—I mean Energy." He points to several evidences of an accumulated energy, both "individual and collective." *Op.cit.*, pp. 29-30.

[47] *Le Culte de la Raison et le Culte de l'Etre Suprême (1793-1794)*, Paris, 1909.

[48] In works already cited; see especially *Les origines des cultes révolutionnaires* . . . , Paris, 1904, and Chapter I of *Contributions à l'histoire religieuse* . . . , Paris, 1907.

April 13, 1790, proclaimed its adherence to the Catholic religion. The new patriotism was at first celebrated through the many avenues of expression which traditional Christianity afforded. For example, after the first notable triumphs of the Revolution, the representatives of the National Assembly or members of other bodies, such as the General Assembly of Paris, would repair to a church to express thanks in a *Te Deum* service. The battalion flags, one of the earliest of the many symbols of the patriotic cause, were sanctified, as we have seen, under Christian auspices. It was from the pulpit that word of the latest blessings of the Revolution was frequently brought to the people. Certain higher ecclesiastics and innumerable priests were among the staunchest supporters of the patriotic cause.

At the same time, there were forms of religious expression which showed an independent tendency. As we have seen, many of the earliest songs of the Revolution were entitled "hymns," and little more than a year elapsed before religious compositions in the French vernacular began to replace the liturgical songs of the Church. Although, so far as I know, there is no instance where patriots set up an "altar to *la Patrie*" in 1789, already in that year literary allusions to the altar of patriotism were not uncommon, the poetic imagination of that day having sensed intuitively the implications of the prevailing idealism. Finally, the sealing of nearly all Revolutionary accords by solemn oaths is indicative not only of the strong "fraternal" impulses which have been mentioned, but also of a conviction that sanctity inhered in the engagements of the new order. At one point in his *Mémoires*, Bailly describes in some detail the taking of an oath by the Assembly—an act which to him was not only "imposing" but also "truly religious."[49] The federative oaths of the citizen-soldiers, taken "before God," "before heaven," and so forth, evince sensations of patriotic reverence comparable to those which Bailly expresses.

Even more important than this nascent ritual was the dawn of what one might call a new cosmic sense. To its devotees, the Revolution seemed to contain the key to all the moral absolutes—to virtue, to truth ("right principles"), and so on. In this connection, anyone interested in the field of comparative religions—where the

---

[49] *Mémoires de Bailly*, Berville and Barrière, eds., Paris, 1821, vol. i, p. 163.

triumph of light over darkness is a recurrent theme—is bound
to be impressed by the degree to which the same imagery permeates
Revolutionary writings. Similarly, the graphic arts of the period
emphasize the thought that the advent of the Revolution is best
conveyed as light—by a rising sun, a shaft of light from heaven,
or a radiant eye (presented after the manner of Masonic symbol-
ism, and indicative also of watchfulness). In paintings and prints
of this genre, the forces over which the Revolution triumphed are
correspondingly shrouded in darkness. In 1789, there was thus
both in art and literature a clearly discernible mythology of the
Revolution represented as the triumph of good over evil. It is entirely understandable that Frenchmen who believed they had discovered spiritual realities of this final character should have regarded them as the direct concern of all mankind, and should have
proclaimed them to be "universal."

Equally suggestive of the new cosmic sense of the Revolutionists
was their concern for what they held to be the everlasting, or
"eternal," nature of their cause. In general, the reformers of this
era seem to have been uninterested in personal immortality, although it is true that Robespierre made the immortality of the
soul a tenet of the Worship of the Supreme Being. What most concerned the devotees of the Revolutionary faith was the hope that
they and their works might be immortalized in the undying memory of future generations. It is difficult to exaggerate the important
part which this sentiment played in the outlook of the Revolutionists. This strong sense of collective immortality was related to other
beliefs, including the notion of a final judgment. So far did the
trend go that Carl Becker could be both witty and just in observing of the Jacobins that "in their theology posterity had elbowed
God out of the judgment seat."[50] Already in 1789 there were inti-
mations of what was to follow, as when a lyrist described the representatives of the nation as "immortals," or expressed the wish that
"they live through all eternity"; or as when a writer reminded citizen-soldiers that their names would be "engraved . . . in the Temple of memory."[51] Such phrases as these might seem entirely inci-

[50] Becker, *The Heavenly City* . . . , p. 144. Of great interest is Becker's discussion
(pp. 140-54) of the Revolutionary "uses of posterity."
[51] These three brief quotations, picked somewhat at random, are from the following songs: *Chanson sur la prise des Invalides* . . . (29), stanza 5; *Nouvel "O Filii"* . . .
(14), stanza 36; *Prise de la Bastille* (31), stanza 8.

dental and pass unnoticed, were it not that they were repeated with marked frequency and with increasing emphasis.

It will serve to elucidate still another aspect of the spirit of 1789 if once again we look beyond that year to the time when the religious impulses of the Revolution were definitely crystallized. It is notable that as the Revolution progressed, certain of its ideals were apotheosized. Not only the Supreme Being, but also Reason, Liberty, Nature, and the Law, etc., became objects of worship. As early as 1791, a representative said, "The Law is my God, I know no other."[52] At a later date a Protestant minister is on record as having expressed substantially the same thought: "I shall henceforth have no other gospel than the Republican Constitution."[53] Gobel, a bishop (until 1793, when he withdrew from the Church), spoke to the Convention of "holy equality."[54] Marie-Joseph Chénier pleaded for a "universal religion, which has neither sects nor mysteries, of which the only dogma is equality . . . and in which the human family burns its incense only at the altar of *la Patrie*, common mother and divinity."[55] These quotations, though too fragmentary to convey the nature of the cults, are given here to suggest that the various elements of the popular faith were ultimately differentiated as separate objects of adoration. To be sure, the worship of individual heroes continued, vivid in appearance but in an essentially weakened form. As heroes became more numerous they lost stature, each one standing for some phase of the Revolution, rather than embodying the cause as a whole.[56] Besides, hero worship as such diminished in relative importance, this simple type of reverence being largely absorbed in the new civic religion, when not superseded by it.

In returning to 1789 we find, by comparison, that the primary devotion of the patriots centered in persons. It is for this reason that I found the function of leadership particularly deserving of attention in the present work. Such concepts or abstractions as lib-

---

[52] Romme, in a statement of November 14, 1791, cited by W. M. Sloane in *The French Revolution and Religious Reform*, New York, 1901, p. 186.

[53] From a speech of Julien de Toulouse, cited by E. Pressensé, in *The Church and the French Revolution* (translated by J. Stoyan), London, 1869, p. 303.

[54] Aulard, *op.cit.*, p. 45.

[55] From Chénier's *Rapport sur l'Instruction publique, du 15 brumaire, l'an II* (November 5, 1793), *Moniteur*, vol. ix, p. 194.

[56] For a word concerning Jacobin martyrology, see page 16, including footnote 39.

erty, law, equality—of signal importance later—were at first contained within the larger idea of the popular cause itself, which Necker and the King (subject to such reservations as have been mentioned) symbolized. Why this dual leadership could not fully serve the purposes of the patriots and was almost certain to end in conflict, has been explained.

But despite the ultimate collapse of this complicated hero worship, the mass of Frenchmen doubtless continued throughout the Revolution to be fundamentally dependent in their political life on personal attachments. Bonds resembling those of the family had long been the basis of social cohesion in France, and, as we have seen, they were found natural and useful in the Revolutionary upheaval of 1789. It stands to reason that habits so deeply ingrained could not at once be reversed—or even radically altered. From this standpoint, one may venture to suppose that under the Republic, Jacobin leadership suffered from want of a strong central human element, which Robespierre even at the height of his power failed to provide. The Directory, with its notable dispersion of power and emphasis on the office rather than on the man, was in this respect even more handicapped. When these governments, which depended for their justification on a somewhat elaborate political theory, were successively overthrown, the traditional principle of the leader was revived—albeit vastly altered to suit Revolutionary ideals—in the person of Napoleon.

The so-called Consulate of the Corsican adventurer, having obliterated the Republic by degrees (1799-1804), was itself finally transformed into the Empire.

This was not the "golden age" men had hoped for in the spring of 1789, but still it was a new day. Men, by and large, were equal; and, although bound by a new regime, were free of Bourbon restraints. If the discipline of the new order should prove more severe than that of the old, Frenchmen might recall that their days of self-reliance had been painful and costly. Who among them would now exclaim, in the spirit of 1789, "All the evils are going to end"? After ten years of cataclysmic change and unprecedented struggle, the proponents of reform had become less sanguine. They would find comfort in being able to depend at last on the single purpose and inexhaustible energy of a *Dieu tutélaire*.

Much more remains to be said concerning this drift from democracy to dictatorship, which serves as a prototype in the history of modern nationalism; but here it can only be added that the transition was effected with ease. The dove of peace which was to have descended upon a free and sovereign people was not sought—by and large, it was not even missed—once the eagle of Napoleonic imperialism was blazoned across the sky.

The spirit of 1789 was thus essentially a religious spirit. To a considerable extent it was made up of inherently conflicting elements, which were reconciled, to appearances at least, and given form in the cults of later years. Although these outward expressions of the Revolutionary faith were short-lived, many of the principles and achievements which the initial faith inspired have endured. Of incalculable importance in their influence on men of later times have been the Revolutionary doctrines of constitutional government, of republicanism, of the essential liberties of man, of man's equality, of brotherhood, and by no means least—and contravening some of the preceding—of nationalism, unforgettably epitomized in the *Marseillaise* as "l'amour sacré de la patrie."

If in this concluding chapter I have added little concerning the magnitude of the achievements of the Revolutionists, it is because the signs of their influence are everywhere about us, and because the debt which we owe them has been many times acknowledged. It seemed more important—and more appropriate to the subject matter of this investigation—to stress the paradoxical aspects of the nascent democratic faith, and to examine the emotional factors in the Revolutionary heritage.

This is by no means to lose sight of the larger significance of the French Revolution; for the very institutions and ideals to which reference has been made may depend for their stability—and perhaps even for their survival—on man's obtaining a fuller understanding of the emotional forces which underlie modern civilization. The twentieth century has introduced an era of psychological awareness that not only points to this need, but also affords some hope of meeting it. No branch of the social sciences can alone exhaust the possibilities of so comprehensive an inquiry, but each—including history—can play a part. This work on the history of popular opinion at the dawn of the democratic era in France is intended as a step in that direction.

BIBLIOGRAPHY

I. A NEW CATALOGUE OF THE POLITICAL
SONGS OF 1789

THE following list provides a catalogue of the political songs which are definitely known to have come out in France in 1789, or which, for various reasons, are ascribable to that year.

At first glance this bibliography may seem a repetition of the work undertaken by Constant Pierre in the "1789" section of his *Catalogue* (published in *Les hymnes et chansons de la Révolution*, Paris, 1904). But the fact is that my investigations have led me to make wide departures from Pierre: i.e., to reject over one-third of the items which he includes, to make a radical rearrangement in the ordering of the remaining pieces, to include some songs which did not come to his attention, to distinguish different editions which he does not signalize, and to add various library references to those which he provides.

A justification for these changes is given in Parts I and II of this Bibliography and in my critique of Pierre's *Catalogue* for 1789, which appears as Appendix A. Together, these three bibliographical chapters are intended to provide a guide to the French Revolutionary songs of 1789.

The song titles which follow are arranged in chronological order, according to the events which they celebrated. Songs which treat of the subject matter of 1789 but were composed later, including anniversary songs, are in general excluded from this list. A few possible exceptions occur—five pieces customarily ascribed to 1789, which in fact may have first appeared slightly later. Each of these is indicated by a dagger (†) preceding the title.

In general, each main entry consists of title, author (when known), and air. Pierre provides first lines in connection with all his entries, but they are introduced here only after the titles of songs which he did not include (the "addenda" mentioned below), and on occasion when a title is not in itself distinctive. The first line, when given, appears in quotation marks.

The great majority of the political songs of 1789 were Revolutionist in sympathy. Exceptions, of which there are ten, are marked "Antirevol."

Variations in style which appear in the titles below result from the use—for the purposes of this Catalogue—of the spelling, capitalization, etc., of the original texts. "Sic" is interpolated only occasionally, for clarity or emphasis. Where texts are multiple and the same titles are not uniform in style, it has seemed advisable to use modern orthography; and this has been done also in a few other cases.

The main and subordinate entries which follow are the result of firsthand investigation unless some indication to the contrary is given. Indeed, an effort has been made to account for all known editions and any exemplifications of them that are extant. Where firsthand investigation has not been possible, I have made acknowledgment to such bibliographers as Martin and Walter, and Monglond. Although I have tracked down most of the numerous leads which Pierre's *Catalogue* affords, it must be added that certain items which Pierre lists, primarily alternative editions or copies, proved to be unobtainable, or were for other reasons not consulted. The attention of the reader is called to such omissions, and a cross reference is provided to Appendix A, where the essential facts, and sometimes explanations, are given. In this way, nothing that Pierre mentions has been lost sight of, and much has been added.

The numbers in parentheses—such as (168), (171), etc.—which follow the song titles below are Pierre's serial numbers for the same items. Reference may thus readily be made to his *Catalogue*, as well as to my annotations thereon in Appendix A. Songs followed by "Ad." in parentheses are addenda to the Pierre *Catalogue*. These several items are numbered in chronological sequence (Ad. 1 through Ad. 14).

Subordinate entries beneath the song titles below reveal the edition, or editions, in which each song is known to have appeared. These entries are followed by cross references to the second part of the Bibliography, thus: (II, A), (II, B), etc. By turning to the section indicated, the reader may obtain information concerning full title, place, and date, etc., of the publication cited, together with library references to indicate where extant copies are preserved. A key to the classification of materials in Part II may be found on page 284.

By way of illustration, in the first two entries below, abbreviations are explained in full. For a further word of explanation, see entry #16.

It is of course true of the French Revolutionary period that new documentary materials still come to light. For this reason no one, including the author, need be surprised if new songs of 1789 (and new editions of those mentioned) are discovered, and if, accordingly, the catalogue which follows has, in the course of time, to be considerably expanded.

ESTATES GENERAL, ANTICIPATION OF

1. *L'Alleluia du Tiers-Etat. "Enfin, le Tiers a triomphé. . . . "* (Ad. 1)
[The first of the items not listed by Pierre.]
    Air: Alleluia.
        Ibid., seconde édition, 1789. (II, B)
            [This single indented entry indicates that the edition cited is the only one known. The publication is described, and its availability indicated, in Part II, section B, devoted to "Songs Published Separately, Words Only."]

2. *Couplets à MM. les députés des bailliages réunis à Metz, nommés le 15 avril 1789, lors de leur départ.* (168) [It is under this serial number

that Pierre lists the same song in his *Catalogue*; the number may be referred to also in Appendix A, where the reader will find annotations on the *Catalogue*.]

> Air: *Regard vif.*
>> Ms. only, *ibid.* (II, G)
>>> [This entry indicates that no printed edition of this song is known; concerning its manuscript form and for library reference see Part II, section G, "Manuscripts."]

3. *Hymne en l'honneur de la Résurrection des Etats-Généraux.* (171)
> Air: *Alleluia.*
>> *Ibid., 1789.* (II, B)

4. *Cahier du Marquis de Fulvy.*
> Air: *Du haut en bas.*
>> a.) *Ibid.,* n.p.n.d., 16 pp., in-8. (II, B)
>> b.) *Ibid.,* n.p.n.d., 16 pp., in-16. (II, B)
>> c.) First stanza and notice concerning appearance of piece in 1789, in *Almanach des Muses, 1790,* p. 315. (II, F)
>> NOTE: the author is Philibert-Louis Orry, marquis de Fulvy, according to Quérard, in *Les supercheries littéraires. . . .*

5. *Arrêté des Habitans de la Grenouillère & du Pont-aux-Choux, de la Rapée & du Gros-Caillou, Adressé à la Nation.* (182)
> Air: *J'veux êt' un chien, &c.*
>> *Ibid.* (II, B)

6. *R'quête en magnier' d'écrit, à Monseigneu le Pervo des Marchands, par un Maît' Pêcheu' du Gros-Caillou.* (182*)
> Air: *Mariniers de la Grenouillère, ou C'est après d'main matin, &c.*
>> *Ibid.* (II, B)
>> NOTE: concerning the possibility of another edition, see Appendix A, 182*.

7. *Le moment désiré, Couplets patriotiques sur les états généraux, par M. Déduit.*[1] (172)

---

[1] In addition to the seven songs which comprise this group, mention may be made of three other items:

(1) *Les Oeufs de Pâques des Français, ou la Résurrection de la félicité publique,* which may belong to this period, although it is ascribed by Pierre to 1790. See Appendix A, 273.

(2) *Chanson nouvelle à la gloire du tiers état. Paris, in-12.—Titre de la 1 chanson.—* such is the brief (and insufficient) entry in A. Monglond, *La France révolutionnaire . . .,* vol. i, col. 524. This item is unknown to me and is not mentioned by Pierre.

(3) *Couplets chantés au festin donné par M. le président du tiers-état, par M. F. de'A - - - -, à Besançon, de l'imprimerie de Couché,* n.d., 4 pp., a song preserved in the Andrew D. White Collection of Cornell University Library. A more fruitful inquiry than I have been able to make into the regional history of Besançon might establish a place for this piece in the list above.

Air: Pourriez-vous bien douter encore.
  a.) Song with music. *Ibid.* (II, A)
  b.) *Ibid.* (followed by) *Discours du Roi à l'Assemblée des Etats généraux . . . au 4 de mai 1789 (extrait)*, according to Martin and Walter, *Catalogue.* . . . (II, D)

ESTATES GENERAL: MAY 5 TO JUNE 20

8. *Chanson nouvelle sur l'assemblée des Etats Généraux, par Mr. B - - - .* (174)
  Air: O filii.
  Song with music. *Ibid.* (II, A)

9. *Chanson nouvelle sur les Etats-généraux, par une D^elle [demoiselle] religieuse de 78 ans nommée Jeanne Rocher.* (175)
  Air: Retire-toi.
  Ms. only. *Ibid.*, p. 1 (also #10, p. 1). (II, G)

10. *Chansonnette sur les Etats-généraux [par Jeanne Rocher]. 20 couplets.* (173)
  Air: O reguigne, oh lon la (misspelled, and partly illegible, in the original).
  Ms. only. *Chanson nouvelle sur les Etats-généraux*, p. 1 (also #9, p. 1). (II, G)

11. *Le Tiers Etat, Adressé à M^r Le Docteur G - - - - .* (179)
  Air: Vous de qui l'amoureuse ivresse.
  a.) Song with music (seven stanzas). *Ibid.* (II, A)
  b.) The first three and the last two stanzas of the above, with slight variations: *Compliments des dames poissardes à leur confrères du Tiers-Etat—avec des Couplets*, in *Plaintes et doléances . . . 1789*, p. 31. (II, D)
  NOTE: Pierre refers to another edition with subtitle, *Couplets chantés le 18 mai à l'Archevêché, par une députation des dames poissardes de la halle*; see Appendix A, 179.

12. *Chanson très-nouvelle. "Le Tiers-Etat/ Depuis long-temps étoit victime. . . . "* (Ad. 2)
  Air: Laysso droumi.
  Ibid. (II, B)

13. (Anti-revol.) *Le chansonnier du Tiers.* (180)
  Air: Pot-pourri.
  Ibid. (II, B)

14. *Nouvel "O Filii" des Etats-Généraux, par A. L. G., le 23 Mai 1789.* (178)
  Air: O filii.
  Ibid. (II, B)

15. *Motion des Harangères [sic] de la Halle.* (181)
     Air: Reçois dans ton galetas.
  a.) Engraved, with black border. *Ibid.* (II, B)
  b.) Ms. (lettering in imitation of the above, without border;
      difference in stanza 3, line 8; text otherwise nearly identical).
      Ibid. (II, G)
  NOTE: concerning other references, see Appendix A, 181.

ROYAL SESSION, JUNE 23 TO JULY 14

16. *Le coup heureux de Versailles du 23 Juin 1789. Chanson grivoise.*
     (187)
     Air: Monsieur, Monsieur, baisez-moi.
       La France régénérée . . . , p. 4 (also #36, p. 1; #24, p. 5; #25,
       p. 7). (II, C)
       [Explanation: Shown here is the page reference for *Le coup
       heureux* . . . , and in parentheses such other songs of 1789 as
       the publication contains. The songs are signalized by their cat-
       alogue numbers, to each of which is prefixed, for clarity, the
       conventional number symbol. This system of cross reference
       is used throughout Bibliographies I and II, i.e., in the case of
       all publications containing two or more songs of 1789.]
       This brochure was first published after July 14. See Appen-
       dix A, 187.

17. *Remerciemens aux Gardes Françaises et aux Gardes Suisses, sur la
     manière patriotique dont ils se sont comportés à Versailles, après la
     Séance Royale du 23 Juin. Au nom des Citoyens du Palais-Royal.*
     "Braves Camarades. . . . " (Ad. 3)
     Air: Le Roi de Sardaigne en passant par Namur.
  a.) *Ibid.* (II, B)
  b.) Under title, *Chanson sur le Patriotisme et la Prudence des
      Gardes Françaises et Suisses, après la Séance Royale de Ver-
      sailles, du 23 Juin 1789. Dialogue entre un Citoyen et un
      Militaire,* and with minor variations in text. (II, B)

18. *Nouveau pot-pourri sur les affaires du temps.* (232)
     Air: Pot-pourri.
       Nouveau pot-pourri . . . , *1789,* p. 1 (also #19, p. 10; #20, p.
       12). (II, C)

19. *Chanson.* "*Notre S. [Saint] Père est un dindon. . . .* " (233)
     Air: O filii.
       Nouveau pot-pourri . . . , *1789,* p. 10 (also #18, p. 1; #20, p.
       12). (II, C)

20. *O filii national.* (234)
     Air: O filii.

a.) Engraved and printed with black border. (II, B)

b.) Ms. (lettering resembling the above; without border; and showing slight differences in orthography). *Ibid.* (II, G)

c.) *Nouveau pot-pourri . . . , 1789*, p. 12 (also #18, p. 1; #19, p. 10). (II, C)

A misprint occurs in first line, "Français envain vous triomphés," the "envain" evidently being a mistake for "enfin," which appears in the other editions. Various differences in orthography from editions "a" and "b."

21. *Chanson poissarde. "Sais-tu, Cadet, que j'somm' du Tiers? . . . "* (180*)

Air: *Aisément cela se peut croire.*

Ibid., édition nouvelle . . . (song accompanied by prose to be spoken). (II, B)

22. *Les trois ordres réunis, par Mr Minier.* (168*)

Air: *Reçois dans ton galetas.*

Song with music. *Ibid.* (II, A)

23. *La réunion des trois ordres. Couplets dédiés à la Nation, par M. Déduit.* (169)

Air: *Avec le jeux dans le village.*

Ibid. (II, B)

NOTE: concerning a second contemporary edition see Appendix A, 169.

24. *Les trois ordres réunis. Suite* (i.e. to #16). (205*)

Air: *Monsieur, Monsieur, baisez-moi,* etc.

La France régénérée . . . , p. 5 (also #36, p. 1; #16, p. 4; #25, p. 7). (II, C)

This brochure was first published after July 14. See Appendix A, 187.

25. *Chanson sur l'Assemblée nationale (par de Joyenval).* (243*)

Air: *Jardinier ne vois-tu pas.*

a.) *La France régénérée . . . ,* p. 7 (also #36, p. 1; #16, p. 4; #24, p. 5). (II, C)

NOTE: no author's name is given with the title, but the final stanza is a "Félicitation à moi-même," which begins "Quant à moi, de Joyenval. . . . " This brochure was first published after July 14—see Appendix A, 187.

b.) An item listed by Martin and Walter, *Catalogue . . . ,* but not known to me at firsthand, appears to be another edition of this song, viz., *Pont-neuf, ou chanson sur l'Assemblée nationale . . . , par de Joyenval . . . , 1789. Ibid.* (II, B)

26. *Couplets sur la bienfaisance de LL AA SS [sic] M^{or} le Duc d'Orleans et Mme la Duchesse D'Orleans dans l'hiver memorable de 1788 à*

1789. Par M Déduit auteur des évenement Patriotiques. "Chantons la bienfaisance. . . . " (Ad. 4)

> Air: Des Bonnes gens.

>> *Ibid., à Paris, avec permission (gravure,* reproduced in H. Gautier, *L'An 1789).* (II, H)

>>> NOTE: my inclusion of this song in this section of the catalogue is based on the conjecture that it relates to the Duke's conspicuous role as a popular leader on the eve of the Bastille uprising. It would thus have come at a time when the Parisians were again suffering acutely from food shortages. But it may have been composed somewhat earlier—or later. As the description (above) of Déduit indicates, the song was subsequent to certain "évenement[s] patriotiques" which that author had already celebrated, but of this earlier work I have found no trace. The title above, with its several orthographical irregularities, corresponds to the original as reproduced by Gautier.

27. *Chanson sur les affaires du temps, par M. le marquis de C - - - P - - .*[2] (230)

> Air: La dance n'est pas ce que j'aime.

>> *Avis au peuple . . . , 1789,* p. 10. (II, D)

28. *Où le bas nous blesse. Chanson à la portée de tout le monde, Enrichie de notes intéressantes.* (206)

> Air: C'est ce qui nous désole.

>> *Ibid. Paris; juillet 1789.* (II, B)

Capture of the Bastille; Royal Visit to Paris, July 17; and Murders of Foulon and Bertier, July 22

29. *Chanson sur la prise des Invalides et de la Bastille, les lundi 13 et mardi 14 juillet 1789. A Paris, ce vendredi 17, jour où l'on attend le Roi devant Messieurs les 300 Electeurs à L'Hôtel-de-Ville; et faite à L'Hôtel de Tours, étant sorti de patrouille, à midi. A mon Parent, M. Moreau de Saint-Merry [sic], Président des 300 Electeurs de Paris. Par le Chevalier de Callières.* (194)

> Air: Dans ma cabane obscure.

>> a.) *Ibid.,* n.p.n.d. (II, B)

>> b.) *Ibid., chez Nyon le jeune . . . , 1789.* (II, B)

30†. *Quelques vers faits le 17 Juillet au sujet de la prise mémorable. P. Rousselet, un assaillant de la Bastille . . . (. . . il faut chanter quelques vers faits . . . etc.). "Amis, des fers de l'esclavage. . . . "* (Ad. 5)

> Air: (none indicated).

>> *Détail intéressant . . . sur la prise de la Bastille . . . ,* p. 28. (II, D)

>> Concerning uncertain date of the *Détail intéressant . . . ,* see

---

[2] The *Cantique nouveau, sur le cantique de saint Roche,* ascribed by Pierre to 1790, may also belong to this period. See Appendix A, 436*.

ibid., Bibliography II, D; concerning song, see page 127, footnote 44.

31. *Prise de la Bastille.* (193)
    Air: Malbrouck.
    Song with music. *Ibid.* (II, A)

32. *Chanson des bourgeois de Paris.* (209)
    Air: Calpigi.
    Song with music. *Ibid.* (II, A)
    NOTE: concerning another contemporary edition (words only), see Appendix A, 209.

33. *Pot-pourri sur les événements arrivez [sic] dans Paris, les 13, 14 et 17 juillet 1789, couplets: "Braves sôldats parisiens . . . , " par un patriote, ce 20 juillet 1789.* (194*)
    NOTE: title only; see Appendix A, 194*.

34. *Chanson nouvelle chantée par les Dames députées du Marché St.-Paul.* (July 20, 1789. The occasion is described in a statement preceding the song, in *Journal de Paris*—see reference below.) (201)
    Air: La Gaieté.
    Journal de Paris, 22 juillet, 1789, p. 912. (II, E)

35. *La Prise de la Bastille. Couplets dédiés à la Nation, par M. Déduit.* "*Que les gardes françaises,/ Sont de bons citoyens. . . .*" (Ad. 6)
    Air: Dans les gardes françaises.
    Ibid. (gravure sur bois coloriée) à Orléans. (II, B)

36. *La France régénérée et les traitres punis. Chanson sur le siège et la prise de la Bastille* (in two parts, including "*Suite. Prise de la Bastille*").[3] (192)
    Air: Matelots.
    a.) *La France régénérée . . . ,* p. 1 (also #16, p. 4; #24, p. 5; #25, p. 7). (II, C)
    b.) Revised version, omitting stanza ten—in place of which three new stanzas are interpolated—and omitting last two stanzas; in fragment commencing "le calotin," p. 5 (also last part of #73, p. 5). (II, C, under Fragment . . .)
    NOTE: the revision is sufficiently in the spirit of the first anniversary of the Bastille to suggest 1790 as the date of this fragment. In any case, it appeared after November 2, 1789 (see Appendix A, 192).

---

[3] At the Cleveland Public Library (W841.04-C452, vol. i, no. 15) is a song by Ladré, entitled *La Prise de la Bastille; la trahison découverte et la punition des traitres (air: En revènant).* (Accents as shown.) This item is not mentioned by Pierre, and I have omitted it from the list above, believing that it may well be an anniversary song attributable to 1790.

37†. *Récit historique de ce qui s'est passé dans la Ville de Paris, depuis le commencement de Juillet, jusqu'au 13, 14, 15 & 16 du même mois de l'année 1789.* (190)
    Air: Henri IV.
      a.) *Entretien d'un Vieillard* . . . , p. 6. (II, C)
          NOTE: concerning uncertainty of date, see Appendix A, 190.
      b.) *Le Savetier bon patriote* . . . [1790], p. 7 (includes also item #437 in Pierre, *Catalogue*). (II, C)

38. *La lanterne merveilleuse.* (199)
    Air: A la façon de Barbari.
    Ibid. (II, B)

39. *Chanson des Dames de la Place Maubert.* (200)
    Air: Ce soir dans ton galetas.
    Ibid. (II, B)

40. *Etats généraux de Bacchus.* (170)
    Air: Ce fut par la faute du sort.
      a.) *Le citoyen en bonne humeur* . . . , *1789*, p. 7 (also #41, p. 10). (II, D)
      b.) Reprinted with final stanza concerning Necker omitted, and with last lines of preceding stanza radically altered, in *Almanach du Bon-Homme* . . . , *Paris, 1793*, p. 130. (II, F)

41. *Le buveur paisible, Chanson de table.* (170*)
    Air: Fanfare de Saint-Cloud.
    Le citoyen en bonne humeur . . . , *1789*, p. 10 (also #40, p. 7). (II, D)

42. *Chanson des dames des Marchés S. Paul, des Quinze-vingts, la Halle et d'Aguesseau, composée par Madame Dupray. Approuvée par M. le Maire de Paris.* (238)
    Air: Reçois dans ton galetas.
    Ibid. (II, B)

43. *La Cocarde du Roi, Couplets patriotiques, Chantés aux Variétés de Bordeaux.* (293)
    Air: Des Dettes, C'est ce qui me console.
    Song with music. *Ibid.* (II, A)

44. *Chanson jettée sur le Théâtre à Brest, le Dimanche 26 Juillet 1789, & chantée par une Actrice. "Amis, nos beaux jours vont renaître. . . ."* (Ad. 7)
    Air: Du serin qui te fait envie.
    Suite de la révolution authentique . . . , p. 4. (II, D)

RETURN OF NECKER, JULY 28, TO INSURRECTION OF OCTOBER 5-6

45. *Couplets en l'honneur de M. Necker revenu à Versailles, par M. de Savigny, patriote. "Necker, notre dieu tutélaire. . . ."* (204)

Air: Vive à jamais (Le bal de Strasbourg, vaud.).
NOTE: title only; see Appendix A, 204.

46. *Bouquet présenté à M. Necker, à son entrée à Paris le 30 juillet
1789. L'Abbé de Courchon. "Assez ta désastreuse absence...."* (Ad.
8)
    Air: Avec les jeux dans le Village.
    Bouquet présenté ..., p. 2. (II, D)

47. *Tribut lyrique ou Vers accompagnés d'une Couronne de Fleurs, et
présentés à M. Necker, à son entrée à l'Hôtel-de-Ville, le jeudi 30
Juillet 1789, par M. Bavouz, Citoyen du District de l'Oratoire.* (202)
    Air: (see below).
    a.) Words only (no air indicated), *ibid., à Paris, chez Froullé
    ...*, n.d. (II, B)
    b.) Words only (no air indicated), *ibid., à Paris, de l'imprimerie
    de Seguy-Thiboust ..., 1789.* (II, B)
    c.) Words only (no air indicated). Title reads "à son arrivée,"
    rather than "à son entrée." *Affiches, annonces ..., 19 août,
    1789,* p. 2394. (II, E)
    d.) Music for same:
       1.) *Musique pouvant se chanter à voix seule, avec symphonie
       et à grand orchestre.*
       2.) *Chaconne du Tiers-Etat, composée par M. Corrette, sur
       les paroles du "Tribut lyrique," que l'on peut exécuter à
       gr. orchestre, sans chanter les paroles, avec trompettes et
       timbales. Chez Mercier, rue des Prouvaires, No. 33: prix
       3 liv.*
    Notices of both scores published under *Avis divers,* in *Affiches,
    annonces ..., 29 avril, 1790,* p. 1132. (II, E)

48. *Le retour de M. Necker, dédié à la nation par MM. C ... et T ...,
"Vive le roi Louis...." (Coulubrier.)* (203)
    Air: La Béquille.
    NOTE: title only; see Appendix A, 203.

49. *Chanson, par Dugazon, Pensionnaire du Roi. "Livrez vos coeurs à
l'allégresse...."* (205)
    Air: Quoi, ma voisine es-tu fâchée?
    Affiches, annonces ..., 1 août, 1789, p. 2233. (II, E)

50. *Couplets à M. le Marquis de la Fayette, présent à la bénédiction
des Drapeaux du District des Cordeliers, le 13 Août 1789, par M. Imbert.* (210)
    Air: (none indicated).
    Almanach des Muses [for] *1790,* p. 161. (II, F)
       In table of contents, *ibid.,* p. 295, Imbert's name is followed
       by "de l'Académie de Nismes."

51. *Chanson sur le brave La Fayette.* "*Lucas, pour chanter sa bergère.*
   . . ." (360*)
   Air: Avec les jeux dans le Village.
   a.) Six stanzas, *ibid.* (II, A)
   b.) The first three and the last three stanzas presented in separate parts, and in inverted order, as follows:
   1.) The last three stanzas only, under same title and with
   same air as above. First line, "Quand le bon la Fayette
   ordonne. . . . " In *La Gazette des Halles* . . . , *No. 1er,
   1789,* p. 10. (II, D)
   2.) The first three stanzas only. First line, "Licas [*sic*], pour
   chanter sa bergère. . . . " *Air: Pourriez-vous bien douter
   encore?* In *La Gazette des Halles* . . . , *No. 1er, 1789,* p. 11.
   (II, D)

52. *Couplets chantés à un Dîner de Corps, où assistoient les trois
   Ordres, par M. B - - - de S - - - - - -.* "*Est-ce l'âge d'Or de la fable.* . . ."
   (Ad. 9)
   Air: Avec les jeux dans le Village.
   Couplets chantés . . . , p. 1 (also #53, p. 2). (II, C)

53. *Autres* [*couplets*]. "*Amis, buvons à la Patrie.* . . . " (Ad. 10.)
   Air: Vive Henri! vive Henri! (de la Bataille d'Ivry).
   Couplets chantés . . . , p. 2 (also #52, p. 1). (II, C)

54. *Couplets pour la Saint-Louis 1789, Bouquet au Roi, dédié à M.
   Bailli, Maire de la Ville de Paris, & à M. le Marquis de la Fayette,
   Commandant général de la Garde Nationale Parisienne, par M. de
   la Boessière, Maître d'Armes.* (213)
   Air: (see "a" below).
   a.) Song with music. *Ibid.* (II, A)
   b.) Announcement of same, and first stanza only, in *Affiches, annonces* . . . , *26 août, 1789,* p. 2450. (II, E)

55. *La Constitution française et les droits de l'homme. Chanson patriotique. Par M. S - - - , Garde National du District de Saint-Gervais.*
   (216)
   Air: Vive Henri IV.
   a.) *Ibid., Paris, chez Garnéry, L'An Premier de la Liberté.* (II, B)
   b.) *Ibid., 3e ed. corrigée et augmentée. Paris, chez Simon & Jacob-
   Sion* . . . , n.d. (II, B)
   This edition differs from edition "a" only in minor respects, such as punctuation, except that here the original
   order of stanzas fifteen and sixteen is inverted.
   c.) *Chansonnier National ou Recueil* . . . , *1790,* p. 2. (II, C)

56. *La Cocarde nationale ou L'Egalité patriotique (par C. Mercier de
   Compiègne).* (217)
   Air: On compteroit les diamants.

a.) First appeared anonymously. Song with music. *Ibid.* (II, A)

NOTE: in later reprints, Mercier's name appeared as author. See "b" and "c," below.

b.) Revised edition under title *Chanson sur la Cocarde Nationale, par le citoyen Mercier de Compiègne,* in *Le Chansonnier de la Montagne, l'an 2* (first, second, and third editions), p. 104. (II, F)

NOTE: for details concerning revision, see Appendix A, 217.

c.) Reprint (edition "b") in Mercier, *Le Temple de la Liberté ... 3e année républ.,* p. 55. (II, F)

In a bibliography of his own works, Mercier made particular mention (*ibid.,* p. 158, item no. 5) of *La Cocarde Nationale.* In reprinting this song in *Le Temple de la Liberté ...* (p. 55), he added the following comment: "Ces couplets furent imprimés au mois d'août 1789 et ensuite en 1792 et 1793."

57. *Couplets, chantés par un soldat citoyen de la garde nationale de Compiègne à la fête donnée le 13 septembre 1789, par les cit. de cette ville, au détachement de la garde nat. parisienne chargé d'escorter le convoi d'armes venant de Maubeuge: Les travaux d'Hercule réalisés par les Parisiens, par M. Mounier, cit. de Compiègne.* (226)

Air: *Mon père était pot.*

Ibid. (II, B)

58. *Couplets chantés à Madame la Marquise de La Fayette. Le 22 Septembre, jour de la Bénédiction du Drapeau de District de St-Etienne-du-Mont, à la suite d'un Repas donné par M. le Commandant du Bataillon de ce District. Par M. Ducray du Minil, Caporal de la quatrième Compagnie du Bataillon du District de St-Etienne-du-Mont, Membre de l'Académie des Arcades de Rome, et de plusieurs Sociétés Littéraires.* (227)

Air: *La Croisée.*

a.) *Ibid., 1789.* (II, B)

b.) Under title, *Couplets chantés le jour de le bénédiction du drapeau de bataillon de S. Etienne du Mont, à un répas où assistaient Madame la Marquise de la Fayette et M. son fils.* S.l., in-12. (Mentioned in Monglond, vol. i, col. 1157, where it is incorrectly attributed to 1790.)

59. *Le voile levé, par M. L. C. D. V.* (220)

Air: *O filii.*

Le voile levé, p. 3 (also #60, p. 12); two editions. (II, C)

60. *Chanson. "Les Français sont des diables. . . . ." Par M. L. C. D. V.* (221)

Air: *Le soir à la croisée.*

Le voile levé, p. 12 (also #59, p. 3); two editions. (II, C)

OCTOBER INSURRECTION

61. *Le Voyage du Roi, de Versailles à Paris, où il fait sa résidence, par un Compagnon de Voyage, Soldat de la Garde Nationale Parisienne.* (240*)
    Air: Vive Henri IV.
      a.) *Ibid.* (II, B)
      b.) *Le voyage du Roi* . . . , p. 1 (also #62, p. 4; #63, p. 5; #64, p. 7). (II, C)
      NOTE: concerning other references, see Appendix A, 240*.

62. *Autre Chanson. "Dans ce monde chacun raisonne. . . . "* (Ad. 11)
    Air: de Tarare.
      Le voyage du Roi . . . , p. 4 (also #61, p. 1; #63, p. 5; #64, p. 7). (II, C)

63. *Départ des poissardes de Paris pour Versailles.* (239**)
    Air: A la bonne huile et v'là l'oignon.
      Le voyage du Roi . . . , p. 5 (also #61, p. 1; #62, p. 4; #64, p. 7). (II, C)

64. *Chanson poissarde. Leur arrivée à Versailles, et leur retour à Paris avec le Roi & la Famille Royale.* (240)
    Air: V'la donc notr' Dauphin bien ravi.
      Le voyage du Roi . . . , p. 7 (also #61, p. 1; #62, p. 4; #63, p. 5). (II, C)

65. *Courage patriotique des Dames de la Halle, dans l'affaire du 5 et 6 oct. 1789, par Labré* [sic, according to Martin and Walter, although presumably *Ladré*]. (Ad. 12)
      NOTE: this title and the bibliographical reference which follows are borrowed from Martin and Walter, *Catalogue.* . . .
      Ni vu ni connu . . . (also #73). (II, C)

66. *Justification des Messieurs et des Dames de la Halle de Paris, sur les crimes de l'exécrable révolution française, notamment de ceux des 5 et 6 Octobre 1789, commis à Versailles, auxquels on les accusoit d'avoir pris part.* (237*)
    Air: Enfin v'la q'c'est donc bâclé [sic].
    Ibid. (II, B)

67. (Anti-revol.) *L'Assemblée nationale ou la France abusée.* (181*)
    Air: Reçois dans ton galetas.
      Etrennes à la nation . . . , *1789*, p. 9 (also #68, p. 13). (II, D)

68. (Anti-revol.) *Chanson. "Le duc d'Orléans reviendra. . . . "* (183*)
    Air: Quand le bien-aimé reviendra.
      Etrennes à la nation . . . , *1789*, p. 13 (also #67, p. 9). (II, D)

69†. (Anti-revol.) *Le troubadour béarnais.* (218)
    Air: (see below).

a.) Ms., with music. *Ibid.* (II, G)

b.) Ms., with music (different score), under title *Chœur béarnais.*
Ibid., p. 1 (also #70†, p. 3). (II, G)

c.) Under title *Chœur béarnais,* in *Actes des apôtres,* no. 29, p.
13. (II, E)

d.) Under title, *Malheurs du Roi et de sa famille, Romance d'un
troubadour béarnois,* in *L'ami du roi, almanach . . . (pour
l'année 1792),* p. 20. (II, F)

NOTE: concerning another reference, see Appendix A, 218.

70†. (Anti-revol.) *Le troubadour parisien, romance, par Gabriel-Joseph
d'Eaubonne.* (243)
Air: (see below).

a.) Ms., *ibid., Autre duo; le même Air* (as *Chœur béarnais,*
above, #69†, ed. "b"). Written at end of song: *Gabriel-
Joseph d'Eaubonne.* In ms. *Chœur béarnais,* p. 3 (also #69†,
p. 1). (II, G)

b.) *Le troubadour parisien* (author's name not given). (II, B)

c.) *Le troubadour parisien, romance* (author's name not given),
in *Actes des apôtres,* vol. iii, no. 61, p. 14. (II, E)

NOTE: concerning other references and uncertainty in regard to
date of first appearance of this song, see Appendix A, 243.

Decree on Church Property, November 2, to End of 1789

71. *Les nouveaux apôtres aristocrates.* (246)
Air: La Lanterne.

a.) Contemporary text known only through a reprint, bearing
subtitle *Couplets à l'occasion du décret de l'Assemblée nationale, qui déclare que les biens possédés par le clergé ap-
partiennent à la Nation,* and reproducing the following imprint, *Se trouvait à la librairie de Valleyre, rue de la Huch-
ette. Poésies révolutionnaires . . . ,* 1821, vol. i, p. 55. (II, H)

b.) For comment on this piece and reproduction of its third
stanza, see *Chronique de Paris, 18 mai, 1790,* p. 549. (II, E)

72. *Chanson nouvelle. Le Requiem aeternam du Clergé de France. Par
M. P. au sortir de l'Assemblée Nationale, du 2 Novembre 1789. "Que
cette journée opportune. . . . "* (Ad. 13)
Air: Du Boudoir d'Aspasie.
Ibid. (II, B)

73. *Ni vu ni connu, j't' embrouille, par M. Déduit.* (245)
Air: Nous nous marierons dimanche.

a.) Text giving three stanzas. *Ibid.* (II, B)

b.) The three stanzas above (with variations which include typographical improvements and the inversion of the seventh and

eighth verses of the first stanza) and a fourth stanza added. *Ibid.* (II, B)

c.) The last part of the third stanza and the fourth stanza mentioned under "b," with variations in text, in fragment commencing "le calotin," p. 5 (also #36, p. 5). (II, C, under Fragment)

d.) Still another edition, according to the *Catalogue* . . . of Martin and Walter: *Ni vu ni connu* . . . (also #65). (II, C)

74. *Couplets, chantés chez le s^r [sic] Bardineau, le 23 novembre 1789, à une fête patriotique, par un volontaire de l'armée.* (248)
   Air: Pot-pourri.
   Ibid., Bordeaux . . . , *1789.* (II, B)

75. *Chanson de MM. les Forts de la Halle et du Port-aux-Bleds.* (252)
   Air: En passant sur le Pont-Neuf.
   a.) *Chronique de Paris,* 7 *décembre, 1789,* p. 422. (II, E)
   b.) Another version, with last part of title reading, *du Port-z'aux-Blés, pour au sujet [sic] du séjour de Roi à Paris, 1790,* and with two additional stanzas, known only from a reprint in *Poésies révolutionnaires* . . . , 1821, vol. i, p. 57. (II, H)

76. (Anti-revol.) *Chanson nouvelle.* "*Guillotin,/ Médecin,/ Politique.* . . ." (250)
   Air: Menuet d'Exaudet.
   a.) *Ibid.* (II, B)
   b.) *Actes des apôtres,* vol. i, no. 10, p. 15. (II, E)
   c.) *Journal des Révolutions de l'Europe en 1789 & 1790, tome 6e à Neuwied, 1790,* p. 19. (II, E)
   d.) With subtitle *sur le nouvel instrument de supplice proposé par le Dr Guillotin, dans la séance du 1er, décembre,* in *Almanach des honnêtes gens* . . . , *7e ed. 1793.* (II, F)
   NOTE: concerning another reference, see Appendix A, 250.

77. (Anti-revol.) *Couplets.* "*Voyant la féodalité.* . . ." (262)
   Air: Jupiter un jour en fureur.
   a.) *Prospectus d'un nouveau journal* . . . , *1789,* p. 13 (also #78, p. 21); and *ibid.,* ed., *1790,* p. 9 (also #78, p. 14). (II, D)
   b.) *Journal général de France,* 8 *janvier, 1790,* p. 31.

78. (Anti-revol.) *Guillotin.* "*Monsieur Guillotin,/ Ce grand médecin.* . . ." (251)
   Air: Paris est au roi.
   a.) *Prospectus d'un nouveau journal* . . . , *1789,* p. 21 (also #77, p. 13); and *ibid.,* ed., *1790,* p. 14 (also #77, p. 9). (II, D)
   b.) *Révolutions de France et Brabant, Paris* (January, 1790), vol. i, no. 8, p. 371. (II, E)

79. *Couplets chantés en l'Assemblée des Compagnies de Grenadiers et de Chasseurs du Bataillon de Bonne-Nouvelle, dont le Drapeau porte pour Devise: "Union, Force, Liberté"; et répétés à celles du Bataillon de L'Oratoire réunies dans le même lieu, le dimanche 20 décembre, 1789. Par M. Charon, ci-devant Officier de la Garde Nationale, Secrétaire-Greffier du District de Bonne-Nouvelle.* (254)
    Air: Aussitôt que la lumière.
      Ibid. (II, B)
      NOTE: concerning another reference, see Appendix A, 254.

80. *Couplets chantés par M. Dugazon, à la suite d'un repas donné le 20 décembre 1789, par la bataillon du district des Cordeliers à MM. les. députés de Montpellier. "Citoyens d'un beau pays. . . ."* (Ad. 14)
    Air: J'aime mieux boire.
      Moniteur, 22 décembre *1789,* vol. i, no. 122, p. 495. (II, E)
      NOTE: the account in the *Moniteur* states, "M. Dugazon, ci-devant officier, et maintenant soldat de la garde nationale de Paris, a chanté couplets de sa composition, analogues à la circonstance." Only one stanza is published, the first line of which is quoted above.

81. *Le grand Noël des Gardes Nationales, ci-devant Gardes-Françaises.* (258)
    Air: Dans les Gardes-Françaises.
      Ibid., 1789. (II, B)

82. (Anti-revol.) *Noël national.* (256)
    Air: Bourgeois de Chartres ou du Noël de la Cour.
      Actes des apôtres, vol. 1, no. 15, p. 12. (II, E)

83. (Anti-revol.) *Noël. "Menons paître nos bêtes. . . ."* (257)
    Air: Pot-pourri.
      Noël, p. 1 (also #84, p. 7; #85, p. 11). (II, D)
      NOTE: concerning the possibility of another edition, see Appendix A, 257.

84. (Anti-revol.) *La lunette* (257*)
    Air: L'amour est un enfant charmant.
      Noël, p. 7 (also # 83, p. 1; #85, p. 11). (II, D)
      NOTE: concerning the possibility of another edition, see Appendix A, 257 and 257*.

85. (Anti-revol.) *Complainte. "O vous, amis de notre reine. . . ."* (261)
    Air: O vous, amans de Gabrielle.
      Noël, p. 11 (also #83, p. 1; #84, p. 7). (II, D)

86. *Chanson Nationale, IIe. Sur la conservation de M. le Maire: de M. le Général: de M. le Ministre des Finances: de toute la Ville de Paris. Par M. le Chevalier de Callières de l'Estang, Ancien Avocat au Parle-*

ment, vieil Caporal du District des Cordeliers. Instituteur du véné-
rable Bataillon des Vétérans. Faite au Corps-de-Garde, le 28 Dé-
cembre 1789; et présentée à Monsieur, le même jour, après avoir
relevé les Sentinelles de son Palais. (259)

    Air: La Fête des Bonnes-Gens.

      Ibid. (II, B)

87†. *La rareté du numéraire.* (253)

    Air: Madeleine a bon droit.

      a.) Song with music. *Ibid.* (II, A)

      b.) Mss., with title *Chanson sur l'état actuel des finances,* and in-
        scription at end of song, *fin Mai 1790.* (II, G)

II. PUBLICATIONS IN WHICH THE POLITICAL SONGS OF 1789 APPEARED

THE following table indicates the divisions of this part of the Bibliography, which aims to disclose, with certain exceptions,[4] all the publications in which the songs of 1789 are known to have appeared:

A. Songs published with music.
B. Songs published separately (words only).
C. Brochures devoted entirely to two or more songs (words only).
D. Pamphlets containing political songs of 1789.
E. Journals in which political songs of 1789 appeared.
F. Almanacs, *chansonniers*, etc., containing political songs of 1789.
G. Manuscripts.
H. Reprints (post-Revolutionary).

The libraries which provided the song materials to which reference is made below, and also in Part III of the Bibliography—with abbreviations used hereafter—are as follows:

Archives nationales, Paris.—Arch. nat.
Bibliothèque de la Ville de Paris, Paris.—Bibl. V.P.
Bibliothèque de l'Opéra, Paris.—Bibl. de l'Opéra.
Bibliothèque du Sénat, Paris.—Bibl. Sén.
Bibliothèque nationale, Paris.—Bibl. nat.
British Museum, London.—Brit. Mus.
Cleveland Public Library, Cleveland, Ohio—Cl. Publ. Libr.
Columbia University Library, New York, N.Y.—Col. Univ. Libr.
Cornell University Library, Ithaca, N.Y.—Cornell Univ. Libr.
Harvard University Library, Cambridge, Mass.—Harvard Univ. Libr.
New York Public Library (DFDT refers to the Talleyrand Collection; DFD to other Collections).—N.Y. Publ. Libr.
Princeton University Library, Princeton, N.J.—Prin. Univ. Libr.

Some items mentioned below are referred to "Coll. C.B.R.," the present writer's collection of French Revolutionary songs and pamphlets.

The entries and library references which follow are based on firsthand investigation save in exceptional instances. In the case of each, an acknowledgment is made—usually by a credit line to one of the following bibliographical aids:

---

4 The exceptions relate to a few library references in Pierre of which I have no firsthand knowledge. The references in question do not provide the bibliographical data needed in Part II. Though not accounted for here, these references are noted in Bibliography I, in connection with the songs to which they relate.

British Museum, *Catalogue of Printed Books,* including the more recent volumes of the *General Catalogue.* Referred to below as "Brit. Mus., *Catalogue* (or *General Catalogue*)."

Hayden, H. E., *French Revolutionary Pamphlets; A Check List of the Talleyrand and Other Collections.* Referred to as "Hayden."

Martin, A., and Walter, G., *Catalogue de l'histoire de la Révolution française: Bibliothèque nationale.* Referred to as "Martin and Walter" or as "M.-W."

Monglond, A., *La France révolutionnaire et impériale, annales de bibliographie méthodique. . . .* Referred to as "Monglond."

Tourneux, M., *Bibliographie de l'histoire de Paris pendant la Révolution française.* Referred to as "Tourneux."

(For fuller data concerning the above, and for mention of other catalogues and guides, see Bibliography IV, A.)

When the publications listed below are known in two or more editions, the different editions are indicated by subdivisions, "a," "b," etc.

Library references are subjoined to each publication and to each edition thereof. For the publications listed in sections A through D, which tend to be rare and are often difficult to obtain, I have attempted to give a key to all copies known to be extant (subject to an exception noted in footnote 4, above). In the case of materials listed in sections E, F, and H, which on the whole are more accessible, this treatment has not seemed necessary; library references in respect to them, although indispensable for many items, serve, for well-known journals and almanacs, merely to indicate the particular copies used in connection with the present work. An explanatory note concerning library reference accompanies the first entry below.

After the title of each publication, an indication is given as to the song, or songs, of 1789, which it contains. This indication usually takes the form of a set of paired numbers in parentheses, which together point to one song. The first number of each group is from the New Catalogue, Bibliography I; the second is the corresponding number in Pierre, as it appears in his *Catalogue* and in Appendix A. An explanation is given in connection with the first entry. It should be added that when reference is made to any of the songs of 1789 which Pierre did not mention (that is, to the "addenda") then only one number, that in the New Catalogue, appears in parentheses. The designations are easy to follow if one observes that the New Catalogue numbers run from 1 through 87 and are in regular type, while Pierre's numbers begin with 168 and are in italics when paired.

In sections A and B, each song in itself comprises a separate publication. Beginning with section C, most of the publications listed contain two or more songs—some contain very many, for various years. It may be said, by way of explaining the matter contained in the parentheses following the titles of such publications, that contents are indicated in respect to the political songs of 1789. The songs are signalized by their numbers, preceded by appropriate page references.

For the various materials listed below (Part II of the Bibliography) the date of publication is either known or held to be 1789, unless a signal to the contrary is given. The titles of works ascribable to "1789 *or* 1790" (date uncertain) are preceded by a dagger (†); those known to have first appeared in 1790 or later are preceded by an asterisk (*).

A. Songs Published With Music

Chanson des bourgeois de Paris, n.p.n.d., 2 pp. (32-*209*) ["32" in the New Catalogue, Bibliography I; "*209*," the corresponding number for the same song in Pierre's *Catalogue*, and in Appendix A.]
> Bibl. Sén., carton 6, cote 204.
>> [The library reference is to the copy of the *Chanson des bourgeois . . .* consulted at the Library of the French Senate, under indicated shelf number. The single reference indicates that, so far as I have been able to determine, this is the only copy extant.]

Chanson nouvelle sur l'assemblée des Etats Généraux, par Mr. B . . . , n.p.n.d., 3 pp. (8-*174*)
> Bibl. nat., Rés Ye 3047.

Chanson sur le brave La Fayette, n.p.n.d., 2 pp. (51-*360**)
> Bibl. Sén., carton 6, cote 210.

Cocarde du roi (La), couplets patriotiques, chantés aux Variétés de Bordeaux, n.p.n.d., 2 pp. (43-*293*)
> Bibl. Sén., carton 6, cote 222.

Cocarde nationale ou l'Egalité patriotique (par C. Mercier de Compiègne), n.p.n.d., 2 pp. (56-*217*)
> Bibl. Sén., carton 6, cote 223.
>> NOTE: it is presumably to this item that Mercier referred when, some years later, he wrote: "Ces couplets furent imprimés au mois d'Août 1789. . . . " This observation appears as a footnote to a revised version of the song, published in the author's *Le Temple de la Liberté . . . 3e année répub.*, p. 55.

Couplets pour la Saint-Louis 1789 . . . , par M. de la Boessière, Maître d'Armes, n.p.n.d., 7 pp. (54-*213*)
> Bibl. nat., Inv. Ye 24883.
>> NOTE: this item is listed in the *Notice* of works of poetry "qui ont paru en 1789," in *Almanach des Muses, 1790*, p. 317.

Moment désiré (Le), couplets patriotiques sur les états généraux, par M. Déduit, à la Syncope, chez Savigny sur le Pont Neuf No. 17, n.d., 2 pp. (7-*172*)
> Bibl. Sén., carton 6, cote 290.

Prise de la Bastille (No. 25, apparently a serial number, is printed on p. 1, but no name of publisher is given), n.p.n.d., 2 pp. (31-*193*)
Bibl. Sén., carton 6, cote 318.

†*Rareté du numéraire (La),* n.p.n.d., 2 pp. (87†-*253*)
Bibl. Sén., carton 6, cote 324.

Tiers Etat (Le), adressé à Mr. le Docteur G - - - - , à Paris, chez Bona-velet, n.d., 2 pp. (11-*179*)
Bibl. nat., Vm⁷ 16683.

Trois ordres réunis (Les), par Mr. Minier, n.p.n.d., 2 pp. (22-*168**)
Bibl. Sén., carton 6, cote 363.

B. Songs Published Separately: Words Only

Alleluia du Tiers-Etat (L'), seconde édition, n.p., *1789,* 8 pp. (1)
N.Y. Publ. Libr., DFDT p. v. 47, no. 2 (also Bibl. nat., according to Monglond, vol. i, col. 523).

Arrêté des Habitants de la Grenouillère . . . , n.p.n.d., 11 pp. (5-*182*)
Bibl. nat., Rés. Ye 3067; Cl. Publ. Libr., W841.04-C452, vol. iii, no. 312.

Cahier du Marquis de Fulvy, n.p.n.d., 16 pp. (4-*184*)
NOTE: the author is Philibert-Louis Orry, marquis de Fulvy, according to Quérard, *op.cit.*
a.) *Ibid.,* in-8.
Bibl. nat., Rés. Ye 3046; Bibl. V.P. 23918, pièce 17; Bibl. Sén., carton 5, cote 95.
b.) *Ibid.,* in-16.
N.Y. Publ. Libr., DFDT p. v. 59, no. 13.
NOTE: in the *Almanach des Muses,* under *Notice* of works of poetry "qui ont paru en 1789," there is mention of the *Cahier du Marquis de Fulvy, Marchands de nouveautés, in-12, de 16 pages. Vingt-sept couplets. . . .* This description corresponds to the editions cited above, except for mention of *Marchands de nouveautés* and for differences in format. *Almanach des Muses, 1790,* p. 315. (II, F)

Chanson des dames de la Place Maubert, n.p.n.d., 4 pp. (39-*200*)
Bibl. nat., Rés. Ye 3064; Bibl. V.P. 19767, no. 12; N.Y. Publ. Libr., DFDT p. v. 63, no. 45; Cl. Publ. Libr., W841.04-C452, vol. i, no. 5.

Chanson des dames des Marchés S. Paul . . . , n.p.n.d., 3 pp. (42-*238*)
Bibl. nat., Ye 54832; Cl. Publ. Libr., W841.04-C452, vol. i, no. 5.

Chanson Nationale, IIᵉ. Sur la conservation de M. le Maire. . . . Par M. le Chevalier de Callières de l'Estang. . . . Faite au Corps-de-Garde, le 28 Décembre 1789; et présentée à Monsieur [de Provence], le même jour . . . , n.p.n.d., 7 pp. (86-*259*)
Bibl. nat., Rés. Ye 3094.

Chansonnier du Tiers (Le), n.p.n.d., 8 pp. (*13-180*)
  Bibl. nat., Rés. Ye 3079; Bibl. nat., Ye 17780; Cl. Publ. Libr.,
  W841.04-C452, vol. iii, no. 315.

Chanson nouvelle. "Guillotin,/ Médecin,/ Politique . . . , " n.p.n.d., 4
  pp. (*76-250*)
  Bibl. nat., Ye 17549.

*Chanson nouvelle. Le Requiem aeternam du Clergé de France. Par M.
  P. au sortir de l'Assemblée Nationale, du 2 Novembre 1789*, n.p.n.d.,
  1 p. (?). (*72*)
  NOTE: owing to the manner in which this item has been mounted and
  bound, it is not possible to determine with certainty the original
  form of publication.
  Cl. Publ. Libr., W841.04-C452, vol. i, no. 120.

*Chanson poissarde. "Sais-tu, Cadet, que j'somm' du Tiers? . . . " Edition
  nouvelle avec additions*, n.p.n.d., 12 pp. (Song with prose to be
  spoken.) (*21-180**)
  Bibl. V.P. 12031, pièce 2; Cl. Publ. Libr., W841.04-C452, vol. i,
  no. 3.

*Chanson sur la prise des Invalides et de la Bastille, les lundi 13 et mardi
  14 Juillet 1789. A Paris, ce vendredi 17. . . . Par le Chevalier de Callières*, 7 pp. (*29-194*)
  a.) *Ibid.*, n.p.n.d.
  Bibl. nat., Ye 16493 (also Brit. Mus., F 348 [5]—*General Catalogue
  . . .* , under Callières).
  This piece was shown at the Exposition on the French Revolution,
  1928, at the Bibliothèque Nationale. See *Catalogue* ("Bibliothèque
  nationale, La Révolution française . . . "), item 41.
  b.) *Ibid., Chez Nyon le jeune, Libraire, Pavillon des quatres Nations,
  1789.*
  Bibl. Sén., carton 5, cote 107; N.Y. Publ. Libr. DBA p. v. 142, no. 2
  and DFDT p. v. 63, no.17; Cl. Publ. Libr., W841.04-C452, vol. i, no.
  12 (also Arch. nat., R. AD I, 100, according to Monglond, vol. i, col.
  515, and Tourneux, vol. iii, no. 12341).

*Chanson sur le Patriotisme et la Prudence des Gardes Françaises et
  Suisses, après la Séance Royale de Versailles, du 23 Juin 1789. Dia-
  logue entre un Citoyen et un Militaire*, n.p.n.d., 4 pp. (*17*)
  Cl. Publ. Libr., W841.04-C452, vol. i, no. 4.

*Chanson très-nouvelle. "Le Tiers-Etat/ Depuis long-temps étoit victime
  . . . , "* n.p.n.d., 1 p. (*12*)
  Cl. Publ. Libr., W841.04-C452, vol. iii, no. 315.

*Constitution française et les droits de l'homme (La). Chanson patri-
  otique. Par M. S. . . . Garde National du District de Saint-Gervais.*
  (*55-216*)

a.) *Ibid., Paris, chez Garnéry, Libraire, rue Serpente, No. 17. L'An Premier de la Liberté.* 8 pp.
  Arch. nat., AD VIII 35, pièce 6; N.Y. Publ. Libr., DFDT p. v. 86, no. 12.
b.) *Ibid., 3ᵉ ed. corrigée et augentée. Paris, chez Simon & Jacob-Sion, Imprimeurs, rue St. Jacques,* n.d., 8 pp.
  Bibl. Sén., carton 5, cote 145; Cl. Publ. Libr., W841.04-C452, vol. i, no. 68.

Couplets chantés à Madame la Marquise de La Fayette. Le 22 Septembre, jour de la Bénédiction du Drapeau du District de St-Etienne-du-Mont . . . , par M. Ducray du Minil . . . , n.p., *1789,* 4 pp. (58-227)
  Brit. Mus., F. 247 (23).

Couplets, chantés chez le sʳ [sic] Bardineau, le 23 novembre 1789, à une fête patriotique, par un volontaire de l'armée. Bordeaux chez Pallandre l'aîné, 1789, 7 pp. (74-248)
  Arch. nat., AD VIII 35.

Couplets chantés en l'Assemblée des Compagnies de Grenadiers et de Chasseurs du Bataillon de Bonne-Nouvelle . . . le dimanche 20 décembre, 1789, par M. Charon . . . , n.p.n.d., 3 pp. (79-254)
  Bibl., V.P., 23918, pièce 24.

Couplets, chantés par un soldat citoyen de la garde nationale de Compiègne à la fête donnée le 13 septembre 1789 . . . par M. Mounier, cit. de Compiègne, n.p.n.d., 3 pp. (57-226)
  Bibl. nat., Ye 48083.

Grand Noël des Gardes Nationales, ci-devant Gardes-Françaises (Le), n.p., *1789,* 9 pp. (81-258)
  Bibl. nat., Rés. Ye 3174.

Hymne en l'honneur de la Résurrection des Etats-Généraux, n.p., *1789,* 15 pp. (3-171)
  Bibl. nat., Ye 35536; Bibl. V.P. 7953 and 25900, pièce 47; Bibl. Sén. carton &, cote 381; N.Y. Publ. Libr., DFDT p. v. 49, no. 21.

Justification des Messieurs et des Dames de la Halle de Paris, sur les crimes de l'exécrable révolution française, notamment de ceux des 5 et 6 Octobre 1789 . . . , n.p.n.d., 2 pp. (66-237*)
  Bibl. V.P. 11945, pièce 1 ter.

Lanterne merveilleuse (La), n.p.n.d. (engraved) 2 pp. (38-199)
  Bibl. nat., Rés. Ye 3072; Bibl. Sén., carton 6, cote 282.

Motion des Harangères [sic] de la Halle, n.p.n.d. (engraved) 2 pp. (15-181)
  Bibl. nat., Rés. Ye 3065; Cl. Publ. Libr., W841.04-C452, vol. i, no. 1.

Ni vu ni connu, j't'embrouille, par M. Déduit. (73-245)
- a.) *Ibid.* Engraved edition giving three stanzas only, n.p.n.d., 2 pp.
  Bibl. nat., Rés. Ye 3103.
- b.) *Ibid.* Engraved edition with a fourth stanza added (concerning variations, see Bibliography I, 71), n.p.n.d.
  Bibl. Sén., carton 6, cote 312.

Nouvel "O Filii" des Etats-Généraux, par A. L. G., le 23 mai 1789,
n.p.n.d., 14 pp. (14-*178*)
     Bibl. nat., Ye 29156.

O filii national, n.p.n.d. (engraved) 2 pp. (20-*234*)
     Bibl. nat., Rés. Ye 3080; Bibl. V.P. 10151; N.Y. Publ. Libr., DFDT p. v. 61, no. 17.

Où le bas nous blesse. Chanson à la portée de tout le monde, Enrichie de notes intéressantes. A la vérité, rue sans gêne, à Paris; Juillet 1789,
30 pp. (of which pp. 11-30 are "Notes faites sur chaque couplet"). (28-*206*)
     Bibl. nat., Rés. Ye 3078; Bibl. V.P. 10156; Coll. C.B.R.; and a fragment of same, pp. 1-16, Bibl. V.P. 23918, pièce 20.

Pont-neuf, ou chanson sur l'Assemblée nationale . . . , par de Joyenval (Paris) impr. de Lottin l'aîné et Lotti de S. Germain, 1789. In-8, 4 pp. (25-*243**)
NOTE: this entry, together with library reference, is borrowed from Martin and Walter, vol. ii, no. 17572.
     Bibl. nat., Ye 24692.

Prise de la Bastille (La). Couplets dédiés à la Nation, par M. Déduit. A Orléans chez Le Tourni, n.d. [woodcut in color]. (35)
NOTE: an original, from the coll. De Vinck, was shown at the French Revolutionary Exposition at the Bibliothèque Nationale, 1928. For a description of this print, see Bibliothèque Nationale; *La Révolution française (Catalogue)*, Paris (1928), p. 159, item 565. Reproductions were made at that time and put on public sale.

Remerciemens aux Gardes Françaises et aux Gardes Suisses, sur la manière patriotique dont ils se sont comportés à Versailles, après la Séance Royale du 23 Juin. Au nom des Citoyens du Palais-Royal,
n.p.n.d., 3 pp. (17)
     N.Y. Publ. Libr., DFDT p. v. 61, no. 8.

Réunion des trois ordres (La). Couplets dédiés a la Nation, par M. Déduit. Chez Goujon, Marchand de musique, Grande Cour du Palais Royal, à côté du Graveur, n.d., 4 pp. (23-*169*)
     Bibl. nat., Rés. Ye 3070; Bibl. V.P. 23918 (also Bibl. nat., 8° Ye. Pièce 4610—M.-W., 9597).
NOTE: this item is listed in the *Notice* of works of poetry "qui ont paru en 1789," in *Almanach des Muses, 1790,* p. 318.

R'quête en magnier' d'écrit, à Monseigneu le Pervo des Marchands, par un Maît Pêcheu' du Gros-Caillou, n.p.n.d. 6 pp. (6-*182**)
Bibl. nat., Rés. Ye 3068; Bibl. V.P. 11945, pièce 3.

Tribut lyrique ou Vers . . . présentés à M. Necker . . . le jeudi 30 juillet 1789. Par M. Bavouz. (47-*202*)
a.) *Ibid., à Paris, chez Froullé, Libraire, Quai des Augustins, au coin de la rue Pavé*, n.d., 4 pp.
N.Y. Publ. Libr., DFDT p. v. 64, no. 7 (also Bibl. nat., Ye 55722 and 8° Ye. Pièce 3910, according to M.-W., vol. i, no. 2124; in this catalogue entry, the author's name is spelled "Bavoux").
b.) *Ibid., à Paris, de l'imprimerie de Seguy-Thiboust, Place Cambray, 1789*, 4 pp.
N.Y. Publ. Libr., DFD p. v. 41 (14th item, unnumbered).
NOTE: *ibid.*, Brit. Mus., F. R. 94 (21), according to *General Catalog . . .* , under *Bavouz.* Edition not specified.

†*Troubadour parisien (Le)*, n.p.n.d. (70†-*243*)
Bibl. nat., Rés. Ye 3099.

Voyage du Roi, de Versailles à Paris (Le) . . . , par un Compagnon de voyage, soldat de la Garde Nationale Parisienne, n.p.n.d., 4 pp. (61-*240**)
a.) *Ibid.*
Bibl. nat., Ye 35087.
b.) According to Monglond (vol. i, col. 530), there is an edition of this item at the Bibliothèque Nationale—shelf reference not given —which is dated 1789.

C. BROCHURES DEVOTED ENTIRELY TO TWO OR MORE SONGS: WORDS ONLY

**Chansonnier national ou Recueil de chanson choisies et patriotiques, sur la Constitution française & les Droits de l'Homme. A Paris, chez Valleyre, rue de la vieille Bouclerie, à l'Arbre de Jessé, 1790*, 12 pp., in-12. (P. 2, 55-*216*; and three other songs)
NOTE: the pretentious title is misleading, since the item itself contains only four songs, two of them nonpolitical. *Chansonnier*, as generally understood and as referred to in II, F., indicates a work of book or booklet size.
Bibl. nat., Ye 35763, pièce 1.

Couplets chantés à un Dîner de Corps, où assistoient les trois Ordres. Par M. B--- de S------. A La Rochelle, chez P. L. Chauvet, Imprimeur du Roi, n.d., 2 pp. (P. 1, #52; p. 2, #53)
Cornell Univ. Libr. 4187, D 19, no. 41.

†*Entretien d'un vieillard avec une jeune bergère. Imprimerie de Val-*
leyre, n.d., 12 pp. (P. 6, 37†-*190;* and two nonpolitical songs)
NOTE: concerning uncertainty of date, see Appendix A, 190.
   Bibl. V.P. 9312, pièce 1.

†Fragment, commencing "le calotin" (pages numbered 5-8), 4 pp., in-
12. (P. 5, 73-*245,* in part only; p. 5, 36-*192*)
NOTE: concerning date, see Bibliography I, 36, b, and Appendix A,
192.
   Bibl. V.P. 9312.

France régénérée et les traîtres punis (La). De l'Imprimerie de Valleyre
l'aîné, n.d., 12 pp. (P. 1, 36-*192;* p. 4, 16-*187;* p. 5, 24-*205*;* p. 7, 25-
243*; p. 10, a nonpolitical song)
   Bibl. nat., Ye 55471-949.

Ni vu ni connu, j' t' embrouille, par Déduit—Courage patriotique des
Dames de la Halle, dans l'affaire du 5 et 6 oct. 1789, par Labré [sic].
(S.l.n.d.). In-12, 4 pp. (73-*245;* #65)
NOTE: this entry, together with library reference, is borrowed from
Martin and Walter, vol. ii, no. 9594; it appears also in Monglond,
vol. i, col. 517.
   Bibl. nat., Ye 19589.

Nouveau pot-pourri sur les affaires du temps. Versailles, imp. de Ma-
dame de Polignac, 1789, 15 pp. (P. 1, 18-*232;* p. 10, 19-*233;* p. 12, 20-
234)
   Bibl. nat., Rés. Ye 3042; Bibl. V.P. 23918, pièce 50.

**Savetier bon patriote (Le). De l'imprimerie de Valleyre,* n.d., 12 pp.
(P. 1, Pierre, #*437;* p. 7, 37†-*190*)
   Bibl. nat., Ye 35763, pièce 2.

Voile levé (Le), par M. L. C. D. V., n.p.n.d., 12 pp. (P. 3, 59-*220;* p. 12,
60-*221*)
a.) *Ibid.*
   Bibl. nat., Rés. Ye 3084; Bibl. V.P. 580, pièce 108; Bibl. Sén., carton 8, cote 457; Cl. Publ. Libr., W841.04-C452, vol. 1, no. 123.
b.) *Ibid.*; reprint of the above (see Appendix A, 220, concerning minor variations).
   Bibl. nat., Ye 34916.

Voyage du Roi de Versailles à Paris, où il fait sa residence (Le), n.p.n.d.,
8 pp. (P. 1, 61-*240*;* p. 4, #62; p. 5, 63-*239**;* p. 7, 64-*240*)
NOTE: the line "Par un Compagnon de Voyage, Soldat de la Garde
Nationale Parisienne" applies not to the brochure as a whole, but
only to the first song, at the end of which it appears, p. 4.
   Bibl. nat., Ye 35763, pièce 13.

D. PAMPHLETS CONTAINING POLITICAL SONGS OF 1789

Avis au peuple sur les événemens présens et à venir, suivi d'une chanson sur les affaires du temps; par M. le Marquis de C - - - P - - - -. Où l'on veut (n.p.) *1789*, 13 pp. (P. 10, 27-*230*)
  Bibl. nat., Rés. Ye 3045.

Bouquet présenté à M. Necker, à son arrivée à Paris le 30 juillet 1789. L'Abbé de Courchon. De L'Imprimerie de Valleyre, l'aîné, n.d., 3 pp. (P. 2, #46)
  Cornell Univ. Libr. 4191, C 564.

Citoyen en bonne humeur (Le). Ouvrage qui a remporté le Prix, non pas à l'Académie Française, mais à l'Académie Bachique en présence de quarante Buveurs renommés. A Bouillon, et se trouve à Paris, chez Belin, Libraire, rue St. Jacques, 1789, 16 pp. (P. 7, 40-*170*; p. 10, 41-*170**)
  Bibl. nat., Rés. Ye 3077; Bibl. V.P. 23918, pièce 21.

†*Détail intéressant, et jusqu'à présent ignoré, sur la prise de la Bastille, et la suite des révolutions, faite par un Assaillant de la Bastille, à un de ses Amis, blessé au même Siége. Se trouve chez l'Auteur Grande Rue du Fauxbourg Saint Antoine, chez le Chandelier, en face de la Cour Saint-Louis* (P. Rousselet), n.d., 32 pp. (P. 28, #30†)
  NOTE: this work appeared after *31 Août* [1789?], a date to which Rousselet refers in the text, p. 22, footnote 1. Victor Fournel (*Les hommes du 14 Juillet*, p. 216, footnote 2) seems to imply that by the time Rousselet was made a member of the Commission of the *Vainqueurs* (March 22, 1790) he was known as the author of the *Détail intéressant*. Though mention of this item is not infrequently made, I have never seen a conclusive statement concerning the date of its publication.
  Coll. C.B.R. (Mentioned in Tourneux, vol. i, no. 1107, with reference to Bibl. nat., Lb[39] 7375.)

Etrennes à la nation, à Rome, de l'Imprimerie du Vatican (n.p.?) *1789*, 14 pp. (P. 9, 67-*181**; p. 13, 68-*183**)
  Bibl. nat., Rés. Ye 3097; also fragment, consisting of the two songs, pp. 9-14, Bibl. V.P. 23918, pièce 30.

Gazette des Halles (La), Dialogue, mêlé de chansons, pour ceux qui les aiment. No. 1er. Imprimé aux dépens des Dames de la place Maubert. De l'Imprimerie de N. H. Nyon, rue Mignon, 1789. 11 pp. (P. 10, #51, ed. "b, 1"; p. 11, #51, ed. "b, 2"; *360**)
  Coll. C.B.R.

Moment désiré (Le), couplets patriotiques . . . [*Suivi d'un extrait du discours du Roi à l'Assemblée des Etates généraux prononcé 4 mai 1789*]. *Paris, imp. de Angeliom* (s.d.). In-fol. obl., fig. (7-*172*)
  NOTE: this entry, together with library reference, is borrowed from

Martin and Walter, vol. ii, no. 9592; it appears also in Monglond, vol. i, col. 82.
Bibl. nat., 8° Lb³⁹ 1674.

Noël, n.p.n.d., 19 pp. (P. 1, 83-*257*; p. 7, 84-*257**; p. 11, 85-*261*; followed by two poems, pp. 17 and 18)
Bibl. nat., Rés Ye 3100; Bibl. nat., Ye 48296; Bibl. V.P. 23918.

Plaintes et doléances des Dames de la Halle et des Marchés de Paris, n.p., *1789*, 32 pp. (P. 31, 11-*179*)
Prin. Univ. Libr., 1509.178.724.

Prospectus d'un nouveau journal, par les auteurs de la Prise des Annonciades, n.p.
a.) Ed., *1789*, 24 pp. (P. 13, 77-*262*; p. 21, 78-*251*)
Bibl. nat., Rés. Ye 3110. (Also mentioned in Tourneux, vol. ii, no. 10395, with reference to Bibl. nat., Lc² 272.)
*b.) Ed., *1790*, 16 pp. (P. 9, 77-*262*; p. 14, 78-*251*)
Coll. C.B.R. (Not mentioned in Tourneux.)

Suite de la révolution authentique & remarquable, arrivée à Brest en Bretagne. A Paris: De l'Imprimerie de N. H. Nyon, rue Mignon, n.d., 4 pp. (P. 4, #44)
N.Y. Publ. Libr., DFDT p. v. 64, no. 48.

E. JOURNALS IN WHICH POLITICAL SONGS
OF 1789 APPEARED

Actes des apôtres (Les).
Vol. i. Nos. 1-30: *commencés le jour des Morts et finis le jour de la Purification* (November 2, 1789, to February 2, 1790: separate issues published at irregular intervals, and not dated. Months given in parentheses below represent careful approximations).
No. 10 (December, 1789) p. 15. (76-*250*)
No. 15 (December, 1789) p. 12. (82-*256*)
*No. 29 (January, 1790) p. 13. (69†-*218*)
Vol. iii. Nos. 61-90: *commencés à la mi-Carême et finis la semaine de la Quasimodo* (March 4, to *cir.* April 11, 1790).
*No. 61 (March, 1790) p. 14. (70†-*243*)
Bibl. nat., Lc² 257; Col. Univ. Libr.; Harvard Univ. Libr., Fr 1325.510.2 (references are to the original edition, to be distinguished from reprint of later date).

Affiches, annonces et avis divers ou Journal général de France.
1789:
No. 213, 1 août, 1789, p. 2233. (49-*205*)
No. 231, 19 août, 1789, p. 2394. (47-*202*)
No. 238, 26 août, 1789, p. 2456. (54-*213*—notice and first stanza only)
Bibl. nat., Inv. v. 28326.

1790:
  *No. 119, 29 avril, 1790, p. 1132. (47-202—notices concerning musical scores)
    Bibl. nat., Inv. v. 28329.

Chronique de Paris.
  1789:
    No. 106, 7 décembre, 1789, vol. i, p. 422. (75-252)
  1790:
    *No. 138, 18 mai, 1790, vol. ii, p. 549. (71-246—editorial comment and third stanza only)
    Bibl. nat., Lc² 218.

Journal de Paris, 22 juillet, 1789, p. 912. (34-201)
  Bibl. nat., Lc² 80.

*Journal des révolutions de l'Europe en 1789 et 1790, à Neuwied sur le Rhin, 1790. vol. vi, p. 19 (76-250)
    Col. Univ. Libr. (Bibl. nat., Lb³⁹ 4472, according to Tourneux, vol. ii, no. 10263, who lists the item under the title which it carried for the first four numbers: Révolutions de Paris en 1789 . . . , n.p., 1789.)

*Journal général de France, 8 Janvier, 1790, p. 31. (77-262)
  Bibl. nat., Lc² 69.

Moniteur (i.e., Gazette nationale ou le Moniteur universel), 22 décembre 1789, vol. i, p. 495. (80)
  NOTE: in the present work, references to the Moniteur are to the original folio edition, not to the Réimpression.
  Col. Univ. Libr.

*Révolutions de France et Brabant, Paris (January, 1790), vol. i, no. 8, p. 371. (78-251)
    Col. Univ. Libr.

F. ALMANACS, CHANSONNIERS, ETC., CONTAINING POLITICAL SONGS OF 1789

* Almanach des honnêtes gens, contenant des prophéties pour chaque mois de l'année 1793, des anecdotes peu connues . . . , septième édition, Paris, chez tous les marchands de nouveautés, 1793. 144 pp. (76-250)
    Bibl. V.P. 22649.

Almanach des Muses, année 1790, à Paris, chez Delalain, l'ainé et fils, Libraires, rue St. Jacques No. 240, n.d., 330 pp. (P. 161, 51-210)
    NOTE: the date in the title is prospective, the book being prepared in the preceding year. In the editor's introduction, p. 2, contributors are instructed to submit material before the first of November. Of some interest is a department appearing at the end of the

    Almanach, "Notice de tous les ouvrages de poésie qui ont paru en 1789," pp. 301-30. Mention is made here of the publication of several songs, as follows: p. 315, *4-184*; p. 317, *54-213*; p. 318, *40-170* (incl. *41-170**) and *23-169.*
        Bibl. nat., Ye 11675; Coll. C.B.R.

* *Almanach du Bon-Homme ou Petit Dictionnaire très utile pour l'intelligence des affaires présents. A Paris, chez les marchands de nouveautés, et Maison de l'Egalité, 1793. L'an 2ᵉ de la République Française, 132 pp.* (P. 130, *40-170*)
        Bibl. nat., Lc²² 45.

* *Ami du Roi (L'), Almanach des honnêtes gens . . . (pour l'année 1792), Paris, chez l'Apothicaire de la Démocratie, au Palais-Royal,* n.d., *102 pp.* (P. 20, *69†-218*)
        Bibl. nat., Lc²² 41; Coll. C.B.R.

* *Chansonnier de la Montagne (Le) ou Recueil de chansons, vaudevilles, pot-pourris et hymnes patriotiques; Par différens auteurs. A Paris, chez Favre, Libraire, maison Egalité, galeries de bois, No. 220. L'an deuxième de la Republique française une et indivisible.* (P. 104 in the three editions below, *56-217*)
    a.) An early edition, presumably the first, 176 pp.
        Bibl. V.P. 18189.
    b.) *Seconde édition, augmentée du Décadaire républicain,* 176 pp.
        Bibl. nat., Ye 17629.
    c.) *Troisième édition, augmentée de l'offrande à la liberté . . . , L'An 2,* 176 pp.
        Bibl. V.P. 702; Bibl. V.P. 22822; Coll. C.B.R.

* *Chansonnier national ou Recueil . . . Paris, 1790;* see *ibid.,* II, C.

* *Temple de la Liberté (Le), Poëms, odes et chansons patriotiques, par C. Mercier de Compiègne. Troisième édition. A Paris. Chez l'auteur, imprimeur-libraire, rue de Coq-Honoré. No. 120. 3ᵉ Année Républicaine. 162 pp.* (P. 55, *56-217*)
        Bibl. V.P. 9291; also, same ed. but with pp. 161-62 missing, Bibl. nat., Ye 27642.

G. Manuscripts

Chanson nouvelle sur les Etats-généraux, par une Dᵉˡˡᵉ [demoiselle] *Religieuse de 78 ans nommée Jeanne Rocher,* n.p.n.d., *2 pp.* (P. 1, col. 1, *9-175*; p. 1, col. 2, *10-173*)
        Bibl. nat., mss., fr. 12755, p. 48.

* *Chanson sur l'état actuel des finances,* n.p., *fin Mai 1790* (appears at end of song, p. 2) *2 pp.* (*87†-253*)
        Coll. C.B.R.

† *Choeur béarnais* (with music), n.p.n.d., 4 pp. (P. 1, 69†-*218*; p. 3, 70†-*243*)
>   NOTE: at the end of the second of the two songs in this ms. is the signature "Gabriel-Joseph D'Eaubonne," which presumably applies only to the latter of the two, but may apply to both.
>   Bibl. nat., mss. n. acq. fr. 6620, p. 37.

Couplets à MM. les députés des bailliages réunis à Metz; nommés lors de leur départ—le 15 avril 1789, par L. D., n.p.n.d. (*2-168*)
>   Bibl. nat., mss. n. acq. fr. 6620, p. 12.

Motion des Harangères [sic] de la Halle, n.p.n.d., 2 pp. (15-*181*)
>   Bibl. nat., mss. n. acq. fr. 6620, p. 7.

O filii national, n.p.n.d., 2 pp. (*20-234*)
>   Bibl. nat., mss. n. acq. fr. 6620, p. 9.

† *Troubadour béarnais (Le)*, (with music), n.p.n.d. (69†-*218*)
>   Bibl. nat., mss. fr. 12755, p. 61.

H. REPRINTS (POST-REVOLUTIONARY)

NOTE: many of the political songs of 1789 were reprinted in post-Revolutionary anthologies, the more important of which are listed in Bibliography IV. This section is reserved for mention of reprinted editions only in cases where contemporary texts are not available.

* Gautier, H., *L'An 1789, événements, mœurs, idées, œuvres et characteres, avec 650 reproductions . . .* , Paris [1889]. (P. 83, the photographic reproduction of a *gravure* containing song #26)

* *Poésies Révolutionnaires et contre-Révolutionnaires, ou Recueil, classé par époques, des hymnes, chants guerriers, chansons républicaines, odes, satires, cantiques des missionaires etc., etc., les plus remarquables qui ont paru depuis trente ans.* Paris . . . , 1821, 2 vols. (Vol. i, p. 55, 71-*246*; vol. i, p. 57, edition "b" of 75-*252*)
>   Bibl. nat., Ye 30324; Coll. C.B.R.
>   NOTE: this work was reprinted in 1827.

III. SONGS AND SONG MATERIALS OF THE FRENCH REVOLUTION OTHER THAN THOSE OF 1789

WHAT follows is not a catalogue, such as that provided in Parts I and II for the political songs of 1789. Part III, below, consists only of publications referred to in the course of the present work as containing political songs for years other than 1789. As explained elsewhere, the total literature, which is voluminous, has been surveyed by Constant Pierre in his *Les hymnes et chansons de la Révolution, aperçu général et catalogue* . . . (concerning this work see pages 6 and 30-31, and the statement which introduces Appendix A).

Several of the publications listed below—especially those in section F—are mentioned in the Introduction as illustrative of the general development of political songs during the French Revolution. Others have been cited in the text in various connections. The greater part, however, are items which Pierre attributed to 1789, but which I have regarded as belonging to other years. Titles of these rejected items are followed by Pierre's serial numbers in parentheses; these serial numbers (unless preceded by "also") constitute main entries in Appendix A, where the problems of dating are discussed and the reasons for rejection stated.

Library references in this part of the Bibliography are not intended to be exhaustive, but they actually are in many instances where the copy identified by a single library reference happens to be the only one known to be extant.

In the arrangement of materials and in the use of symbols and abbreviations, this part of the Bibliography corresponds to Part II; see introductory statement, pages 284-86.

A. SONGS PUBLISHED WITH MUSIC

Couplets au peuple français par Bastide Régnier, n.p.n.d., 4 pp. (*223*; also *1764*)
  Bibl. Sén., carton 6, cote 226.

Couplets sur l'Assemblée des Notables, par M. du Croisi, n.p.n.d., 2 pp. (*177*)
  Bibl. nat., Vm⁷ 16461.

B. SONGS PUBLISHED SEPARATELY: WORDS ONLY

Chanson nouvelle, chantée par un soldat de l'armée révolutionnaire, à la société républicaine de Provins. "Ce noble que l'on balotte. . . ." *Air: Belle Raimonde. De l'Imp. de Lion, Imp. de la Section du Panthéon-Français* [Paris], n.d., 3 pp. (Not mentioned in Pierre)

NOTE: the following appears on p. 3: "Extrait du registre des délibérations de la Section du Panthéon Français, du 10 Brumaire, l'an 2ᵉ . . . : L'assemblée générale . . . en arrête l'impression . . . et l'envoi aux 47 Sections et aux Sociétés populaires."
Coll. C.B.R.

Chant Républicain, sur la Bataille de Fleurus, par le Citoyen Lebrun. . . . Exécuté au concert du Peuple, musique de Catel. De l'Imprimerie de la Commission de L'Instruction Publique [Paris], n.d., 4 pp. (*Hymne* #66 in Pierre, *op.cit.*, p. 332, but this edition not cited)
NOTE: the imprint states: "La Commission de l'Instruction Publique arrête l'impression . . . le 16 Messidor, l'an deuxieme de la République."
Coll. C.B.R.

Considérations politiques des Notables de la Halle au pain, sur les affaires du tems. "Les Notables ont fini. . . ." Air: *Reçois dans ton galetas.* N.p. [1788], 3 pp.
Coll. C.B.R.
NOTE: for another edition of this song see [*Premier*] *1ᵉʳ Envoi à M. Necker* . . . , in section D, below.

Journée de Louis XVI (La) ou Discours du meilleur des Rois, par Mʳ Déduit, auteur patriotique, à Paris, chez les frères Savigny . . . [1790], 2 pp. (*212*)
Bibl. Sén., carton 6, cote 281.

C. Brochures Devoted Entirely to Two or More Songs: Words Only

Alexandrine à Paris, venant rejoindre Fleur-d'Epine, Cavalier nationale de Paris, Senlis, 1790, 8 pp. (P. 2, *249*; and several nonpolitical songs)
Bibl. V.P. 9308.

Chanson patriotique. "Oui, je suis soldat, moi. . . ." N.p.n.d., 2 pp. (*195*; also *328*)
Bibl. V.P. 9312.

Chansons sur les affaires du temps, n.p.n.d., 4 pp. (*231*; and a second song not mentioned by Pierre—see Appendix A, *231*)
Cornell Univ. Libr. 4187, C 43, no. 24.

Chanson sur les émigrants . . . , imp. *F. D. Thierry,* n.d., 4 pp. (*198*; also p. 1, *695**)
Bibl. nat., Ye 17595 *bis.*

Heureux retour du Parlement (L'), chanson patriotique, n.p. [1788], 4 pp. (P. 1, *178**; p. 4, *235**)
Bibl. V.P. 23918.

Tonsure (La) ou Plaintes des perruquiers à l'Assemblée nationale.
    Impr. Gironard, n.d., 4 pp. (P. *3, 188*; also *405* and *413*)
        Bibl. Nat., Rés. Ye 3131.

D. Pamphlets Containing Political Songs

Numéraire aux Parisiens (Le), ou les écus parlans, n.p.n.d., 16 pp. (P.
    15, *228**)
        Bibl. nat., Lb³⁹ 2604.

[Premier] 1ᵉʳ envoi à Mʳ Necker. De la Halle ci 23 Xᵇʳᵉ 1788, n.p.n.d.,
    4 pp., engraved. (The *envoi* is followed, p. 2, by the song, *Considéra-
    tions politiques des Notables . . .* ; see B, above)
        N.Y. Publ. Libr., DFDT p. v. 28, no. 35.

*Récit de tous les incidents qui ont dû intéresser les Députés de la
    Garde-Nationale de Rouen, à la Fédération de Versailles, jusqu'au
    moment où ils sont rentrés dans leurs compagnies respc.; contenant:
    Les détails de toutes les Fêtes remarquables qui ont accompagné et
    suivi cette Fédération et celle de Paris; une partie des couplets qui y
    ont été chantés; les descriptions des deux Camps; les inscriptions
    qu'ont y lisoit et les réflexions qu'elles ont fait naître: dédié—A tous
    les bons Français, et principalement à ceux de ses Frères-d'Armes
    avec lesquels il s'est trouvé à toutes ces fêtes. Par F. A. Bagneris . . . ,
    Avocat, ci-devant Secrétaire de l'Intendance de Rouen. . . . A Rouen
    . . . , 1790,* 92 pp.
        Arch. nat., AD viii 19.

Requête des curés de France au roi, n.p.n.d. [1788], 15 pp. (P. *4, 231*)
        Bibl. nat., Rés. Ye 3092; Bibl. V.P. 25900, pièce 38; etc.[5]

*Satyres, ou choix des meilleures pièce de vers qui ont précédé ou suivi
    la Révolution, Paris, l'an premier de la Liberté* [1790; see Appendix
    A, 255] 32 pp. (P. 12, *255*; p. 20, *255**)
        Bibl. nat., Ye 20150, Ye 20151, and Rés. 3138; Cornell Univ.
        Libr. 4191, C 268.

F. Almanacs, *Chansonniers*, etc., Containing Political Songs

NOTE: Among the numerous songs contained in the publications listed
below, only those which are treated in Appendix A as incorrectly
ascribed by Pierre to 1789 are signalized (by Pierre's serial numbers in
parentheses). The "etc." following serial numbers indicates that the
work cited contains other songs as well—i.e., such as are unrelated to
the problems of 1789.

---

[5] "Etc." following library references in Bibliography III indicates that Pierre (see
op.cit., under song nos. and pp. 153-69) provides library references in addition to
those given here.

Almanach de la Mère Gérard, pour l'Année Bissextile 1792, ou les Droits de l'homme et du citoyen, mis en vaudevilles. . . .

    a.) *Ibid.*, with remainder of title: *et dédiés à le Mère Gérard, pour l'amusement et l'instruction de ses petites-filles. A Paris, chez Bouqueton, imprimeur . . . , l'an III de la Liberté,* 64 pp. (P. 32, *215;* etc.)

        Bibl. V.P. 23918; Bibl. nat., Lc²² 39.

    b.) *Ibid.*, with remainder of title: *suivi de Noëls Civiques et Patriotiques, pour l'amusement et l'instruction des petites-filles de la Mère Gérard. A Paris, chez les Marchands de Nouveautés, l'an III de la Liberté,* 127 pp. (P. 32, *215;* p. 65, *235;* etc.)

        Bibl. nat., Lc²² 39 A.

    NOTE: the author of this anonymous work is presumably T. Rousseau; see Appendix C.

Almanach républicain chantant, pour l'an 2 de la République française . . . , par le citoyen B - - - , à Paris chez Lallemand, à Amiens chez Marielle [1793], 127 pp. (P. 55, *196;* etc.)

    Bibl. V.P. 22624.

Ame du peuple et du soldat (L'), chants républicains, par Th. Rousseau (seven "cahiers"—six of 16 pp. and one of 4 pp.), Paris, n.d. (None of the cahiers are numbered; they can best be identified by the opening songs. Cahier commencing with *Le Triomphe de l'Egalité,* p. 1, *208,* and p. 7, *185;* with *Départ des sans-culottes . . . ,* p. 9, *196,* and p. 11, *235;* with *Hymne pour la fête d'un citoyen soldat,* p. 7, *214;* with *Hymne en l'honneur des Marseillois . . . ,* p. 6, *247.*)

    One or more brochures, but not complete at any one library: Bibl. Sén.; Bibl. V.P.; Arch. nat. Complete set of seven—Coll. C.B.R.

Chansonnier de la Montagne (Le), ou recueil de chansons, vaudevilles, pot-pourris et hymnes patriotique; par différens auteurs. A Paris, chez Favre . . . , l'an III. 156 pp.

    Bibl. nat., Ye 17630; Coll. C.B.R.; etc.

Chansonnier de la République pour l'an III, dédié aux amis de la Liberté; hymnes patriotiques avec airs notés. Bordeaux et Paris.

    Bibl. V.P. 18238; etc.

Chansonnier patriote (Le), ou Recueil de chansons nationales, et autres, choisies, composées et chantées par Ladré Père, accompagné de son Fils. Senlis, 1791, 8 pp. (*244;* etc.)

    Bibl. nat., Ye 35763, pièce 5.

Chansonnier patriote (Le), ou Recueil de chansons, vaudevilles et pots-pourris patriotiques par différents auteurs. Paris, chez Garnéry. An 1ᵉʳ de la République française, 171 pp. (*185, 208, 214, 235;* etc.)

    Bibl. nat., Ye 10659; etc.

Chansons patriotiques, à Paris chez André, libraire, n.d. [probably late 1792], 156 pp. (P. 49, *196*; etc.)
>   Bibl. nat., Ye 17941.

Chansons patriotiques, par le citoyen Piis . . . , Paris . . . , an 2ᵉ, 108 pp.
>   Bibl. nat., Ye 11287.

Chants du patriotisme (Les), avec des notes dediés à la jeunesse citoy-enne, par M. T. Rousseau, citoyen Français, Paris, 1792, 314 pp., 2 vols. (P. 3, *183*; p. 11, *185*; p. 19, *186*; p. 49, *191*; p. 65, *196*; p. 73, *197*; p. 89, *208*; p. 96, *214*; p. 105, *224*; p. 113, *228*; p. 145, *229* and *237*; p. 153, *239* [by Maréchal]; p. 161, *241*; p. 193, *242*; p. 265, *235*; p. 281, *247*; etc.)
>   Bibl. nat., Ye 32546; etc.

Constitution en vaudeville (La), suivie des Droits de l'homme, de la femme et de plusieurs autres vaudevilles constitutionnels, par M. Marchant. Paris, chez les libraires royalistes, 1792, 160 pp.
>   Bibl. nat., Lc²² 42; etc.

Constitution française en chansons (La) . . . , par Sylvain Maréchal, Paris, chez Gueffier . . . , 1792, 125 pp. (P. 54, *239*; p. 59, *236*; etc.)
>   NOTE: Pierre incorrectly treats this work and the songs it contains as anonymous; see *op.cit.*, p. 154, no. 52, and the songs he refers to under that entry.
>   Bibl. nat., Ye 18976.

Grande bible des Noëls (La) et des cantiques en l'honneur de la Li-berté, ou le Calendrier républicain, par le citoyen T. Rousseau . . . , Paris . . . , 2ᵉ ed., n.d., 108 pp.
>   Bibl. V.P. 18236; etc.

Noëls civiques et patriotiques, dediés à tous les amis de la Constitution, par T. Rousseau, Paris, 1792, circ. 48 pp. (P. 1, *235*; etc.)
>   Bibl. V.P. 9293.

Nouveau chansonnier patriote ou recueil de chansons, vaudevilles et pots-pourri patriotiques par différentes auteurs. Lille; Paris. L'an 2ᵉ.
>   Bibl. V.P. 18235; etc.

Recueil chronologique des hymnes et chansons patriotiques, qui ont paru depuis la Révolution française, à Saint-Lo, chez J. Marais, Im-primeur . . . VIIIᵉ année de la République, 305 pp. (plus iv and xi). (P. 2, *185*; p. 7, *208*; p. 9, *214*; p. 12, *235*; p. 16, *260*; etc.)
>   Bibl. Opéra 113-B.

Recueil de chansons civiques et martiales, Commercy, impr. Denis, n.d., 36 pp.
>   Bibl. Sén., carton 5, cote 167.

Recueil de chansons patriotiques, dédiées aux vrais Républicains, par les Citoyens Leveau, dit Beauchant, et Baptiste, dit le Divertissant, chanteurs des Menusplaisirs des Sans-Culottes . . . [Paris], n.d., 4 pp.
  Bibl. nat., Ye 35763; etc.

Triomphe de la Liberté et de l'Egalité (Le), Almanach Républicain, chansons analogues aux années 1789, '90, '91, '92, par la citoyenne veuve Ferrand. Followed by *Calendrier pour l'An de grace MDCCXCIII. Paris*, n.d., 115 pp. (plus 24 unnumbered pages). (P. 9, *239**; etc.)
  Bibl. nat., Ye 34121.

G. Manuscripts

Assemblée des notables (L'), pot-pourri, n.p.n.d. (1787), 4 pp. (*176*)
  Bibl. nat. mss. fr. 7004, p. 39.

Couplets pour les gardes françaises lorsqu'ils n'ont pas voulu tirer sur le peuple à Veresailles, par Fardeau, sapeur des Arcis, n.p. (is inscribed, "mss. therm. an II"). (*237***; also *416** and *1576**)
  Arch. nat. F¹⁷ 1010 D (Dos. 3961).

H. Reprints (Post-Revolutionary)

NOTE: The *Chanson patriotique* (*181***), which Pierre attributes to 1789, is known to me only as reprinted in the work mentioned below. See Appendix A concerning this song, which appears to relate to 1787.

Damade, L., ed., *Histoire chantée de la première République (1789 à 1799)* . . . , Paris, 1892. (P. 76, *181***)

IV. GUIDES; DOCUMENTARY COLLECTIONS; AND PRIMARY SOURCES OTHER THAN THOSE CONTAINING SONGS

A. GUIDES

Apollinaire, G., F. Fleuret, and L. Perceau, *L'Enfer de la Bibliothèque nationale, nouv. ed.*, Paris, 1919.

Archives parlementaires, première série (1787 a 1799), indexes in vols. vii, xxxii, xxxiii, li, and lxxi (in two parts).

Barbier, A.; see Quérard, J. M.

Bibliothèque nationale, La Révolution française, Janvier-Mars, 1928 [*Catalogue de l'Exposition de 1928*], Paris [1928]. Note: see also Martin, A., below.

British Museum: *Catalogue of Printed Books*; since 1931, *General Catalogue of Printed Books*.

Caron, P., *Manuel pratique pour l'étude de la Révolution française*, Paris, 1947.

Grand-Carteret, J., *Les almanachs français: bibliographie-iconographie des almanachs, années, annuaires, calendriers, chansonniers, étrennes, états, heures, listes, livres d'adresses, tableaux, tablettes et autres publications annuelles éditées à Paris (1600-1895)*, illus. Paris, 1896.

Hatin, E., *Bibliographie historique et critique de la presse périodique française* . . . , Paris, 1866.

Hayden, H. E., *French Revolutionary Pamphlets; a Check List of the Talleyrand and Other Collections*, in *Bulletin of the New York Public Library*, vol. xliii, 1939 (articles commencing on pages 3, 359, 432, 513, and 563); and also published separately, New York, 1945.

Hyslop, B. F., "Historical Publication since 1939 on the French Revolution" [a guide to important periodical literature, as well as to recent books—see especially page 233, note 4, concerning special numbers of learned journals issued for the sesquicentennial of the French Revolution] in *The Journal of Modern History*, vol. xx (1948), pp. 232-50.

Martin, A., and G. Walter, *Catalogue de l'histoire de la Révolution française: Bibliothèque national*, 1936-1943, vols. 1-3 (Abassol-Piis), and vol. 5 (Journeaux et Almanachs).

Monglond, A., *La France révolutionnaire et impériale, annales de bibliographie méthodique et description des livres illustrés* . . . (especially vols. i and ii, including *Index des tomes I et II, années 1789-1793*), Grenoble, 1930-38, 5 vols.

Moniteur universel (Le), Tables alphabétiques (also those of *Réimpression de l'Ancien Moniteur*)

Pierre, C., *Les Hymnes et chansons de la Révolution: aperçu général et catalogue avec notices historiques, analytiques et bibliographiques (Ville de Paris, Publications relatives à la Révolution française) Imprimerie nationale*, Paris, 1904.

Procès-verbal de l'Assemblée nationale . . . *: Tables des matières, des noms de lieux et des noms de personnes* . . . Camus, ed., Paris, an XIV, 5 vols.

Quérard, J. M., *Les supercheries littéraires dévoilées, seconde édition, considérablement augmentée, publiée par MM. Gustave Brunet et Pierre Janet, suivi du Dictionnaire des ouvrages anonymes par Ant.-Alex. Barbier, troisième édition, revue et augmentée par M. Olivier Barbier* . . . , Paris, 1869-79, 7 vols.; and *Supplément à la dernière édition de ces deux ouvrages, par Gustave Brunet*, Paris, 1889.

Stewart, J. H., *France, 1715-1815—a Guide to Materials in Cleveland; being a Representative Selection from the Principal Holdings of the Libraries of Western Reserve University, the Cleveland Public Library, and the Western Reserve Historical Society*, Cleveland, 1942.

Tourneux, M., *Bibliographie de l'histoire de Paris pendant la Révolution française (Ville de Paris, Publications relatives à la Révolution française)*, Paris, 1890-1913, 5 vols.

B, 1. DOCUMENTARY COLLECTIONS; SONGS

Pre-Revolutionary

Lincy, L. de, ed., *Recueil de chants historiques français depuis le XIIᵉ jusqu'au XVIIIᵉ siècle* [completed only through the sixteenth century], Paris, 1841-42, 2 vols.

Raunié, E., ed., *Chansonnier historique du XVIIIᵉ siècle*, Paris, 1879-84, 10 vols.

Recueil général, de toutes les chansons mazarinistes. Et avec plusieurs qui n'ont point estées chantées. A Paris, 1649, 27 pp.

Moreau, no. 3055. N.Y. Publ. Libr. 9-DEN p. v. 10; no. 6.

Revolutionary (Modern Collections)

Damade, L., ed., *Histoire chantée de la Première République (1789 à 1799).—Chants patriotiques, révolutionnaires et populaires*, Paris, 1892.

Pierre, C., ed., *Musique des fêtes et cérémonies de la Révolution française. Oeuvres* [i.e., scores reproduced] *de Gossec, Chérubini, Lesueur, Méhul, Catel, etc. (Ville de Paris, Publications relatives à la Révolution française)*, Paris, 1899.

Poésies nationales de la Révolution française, ou Chants, Hymnes, Couplets, Odes, Chansons patriotiques, Paris, 1836.

Poésies Révolutionnaires et contre-Révolutionnaires, ou Recueil . . . [see *ibid.,* II, H], in *Collection des pièces importantes, relatives à la Révolution française,* Paris, 1821, 2 vols.

B, 2. DOCUMENTARY COLLECTIONS, GENERAL

Actes de la Commune de Paris pendant la Révolution, S. Lacroix and R. Farge, eds., Paris, 1894-1914, 16 vols.

Archives parlementaires de 1787 à 1860, Recueil complet des débats législatifs et politiques des chambres françaises, imprimé par ordre du Sénat et de la Chambre des députés, première série (1787 à 1799), 82 vols. [extending only to January 4, 1794], Paris, 1868-1913. Note: concerning certain defects in the preparation of this work, see P. Caron, *op.cit.*

Collection complète des lois promulguées sur les décrets de l'Assemblée nationale, imprimée par ordre de l'Assemblée nationale, sous la surveillance du Ministre de la Justice. A Paris, de l'Imprimerie nationale, 1791.

Collection de documents relatifs à l'histoire de Paris pendant la Révolution française et l'époque contemporaine publiée sous le patronage du Conseil municipal. See in this section: *Actes de la Commune . . . ; Les élections et les cahiers . . . ; L'Etat de Paris . . . ;* and *Le mouvement religieux. . . .*

Collection des documents inédits sur l'histoire de France. See in this section: *Procès-verbaux du Comité d'instruction publique . . . ; Recueil de documents relatifs à la convocation . . . ; Recueil des actes du Comité de salut publique . . . ;* and *Recueil des actes du Directoire exécutif. . . .*

Elections et les cahiers de Paris en 1789 (Les); documents . . . , Ch. L. Chassin, ed., Paris, 1888-89, 4 vols.

Etat de Paris en 1789 (L'); études et documents sur l'ancien régime à Paris, H. Monin, ed., Paris, 1889.

Mouvement religieux à Paris pendant la Révolution (Le), J. F. E. Robinet, ed., Paris, 1896-98, 2 vols.

Procès-verbal de l'Assemblée nationale, imprimé par son ordre, Paris, n.d., 75 vols.

Procès-verbaux du Comité d'instruction publique de la Convention nationale, J. Guillaume, ed., Paris, 1891-1907, 6 vols.

Recueil de documents relatifs à la convocation des Etats généraux de 1789, A. Brette, ed., Paris, 1894-1915, 4 vols.

Recueil des actes du Comité de salut publique avec la correspondance officielle des représentants en mission et la registre du Conseil exécutif provisoire. F.-A. Aulard, ed., Paris, 1889-1933, 27 vols.

Recueil des actes du Directoire exécutif . . . , A. Debidour, ed., Paris, 1910-17, 4 vols.

Select Documents Illustrative of the History of the French Revolution— The Constituent Assembly, L. G. W. Legg, ed., Oxford, 1905, 2 vols.

C. PRIMARY SOURCES
OTHER THAN THOSE CONTAINING SONGS

NOTE: Although a few items have been added, the following list is primarily a résumé of works mentioned in the text. No attempt is made to account here for the incomparably larger number of works which have been consulted. The reader is referred instead to such guides to the sources as are mentioned in section IV, A. The *Manuel* of Caron is particularly good for general use. Indispensable guides to the voluminous pamphlet literature of the Revolution are listed under Hayden, Martin and Walter, Monglond, and Tourneux.

C, 1. PAMPHLETS (IN ADDITION TO THOSE LISTED ABOVE, IN II, D AND III, D)

NOTE: Library references are provided only for pamphlets not mentioned in Tourneux, *op.cit.*

Adresse des Gardes-françoises enlevés des Prisons de l'abbaye, au Roi. Au Palais Royal . . . 2 juillet, 1789, n.p.n.d., 8 pp.

Boissel, F., *Le catéchisme du genre humain . . . ,* n.p., *1789,* 132 pp.
    For different editions and library references see M.-W., vol. i, no. 3846.

Confession de M. Necker (La), au moment de son agonie (1er octobre). [Signed:] *Nérac. Imp. du Postillon,* n.p.n.d., 8 pp.

Desmoulins, C., *La France libre, par M. Desmoulins . . . , troisième édition,* n.p., *1789,* 76 pp.
    N.Y. Publ. Libr., DFD p. v. 70, no. 1.

Entrée triomphante de M. Necker à l'Hôtel-de-Ville, accompagnée du compliment de M. le marquis de la Fayette & de M. Bailly, maire; suivi de la réponse de M. Necker, & de la présentation du bouquet des poissardes. De l'Imprimerie de P. R. C. Ballard, Imprimeur, rue des Mathurins [Paris], n.d., 4 pp.

Extrait d'un Discours adressé par M. le Marquis de la Fayette, vers la fin d'Octobre, aux Officiers de la Garde Nationale, assemblés chez lui [and a *Lettre* in reply]. *A Paris, chez Grégoire . . . ,* n.d., 8 pp.
    N.Y. Publ. Libr., DFD p. v. 70, no. 12.

Fauchet, C., *Discours sur la liberté françoise, prononcé le Mercredi 5 Août 1789, dans l'Eglise Paroissiale de S.-Jacques & des SS. Innocens, durant une Solemnité consacrée à la Mémoire des Citoyens qui sont morts à la prise de la Bastille, pour la défense de la Patrie. Par M. l'Abbé Fauchet. . . . A Paris . . . , M.DCC.LXXXIX,* 16 pp.

This item appears in Tourneux, vol. iii, no. 16614, but in the Index, vol. v, the *Discours* is incorrectly dated "31 août."

———, (contemporary English translation of the above) *A Discourse by M. L'Abbé Fauchet, on the Liberty of France, delivered Wednesday the 5th of August, 1789. . . . Translated from the French by William Harvest, London, 1790,* 24 pp.

N.Y. Publ. Libr., DFD p. v. 66, no. 3.

Fédération de Montélimart, en Dauphiné [13 décembre, 1789], n.p.n.d., 14 pp.

N.Y. Publ. Libr., DFD p. v. 17, no. 2.

Géant devenu pygmée (Le), ou Necker au grand jour. A Masulipatan, Chez Christophe Lerond, le jeune, 1790, 15 pp.

Joie des Française (La), L'Arrivée de M. Necker. Chez Momoro, Libraire, rue de la Harpe, No. 160. De l'Imprim. de Crangé [sic], n.d., 3 pp.

Cornell Univ. Libr., 4191, C564.

Lebois [according to Tourneux, vol. iv, no. 24512], *Lettre des Parisiens à M. Necker, pour l'inviter à reprendre sa place. Par M. F. R. Leb. . s. Imp. Rue de la Parcheminerie, 1789,* 4 pp.

Lettre de M. Necker, du 24 Juin 1789; et Discours prononcés dans la Séance de l'Assemblée Nationale, du 25 Juin 1789, n.p.n.d., 18 pp.

Lettre des Gardes-françoises au Roi, pour remercier sa Majesté de la grace qu'elle vient de leur accorder. Le 2 juillet. n.p.n.d., 3 pp.

N.Y. Pub. Libr., DFDT p. v. 61, no. 11.

Ma Confession; Avis au Peuple; Mon Secret, n.p.n.d., 16 pp.

[Marat, J. P.], *Offrande à la patrie ou Discours au tiers-état de France. Au temple de la Liberté,* n.p., *1789,* 62 pp.

N.Y. Pub. Libr., DFDT p. v. 32, no. 19.

Necker jugé par le tribunal de la lanterne (with subheading, *Français, lis ce jugement, et rougis de ton erreur*), n.p.n.d., 30 pp.

Récit de ce qui s'est passé à Versailles le 23 Juin 1789, depuis six heures du soir jusqu'à neuf heures, au sujet de M. Necker. Par un témoin oculaire, n.p.n.d., 7 pp.

Mentioned by Tourneux, vol. i, no. 1009, but apparently not included in Index, vol. v.

Robbins, Chandler, *An Address delivered at Plymouth, on the 24th day of January, 1793, to the inhabitants of that town, assembled to cele-*

brate the victories of the French Republic over their invaders ... (including, p. 19, "An Ode to Liberty, composed by Mr. Joseph Croswell, and sung at the Civic Feast at Plymouth, January 24, 1793"), *Boston, 1793,* 20 pp.

N.Y. Pub. Libr., *KD.

Rutledge, J.-J., *L'astuce dévoilée, ou origine des maux de la France, perdue par les manoeuvres du Ministre Necker ... , par M. Rutofle de Lode* [pseud.], n.p., *1790,* 114 pp.

Sieyès, E., *Qu'est-ce que le tiers-état?* [author's name not given], *seconde édition, corrigée,* n.p., *1789,* 130 pp.

N.Y. Publ. Libr., DFDT p. v. 35, no. 12.

——, *Quelques idées de Constitution applicables à la ville de Paris, en juillet, 1789. Par M. l'Abbé Sieyes* [sic., without accent]. *A Versailles, chez Baudouin ... ,* n.d., 37 pp.

Suite des nouvelles d'hier, mardi 23 juin 1789, n.p.n.d., 7 pp.

N.Y. Pub. Libr., DFD p. v. 41 (fifth of unnumbered items).

Tribut de reconnoissance de la Nation Françoise au meilleur de ses amis. Août 1789 (date follows title, on title page). *De l'imprimerie de Cailleau, père, rue Galande, No. 64,* 8 pp.

Vialla, *Compliment à M. Necker, fait et prononcé par un Garde-Françoise, au nom des Compagnie* [sic] *de Versailles. Par M. Vialla, Bachelier en Droit & Garde-Françoise de la Compagnie de M. le Comte de Roussy. A Paris, de l'Imprimerie de Seguy-Thiboust, Place-Cambray, 1789,* 4 pp.

N.Y. Publ. Libr., DFD p. v. 41 (sixth of unnumbered items); Cornell Univ. Libr. 4191, C 550.

Vidaillet, *Confession de tous ceux qui ont cherché à trahir la Nation Françoise,* "signed:" *Vidaillet, ...* "for omitted matter see below." *De l'impr. de Cailleau,* 8 pp.

    a.) *Ibid., 31 juillet 1789,* in-8, mentioned in Tourneux, vol. i, no. 1192.

    b.) *Ibid., seconde édition, Août 1789,* in-12.

    N.Y. Publ. Libr., DFD p. v. 70, no. 8.

C, 2. JOURNALS, MEMOIRS, ETC.

NOTE: Journals mentioned below were published in Paris, unless otherwise indicated; those for which no date of commencement is given were published throughout the year 1789.

Actes des apôtres (Les), from November 2, 1789.

Affiches, annonces et avis divers ou Journal général de France.

Ami du peuple (L'), ou le Publiciste parisien, journal politique, libre et impartial, par une société de patriotes, et rédigé par M. Marat ... , from September 12, 1789, with the first five numbers under the title, *Le Publiciste parisien*. . . .

Annales patriotiques ou littéraires de la France, et affaires politiques de l'Europe, journal libre . . . *dirigé par* M. *Mercier*, from October 3, 1789.

Bailly, J. S., *Mémoires de Bailly* (in *Collection des mémoires relatifs à la Révolution française*, Berville and Barrière, eds.), Paris, 1821-22, 3 vols.

Barère de Vieuzac, B.; see *Le point du jour*.

Bastille dévoilée (La) ou Recueil de pièces authentiques pour servir à son histoire [9 *livraisons*], Paris, 1789-90.

Brissot de Warville; see *Le Patriote français*.

Chronique de Paris, from August 24, 1789.

Courrier de Provence (Le), from July 24, 1789.
    NOTE: this is a continuation of the *Lettres du Comte de Mirabeau à ses commettans* (see below).

Décret de L'Assemblée Nationale sur la réformation de quelques points de la jurisprudence criminelle. (Procès-verbal, des 8 & 9 octobre 1789, vol. v.)

Desmoulins, C., *Oeuvres de - - - - -*, J. Claretie, ed., Paris, 1894, 2 vols.
——; and see below, *Révolutions de France et de Brabant*.

Ferrières, *Mémoirs du Marquis de - - - - - (Bibliothèque des mémoires relatifs à l'histoire de France, pendant le 18ᵉ siècle, nouvelle série*, M. de Lescure, ed., vol. xxxv), Paris, 1880.

Gazette nationale ou le Moniteur universel [commonly referred to as *Le Moniteur*], from November 24, 1789, the numbers from May 5 through November 23 being the result of a compilation made in *l'An IV*.
    NOTE: references in the present work are to the original folio edition, rather than to the *Réimpression*.

Journal de Paris.

Journal des débats et des décrets, Versailles [later, Paris], from August 29, 1789.

Journal des Etats-Généraux . . . , from cir. June 1, 1789, and written retrospectively to cover the period from April 27, 1789.

Journal des révolutions de l'Europe en 1789 et 1790 . . . , Neuwied sur le Rhin . . . , 1790.

Journal général de France.
    NOTE: this was an edition of part of the *Affiches, annonces et avis divers* . . . , mentioned above.

Journal politique-national des Etats-généraux et de la Révolution de 1789. Publié par M. l'abbé Sabatier, & tiré des Annales manuscrites de M. le Comte de R*** [Rivarol], Cambrai, 1790.
> NOTE: this is a reprinted edition of the *Journal politique-national . . .* , which, according to Hatin, appeared first at Versailles on July 12, 1789.

La Fayette, *Mémoires, correspondance et manuscrits du Général Lafayette*, Paris, 1837-38, 6 vols.

Lettres du Comte de Mirabeau à ses commettans, nos. 1-19, n.p., from May 10 to July 24, 1789.
> NOTE: this is a continuation of Mirabeau's earlier *Etats-Généraux*, 2 nos.; it was followed, in turn, by his *Courrier de Provence* (see above).

Mallet du Pan, *Memoirs and Correspondence*, A. Sayous, ed., London, 1852, 2 vols.

Marat, J. P.; see *L'Ami du peuple.*

Mercure de France, dédié au Roi, par une société de gens de lettres . . . , [founded as *Le Mercure galant* in 1672].

Mirabeau, Comte de; see *Courrier de Provence* and *Lettres du Comte de - - - - -.*

Moniteur universel (Le); see *Gazette nationale. . . .*

Morris, G., *A Diary of the French Revolution by Gouverneur Morris*, B. C. Davenport, ed., Boston, 1939, 2 vols.

Mounier, J. J., *Exposé de la conduite de M. Mounier, dans L'Assemblée nationale, et des motifs de son retour en Dauphiné* [Paris], 1789, 120 pp.

Necker, J., *Mémoire lu par le premier Ministre des Finances à l'Assemblée nationale, le 14 novembre 1789, et imprimé par ses ordres (Procès-verbal . . .* , vol. 7).

———, *La Révolution françoise* (in *Oeuvres complètes de M. Necker . . .* , Paris, 1821, vol. ix).

Patriote français (Le), journal libre, impartial et national . . . , dirigé par J.-P. Brissot de Warville, commenced (except for a single number in May) July 28, 1789.

Point du Jour (Le), ou Résultat de ce qui s'est passé la veille à l'Assemblée nationale . . . [Barère, ed.], from June 19, 1789, the period from April 27 to June 7, 1789, being covered retrospectively in a later volume.

Projet de l'organisation du pouvoir judiciaire, proposé à l'Assemblée Nationale par le Comité de Constitution; and *Suite du Projet . . . (Procès-verbal . . . , 21 décembre, 1789*, vol. x).

Révolutions de France et de Brabant . . . , par M. Desmoulins . . . , from November 28, 1789.

Révolutions de Paris, dédiées à la Nation et au district des Petits-Augustins. Published by Prudhomme, from July 12, 1789.

Staël, Madame de, *Considérations sur les principaux événemens de la Révolution françoise, ouvrage posthume . . . , publié par M. le Duc de Broglie et M. le Baron de Staël,* 3rd ed., Paris, 1820, 3 vols., esp. vol. i.

Talleyrand, *Motion de M. l'Evêque d'Autun sur les Biens ecclésiastiques, 10 octobre 1789* (*Procès-verbal,* vol. 6).

Young, Arthur, *Travels in France During the Years 1787, 1788, 1789,* Betham-Edwards, ed., London, 1900.

V. SECONDARY WORKS

NOTE: Works mentioned below belong primarily to the following categories: those which bear particularly on the year 1789 in France, or which contain important chapters concerning that year, except that general histories of the Revolution are included only if referred to in the text; books which concern political songs or festivals; and works bearing on the spirit and morale of the Revolution, especially in its first phases.[6] Even within these limits, the list is highly selective.

Acton, J., *Lectures on the French Revolution*, London, Macmillan, 1910.

Andrews, G. G., *The Constitution in the Early French Revolution (June to September, 1789)*, New York, Crofts, 1927.

——, "Early Revolutionary Newspapers," in *Persecution and Liberty; Essays in honor of George Lincoln Burr*, New York, Century, 1931, pp. 421-43.

Aulard, A., *Le Culte de la Raison et le Culte de l'Etre Suprême (1793-1794)*, Paris, Alcan, 1909.

——, *Etudes et leçons*, especially *première série*, and *troisième série*, Paris, Alcan, 1893 and 1902.

——, *Histoire politique de la Révolution française*, Paris, Colin, 1921.

——, *Le patriotisme français de la Renaissance à la Révolution*, Paris, Chiron, 1921.

——, *Le patriotisme selon la Révolution française*, Paris, Cornély, 1904.

——, *La Révolution française et le régime féodal*, Paris, Alcan, 1919.

Bainville, J., *Histoire de France*, Paris, Tallandier, 1926, 2 vols.

Barzun, J., *The French Race: theories of its origins and their social and political implications prior to the Revolution*, New York, Columbia University Press, 1932.

Becker, C. L., *The Heavenly City of the Eighteenth-Century Philosophers*, New Haven, Yale University Press, 1932.

Blanc, L., *Histoire de la Révolution française*, Paris, Lacroix, ed. of 1878, 15 vols., especially vols. 3 and 4.

Bliard, P., *Fraternité révolutionnaire*, Paris, Emile-Paul, 1908.

Blum, E., *La Déclaration des Droits de l'homme et du citoyen*, 4th ed., Paris, Alcan, 1904.

Boursin, E., and A. Challamel, *Dictionnaire de la Révolution française; institutions, hommes et faits . . .*, Paris, Jouvet, 1893.

Braesch, F., "*1789—L'année cruciale*," Librairie Gallimard, 1941.

---

[6] Concerning recent periodical literature, see Bibliography IV, A, under B. F. Hyslop.

Brinton, C., *A Decade of Revolution, 1789-1799* [contains "Bibliographical Essay," pp. 293-322], New York and London, Harpers, 1934.

———, *The Jacobins—An Essay in the New History*, New York, Macmillan, 1930.

Cahen, L., *Condorcet et la Révolution française*, Paris, Alcan, 1904.

Cambridge Modern History, vol. viii: *The French Revolution*, New York and London, Macmillan, 1908.

Carré, H., *La fin des Parlements (1788-1790)*, Paris, Hachette, 1912.

———, and P. Sagnac and E. Lavisse, *Le règne de Louis XVI (1774-1789)*, Paris, Hachette, 1910 (tome ix, 1st part, in the series *Histoire de France depuis les origines jusqu'à la Révolution*, E. Lavisse, ed.).

Challamel, A., *Histoire-musée de la République française depuis l'Assemblée des Notables jusqu'à l'Empire; avec les estampes, costumes, médailles, caricatures, portraits historiés et autographes les plus remarquables du temps*, 3rd ed., Paris, Bollay (1857-1858), 2 vols.

Champion, E., *Esprit de la Révolution française*, Paris, Reinwald, 1887.

———, *La France d'après les Cahiers de 1789*, 5th ed., Paris, Colin, 1921.

Chapuisat, E., *Necker (1732-1804)*, Paris, Sirey, 1938.

Chérest, A., *La chute de l'Ancien Régime (1787-1789)*, Paris, Hachette, 1884-86, 3 vols.

Cochin, A., *La Révolution et la libre-pensée*, 4th ed., Paris, Plon, 1924.

———, *Les sociétés de pensée et la démocratie*, Paris, Plon-Nourrit, 1921.

Conard, P., *La peur en Dauphiné*, Paris, Bellais, 1904.

Dreyfous, M., *Les arts et les artistes pendant la période révolutionnaire (1789-1795), nouvelle édition, augmentée d'une Préface par Anatole France et illustrée de reproductions de documents de l'époque*, Paris, Paclot [1906].

Droz, J., *Histoire du règne de Louis XVI pendant les années où l'on pouvait prévenir ou diriger la Révolution française*, Paris, Renouard, 1839-42, 3 vols.

Duclos, P., *La notion de Constitution dans l'oeuvre de l'Assemblée Constituante de 1789*, Paris, Dalloz, 1932.

Elton, G., *The Revolutionary Idea in France, 1789-1871*, London, Arnold, 1923.

Farmer, P., *France Reviews Its Revolutionary Origins: social politics and historical opinion in the Third Republic*, New York, Columbia University Press, 1944.

Faÿ, B., *L'esprit révolutionnaire en France et aux Etats-Unis à la fin du XVIIIᵉ siècle*, Paris, Champion, 1925.

Faÿ, B., *La Franc-Maçonnerie et la révolution intellectuelle du XVIIIe siècle*, Paris, Cluny, 1935.

Flammermont, J., ed., *La journée du 14 juillet 1789 . . . de Pitra*, Paris, La Société, 1892.

Fling, F. M., *Mirabeau and the French Constitution in the Years 1789 and 1790*, Ithaca, Journal Job Printing House, 1891.

Fournel, V., *Les hommes du 14 Juillet, Gardes-Françaises et Vainqueurs de la Bastille*, Paris, Levy, 1890.

Funck-Brentano, Frantz, *L'Ancien Régime*, Paris, Fayard, 1926.

Garrett, M. B., *The Estates General of 1789; the Problems of Composition and Organization* [including a bibliography of pamphlets published between July 5, 1788, and January 24, 1789], New York, Appleton-Century, 1935.

Gautier, H., *L'An 1789, événements, moeurs, idées, oeuvres et caractères, avec 650 reproductions . . . de vignettes, d'estampes et de tableaux de l'époque*, Paris, Delagrave [1889].

Gershoy, L., "Barère in the Constituent Assembly," in *The American Historical Review*, vol. xxxvi (1931), pp. 295-313.

———, *From Despotism to Revolution, 1763-1789*, New York and London, Harpers, 1944.

———, *The French Revolution and Napoleon*, New York, Crofts, 1933.

Goncourt, E. de, and J. de Goncourt, *Histoire de la société française pendant la Révolution*, Paris, Charpentier, ed. of 1880.

Gooch, G. P., "The French Revolution," Chapter xiii in *History and Historians in the Nineteenth Century*, 4th impression, London, Longmans, 1928.

Gorce, P. de la, *Histoire religieuse de la Révolution française*, Paris, Plon-Nourrit, 1925, 5 vols.

Gosselin, L.; see Lenotre, G. (pseud.).

Gottschalk, L. R., *The Era of the French Revolution (1715-1815)*, Boston, Houghton Mifflin, 1929.

———, *Jean Paul Marat, a Study in Radicalism*, New York, Greenberg, 1927.

———, "Philippe Sagnac and the Causes of the French Revolution," in *The Journal of Modern History*, vol. xx, pp. 137-48.

Hayes, C. J. H., *Essays on Nationalism*, New York, Macmillan, 1926.

———, *The Historical Evolution of Modern Nationalism*, New York, Richard R. Smith, 1931.

Hazen, C. D., *The French Revolution*, New York, Holt, 1932, 2 vols.

Henderson, E. F., *Symbol and Satire in the French Revolution*, New York and London, Putnam, 1912.

Hérissay, J., *Le monde des théâtres pendant la Révolution (1789-1800)*, Paris, Perrin, 1922.

Hyslop, B. F., *French Nationalism in 1789 according to the General Cahiers*, New York, Columbia University Press, 1934.

———, "The Theatre during a Crisis: The Parisian Theatre during the Reign of Terror," in *The Journal of Modern History*, vol. xvii (1945), pp. 332-55.

Jalliffier, R., *Histoire des Etats généraux (1302-1614)*, Paris, Cerf, 1885.

Jauffret, E., *Le théâtre révolutionnaire (1788-1799)*, Paris, Furne-Jouvet, 1869.

Lavisse, E.; see Carré, H.

Le Bon, G., *La Révolution française et la psychologie des révolutions* (new ed. of 1913), Paris, Flammarion, 1925.

Lecesne, E., *Plantation de l'arbre de la liberte à Arras, en 1792* [Arras, 1879]. Note: this is known to me only as a separate brochure, with pagination 285-301, being apparently an extract from a periodical.

Lecocq, G., *La Prise de la Bastille et ses anniversaires d'après des documents inédits*, Paris, 1881.

Lecomte, G., *Au chant de la Marseillaise*, Paris, Fasquelle, 1929.

Leconte, A., *Rouget de Lisle; sa vie, ses oeuvres, la Marseillaise*, Paris, Librairies-Imprimeries Réunis, 1892.

Lefebvre, G., *La grande peur de 1789*, Paris, Colin, 1932.

———, *The Coming of the French Revolution*, Princeton, Princeton University Press, 1947; translation by R. R. Palmer, of *Quatre-vingt-neuf*, Paris, 1939.

Lenotre, G. (pseud.), *Le mysticisme révolutionnaire; Robespierre et la "Mère de Dieu,"* 11th ed., Paris, Perrin, 1926.

Le Roy de Sainte-Croix, *Le chant de guerre de l'armée du Rhin ou la Marseillaise*, Strasbourg, Hagemann, 1880.

McCarthy, J. H., *The French Revolution*, London, Chatto and Windus, 1890-1897, 4 vols.

Madelin, L., *The French Revolution*, New York, Putnam, 1916; translation by F. S. Barr, of *La Révolution*, Paris, Hachette, 1911.

Marion, M., *Histoire financière de la France depuis 1715*, Paris, Rousseau, 6 vols. 1914-31, especially vol. ii (*1789-1792*).

Martin, G., *La Franc-Maçonnerie française et la préparation de la Révolution*, 2nd ed., Paris, Presses Universitaires, 1926.

Masson, E., *La puissance paternelle et la famille sous la Révolution*, Paris, 1910.

Mathiez, A., *Contributions à l'histoire religieuse de la Révolution française*, Paris, Alcan, 1907.

———, *The French Revolution*, London, Williams and Norgate, 1929, translation by C. A. Phillips, of *La Révolution française*, Paris, Armand Colin, 1922-27, 3 vols.

Mathiez, A., *Les origines des cultes révolutionnaires (1789-1792)*, Paris, Bellais, 1904.

———, *La Révolution et les étrangers*, Paris, La Renaissance du Livre, 1918.

———, *La Théophilanthropie et le Culte décadaire 1796-1801*, Paris, Alcan, 1904.

Mirkine-Guetzévitch, B., P. Sagnac, and others, *Cahiers d'histoire de la Révolution française*, New York, Editions de la Maison Française, 1946.

Monseignat, Ch. de, *Un chapitre de la Révolution française ou Histoire des journaux en France de 1789 à 1799 . . .* , new ed., Paris, 1878.

Moore, A. P., *The Genre Poissard and the French Stage of the Eighteenth Century*, New York, Columbia University Press, 1935.

Mornet, D., *Les origines intellectuelles de la Révolution française (1715-1787)*, Paris, Colin, 1933.

Moulonguet, P., *La souveraineté de Béarn à la fin de l'Ancien Régime*, Toulouse, 1909.

Nisard, C., *Des chansons populaires chez les Anciens et chez les Français, étude historique . . .* , Paris, Dentu, 1867, 2 vols.

———, *Etude sur la langue populaire ou Patois de Paris et de sa banlieue*, Paris, Franck, 1872.

Padover, S. K., *The Life and Death of Louis XVI*, New York and London, Appleton-Century, 1939.

Parker, H. T., *The Cult of Antiquity and the French Revolutionaries; a study in the development of the Revolutionary spirit*, Chicago, University of Chicago Press, 1937.

Pellet, M., *Elysée Loustallot et les Révolutions de Paris (juillet 1789-septembre 1790)*, Paris, 1872.

———, *Les actes des apôtres (1789-1791)*, Paris, 1873.

Pressensé, E., *The Church and the French Revolution* (translation by J. Stroyan), London, Hodder and Stoughton, 1869.

Quinet, E., *La Révolution*, Paris, Lacroix, 1865, 2 vols.

Robinson, J. H., "The Principles of 1789," Chapter VII in *The New History*, New York, Macmillan, 1922.

Rocquain, F., *L'esprit révolutionnaire avant la Révolution, 1715-1789*, Paris, Plon, 1878.

Rose, J. H., *Nationality in Modern History*, New York, Macmillan, 1916.

Sagnac, P., *La Révolution (1789-1792)*, Paris, Hachette, 1920 (in the series, *Histoire de France contemporaine*, E. Lavisse, ed.).

Sagnac, P., *La fin de l'ancien régime et la Révolution américaine (1763-1789)*, Paris, Presses Universitaires, 2nd ed., 1947 (vol. xii in the series, *Peuples et civilizations; Histoire générale*, L. Halpern and P. Sagnac, eds.).

———, *La révolution des idées et des mœurs et le déclin de l'ancien régime*, Paris, Presses Universitaires, 1946 (vol. ii of *La formation de la société française moderne*).

———, and J. Robiquet, *La Révolution de 1789 d'après Michelet—E. Quinet—Thiers. . . . Iconographie de l'époque réunie sous la direction de Jean Robiquet*, Paris, Editions Nationales, 1934, 2 vols.

———, see also Carré, H.

Sée, H., *La France économique et sociale au XVIIIᵉ siècle*, Paris, Colin, 1925.

Sepet, M., *La chute de l'Ancienne France—La Fédération*, Paris, Retaux, 1896.

———, *Louis XVI, Etude historique*, Paris, 1910.

Siegfried, A., *France, a Study in Nationality*, New Haven, Yale University Press, 1930.

Sloane, W. M., *The French Revolution and Religious Reform . . .* , New York, Scribners, 1901.

Soboul, A., *1789, l'An I de la Liberté, étude historique, textes originaux*, Paris, Editions Sociales Internationales, 1939.

Stryienski, C., *Le dix-huitième siècle*, Paris, Hachette, 1913.

Taine, H., *L'Ancien Régime*, 31st ed., Paris, 1926-27, 2 vols. (Part I of *Les origines de la France contemporaine*, 12 vols.)

Thompson, J. M., *The French Revolution*, New York, Oxford University Press, 1945.

Tiersot, J., *Les fêtes et les chants de la Révolution française*, Paris, Hachette, 1908.

———, *Histoire de la Marseillaise*, Paris, Delagrave, 1915.

———, *Rouget de Lisle, son oeuvre, sa vie*, Paris, Delagrave, 1892.

Tocqueville, A. de, *L'Ancien Régime*, G. W. Headlam, ed., Oxford, 1904.

Trahard, P., *La sensibilité révolutionnaire (1789-1794)*, Paris, Boivin, 1936.

Van Deusen, G., *Sieyes: His Life and His Nationalism*, New York, Columbia University Press, 1932.

Welschinger, H., *Les almanachs de la Révolution*, Paris, Librairie des Bibliophiles, 1884.

Wilkinson, S., *The French Army before Napoleon*, Oxford, Clarendon Press, 1915.

APPENDIX

APPENDIX A

*Les hymnes et chansons de la Révolution, aperçu
général et catalogue,* Paris, 1904, in quarto, 1040 pp.

THE *Hymnes et chansons* of Constant Pierre forms part of one of the
greatest bibliographical undertakings in the historiography of the
French Revolution. Along with the *Répertoire général des sources
manuscrites . . .* of Alexandre Tuetey, and the *Bibliographie de l'histoire de Paris . . .* of Maurice Tourneux, it appeared in the *Publications
relatives à la Révolution française* which the City of Paris began to
publish in 1890.[1]

All in all, Pierre's work makes mention of several thousand items,
and is the only great compendium of information on the songs of the
French Revolution. To one interested in this particular field, it is
highly important to know what reliance can be placed on Pierre's comprehensive survey. From the standpoint of this larger question, my
critique of Pierre's *Catalogue* for 1789 may be of interest. It is, besides,
an essential part of the present study of the songs of that year.

Within the limit specified, it must be said that Pierre's *Catalogue* is
unreliable. That this is so will be sufficiently demonstrated, I believe,
in subsequent paragraphs and in the annotations which follow.

It should be emphasized, however, that I am analyzing the *Catalogue*
at one point in time only, and that the songs of 1789 constitute but four
percent of the total literature which Pierre surveys. Furthermore, I am
convinced by a study of the *Catalogue* as a whole that in the all-important matter of properly dating songs, errors are numerous for the
early years of the Revolution, especially the first, and become proportionately much fewer as the Revolution progressed. This discrepancy is
readily explainable: *brochures* and *feuilles volantes* for the early period
are usually undated (and they are frequently enigmatic and difficult to
allocate); while most publications at the height of the Revolution carry
a complete publisher's imprint. By that time Frenchmen had the sense
that they were making history, and they were apt proudly to establish
the date of every new event—including publishing events—in terms of
the new Revolutionary calendar.

Also in regard to chronology, mention should be made of Pierre's
handling of anniversary and other retrospective songs. Some of these
Pierre ascribes to the year in which they were written (which is doubtless the correct procedure); but many of them he assigns to the year of
the events which they celebrated, although they almost invariably show
the influence of a later point of view. Many of the songs which I have

[1] The title was expanded in 1908 to read " . . . *et à l'histoire contemporaine de
Paris,*" so that the subsequent period of modern history might be included.

been obliged to reject, in considering Pierre's *Catalogue* for 1789, are of this nature.

Another disturbing feature of his book is want of consistency in the treatment of multiple editions. Frequently different editions of a given song, pamphlet, or larger work are elaborately set forth, and the user of the *Catalogue* may at first be led to suppose that it is exhaustive in this respect; but presently he discovers elsewhere that multiple library references which seem to point to a single printing actually lead in the library to two or more different editions. These and other defects, and the precautions which have to be taken, are disclosed in detail in the annotations below.

Of the 115 songs which Pierre attributes to 1789,[2] the texts of all have been examined, except six which proved to be unavailable.[3] Of the 109 available songs, it has been necessary to reject forty-two:

    (1) seven as having appeared before 1789;
    (2) thirty-five others as having first appeared in print one or more
        years later.

The remaining sixty-seven are included in my "New Catalogue of the Political Songs of 1789," Bibliography I. Also included in that Catalogue are three items (Bibliography I, 43, 51, 77)[4] which Pierre ascribed by error to 1790; and fourteen additional songs which are not mentioned in his *Catalogue*.[5]

It is not surprising that new songs have come to light—indeed, of these, several appear to be obtainable only in American collections—but it is highly significant, from the standpoint of serious historical inquiry, that an analysis of Pierre's inclusions for 1789 should expose a ratio of error of approximately forty percent.

Certain of the foregoing remarks imply sweeping criticisms which relate in a measure to Pierre's work as a whole, and not simply to that part devoted to 1789. In all fairness, however, much remains to be explained. Pierre's *Hymnes et chansons* consists of several parts. It opens with a long introductory statement of considerable merit. The work includes, besides, valuable bibliographies, which precede the *Catalogue* itself. Furthermore, Pierre analyzed musical scores, for the most part not considered here. Besides, he investigated with unusual thoroughness the most famous of the Revolutionary songs, on which he reports at length. Errors in dating, so serious for 1789, are, as already said,

---

[2] Pierre lists 116 items under 1789, but one of these may be combined with another item. See Appendix A, 207.

[3] These six are 194*, 203, 204, 211, 222, and 228**.

[4] Pierre serial numbers 293, 360*, and 262 respectively; concerning Pierre's errors in dating these items, see same, Appendix A.

[5] This accounts for eighty-four of the eighty-seven items listed in Bibliography I. The other three items consist of titles taken from Pierre (33-*194**; 45-*204*; 48-*203*), though the texts of these songs were, and presumably still are, unavailable; see same, under Pierre serial numbers, in Appendix A.

less frequent for later years. Whereas Pierre's arrangement of material is often unacceptable from the historical standpoint, it should be emphasized that he (and such collaborators as he may have had) combed the important libraries of Paris and the British Museum for song literature. Much of what they found does not appear in library catalogues. Thus was accomplished, one might say, a great work of excavation; and no student of the songs of the French Revolution can afford to be without the *Hymnes et chansons* of Constant Pierre. Finally, there are at the conclusion of Pierre's work no less than six indices, the first five of which are immensely valuable. It is true that errors and inaccuracies mar the book, and that new material has come to light since 1904. It is to be hoped that in time a Supplement containing errata and addenda will appear—the product of detailed studies which would give to Pierre's work the definitive quality that such a bibliographical guide should possess.

In the annotations which follow, songs are identified only by numbers. The initial number of each of the entries (beginning "168") is the serial number from Pierre's *Catalogue*. At some point in his preparations, after a complete sequence had been established, Pierre interpolated additional songs, and the titles of these he signalized by numbers already assigned, with an asterisk added (thus, "168*"). For a double interpolation, there is a second asterisk, and so on. In the entries below, a number in parentheses following Pierre's serial number, is the corresponding number of the same song in the New Catalogue, Bibliography I. All Pierre's numbers for 1789 (with corresponding New Catalogue numbers) have been entered below—even in instances where there has been no occasion for comment—in order to sustain an unbroken sequence for purposes of cross reference.

Concerning abbreviations used in this Appendix see statement introducing Bibliography II, pages 284-86.

168. (2)

After title add *par L. D.*

Pierre begins his *Catalogue* with this song, relating to April 15, 1789, but should have preceded it by several items which he includes subsequently: three songs (177, 178*, and 235*) attributable to 1788; three other songs (176, 181**, and 231) attributable to 1787; and one other item (211), which may have been earlier still. Concerning the dating of these seven items see below under numbers mentioned.

168*. (22)

Both 168* and 169, which follows, concern the so-called "reunion" of the three orders. Pierre evidently takes this to mean the gathering of the Estates General, May 5, 1789; whereas it signifies, as is borne out by internal evidence, the union of the three orders commanded by the King on June 27. The piece should rightly follow 187.

169. (23)

This song, *La réunion des trois ordres*, also relates to June 27, and should follow 187; see 168*. To title, add *Couplets dédiés à la Nation*.

A text published in the anthology *Poésies Révolutionnaires . . . ,* Paris, 1821, vol. i, p. 26, indicates that there was a second contemporary edition of this song (though no copy of the original is known). This reprint bears the title *L'Alégresse du Peuple français, à l'occasion de la réunion des trois ordres, après la mémorable séance du jeu de paume. Juin 1789. M. de Castella* (rather than Déduit) appears as author. Variations of phrasing, though not of essential meaning, occur in eleven of the forty lines of the song.

> See *La réunion . . .* , Bibliography ii, B, for publisher's name and for evidence of the work having appeared in 1789. To the library reference given, add *Bibl. V.P. 23918* (same edition).

170. (40)

This piece, which appears with 170* in the pamphlet *Le Citoyen en bonne humeur, 1789*, is post-Bastille and, accordingly belongs with the Pierre group 189-194*.

> The two library references to this pamphlet are to the same edition. To *Le Citoyen . . .* , etc., add *1789*. To the Bibl. V.P. reference, add *pièce 21*.
>
> To the reference *Alm. du Bonhomme . . .* , add *1793*. As reprinted here, the song has lost its originally jovial character, revisions bringing it to a close on a grim note: "sabrons même les plus gothiques . . ." etc. For further comment, see Bibliography i, 40, b.

170*. (41)

Published in *Le Citoyen en bonne humeur* with 170: see same, concerning corrected chronology and library references.

171. (3)

Pierre omits the date *1789*, which appears on the brochure containing this song.

> All four library references are to the same edition. For *p. 47* in the last of these, read *pièce 47*.

172. (7)

Published with music: add *Chez Savigny*.

Concerning another edition see Bibliography i, 7, b.

173. (10)

Add after title [*par . . . Jeanne Rocher*]. Some indication should be given to relate this piece to song 175. Both appear in the same manuscript and in the same handwriting, as does the signature, *par une D^{elle} [demoiselle] religieuse de 78 ans, nommée Jeanne Rocher*. This signature appears to apply not only to 175, as Pierre indicates, but to this piece as well.

174. (8)

175. (9)
  With 173 (see above).
  To manuscript reference, add *p. 48.*

176.
  L'Assemblée des notables pot-pourri. Incorrectly listed under 1789.
This satiric piece attacks Calonne and the Assembly of Notables, and
belongs, therefore, to the year 1787.

177.
  As the title indicates, this piece concerns the *Assemblée des notables.*
Internal evidence suggests that the subject is the first gathering, which
met in 1787. In the opening stanza, a tribute is paid to Eschouchard,
who, according to a footnote appearing in this song, "made an excellent
discourse on the Assembly of Notables in 1787." The fact that the year
is thus specified would seem to indicate that the piece in question was
not published until a subsequent year, which one may judge from internal evidence to have been 1788.

178. (14)
  Le 23 Mai 1789, which Pierre has set off in parentheses, is subjoined
to the title; it serves as a caption to introduce the first three stanzas, at
least, and perhaps the song as a whole.

178*.
  Attributable to 1788. This piece, *L'heureux retour du Parlement,*
contains the following lines,

  Les trois ordres assemblées
  Pour le salut de la France . . . ,

which at first sight seem to indicate the gathering at Versailles, 1789.
On closer inspection, one finds the reference to be to the meeting of
the three orders in Dauphiné the preceding year; the *parlement* referred to in the title being that of Grenoble. There are repeated tributes in the song to the "premier Président" and specific mention of
Berulle (stanza 8), who was the First President of the Grenoble *Parlement.* This song is followed by another piece, 235*, which is a diatribe
clearly directed against Brienne, who was Minister at the time of the
Dauphiné uprising.
  In the listing in the Pierre *Catalogue,* strike out *par Berulle,* whose
name, as indicated above, appears in the text of the song. There is no
authorship indicated in the one extant copy of the piece.
  The verb *remplis,* not *accomplis,* appears in the first air indicated in
the text.

179. (11)
  Pierre gives two library references, both to items at the Bibliothèque Nationale. The first of these, *Vm⁷ 7094,* is reported there as

having been lost. The references are apparently to different editions, since the one available does not contain the lines which Pierre quotes, *Couplets chantés le 18 mai . . .*, etc.

The second reference should be completed to read *Vm⁷ 16683*. Add a third reference, *Plaintes et doléances . . . 1789*, p. 31; see Bibliography I, 11, b.

180. (13)

This piece satirizes the sixteen commissioners chosen by the Third Estate on May 19, to bring about an agreement between the three orders. It is a precursor of the anti-Revolutionary songs which appeared later in the year, and, so far as is known, is the only song of its kind ascribable to the spring of 1789.

The word *pot-pourri* given by Pierre is descriptive; it does not appear in the text.

The two references are to the same edition. The second Bibl. nat. reference should read *Rés. Ye. 3079*.

180*. (21)

In one of the prose passages interpolated in this *chanson poissarde* a tribute is paid to the nobles who have voluntarily joined the Third Estate (in the song itself, the Duke of Orleans is praised for having done so), and there follows a threat against those who should fail to follow their example. This indicates that the piece was composed after July 25, the date when Orleans joined, and presumably before the Royal Session of June 27, which settled the controversy. In the Pierre listing, it should follow 187.

This item bears the imprint, "édition nouvelle." To the reference given, add *pièce 2*.

181. (15)

The first reference is to an item reported lost at the Bibliothèque Nationale; see 179. Concerning the next two items, see Bibliography I, 15, a and b. In respect to these two editions, for Pierre's spelling, *harengères*, read *harangères*. Text at British Museum not consulted.

181*. (67)

This song, in which reference is made to the King's residence at Paris as a result of the October insurrection, belongs with the Pierre group 237*-243.

It is anti-Revolutionary, and appeared, along with 183*, in *Etrennes à la nation*, which bears the date *1789*. Pierre does not mention the date either in connection with the song (*Catalogue*, p. 400), or in his bibliographical listing of the pamphlet (*ibid.*, p. 167, no. 327).

For an additional reference, see *Etrennes . . .*, Bibliography, II, D.

181**. *Chanson patriotique.* Air: *d'Azemia.*

The first line, "Parlons un peu de ces édits," refers to the edicts of Brienne which the *Parlement* refused to register and which caused a crisis in the summer of 1787. Although Brienne is not named in the song, mention is made of Lamoignon, who supported the edicts, and there are allusions to *lettre de cachet* and *lit de justice,* as well as to other phases of the crisis that led to the exile of *Parlement* in August, 1787. One may say categorically that in attributing this song to 1789, Pierre is in error, as is, also, Damade, who in the *Histoire chantée . . . ,* pp. 76-77, gives it under 1790. I have depended on the text as it appears in Damade, since the original was not among the items in the *dossier* (Bibl. V.P. 23918) to which Pierre makes reference.

182. (5)

The position which Pierre gives to this song, as coming at the end of the gathering of the Estates General, is misleading. The piece celebrates the double representation accorded to the Third Estate on December 27, 1788, and ends in praise of Louis for having convoked the Estates General. It was presumably written in anticipation of the gathering, and may be regarded as one of the first songs of 1789. To title as given, add *Addressé à la Nation.* In "air," for *et' chien* read *êt' un chien.*

182*. (6)

This song, as is the case with the one above, should come considerably earlier in the Pierre listing; for it, too, appears from internal evidence to have been written in anticipation of the gathering of the Estates General.

The first two references are to the same edition. Text at British Museum not consulted.

183.

A retrospective piece by T. Rousseau, first published in 1792. See Appendix C.

183*. (68)

This is an anti-Revolutionary song, published in *Etrennes à la nation,* which appeared after the October insurrection; see 181*. It belongs with the Pierre group 237*-243.

Concerning references, see *Etrennes . . . ,* II, D.

184. (4)

Internal evidence suggests that this song appeared somewhat earlier than Pierre's listing indicates.

Of the four references given, the first three are to the same edition. To the reference *Bibl. V.P. 23918* add *pièce 30.* Another edition has come to my attention in the New York Public Library; see Bibliography II, B, under *Cahier du Marquis de Fulvy.* Concerning Pierre's fourth reference, *Almanach des Muses . . . 1790*, see *ibid.*, II, F.

185.

A retrospective piece by T. Rousseau, first published in 1792; see Appendix C.

Le Chansonnier patriote bears the date *an 1 de la République*.

In addition to the Bibl. Sén. reference given for *L'Ame du peuple et du soldat*, add *Arch. nat.* A.D. VII *35, pièce 35.*

186.

A retrospective piece by T. Rousseau, first published in 1792; see Appendix C. To title add *par T. Rousseau.* (The song is from his *Les Chantes . . . etc.*, 1792.) In quotation of the first line, for *maîtres* read *Ministres.*

187. (16)

This song celebrates the stand taken by the Third Estate in defying Louis's command on the occasion of the Royal Session, June 23, 1789. The fact that it appeared only in *La France régénérée . . .* indicates, as shown below, that it was not published until some weeks later.

La France régénérée . . . is a brochure containing in addition to this piece other songs as follows: 205*, in praise of the clergy and nobles who voluntarily joined the Third Estate; 243*, in praise of the National Assembly; and 192, celebrating the capture of the Bastille.

188.

La Trahison du Prince Lorrain. This patriotic piece is an attack on Lambesc, and refers apparently to July 12, 1789. Its first known appearance, however, was with two other pieces, Pierre 405 and 413, the latter of which fixes the date of publication as coming after the massacre of Nancy in August, 1790. For this reason, and because internal evidence suggests a later mood, it seems advisable to assign it, not to 1789, but to the following year.

The author's name, Bernard Cercey, should not be in brackets, as it appears in print at the end of this song.

Precede library reference by *La Tonsure ou Plaintes . . .* , p. 3.

(For fuller entry, see same, Bibliography III, C.)

189.

The general atmosphere of this song, together with mention of the fact that the Bastille has been razed and inclusion of lines addressed to the *Gardes Françaises réunis*, indicate that the song relates to the Festival of Federation on the anniversary of the capture of the Bastille, and that it should therefore be assigned to 1790.

Par Mlle Disdier is not in the text at the Bibl. Sén., in which the song is anonymous, nor is there any mention of the publisher Coulubrier. The other reference which Pierre gives is to an item that has been reported lost at the Bibl. nat.; see 179.

190. (37†)

This song on the capture of the Bastille appeared in print twice, on each occasion in a small brochure of songs published by Valleyre. It is difficult to determine whether the earliest publication of the piece was at the time of the capture in 1789, or at that of the anniversary celebration of the following year.

Certainly one of the brochures, *Le Savetier bon patriote*, must be ascribed to 1790, for it contains a song by Ladré (Pierre #437) on the law abolishing titles of nobility. This law was passed June 19, 1790, and one may suppose that the song on the Bastille was added because of the excitement which prevailed at about that time over the celebration of the first Bastille anniversary.

In regard to the Ladré song, the serial number in the Pierre *Catalogue* should, according to my view, be not 437, which relegates it to the latter part of the year 1790, but 299 approx., which would place it ahead of songs on the Festival of Federation.

There is no similar means by which to fix the date of the other brochure, since in it the song on the Bastille is accompanied by popular lyrics of no political import. This brochure, *Entretien d'un vieillard . . .* , might also have come out in 1790; or it might have been brought out shortly after the capture, and the song on the Bastille rerun nearly a year later when the subject was again topical. I see no way of settling the matter definitely, and in ascribing this piece to 1789, I have done so with reservations, which are referred to in the text.

The two library references should be separated, as they refer to different editions; see Bibliography I, 37†.

191.

A retrospective piece by T. Rousseau, first published in 1792; see Appendix C.

191*.

La prise de la Bastille ou Paris sauvé, chant national, par un citoyen de Paris, musique de P. Ligny. Date uncertain, but later than 1789. That the piece is retrospective is indicated in the opening stanza—"Already the threads of memory . . . consecrate this noble deed in our history"; and by the style, which is artificial and does not suggest the enthusiasms of the moment.

This song on the capture of the Bastille is known only through its appearance in post-Revolutionary anthologies. One of these, *Poésies revolutionnaires . . .* 1821, is cited by Pierre (for *p. 28*, read *vol. 1, p. 28*). An additional reference is as follows: *Poésies nationales . . .* , 1836, p. 13.

192. (36)

In title, after *le siège*, add *et la prise*.

There are two versions of this song on the Bastille, concerning which see Bibliography I, 36. The first publication of the piece appears to have been in *La France régénérée* (edition "a"), which contains in addition to this item three songs inspired by the events of June—see 187. The second version of 192 carries three new stanzas, in which tributes are paid to individual heroes; this version appears in a fragment which contains also Déduit's *Ni vu ni connu*, written subsequent to November 2—see 245.

Pierre's two references are not to the same edition, as would appear in the *Catalogue*, and should be supplemented with the information given in Bibliography I, 36.

193. (31)

In the original, the air is *de Malbrouck*, not *de Malborough*, which Pierre gives.

194. (29)

For reproduction of all matter on title page see Bibliography I, 29. This piece was shown at the *Exposition de la Révolution française* of the Bibliothèque Nationale, 1928. It is item 41 (p. 21) in the catalogue of the exposition.

Pierre's two references are to different editions; concerning these, and for additional library references, see *Chanson sur la prise . . .*, Bibliography II, B.

194*. (33)

The only reference given by Pierre is to an item reported lost at the Bibl. Nat. The shelf number is Vm⁷ 7094, which as one may determine from one of Pierre's tables (*op.cit.*, p. 176), refers to a group of eight songs published with music (in the table, *194*, should read *194**). Of the eight songs, five are known by other copies or editions; but, besides 194*, two others, 203 and 204, are known only in connection with this group.

195.

La conversion des aristocrates. This is an amusing piece, in which the aristocrat is pictured as overwhelmed by his plight; filled with remorse over the privileges he has enjoyed, he now says his *mea culpa*. Ridicule of exactly this sort was prevalent in popular writings just after the Assembly abolished titles of nobility, June 19, 1790. Pierre, I have no doubt, is wrong in ascribing this piece to 1789, especially since its only known appearance was in a brochure with a *Chanson patriotique* (Pierre, *op.cit.*, p. 494, song 328) which refers explicitly to the abolition of the titles of nobility, and which Pierre himself ascribes to 1790.

196.

A retrospective piece by T. Rousseau, first published in 1792. See Appendix C.

197.

Also T. Rousseau, 1792. See Appendix C.

198.
Couplets patriotiques. Date uncertain; presumably later than 1789. The only known appearance of the song was in a brochure which contained also *Chanson sur les émigrants,* a piece which Monglond (*op. cit.,* vol. i, col. 1157) lists under 1789, but which Pierre (*op.cit.,* p. 565, no. 695**) ascribes to 1792. Although I do not know on what basis Pierre selected the latter date, internal evidence suggests that the *Chanson sur les émigrants* and hence the brochure itself, were later than 1789.

> Precede library reference by *Chanson sur les émigrants* (see *ibid.,* Bibliography III, C).

199. (38)
The two references are to the same edition.

200. (39)
The two references are to the same edition. To *Bibl. V.P. 19767,* add *No. 12.*

201. (34)
The first title which Pierre gives for this song is that which appears over the only known contemporary text, published in the *Journal de Paris,* July 22, 1789.

As far as I can discover, the *autre titre* which he subjoins without explanation or reference occurs for the first time in Damade's *Histoire chantée* . . . , 1892, p. 18. The information conveyed in Damade's title, *Couplets composés et chantés,* etc., is to be found in a prose passage which preceded the song in the *Journal de Paris.*

202. (47)
At end of title (after *1789*) add *par M. Bavouz, Citoyen du District de l'Oratoire.*

> Pierre's reference to the words of this piece, which was originally published as a poem and subsequently put to music, should be completed to read: *Affiches, Annonces . . . ou Journal général . . . , 19 août 1789,* no. 231, p. 2394. His reference to "Musique . . . (etc.)" is perhaps misleading; since no score is given in the *Affiches, annonces . . .* of April 29, 1790, but simply the notice, which Pierre quotes.

> Reference should be given to the separate publication of this song in a leaflet, of which there are two editions. See *Tribut lyrique . . . ,* Bibliography II, B.

203. (48)
The only reference given by Pierre is to an item reported lost at the Bibliothèque Nationale; see 179.

204. (45)
Ditto (203).
This piece, as the title indicates, is in celebration of the return of

Necker to Versailles. As a matter of chronological exactitude, I have placed it ahead of 202, which concerns the reception accorded Necker on his arrival at Paris. In his biographical work, *Necker (1732-1804)*, Chapuisat brings together interesting information concerning the Minister's return from Basel; his reception at Versailles, July 28 and 29 (see letter of Tronchin to Puerari, pp. 313-14); and concerning his visit to Paris, July 30 (see pp. 191-92).

205. (49)

205*. (24)

This song *Les trois ordres réunis*, concerning June 27, 1789, is known only through its appearance in *La France régénérée . . .* , published after July 14. See 187.

After title, add *Suite* (relative to 187, which precedes this piece).

206. (28)

A high degree of precision is possible in establishing this piece chronologically. It bears the date "Juillet, 1789"; furthermore, as an allusion in the text to the cooperation of the King and his Minister reveals, it appeared before the 12th of that month, when news of Necker's dismissal reached Paris. It should therefore have been listed by Pierre with his pre-Bastille group, previous to 188.

In title, for *bât* read *bas*. For reproduction of all matter on title page, see Bibliography I, 28.

All three references are to the same brochure, *Où le bas . . .* , in-8°, 30 pp.; the third, however, *Bibl. V.P. 23918* (to which add *pièce 20*) is to a fragment of the same, pp. 1-16.

207.

This entry does not refer to the text of a song, but rather to a musical score, which was mentioned, but not printed, in the *Affiches, annonces . . .* for April 29, 1790. The music is to accompany the words of *Tribut lyrique*, see 202.

This is one of two such notices, both in the *Affiches, annonces . . .* of the same date. Pierre separates them, mentioning one under the entry 202, and listing under a new number the one under consideration here. In thus isolating the latter, he should assign it to 1790, rather than to 1789. It has seemed to me preferable to treat both scores alike and to mention them both in connection with *Tribut lyrique*; see Bibliography I, 47, d.

Chacone, the title word, is the name of a popular dance; in the original it is spelled *Chaconne*.

208.

A retrospective piece by T. Rousseau, first published in 1792. See Appendix C.

To *Chansonnier patr., an 1ᵉʳ*, add *de la Répub*. To *Rec. chrono-*

logique, add *VIIIᵉ année de la Répub. fr.* To the references given, add *L'Ame du peuple* . . . , *Arch. nat. VIII 35, pièce 34.*

209. (32)

This song, *Chanson des bourgeois de Paris*, is in celebration of the capture of the Bastille, and belongs with the Pierre group 189-194*.

The first reference is to an item reported lost at the Bibliothèque Nationale; see 179. The only copy of this piece which I have found is that at Bibl. Sén. I have no knowledge of the text listed as having been in the Bibl. Paul Lacombe, except that Pierre's mention of *Paroles, imp. Gueffier* indicates a different edition from the one consulted.

210. (50)

After title add *par M. Imbert.* (The author is described as a member of the *Académie de Nismes.* See Bibliography I, 50.)

To *Alm. des Muses, 1790,* add *p. 161.*

211.

Les bienfaits du roi. Air: Bonnes gens.

The only text referred to by Pierre is reported as having belonged to the collection of J.-B. Weckerlin. The collection was sold subsequent to the publication of Pierre's book, and I have been unable to trace the item in question. It may be that this piece, which Pierre identifies as No. 350* in the music series of Frère, should be ascribed to a year considerably earlier than 1789. In any case, on the basis of Pierre's own survey of Frère publications (*Les hymnes et chansons* . . . , p. 117), a song in that series numbered 350* would seem to be ascribable to approximately 1784.

212.

This piece, entitled *La journée de Louis XVI, ou discours du meilleur des rois*, refers, I take it, to February 4, 1790, when Louis XVI made a highly conciliatory speech before the National Assembly. Among other telling allusions in the text of the song is that to the King's promise—made at that time—to inculcate in the Dauphin a proper respect for the principles of reform. This promise, which had popular appeal, was given immediate publicity by patriotic writers. There are other allusions in the song suggestive of the speech on February 4, notably the emphasis on *la loi*, in the sense of Louis' professed endorsement, February 4, of the Constitution.

In the title, as given by Pierre, insert *ou* before *discours.* In the original, *pot-pourri* does not appear as part of the title; and Déduit's name is followed by the words *auteur patriotique.*

213. (54)

For reproduction of a dedication following the title, see Bibliography I, 54.

Only the first of Pierre's references is to a complete text. His citation of the *Affiches, annonces* . . . , *du 26 août* (add *1789*) should be corrected to indicate that not the "paroles," but a notice and the first stanza only, appear in this journal.

To the reference *Alm. des Muses*, add *1790, p. 317.*

214.

A retrospective piece by T. Rousseau. None of the four works to which Pierre refers this song antedate 1792. See Appendix C. The item which Monglond lists (see below) may have been somewhat earlier.

To *Les chants du patr.*, add *1792, p. 96.*

The following entry appears in Monglond (vol. i, col. 524): *Déclaration des droits de l'homme et du citoyen, les 20, 21, 22, 23 et 26 avril* [sic.—i.e., Monglond] *1789, (Paris), imp. de Migneret, in-8.* [N.d.]

215.

This song appeared in the *Almanach de la mère Gérard*, which is mentioned in many bibliographies, being everywhere described, so far as I know, as anonymous. In Appendix C, I give reasons for ascribing this work to T. Rousseau. The date of publication is presumably 1791.

To Bibl. V.P., add *pièce 51.*

216. (55)

The two library references are to different editions (see Bibliography I, 55); and *Imp. Garnery . . .* , etc., which follows the title in Pierre's entry applies only to the item referred to at Arch. nat. Add as an additional reference *Chansonnier national ou recueil . . . , 1790, p. 2.* Concerning this item, see same, Bibliography II, C.

217. (56)

This piece, *La Cocarde nationale . . .* , was originally published, in 1789, anonymously. Years later it was revised and appeared under the name of *C. Mercier de Compiègne*; see Bibliography I, 56. Pierre gives Mercier's name, but in brackets without explanation.

The statement which Pierre provides concerning successive editions is from *Le Temple de la Liberté . . .* , p. 57, where it appears as a footnote. The first printing—"in the month of August, 1789"—no doubt refers to the item at the Bibl. Sén. The text in this edition praises Louis and Necker, and is entirely in the spirit of the first year of the Revolution.

The song next appeared in *Chansonnier de la Montagne . . . , l'an 2,* with the second stanza omitted, and with some interesting modifications, among them replacement of the line,

"Necker revient, un astre brille,"
by the line,

"L'astre de la liberté brille";
and replacement of the lines,

"Le blanc est la couleur de lis,
De l'Etat les lis sont l'image,"

by the lines,

> "Le blanc annonce la candeur
> D'âme vraiment républicaine."

To the reference *Chansonnier de la Mont*, add *l'an 2* (this work had a sequel, *l'an 3*). Add, also, *p. 104*. Concerning various editions and corresponding library references, see same, Bibliography II, F.

To *Le Temple de la Liberté*, add *3e Année Répub.*

218. (69†)

The position given in the *Catalogue* to *Le troubadour béarnais* is misleading, for the song concerns the plight of the King after the October insurrection. It should follow Pierre's group 236-40*.

This is a Royalist song, of which there are two manuscript editions, both with music, at the Bibl. nat. The opening measures reproduced by Pierre correspond to the score in mss. fr. 12755, which consists of this one piece. The other manuscript edition, in which this piece appears under the title *Choeur béarnais*, includes, also, the Royalist song 243, below.

The earliest publication of *Le troubadour béarnais* with which I am familiar is that in *Les actes des apôtres*, no. 29, which appeared in January, 1790. I am not familiar with the item referred to by Pierre as having been in the Bibl. P. Lacombe.

Pierre refers to a musical score printed in *Les actes des apôtres*, no. 28, p. 13, as does also M. H. Monin in his *Etudes révolutionnaires: La chanson historique pendant la Révolution . . .*, in the *Revue bleue*, February 8, 1890, p. 177. I have never seen the score, and presume that it may have been detachable, as I have examined three different copies of no. 28 of *Les actes des apôtres*, which, though apparently intact, do not contain it.

To references given add *Actes des apôtres, No. 29, p. 13*. Concerning Pierre's reference to no. 28 of this journal, see paragraph above. To reference *L'ami du roi . . .*, add *almanach . . . pour l'année 1792*.

219.

Later than 1789. This piece warns against the plots of the reactionaries; praises Marat. There is an allusion in the text to the complaint of the merchant that the people have no wealth save *assignats*. The *assignats* were not voted by the Assembly until December 19, 1789, and did not come into general use until considerably later.

This song has been bound with other pieces in a volume at the Bibliothèque Nationale, marked 1789, a misleading inclusion, as indicated by the evidence in the preceding paragraph.

The two references are to the same edition.

220. (59)

In this song an anonymous author inveighs, for fifty-six stanzas of four lines each, against the clergy. There is nothing by way of internal evidence to establish its date beyond question, but the piece has several of the features of the songs of 1789 and apparently reflects certain events and trends of late August and September of that year. For further discussion, see pages 201-03.

The absence of any reference in the song to acts of an anticlerical nature, such as began to go into effect from the end of 1789, though not in itself conclusive, helps to confirm my impression that the piece did not appear later than that year. These acts included the confiscation of Church property, November 2 and December 19, 1789; the abolition of monasteries and convents, February 13, 1790; and the Civil Constitution of the clergy, July 12, 1790. Anticlerical songs written subsequent to these acts customarily alluded to them, or to their effects.

> The four references are to the same brochure, *Le voile levé*. There were at least two printings of this work, as indicated by minor variations in the text of the item at Bibl. nat. Ye 43916 (cf., for example, stanza 1, v. 3) from the texts of the other three items mentioned. The four available copies are alike in make-up, bear identical colophons (pp. 3 and 12), and are apparently by the same publisher, whose name is not given.
>
> Complete second Bibl. nat. reference to read *Rés. Ye 3084*. Delete asterisk after Bibl. V.P. reference, and add *pièce 108*.

221. (60)

This piece, an anticlerical satire, appears in *Le Voile levé* with 220, above.

> To references given add *Bibl. nat. Rés. Ye 3084* and *Bibl. Sén., carton 8, cote 457*. Concerning a second printing, and correction of Bibl. V.P. reference, see 220, above.

222.

Chanson nouvelle, sur l'air de la "Vieille méthode": "Puisque j'ai loisir. . . . "

The library reference given by Pierre is incomplete, and I have been unable to locate this item at the Bibliothèque Nationale, or elsewhere.

223.

Romance de Mlle. de ----, adressée au chevalier de ---- par M. Goidard. This piece appears to me to be nonpolitical and to show no evidence of relating to the year 1789. It belongs to the Frère series of musical publications, issued in the form of *feuilles volantes*, and bears the Frère serial number 612; printed with it is Frère No. 789, which Pierre ascribes to 1795 (*op.cit.*, p. 758, song 1764). There is some reason to suppose that Pierre has attempted to date the *Romance* . . . on the basis of the Frère serial number; see *op.cit.*, p. 117. But since most of the Frère publications are lost—only one, No. 417, remaining between this piece and No. 323, which goes back to 1783—the Frère serial numbers of this period are of little help in dating.

Precede Bibl. Sén. reference by *Couplets au peuple français . . .* (see in Bibliography III, A).

224.

A retrospective piece by T. Rousseau, first published in 1792; see Appendix C. For *Cornalie* read *Cornélies*.

225.

This "Chanson," published in the *Chronique de Paris, 12 septembre, 1789,* was designated in an editorial comment as "faite en 1776."

To *Chronique de Paris* reference, add *1789.*

226. (57)

227. (58)

For titles following author's name (spelled in the original, *Ducray du Minil*) see Bibliography I, 58.

The text at the British Museum comprises a four-page leaflet.

Pierre's reproduction is of the first stanza only.

Concerning mention by Monglond of another edition see Bibliography I, 58, b.

228.

A retrospective piece by T. Rousseau, first published in 1792. See Appendix C.

228*.

The line "Sur le don de l'argenterie du roi," which Pierre appends to the entry on this song, does not appear in the published text, and is apparently his explanatory comment. To me, however, it seems erroneous, for I take the song, which opens "Ta démarche sublime . . . ," to refer to the King's speech before the National Assembly on February 4, 1790. Louis spoke at that time without an express invitation and supposedly without prompting (though it has since become well known that this was not the case). "Démarche" was the word currently used, both in and out of the Assembly, to describe his sudden and welcome visit. (Mention of this occasion is made also in connection with song 212.)

Another indication that "démarche sublime" referred to this appearance of Louis before the Assembly is the emphasis, occurring both in the song and in prose that accompanied it, on a prospective reconciliation of the aristocrats with the Revolution, something which Louis had stressed in his speech at that time, and of which much was made by the patriots.

Furthermore, there is evidence that the pamphlet *Le numéraire aux Parisiens,* in which this song appeared, was published at about the time of Louis' speech of February 4. In a prose passage, *ibid.,* p. 1, the complaint is made that the *écus* have been scarce for eight months, since Frenchmen became free. The eight months should date from July, or possibly June, 1789.

This view, arrived at independently on the basis of internal evidence, I find confirmed in Tourneux, who mentions *Le numéraire aux Parisiens* . . . (vol. iii, no. 12943) and describes the song which it contains as having been made "en honneur du discours prononcé par Louis XVI, le 4 février, 1790."

228**.

Sur le don patriotique des boucles d'argent, par Piis.

The only source which Pierre gives for this entry is "Chansons nat . . . , p. 68." Contrary to his usual practice, he has failed to designate a library reference. I have examined a number of works, especially those by Piis, but have been unable to find the song. It does not appear in that author's *Chansons patriotiques, Paris, an 2ᵉ*.

229.

A retrospective piece by T. Rousseau, first published in 1792; see Appendix C.

230. (27)

This song celebrates the King's command, June 27, 1789, that the two noble orders meet with the Third; and there are indications in the text which suggest that the piece appeared before the July events. On the basis of this analysis, it should be advanced from its present position in the *Catalogue* with the items of September, to follow Pierre's item 187.

231.

Chanson sur les affaires du temps, a quaint and homely protest against privilege, is attributable to 1788. Various lines of the piece suggest that it was composed before the summoning of the Estates General. A pamphlet in which it was published, *Requête des curés de France au roi*, presumably relates to the *Remonstrances* of the clergy to the King, June 15, 1788. Two of Pierre's three references are to this item; his third is to Bibl. Paul Lacombe, a collection which I have been unable to locate.

The song is available in a different edition from the one mentioned above, in the White Collection of the Cornell University Library (4187, C 43, no. 24). It appears here as the first of two songs in a four-page leaflet, entitled *Chansons sur les affaires du temps*. The second of the two songs, which opens "Du haut en bas,/ Et les Prélats & la Noblesse . . . ," is not mentioned by Pierre. This piece was inspired, one may infer, by announcement of the summoning of the Estates General. It was written perhaps shortly after the recall, August 25, 1788, of Necker, to whom there is a tribute in the final stanza.

The Bibl. nat. reference should be completed to read *Rés. Ye 3092*. It should follow *Requête des curés* (etc.), as does the reference to Bibl. V.P. Add mention of edition in *Chansons sur les affaires du temps*; see above, and *ibid.*, Bibliography III, C.

232. (18)
This song, together with 233 and 234 below, appeared in the brochure *Nouveau pot-pourri sur les affaires du temps*, dated *1789*. The topical allusions contained in these songs are all to the events of late June. In stanza 12 of 232, resentment is expressed against De Juigny, the unpopular Archbishop of Paris who was attacked by a mob on June 24. Song 233 touches on the same theme; 234 celebrates the day, June 25, when the Duke of Orleans and other nobles joined the newly created National Assembly. These pieces appear to have been written before July 14, and presumably should be listed in the *Catalogue* of Pierre previous to the group 189-94*.
For *du Mis*, read *de Madame*.
Insert before the library references, *Nouveau pot-pourri . . . , 1789, p. 1*. To *Bibl. V.P. 23918* add *pièce 50*. The two references are to the same edition.

233. (19)
The only known printing of this piece was in the brochure *Nouveau pot-pourri . . .* , concerning which see 232.
To *Nouveau pot-pourri* add *1789*. Concerning library references see note, 232 above.

234. (20)
This song was included with the two above in the *Nouveau pot-pourri . . .* , concerning which see 232. The first line of the song, as it appears in this brochure, is faulty; see Bibliography I, 20, c. The imprint line which Pierre subjoins to the title relates to the *Nouveau pot-pourri*, but to none other of the items to which reference is made. For *M. de Polignac*, read *Madame de Polignac*.
The library references, as given, are jumbled: only the first and fourth which follow *Nouveau pot-pourri . . .* refer to that work. To the latter of these, add *pièce 50*. The second reference should be separate. The third relates to Edition gravée (mentioned on the line below) as does the Bibl. nat. reference which follows that entry. For a recapitulation of the editions by which this song is known, see Bibliography I, 20.

235.
A retrospective piece by T. Rousseau, first published in *Alm. de la mère Gérard* (1791). See Appendix C.

235*.
Attributable to 1788. See 178*, with which this song appeared.
Precede reference by *L'heureux retour du Parlement . . .* , p. 3.

236.

This piece, *Complainte de Marie-Antoinette* . . . , appeared only in *La Constitution française en chansons* . . . , published in 1792. This work (published anonymously) was by Sylvain Maréchal, whose name may be added as author of the song.

To *La Constitution*, etc., add *1792*.

237.

A retrospective piece by T. Rousseau, first published in 1792. See Appendix C.

237*. (66)

To reference given, add *pièce 1-ter*.

237**.

This song cannot safely be assigned to 1789; it seems to have been composed later, and is preserved only in a manuscript which, as Pierre indicates, bears the date "therm. an II." (For entry concerning same, see Bibliography III, G, under *Couplets pour les gardes françaises*. . . .)

The Arch. nat. reference should read F^{17}, *1010^D (Dos. 3961)*. This correction is occasioned by the revised system of cataloguing adopted by the Archives Nationales since the appearance of Pierre's work.

238. (42)

Internal evidence suggests that this piece (for consideration of, see page 143) relates to the summer of 1789. It should have been listed by Pierre presumably with the post-Bastille group of songs, and certainly not, as is the case in the *Catalogue*, with those concerning October 5-6.

For *par Mme Dupray*, read *composée par Mme Dupray*; and add *Approuvée par M. le Maire de Paris*.

239.

Le beau Varicour . . . , a romantic piece concerning the October insurrection, appeared in two works, *Le Constitution française en chansons* . . . by Sylvain Maréchal, and *Les chants du patriotisme*. . . . by T. Rousseau, both published in 1792. Pierre incorrectly attributes the song to T. Rousseau; though Monin (*op.cit.*, p. 176) had recognized Maréchal as the author. To dispel any doubt, one has only to refer to the statement made by Rousseau in his *Les chants du patriotisme*, p. 156. Concerning *Le beau Varicour*, he explains in a footnote: "Cette pièce est de M. Sylvain Maréchal . . . ce jeune auteur qui vient de nous donner la 'Constitution Française en chansons. . . .'"

239*.

This song on the October insurrection is known only by its inclusion in a book of songs by "la citoyenne veuve Ferrand," which carried a calendar for 1793 and presumably appeared late in the preceding year.

To *Triomphe de la liberté*, add [*1792*].

239**. (63)

This piece is the third in a brochure, *Le voyage du roi . . .*, etc., which contains four songs: p. 1, 240*; p. 4, *Autre chanson—"Dans ce monde chacun raisonne . . ."* (an item not included in the Pierre *Catalogue*); p. 5, the item referred to here; and p. 7, 240.

> *Le Voyage du roi . . . , p. 5* should precede library reference. To *Bibl. nat. Ye 35763*, add *pièce 13*.

240. (64)

Concerning the brochure in which this song appears, see 239**.

> *Le Voyage du roi . . . , p. 7* should precede library reference. To *Bibl. nat. Ye 35763*, add *pièce 13*.

240*. (61)

This piece, *Le voyage du roi . . .*, is the leading item in the brochure first mentioned in connection with 239**, above. The pamphlet, 8 pp., is in-12. The song was also published separately, 4 pp., in-8. Monglond, *op.cit.*, vol. i, col. 530, mentions the edition in-12, and an edition in-8, dated 1789. I have no knowledge of the item attributed to Bibl. P. Lacombe.

> The two Bibl. nat. references should be separated; the second to be preceded by *Le voyage du roi . . . , p. 1*, and followed by *pièce 13*.

241.

This piece by T. Rousseau on the *Installation de l'Assemblée nationale constituante à Paris le 19 octobre 1789*, appears in his *Les chants du patriotisme . . . , 1792*, as one of a series of songs written to celebrate "les époques les plu intéressantes de la Révolution." The song probably dates from 1792, though possibly an edition referred to by Pierre as having been in the Bibl. P. Lacombe came earlier. In general, there is no proof that Rousseau was engaged as early as 1789 in celebrating the Revolution in song, and ample evidence that the songs which he wrote concerning the events of that year were part of an educational program undertaken by him about 1791.

242.

A retrospective piece by T. Rousseau, first published in 1792; see Appendix C.

243. (70†)

Romance du troubadour parisien; but the title more generally used seems to be *Le troubadour parisien, romance*; see Bibliography 1, 70†.

This anti-Revolutionary piece on the King's residence at Paris following the October insurrection was published in *Les actes des apôtres*, no. 61, which appeared about March 1, 1790. The song was published also in an undated brochure (Bibl. nat. Ye 3099) which may have appeared considerably earlier. There are two references (Bibl. nat. Ye

21001 and 3022) which I have not consulted. The following lines in stanza 11,

> "Qu'il aille au nouveau printemps
> Voir ses château de plaisance!"

suggest, though they do not prove absolutely, that the song was composed after the turn of the year. In the absence of fuller information, I am inclined to classify this piece as possibly 1789, probably 1790; though Pierre in his Introduction (*op.cit.* pp. 35-36) writes categorically, "De cette année [1789] datent la fameuse romance royaliste 'le Troubadour béarnais' [69†-*218*] et sa parodie 'le Troubadour parisien.'"

Concerning the manuscript edition of this song, see Bibliography I, 70†, a.

In the reference to *Actes des apôtres,* for *p. 4,* read *p. 14.*

243*. (25)

The *Chanson sur l'Assemblée nationale* was known to Pierre through its publication in *La France régénérée,* of which the leading piece (see 192) celebrates the capture of the Bastille. Song no. 243* relates to the events of June, and one is at a loss to know why Pierre assigns it to the autumn of 1789, unless he took the lines, "Les Nobles abandonnant Tous droits pécuniaires," as an allusion to the August decrees. The general tenor of the song, and the phrasing of the particular allusion, indicate that reference is made to the abolition of the *droits pécuniaires* on May 20-23. After title, add *(par de Joyenval);* see Bibliography I, 25, a.

Concerning possibly another edition, see Bibliography I, 25, b.

244.

Pierre indicates as the only known text of this anticlerical song that in *Le chansonnier patriote, ou recueil* . . . of Ladré, which is dated 1791. (Other pieces in this eight-page brochure are those listed by Pierre, *op.cit.,* as 464, 549*, 570*, and 571*.) I am inclined not to attribute this piece to 1789, even though the song appears in an apparently undated item (mounted and bound, with page numbers, etc., obliterated) at the Cl. Publ. Libr. (W841.04-C452, vol. i, no. 117).

The reference *Bibl. nat. Ye 35763* should be preceded by *Le chansonnier patr. ou recueil . . . , 1791,* and followed by *pièce 5.*

245. (73)

There is an allusion in stanza three of this song to the distress of the clergy occasioned by *des nouvelles loix,* namely—as internal evidence indicates—the decrees on the Church lands, passed by the Assembly on November 2, 1789.

The two library references should be broken down to indicate different editions; and a third reference, Bibl. V.P. 9312, added. For a résumé of same, and for mention of yet another edition, see Bibliography I, 73.

246. (71)

Pierre's sole reference, *Chronique de Paris, 18 mai, 1790,* is to the reproduction of but the third stanza of this piece, which is cited in the course of journalistic comment on the song. One may, however, find a text which appears to be complete and which is accompanied by information concerning the publisher, in a post-Revolutionary work; see Bibliography I, 71, and reference below.

Add *Poésies révolutionnaires . . . , 1821, vol. i, p. 55.* Qualify reference to *Chronique de Paris* in accordance with paragraph above.

247.

A retrospective piece by T. Rousseau, first published in 1792; see Appendix C.

The title under which Pierre lists this song is from *Les chants,* etc., the alternative title being from *L'âme du peuple et du soldat.*

As an additional reference for *L'âme du peuple et du soldat,* add *Arch. nat.* A.D. VIII *35, pièce 35.*

248. (74)

249.

This *chanson poissarde* on the October insurrection is known only through its inclusion in a brochure which is dated 1790. It is a piece which may be regarded as retrospective rather than contemporaneous in tone.

The date in brackets which Pierre subjoins to the title is taken apparently from an inscription in ink on page 1 of the brochure, commencing "permis de vendre les chansons . . . ," and ending, "le 5 mai, 1790."

Precede library reference by *Alexandrine à Paris . . . , Senlis, 1790, p. 2.*

250. (76)

This is the somewhat famous *guillotine* song, which was launched in *Les actes des apôtres* in December, 1789. It seems strange that in his list of references, Pierre fails to mention its appearance in this journal.

The piece appeared not only in Royalist publications, but also in the patriotic *Journal des Révolutions de l'Europe . . . ;* see note below.

There is an edition of the song published separately (Bibl. nat. Ye. 17549); and an item at the British Museum, which I have not consulted, would appear from Pierre's listing to be substantially the same.

Pierre's reference to *Alm. des honnêtes gens . . .* is incomplete, there being several editions of this work. The precise item which he intended to indicate cannot be discovered through the Bibl. nat. reference, for the serial number given by him does not correspond to any at the library. The song is not contained in the several editions of *Alm. des honnêtes gens* which I was able to obtain at the Bibliothèque Nationale, but is to be found in the *7e edition, 1793*, at Bibl. V.P. 22649.

To references, add *Actes des apôtres, 1er vol., no. 10, p. 15*, and *Journal des Révolutions de l'Europe . . . , Neuwied, 1790, 6e vol., p. 19*.

251. (78)

The first edition of the *Prosp. d'un nouv. journal*, in which this song appeared, is dated 1789. Contained in the same pamphlet is another song, which Pierre incorrectly ascribed to 1790; see 262, below.

To the reference *Prosp. d'un nouv. journal*, add *1789, p. 21*. As additional references, add *ibid., 1790, p. 14*, and *Révolutions de France et Brabant, 1er vol., no. 8, p. 371*.

252. (75)

The text of this song is known through its publication in the *Chronique de Paris*, December 7, 1789.

For indications that a second, enlarged, edition appeared in 1790, see Bibliography I, 75, b.

253. (87†)

I have come into possession of a manuscript edition of this song, which bears a different title and is dated 1790; see Bibliography I, 87†, b.

254. (79)

To *Bibl. V.P. 23918*, add *pièce 24*. Of the two references given, I have consulted only the second. According to the system of Pierre, the references are presumably, though not necessarily, to different copies of the same item.

255.

This song is an obscene satire on Marie Antoinette, which was maliciously attributed by an anonymous publisher to M.-J. Chénier. It was included in the pamphlet, *Satyres, ou choix des meilleures pièces de vers qui ont précédé et suivi la Révolution, l'an premier de la Liberté.*

Most of the pieces included in this brochure, the *avertissement* states, "ont paru depuis 1786 jusqu' en 1790." This phrasing suggests that the pamphlet was prepared in the course of the year 1790. More precise information concerning the date of its appearance is provided by a letter of Chénier, published in the *Chronique de Paris* of June 18, 1790. In the course of a protest against the use of his name, Chénier referred to the *Satyres, ou choix . . .* as "un libelle qu' un barbouilleur . . . a publié ces jours derniers."

Tourneux does not mention the *Satyres, ou choix . . .* , but Monglond lists it, with the following note: "Contient quelques vers de Camille Desmoulins. Apollinaire signale un exemplaire (Enfer, 764) qui porte: A Paris l'an premier de la Liberté, 32 pp., frontispiece, et pour laquelle il propose la date de 1790."

In attributing this item to 1789, it may be that Pierre was guided by the date line, "l'an premier de la Liberté." Whereas "les ans de la Liberté" were frequently used by patriotic writers to correspond to the years of the Christian calendar, there is ample evidence to prove—the *Satyres, ou choix* . . . being a case in point—that there were other patriots who regarded the years of Liberty as dating from the capture of the Bastille, July 14, 1789, and extending to the same date of each successive year. Similarly, when the Revolutionists officially inaugurated their own Republican calendar, they used September 22, 1792, as the point of departure, with the result that each Republican year spanned parts of two years of the Christian calendar.

In the third reference, for *Rés. 3130* read *Rés. 3138.*

255*.

This is another of the songs which was published in the *Satyres, ou choix* . . . , attributable to 1790; see 255, above.

> Both the entry *Satyres,* and the library references to it, should be completed to resemble those given by Pierre under 255, except that the correction Bibl. nat. *Rés. Ye 3138* (for *Rés. 3130*) applies here also.

256. (82)

After *air des,* for *Bourgeois de Châtres,* read *Bourgeois de Chartres ou du Noël de la Cour.*

257. (83)

This piece is the leading item in a brochure which has as its only title that of this song, *Noël.* Also included in the brochure are songs 257* and 261. These pieces are anti-Revolutionary.

> The first three library references are to the same edition; they should be preceded by *Noël (etc.) p. 1.* I have no knowledge of the item indicated as having belonged to the Bibl. P. Lacombe.

257*. (84)

Concerning the brochure in which this piece was published, see 257, above.

> Precede the first two library references with *Noël (etc.) p. 7,* and add *Bibl. nat. Ye 48296.* Concerning reference to Bibl. P. Lacombe, see 257, above.

258. (81)

259. (86)

Pierre has modified the title, which appears in the original as *IIe Chanson nationale, Sur la conservation* . . . (etc.). The piece is by Callières. One may suppose that he had in mind his song on the capture of the Bastille (194) as his first *chanson nationale*, though it did not bear that designation.

For the reproduction of interesting matter contained on the title page of the original, see Bibliography 1, 86.

260.

A trivial, anticlerical piece of only five lines, which might have come out at almost any stage of the Revolution, and which, so far as is known, was published only in an anthology in the year VIII of the Republic.

> After *Bibl. de l'Opéra*, for *nº 6097* read *113 B*, this change being occasioned by a reclassification of material at the library since the appearance of Pierre's work.

261. (85)

Concerning the brochure in which this piece was published, see 257.

> Precede the library references given, by *Noël (etc.) p. 11*, and add *Bibl. nat. Ye 48296*, all three references being to the same edition.

262. (77)

This is the first of the items which Pierre lists under 1790. It was published in the *Prospectus d'un nouveau journal*, an edition of which is dated *1789*. See 251. Concerning this song and others in the same brochure, see text, page 227, including footnote 12.

> To the reference *Prospectus d'un nouv. journal*, add *1789, p. 13*. As an additional reference, add *ibid., 1790, p. 9*.

273.

Pierre assigns to the spring of 1790, *Les oeufs de Pâques des Français, ou la résurrection de la félicité publique; air "O filii et filiae."* There is no internal evidence in this brief piece by which conclusively to fix the date; but the title, the whole atmosphere of the song, and the air used, all suggest the spring of 1789. Though I have not assigned this piece categorically to that year, I have made mention of it in connection with the group "Anticipation of Estates General" in Bibliography 1 (page 269, footnote 1).

293. (43)

La cocarde du roi, published with music in a two-page leaflet, bears no date, but clearly should be assigned to 1789 (rather than to the following year, where Pierre places it). Stanza 2, containing the line "Les trois Ordres sont réunis," refers to the events of June 27, 1789. There are other allusions to the same time. The concluding stanza refers (as does the title) to Louis's acceptance of the tri-color cockade on the occasion of his visit to Paris, July 17 ("Louis la Cocade au chapeau/ N'aura jamais d'instant plus beau."). The final allusion is to the recall of Necker ("Pour mettre le comble à cela/ Oui par nous *Necker* restera").

315.

Ah ça ira! song by Ladré. Pierre (*op.cit.*, pp. 477-93) gives a résumé of conflicting views concerning date, authorship, editions, etc., of this famous Revolutionary song. In the course of an extended analysis, he takes into account the contention—supported by Castil-Blaze, G. Kastner, and G. Chouquet—that *Ça ira* made its appearance as early as 1789. Pierre nevertheless concludes, as do most other students of the subject, that the piece first appeared on the eve of the Festival of Federation of July 14, 1790.

There is an interesting discussion by A. Granier de Cassagnac, published in the *Feuilleton du Constitutionnel, 15 octobre, 1851*, which Pierre fails to mention. In this article, Cassagnac reproduces the text of a letter (from a manuscript in the "Papiers de Robespierre, Archives de la préfecture de police") written by Ladré to Robespierre, July 1, 1794, in which Ladré subjoined to his signature, "auteur de *Ça ira* de 1789, vieux style." But this bit of evidence, which at first glance seems telling if not entirely conclusive, is offset by other documentary evidence, viz., Ladré's communication to the *Comité de Sûreté générale* requesting a recompense as being "l'auteur des paroles du *Ça ira* de 1790 . . ." (cited in Pierre, *op.cit.*, p. 485).

For several reasons, which it is perhaps unnecessary to survey here, I am inclined to adhere to the generally accepted view. It is true that Cassagnac purported to find in the text itself of *Ça ira* proof that its words were composed in 1789; but his argument from internal evidence is far less compelling than he would have the reader believe (for example, he gives an entirely false impression concerning the date of the actual disposal of Church lands). As for the letter to Robespierre, it is possible that Ladré might casually have attached to the title of his great hit the words, "of 1789," in the sense that that year—marking the Revolution's origin—had become, according to a certain usage, synonymous with the Revolution itself.

There are countless evidences of the existence and popularity of *Ça ira* in 1790; in the absence of substantial proof that the piece was already out a year earlier, it has seemed to me permissible to devote only this passing mention to the still tenuous thesis that *Ça ira* had an obscure existence for nearly a year before it burst into sudden popularity.

360*. (51)

This is a song of six stanzas in praise of Lafayette. The only text to which Pierre refers is undated, and he apparently assumed that the lyrics were inspired by the popularity of Lafayette at the time of the Festival of Federation, for he assigns the piece to July, 1790. The song belongs, however, to the preceding year, as is indicated by its inclusion in *La Gazette des Halles* . . . , *No. 1ᵉʳ*, which is dated 1789. See Bibliography 1, 51, b.

436*.

The *Cantique nouveau,* which Pierre lists under 1790, may well belong to the preceding year. In any case, Monglond, who refers to the same text that Pierre cites, assigns the piece to 1789. In this song, the King is advised to take strong measures against the evils which surround him. Although there is no definitive topical allusion, the warning seems to refer to the circumstances of June or early July, 1789. In the absence of fuller knowledge, I have not included this as a regular item in Bibliography 1. The possible relevance of the piece, however, is noted (page 273).

APPENDIX B

*Histoire chantée de la Première République, 1789 à 1799; chants pa-
triotiques, révolutionnaires et populaires; recueillis par Louis Damade,
attaché à la Bibliothèque de l'Opéra,* Paris, 1892.

THIS is the most readily available collection of songs of the French
Revolution. The editor, however, had little understanding of the historical problems involved in the proper preparation of such a work.
The following analysis of the selections which Damade made for the
first year of the Revolution may serve to indicate the fallacious arrangement of materials in the *Histoire chantée.*

The orthography used by Damade is modern. Even when allowance
is made for this fact, the reprinted texts are not always accurate tran-
scriptions of the originals. Many of the titles appear to have been
devised by the editor.

Damade presents 25 songs under the heading "1789." Of this number, 3 are nonpolitical and need not be considered. Of the remaining
22, I am inclined to regard only 7 as belonging to 1789.

The acceptable songs are: *Recit historique* . . . (37†-*190*), p. 8;
Couplets sur la cocarde nationale (*56-217*), p. 16; *Couplets . . . par les
Dames* . . . (*34-201*), p. 18; *Couplets à Monsieur le Marquis de Lafa-
yette . . .* (*50-210*), p. 22; *Couplets chantés en l'Assemblée des Companies
de Grenadiers . . .* (*79-254*), p. 38; *O filii nationale* (*20-234*), p. 53; and
Chanson (*19-233*), p. 63.

There are in addition 3 songs which might conceivably have appeared in 1789, but which, judged by internal evidence, seem to be
more suitably assigned to the following year. These are (by Pierre
serial numbers) *330*, p. 32; *249* (concerning this item see Appendix A),
p. 40; and *328*, p. 50.

Of the songs which Damade ascribes incorrectly to 1789, 5 are retrospective pieces by T. Rousseau. These are (by Pierre serial numbers)
185, p. 1; *528*, p. 3; *208*, p. 19; *214*, p. 23; and *215*, p. 56. (The last of
these is not signed by Rousseau, but is identifiable as his work.) None
of the first three of these five items was published before 1792. The
fourth may have appeared somewhat earlier; the last mentioned was
published in 1791. See Appendix C concerning Rousseau's works,
which are not contemporaneous with the first phase of the Revolution
and which reflect a later point of view.

The remaining 7 songs which Damade attributes to 1789 have no
place whatsoever in an anthology of that year. The *Hymne,* p. 6, was
first published, so far as is known, in year VIII of the Republic; this
piece (*378*) Pierre regards as having been inspired by the first anniversary of the Bastille, but internal evidence suggests a subsequent

anniversary. Another *Hymne*, p. 13 (Pierre *1828*), belongs to a much later period (*circa* 1796). A *Chanson*, p. 26, concerns the Jacobin factions, and relates to 1793 (so listed by Pierre, *1145*). The *Chant patriotique*, p. 27, is assigned by Pierre to 1790, though it was first published with *L'emprunt forcé* (*1051*) in 1793, and seems to relate to that year. On p. 46, Damade includes as of 1789 a piece in denunciation of the "regicides" (*1570*), which obviously could not have appeared until years later. Two other pieces which he assigns to 1789—*724*, p. 48, and *719*, p. 52—are strikingly out of place, the titles of each containing the words "ci-devant Roi."

Obviously this mélange of material which Damade presents under 1789 is entirely misleading as an expression of the spirit of that year. If the 3 doubtful pieces are conceded, these added to the 7 which are clearly of 1789, leave a score of 10 correct items, and of 12 in error.

It should be said, furthermore, that in sections of Damade's book devoted to later years one may discover two other songs of 1789. One of these, *Chanson contre l'Assemblée nationale* (68-*183**), Damade lists, p. 95, under 1790, although it was published in the *Etrennes à la nation . . .* , which bears the date 1789. The other, *Cahier de Marquis de Fulvy* (4-*184*), Damade presents (p. 422) under the title *C'est mon avis*, with subtitle, *Chanson de 1794*. One is bound to have difficulty in discovering the basis on which Damade assigned this piece to so late a year. Possibly the following lines from the fifth stanza provide a clue, inasmuch as there was a French victory at Mont-Cenis in 1794:

> "C'est mon avis,
> De tout abbé que le roi nomme,
> Que les Louis
> Ne pássent plus le Mont-Cenis."

And yet this obviously refers to the payment of *annates* to the Pope, the "Louis" signifying coins. These payments passed via the Italian town of Mont-Cenis until they were abolished by the Assembly in 1789.

APPENDIX C

NOTE ON THE SONGS OF T. ROUSSEAU

THE most prolific writer of Revolutionary songs was Thomas Rousseau, who under the Republic served as archivist of the Jacobin Society. This author undertook to celebrate in song all the memorable days and chief events of the Revolution. Many of his lyrics concern the events of 1789, and scholars frequently assign certain of his works to that year, as did Pierre and Damade. It is important to note, however, that Rousseau did not interest himself in this sort of writing until 1791, and that most of his songs celebrating the events of the Revolution were written in 1792 and 1793. Furthermore, Rousseau makes no effort to recapture the atmosphere of 1789, but expresses the mood of later years.

Rousseau brought out his songs in *L'âme du peuple* and in *Les chants du patriotisme*, both serial publications, and in small books, such as *Noëls civiques et patriotiques* and *La grande bible des Noëls*. For complete entries, see Bibliography III, F.

He appears, also, to have been author of the *Almanach de la mère Gérard pour l'année bissextile 1792 . , . suivi de Noëls civiques et patriotiques*. This work—which no doubt owed its title to the success of Collot d'Herbois' *Almanach du père Gérard*—is carried in Revolutionary bibliographies as anonymous. I take it to have been an experimental work of T. Rousseau, which he did not sign—the first of his several song collections. In the *Almanach de la mère Gérard* are fifteen songs. Of these, two (Pierre's *516* and *550**) do not appear elsewhere; one (*215*) was published separately, unsigned. The remaining twelve were recurrently reprinted in the four works of T. Rousseau mentioned above. Three of them (*527, 542, 572**) were reprinted once; two of them (*535** and *573**) appear in two of the works; and seven (*235, 529, 543***, 566**, 567**, 567***, and 589*) were reprinted in three out of the four works which bear Rousseau's signature. In other words, the *Almanach de la mère Gérard* is made up primarily of songs, all of which are in Rousseau's style and the greater part of which he later claimed.

INDEX

DATE DUE